CONNECTING THE DOTS OF IDENTITY-2

MODERN ABSTRACT RELIGIOUS VERBAL IMPRESSIONISM
ROLEPLAY IDENTITY ARRAY

JOHN LOUIS THOMAS

COPYRIGHT AND DISCLAIMER

REDNLOVE

Rednlove2@gmail.com

Connecting the Dots of Identity-2

Internet references are taken from popular web browsers in the years 2019, 2020, 2021, 2022, and 2023. Some sources may require updates or additional information regarding the validity of their content.

Briefly, this license allows intellectual property to be shared among content creators within limits. If you alter the material, you may not distribute it. You may copy and redistribute the material but not for commercial purposes. If your platform is commercially oriented and you post *Connecting the Dots of Identity* content you violate the terms of the Creative Commons License. This is the letter of the law. In the spirit of the law, if you profit from the content, you incur an obligation to remit a portion of the profit to the license holder. The license holder provides content, the content creator extends content.

The main goal in granting a Creative Commons license is to facilitate the distribution of the work by screen capture, text, voice, closed captioning, subtitles, or sign language. By extension, this includes translation from the English language.

Content creators may reproduce a chapter not to exceed the length of one chapter per 30-day period on the same website or URL (Universal Resource Locator). Any chapter may be selected. Permission is granted to

Name or link to purchase the publication.

Text To Speech (TTS). This is a service that converts written material to an audio program that simulates the human voice. These paid and free services assist those who are visually impaired, have limited reading opportunities, or prefer narration for distinct reasons. Consider TTS for someone to access *Connecting the Dots of Identity* on Android, IOS, Windows, and other platforms using a desktop, laptop, tablet, or smartphone.

Connecting the Dots of Identity is not intended to modify, subvert, or infringe on Christian orthodox theology.

Connecting the Dots of Identity is strictly an artistic verbal impression of religious principles. It is an art project rendered by an artist.

Connecting the Dots of Identity expressly discourages any representation as a church.

Connecting the Dots of Identity does not qualify as a church. The essential elements of a church include order of service, worship, discipleship, prayer, sacraments, discipline, leadership, teaching, missions, and fellowship.

Connecting the Dots of Identity supports the local church, away church, and spiritual social gatherings.

Editor: Polgarus Studios

Cover Design: Sidney Nicholas

DEDICATION

Love to you 100 percent human Roleplayers

Table of Contents

GLOSSARY OF COLORS

These are some of the primary, secondary, and tertiary colors used to paint Modern Abstract Religious Verbal Impressionism-Roleplay Identity Array. There is no other way to present *Connecting the Dots of Identity* other than to make use of vivid expressions.

AGNOSTICISM

The conclusion that knowledge of a Supreme Being, or God, is doubtful, inaccessible, and unknowable. Therefore, theism and atheism cannot be known or proven. Proof of non-conversion to theism, and the ongoing lifestyle as an atheist, confirm an agnostic's conviction that theism is man-made.

Agnosticism doesn't acknowledge the doctrine of spiritual blindness, that God intentionally withholds knowledge of Himself. However, they must admit to blindness in the sense they have no spiritual eyesight. They do not perceive God. He’s incomprehensible. He's also incomprehensible to everyone else.

Initially, this is true. Spiritually seeing God is an involuntary action by the Holy Spirit as proof of God's Election-Predestination program existing before the foundation of the world. Scripture asserts no one perceives and then chooses to follow Jesus Christ unless God initiates the process. The default position from birth is a belief in the self and disbelief in the God of the Bible. This is the Demonstration of Free Will.

ANGELS

First-Class Angels—accept God's will for their life.

Second-Class Angels—Satan and others decline God's will for their life, but do not abandon Heaven.

Third-Class Angels—Abaddon (Hebrew), or Apollyon (Greek), and others are those that left Heaven for the Earth in the hope of securing a redeemer for angels via procreation with human females. An audacious mission to match God's solution to human disobedience.

ARMINIANISM

The religious doctrine attributed to Jacobus Arminius (1629-1725) that affirms man's Free Will in the salvation plan of God rather than God's determined will as the only factor.

ATHEISM

The system of thought that a Supreme Being, or God, does not exist. Although they are proponents of objectivity and science, atheists possess no knowledge or proof of their negative position or agreed-upon evidence of absence.

Atheists reject the Reformed theology principle that God withholds knowledge of Himself except to the Elect. Though their knowledge of God is from General Revelation (nature) and Special Revelation (scripture), atheists are spiritually blind. Being so blinded, they are functionally agnostics. They can't know God and, therefore, you can't know God either. Otherwise, we would all know God. Why wouldn't we?

This contrasts with theism, which holds that an Intelligent Essence has always existed throughout various belief systems and makes itself known in a variety of means.

AUTHENTIC AND INAUTHENTIC IDENTITY

Authentic identity is the primary identity of a 100 percent human being that is recognized by the Lord before the foundation of the world. This is referred to as the Super-Spiritual Identity or SSID.

The inauthentic identity is a secondary identity engaged in the Demonstration of Free Will initiated by Adam and Eve subject to the forces of heredity, environment, and experiences.

The inauthentic identity may be transformed by the Holy Spirit (Holy Spirit Identity or HSID). They are born-again. Those who are not transformed are:

a) The control group that proves unless the Holy Spirit intercedes, no one ever perceives or chooses to follow God. Their Roleplay ends. They join the SSIDs.

b) Compromised by evil spirits (Evil Spirit Identity or ESID). They may not be 100 percent human. An inauthentic identity must be transformed at death, before death, or after death or will have no corresponding SSID in Paradise on Judgment Day.

BLIND EYES CHART

The Blind Eyes Chart is an informal attempt to highlight nonphysical aspects of identity-array Roleplay blindness using a questionnaire and a brief essay.

Nonphysical Roleplay blindness refers to spiritual blindness, intentional blindness, and unintentional blindness. This follows from an inability or unwillingness to perceive objective morality, thereby deferring to subjective morality. The intent of the chart is to help clarify the disparity in Roleplayers' perceptions of good/bad and right/wrong. (Glossary—Objective Morality and Subjective Morality).

A thirty-point yes/no questionnaire on spiritual blindness follows with a brief essay defining spiritual, intentional, and unintentional blindness. (*Connecting the Dots Of Identity-1* Chapter 17, *Connecting The Dots Of Identity-2* Chapter 17).

BOOK OF LIFE / LAMB'S BOOK OF LIFE (spiritual books)

The blessed heavenly "book" that contains (God-given) names of the individual persons who are assured of salvation before God created the world (refers to bible verses implying names, writings, books, etcetera).

CALVINISM

The belief system of John Calvin (1615-1772) declares grace (salvation by the grace of God) rather than works (salvation by man's efforts). Five primary points feature the acronym

T.U.L.I.P. (Total depravity, Unconditional election, Limited atonement, Irresistible grace, Perseverance of the saints).

CREATIONISM

Creationism is a secondary view (following Traducianism and Designationism defined in this section) that centers around WHEN souls or spirits are created and HOW souls or spirits are created.

When — (1) at conception (2) before conception, or (3) after conception.

How — (1) by parents, or (2) by God.

Creationism follows that the SOUL or SPIRIT is created by God at conception. This may include fractions of time before conception or after conception. A human being's BODY (physical identity/mental identity) is created in sin by sinful parents. God cannot be the creator of sinful persons. Creationists hold a man is essentially a soul WITH a body versus traducianists, who hold a man is both soul AND body.

CHRISTIAN REFORMED IMPRESSIONISM

The imagery of Christian Reformed theology as spiritual impressions featuring suppositional constructs outside orthodoxy. This includes:

- A pre-life ontological identity based on Election/Predestination.

- An inauthentic present-life Roleplay identity based on heredity, environment, and experiences.
- Everyone who is 100 percent human goes to Heaven based on Election/Predestination.
- Only those less than 100 percent human, Satan, and his angels go to Hell.
- Jesus Christ as the 100 percent human (and 100 percent God) perfect Roleplayer assured salvation for Elect Roleplayers.
- Life is a Demonstration of Free Will initiated by Adam and Eve, and also influenced by the Nephilim (fallen angel/human female offspring).
- Salvation is by grace and not by works. Free Will to choose God was abrogated when Adam and Eve chose their own will for their lives rather than God's will for their lives. Only a flawless person can choose God; a flawed person cannot. All progeny from Adam and Eve are flawed. By grace, the Holy Spirit affirms salvation to inauthentic Roleplayers, confirming unless He arrives, Roleplayers cannot, do not, and will not choose God's will for their life.
- Since the UNSANE (Glossary) aren't able to open their spiritual eyes, and the SANE (Glossary) aren't able to do so for them, the responsibility of the SANE is to serve God by reintroducing God to the UNSANE. This is done by illustrating that God saved them before they were born. Who they are presently is a construct of heredity, environment, and experience derived from a Demonstration of Free Will, in contrast to God's Determined Will for human beings—AND angels—before the foundation of the world.

DESIGNATIONISM

A third view regarding WHEN and HOW a soul is created is Designationism (see Creationism and Traducianism defined in this section).

God has determined specific souls before He created the world, which correspond to specific humans conceived after creation. The soul, or spirit

(Spiritual Identity-SID), is created in sin as SID-Negative. Moving from pre-birth to birth through childhood, the child gravitates SID-Positive or SID-Negative depending on heredity, environment, and experiences.

Therefore, Designationism comes first. God elects souls before He creates the world. Traducianism comes second from parents. Creationism comes third as God identifies the Pre-Life Elect by giving the Holy Spirit—a reborn soul. (From Christian Reformed Impressionism)

EGO-CENTRACISM

The belief that it is the right of a living creature is to demand and pursue the best interests of said creature. Restriction of this right therefore undermines the viability and autonomy of a flawless living creature. It's my life and not God's life through me. Otherwise, I may not be actually alive.

EGO-SKEPTICISM

A result of uncertainty regarding the nature of identity (who am I, what should I be doing, why am I here?). This includes unreliability of General Revelation (nature or science), Special Revelation (scripture), sense perception, and limitations of mental ability. Generally, a begrudging acknowledgment that autonomic systems of the body such as heart, lungs, glands, and brain, and other immutable aspects of the body such as race, height, and age, contribute to confirming a lack of access and authority regarding identity.

Where God's Determined Will is perceived as non-religious natural forces of macroevolution, similar feelings of Ego-Skepticism apply.

Lucifer – A lack of confidence in God's Determined Will that restricts the freedom of a flawless creature leading to resentment and discontent with life.

Serpent, Adam, Eve – Doubt and lack of confidence stemming from a lack of access to the control of essential determining factors that define physical, mental, and spiritual details of identity.

Roleplayers – Helplessness at lack of access to physical, mental, and spiritual details that confirm the utter dependence on heredity, environment, and experiences affecting the purpose and reason to live. Additionally, given the limited access to the self, access to the knowledge of others is also limited. Therefore, the ability to communicate and coordinate with others elicits feelings of suspicion, mistrust, and uncertainty.

EXCLUSIVISM

The belief that there is one way and one way only that will satisfy God's provision for salvation, such as Jesus Christ. The view includes religious liberty as everyone's right to freely worship without prohibition. It is the opposite of INCLUSIVISM (Glossary).

FREE WILL DEMONSTRATION

Human life as it began in the Garden of Eden, whereby flawless living creatures (the Serpent, Adam, and Eve) illustrate freedom to pursue God's will for their lives or pursue their own will for their lives. Roleplay (pursuit of Free Will based on heredity, environment, and experiences) provides conclusive proof that Free Will leads to death and eternal damnation.

GENERAL REVELATION AND SPECIAL REVELATION

The biblical explanation of how God is revealed to us. General Revelation by the way we perceive the world through our senses, experiences, and natural laws of the universe. Special Revelation by the words God has given through oral tradition and the written word.

GODLY MARRIAGE MATERIAL

The person who accepts who they are as the *inauthentic* identity imposed by heredity, environment, and experience. Therefore, if the *authentic* identity is recognized by God who granted salvation before the foundation of the world, life is a responsibility to assist the Holy Spirit in healing spiritual blindness. The secondary responsibility is addressing intentional and unintentional blindness as defined by the Blind Eyes Chart. In the interim, every effort is made to overcome the effects of identity flaws that inhibit the attractiveness to bond with others who follow Connecting the Dots of Identity, especially Single-Persons Champions.

GOD'S DETERMINED WILL

God's provision that established salvation for His Elect individuals before He created the world is His Determined Will. This affirms that autonomous human beings and spirit beings possess everlasting life. God's Determined Will is that flawless identities possess autonomy but will never disobey His will for their life. There are two classes:

1) Super-Spiritual Identities (SSIDs) – The Pre-Life Elect individuals identified in scripture who are guaranteed salvation before the foundation of the world. Also portrayed as Christian Reformed Impressionism and Election-Predestination.

2) First-Class Angels – Spirit creatures who never exercise Free Will to disobey God.

The contrast is:

Non-Limited Free Will: Free Will to obey or disobey God. The Second-Class Angels, Third-Class Angels, the Serpent, Adam, and Eve were created flawlessly with this status.

Limited Free Will: The Serpent, Adam, and Eve became estranged from God by exercising Non-Limited Free Will to disobey God. Second and Third-Class Angels also became estranged from God when they disobeyed. Disobedience to God becomes Limited Free Will as there is no longer an ability to obey God flawlessly.

IDENTITY ARRAY

The 8-part identity model of personhood — SSID, HSID, SID, ESID, PID, MID, CID, MID. They are Super Spiritual ID, Holy Spirit ID, Spiritual ID, Evil Spirit ID, Physical ID, Mental ID, Childhood ID, and Dream ID.

INCLUSIVISM

The belief system asserts there are many paths to God. No one path or set of paths is more efficacious to salvation than others. It is the opposite of EXCLUSIVISM (Glossary) which maintains there is only one path to salvation – such as Jesus Christ.

INSANITY CHART (See complete chart in Chapter 17 and Chapter 27, and *Connecting the Dots of Identity-1*, Chapter 17).

A crude shortcut to a classification of thinking and behaving.

SANE

The status of Pre-Life Elect individuals (Holy Spirit Identity-HSID) who possess a Christian worldview while continuing the Demonstration of Free Will through heredity, environment, and experience. They affirm objective morality as the standard of thinking and behaving based on the transcendent, universal, top-down imperative from God of the Bible. The sane include people who are Holy Spirit immature: spiritually-minded people who have yet to receive the Holy Spirit, and people whose mental impairment prevents them from consistent Christian participation.

UNSANE

People who ascribe to atheists, agnostics, and non-Christian worldviews. They are spiritually blind, but broadly mentally competent. Their profile is a cynical, derisive, contemptible view of objective morality—the standard of thinking and behaving based on the transcendent, universal, top-down imperative from God of the Bible. They are against godliness unless God overrides their Free Will. They portray the Demonstration of Free Will through heredity, environment, and experience. (See Blind Eyes Chart)

INSANE

Group A—A group of people who are 100 percent human, who suffer mental impairment from heredity, environment, and experience. They may be sane, adult Christians, but in general, are mentally irresponsible. Additionally, the unsane also may suffer insanity from the effects of heredity, environment, and experience.

Group B—A group of people who are less than 100 percent human. Their mental identity also suffers the effects of heredity, environment, and experience. These are most likely ancestors of the Nephilim.

LUCIFER'S POSTULATE

Before "Lucifer" became Satan, a leading angel (X) inquired of God to receive unlimited freedom of behavior (omnipotence). The essence of living for a flawlessly created being is to behave as one desires without negative consequences. Considering God is omnipresent, omnipotent, and omniscient, He is capable of correcting any misbehavior on-the-fly. This renders true autonomy and freedom to the flawlessly created being while eliminating any negative aspects of actions.

God declined the request, based on granting omnipotence to a created being without granting omniscience. However, God will provide a live Demonstration of Free Will. Non-angelic flawless created beings will have limited omnipotence (behavior) and limited omniscience (knowledge).

The Demonstration will help prove God's will for His creatures is better than the creature's will for itself.

MARVI-RPIA

Modern Abstract Religious Verbal Impressionism-Roleplay Identity Array. The name intends to convey a pseudo-orthodox view of religion featuring an artistic impression of Reformed theology.

MINISTER OF ART

Your humble servant, the author of CD1/CD2. Also, anyone who appreciates the artistry of Christian Reformed Impressionism by promoting or improving the imagery.

MONISM

The thoughts regarding the source of reality. Broadly, monism holds that everything is derived from one primary source INDEPENDENT of everything else. It differs from PHYSICALISM (materialism) in that physicalism holds that everything is derived from one primary source, though that source is NOT independent of everything else. Monism affirms a distinction in physical, mental, and spiritual states. Physicalism affirms a "meat all the way down" aspect of human identity, which includes consciousness and mental states as products of the physical brain and other anatomical systems.

MORAL RELATIVISM

The view is that any standard of thinking and behaving is dependent upon the individual and circumstances. Context rules the adjudication of an agent to express themselves in any manner that enhances the quality of life, irrespective of other factors. Objective moral standards, such as rape, murder, and theft, are without standing and subject to reformation.

NEPHILIM AND NEPHILIM ONE-DROP RULE

The Nephilim are the living product of the sons of God (Third-Class Angels) and the daughters of men (human females). The offspring are destroyed in the Flood with every other person except the eight people of Noah's family. One (or more) of the eight persons saved is thought to genetically pass on a fraction of Nephilim genetic material from a relative who perished in the Flood. Since Noah and Missus Noah are ostensibly blessed by God, and the three sons were blessed by God in scripture that leaves one or more of the three wives of Noah's sons as suspects.

Given that Shem was the progenitor of Abraham, and from Abraham came Jacob, and from Jacob came Judah, and then forward to Jesus, Missus Shem was most likely pure. Given that Canaan is cursed by Noah, and Canaan is a son of Noah's blessed son Ham, perhaps Canaan has the so-called drop of Nephilim blood from Missus Ham. This may also set the example for the children of Missus Japheth. It should also be noted that, even though Jesus avoided the cursed line that included Jeconiah, Jeconiah's curse was later modified. Even more so, all of the ancestors of Jesus's mother and stepfather were sinners (cursed) until blessed by Jesus's birth. Every 100 percent human being was cursed until redeemed by Jesus.

(This One-Drop Rule refers to the dominant status of Negro blood in any ambiguous Negro person thereby, classifying them as Negro. This one-drop-of-blood practice was legally and socially in effect in times past, especially in the United States, but also elsewhere, and currently in effect among some Native American and Alaska Native tribes as proof of eligibility for membership).

OBJECTIVE MORALITY

Standards of thinking and behaving are based on transcendent, universal, top-down imperatives from the God of the Bible that apply to everyone. This contrasts with Subjective Morality, which bases standards of thinking and behaving on individual human preference rather than God.

ONTOLOGICAL STATUS

Human individual identity BEFORE the world was created. The essence of individual personhood being of necessity by the assertion from multiple examples in scripture. A determined, uncreated, identified immaterial essence.

PARADISE

The secondary name used for Heaven and/or the location with the Lord outside of time.

PELAGIANISM

Pelagianism is a heterodox Christian theological position.

Pelagius (354-418 AD): Theologian. Philosopher. The British Isles. Noted antagonist to Saint Augustine. Believed no sin nature came from Adam; we are born spiritually neutral. We can choose God by individual Free Will. No such thing as predestination. Denied atonement by Jesus Christ. We should emulate Jesus. We are able to lead a sinless life or God would not command what man cannot achieve. Denounced as a heretic at the Council of Carthage (418), Council of Ephesus (431), and Council of Orange (529).

Semi-Pelagianism: Denial of full efficacy of grace for salvation until human initiative begins.

PHYSICALISM

Holds everything is derived from one primary source, but that source is NOT independent of everything else. Physicalism affirms a "meat all the way down" aspect of human identity, which includes consciousness and mental states as products of the physical brain and other anatomical systems. As opposed to MONISM, everything is derived from one primary source that is INDEPENDENT of everything else.

PLURALISM (RELIGION)

The belief is that all religions have the blessing of God to achieve salvation. God honors sincere efforts to pursue love, honor, and peace with others, especially other religious belief systems. A community where diverse religious rights are protected from non-religious entities. This view relates to religious liberty.

PRE-LIFE ELECT

Individual persons (as opposed to a collective group of persons) guaranteed salvation before birth and before the world was created, and function as Roleplayers of Free Will.

REDEEMER/ANTIDOTE/REMEDY/SOLUTION/MEDIATOR

The embodiment of God Himself via procreation of the Holy Spirit and Virgin Mary. By becoming 100 percent human and retaining 100 percent divinity, He provides correction to the error posed by Adam and Eve that created (physical) death and eternal damnation (spiritual non-life).

ROLEPLAY

Autonomous human beings were created by God to demonstrate Free Will beginning with Adam and Eve. Also, Jesus Christ, being 100 percent God and 100 percent human, became a Free-Will Roleplayer as a 100 percent human to live a perfect life in place of Adam and Eve. After living perfectly, He died so as to conquer death by resurrection for all 100 percent human beings.

Our identity emanates from three basic influences: heredity, environment, and experience. HEVEX is the acronym.

Heredity-Roleplay

The identity we possess is a composite of ALL the identities in the TOTAL ancestral line. Heredity isn't as basic as mother, father, grandparents, and great-grandparents. Heredity isn't necessarily a research project that discovers the ancestral line of the past 100 to 500 years.

Heredity from the biblical record is comprised of EVERYBODY back to Mister and Missus Noah. The Nephilim, being less than 100 percent human, are also a possible ancestral component. Receding further, our identity begins with Adam and Eve—flawless humans who became flawed. Coming forward, the environment and experience contribute to determining what essentially an inauthentic identity is.

Environment-Roleplay

Parenting. Family members. Friends. Peers. Neighbors. Education. Associates. Culture. National Government. Local Government. Neighborhood quality. Air quality. Water quality. Soil quality. Nutritional quality. Ambient Sound quality. Weather quality. Personal products. Medicines. Toxins. A collective of material and immaterial components that contribute to identity.

Experience-Roleplay

Life events that are remembered, forgotten, repressed (accessible but avoided), subconscious (inaccessible), embellished, or inaccurate. This includes non-physical "experiences" such as imaginations, dreams, and impressions.

Other than birth and death, the most significant event upon inauthentic identity is the Holy Spirit's arrival. Preceding this, who we are could be summarized by heredity, environment, and experience until we join our authentic identity in Paradise. In the interim, our identity doesn't respect OBJECTIVE MORALITY, the standard of thinking and behaving defined by God. We respect SUBJECTIVE MORALITY, standards of our own defined as we see fit. This state of mind is spiritual blindness. It's the default position that NEVER changes until the Holy Spirit intercedes.

In this regard, what we see in Free Will Roleplay is sanity and unsanity (see Insanity Chart):

1–Sane persons who project a high level of individual integrity.

2–Sane persons who project low to high levels of individual integrity.

3–Unsane persons who project low to medium levels of integrity.

ROLEPLAYER—TEAM PLAYER—TEAM COMPANION

ROLEPLAYER is a term to imply a contrived, temporary, inauthentic identity. It is the manifestation of heredity, the environment, and experiences before birth, at birth, and beyond birth. God developed procreation through Adam and Eve for two reasons: to prove the error of their Free Will through successive generations and correct their error via the Antidote Jesus Christ. Like actors on a stage, we assume the character imposed on us, though it is not our true identity (Super-Spiritual Identity or SSID).

TEAM PLAYER is the union of two or more Roleplayers. A Roleplayer loses their Roleplayer status by a 100 percent commitment to combine identities, typically through marriage. Roleplayers retain their contrived, temporary, inauthentic identity. As Team Players, they continue the Demonstration of Free Will, susceptible to procreation, thereby creating new Roleplayers who join the team. Ideally, both parties follow the impression conveyed by *Connecting the Dots of Identity*, which suggests Godly Marriage Material, Team Companion, and Single-Persons Champion before reaching Team Player status.

TEAM COMPANION is a relationship to a person or persons who communicate heart-to-heart regarding Connecting The Dots Of Identity impressions.

Godly Marriage Material (dating): Bronze.

Team Companion (friend, not marriage material): Silver.

Single-Persons Champion (unattached, not dating): Gold.

Team Player (engaged or married): Gold.

If you come to accept some of the tenets of MARVI-RPIA, you could be in the process of becoming Godly Marriage Material, assuming you are unattached. The next step is being a suitable Team Companion to a Single-Persons Champion. The process you go through begins with being the best single person you can be. As you evaluate the effects of heredity, environment, and experience that formed what could be considered your inauthentic identity, you realize you're not limited by your appearance, your intellect, or your experiences.

SINGLE-PERSONS CHAMPION

Someone who never married, is divorced, or widowed. A person who has yet to meet another person worthy of changing their single-person status. In the interim, they think and behave in a manner that gives honor and service to the Lord by exemplifying and promoting Jesus Christ with 100 percent commitment.

Although finding a spouse has never been easier than it is today, the Single-Persons Champion doesn't pursue marriage. They're as neutral as possible, even while casually dating and making friends. The Single-Persons Champion motto is: “It’s up to YOU to make it impossible for ME to remain single.”

SPECIAL REVELATION AND GENERAL REVELATION

The biblical explanation of how God is revealed to us. General Revelation by the way we perceive the world through our senses, experiences, and natural laws of the universe. Special Revelation by the words God has given through oral tradition and the written word.

SUBJECTIVE MORALITY

The reliance on human definitions for good/bad, right/wrong, and risk/reward rather than a theistic definition. It is characterized by a cynical, derisive, contemptible view of objective morality.

SUPRALAPSARIAN (ANTELAPSARIAN) (refers to a lapse in time)

Refers to the timing when God decrees individuals to salvation. This view maintains that (1) God chose individuals before He created the world, and (2) He creates the world. Contrast is then shown between the saved and unsaved of the world.

SUBLAPSARIAN and INFRALAPSARIAN (refers to a lapse in time)

This view holds that (1) God created all individuals, and (2) They all sin. Then God provides salvation to an elect number.

TRADUCIANISM

Traducianism is a secondary view (following Creationism and Designationism defined in this section) that centers around WHEN souls or spirits are created and HOW souls or spirits are created.

When: (1) at conception (2) before conception (3) after conception

How: (1) by parents (2) by God

Traducianism proposes the soul or spirit is created at conception by one or both parents. Although the soul is essentially immaterial, it is nonetheless transferred through procreation. The child is created in sin inherited by the parents.

Traducianism continues that God initiated physical and spiritual essence all at once with Adam and Eve. They were not conceived in sin. Only afterward when Adam and Eve fell was sin inherited from parents, not from God. The question of Jesus inheriting sin from the Virgin Mary is mitigated by the Holy Spirit, who implemented procreation.

UNIVERSALISM

In the sense of a religious principle, Universalism teaches that God's presence is in all individuals and is sufficient to assure all will achieve salvation, and that none be condemned. God is love. His love covers any and all circumstances from conception to death. Hell is not a physical place of eternal torment for human beings. No humans go there. All humans go to Heaven. Jesus Christ paid for all sin for all time.

PREFACE

The first *Connecting the Dots of Identity* book served to present a dynamic image of Christian Reformed Impressionism. It illustrated the basic image of a Minister of Art, painting a mural on the architecture of spirituality. *Connecting the Dots of Identity-2* seeks to provide the reader with support for CD-1 content and some applications that follow from the imagery.

As I took notes on life, it led to a notebook, which led to a journal, which led to a manuscript. As the journal grew, it became appropriate to divide it into subjects. The most important subjects were religion, philosophy, psychology, and sociology. Religious materials became 90 percent of the content.

I developed a personal "perfect" prayer. I developed a Spiritual Day once a month devoted to only spiritual things. I honored the Sabbath Day. I became a member of a church for twenty-five years. Then, the pandemic hit. No physical church attendance for the time being. But that was not a time to relax. It was a time for fellowship and communication in other ways. Here was an opportunity and a challenge to continue spiritual growth and support religious organizations.

The background of my research over the years of religious study centered on question-and-answer programs: thousands of questions and thousands of answers. This helped formulate an image of spiritual reality and how that coincided with physical and mental experiences. In the task of collating and preserving thirty years of notes into the computer, an idea began to form. This led to the possibility of an unorthodox religious project. Rather than promote the project as theology, it seemed more effective to simply share the project as an artistic, theological impression.

This was especially fitting as I have no aspirations of ministry, teaching, or writing.

The impetus for presenting this material is to offer a viable alternative to the current imagery of theism, agnosticism, and atheism. By *Connecting the Dots of Identity via Modern Abstract Religious Verbal Impressionism*, who I am, who you are, and what is happening has an exciting new image. God could have a similar plan. Certainly, His Plan A is flawless, but this artistic Plan B is an image that may complement His.

And Plan B doesn't have to be true. It doesn't have to be orthodox. It just has to make as much sense as any other worldview to be helpful.

INTRODUCTION

People do not know of an AUTHENTIC identity. Therefore, they accept an INAUTHENTIC identity based on heredity, environment, and experiences. Authentic identity is described as individuals recognized by God before the creation of the world. The implication is salvation for the individual has already occurred. Everyone who is to be saved in the present was saved before they were born. Past tense. From this, an IMPRESSION of the Bible becomes a book of verbal art.

Adam and Eve did NOT begin with an authentic identity. They began with an *immaculate inauthentic identity.* Their identity was virtuous and uncorrupted. When they knowingly disobeyed God, virtue left them. Their identity became corrupted. They didn't lose their salvation, they gained death. Physical death, that is, not spiritual death.

Primarily, procreation was the manner that God initiated to correct their error through the birth of Jesus Christ. Secondly, procreation conclusively proves the futility of their Free Will error. This becomes the Demonstration of Free Will. Even so, Free Will is heavily influenced by the circumstances of heredity, environment, and experiences. From this comes frustration, resentment, and aberrant behavior as a range of possible responses to a lack of control over physical and mental attributes imposed without your knowledge or consent. You get whatever your ancestors and immediate family transfer to you during conception and, later, at birth.

Think of a surprise gift box. You're inside. You are to be delivered sometime in history to some parent or parents. You may be aborted, stillborn, or miscarried. No idea of ethnicity, height, weight, health, looks, intelligence, or talent. You're in the queue to be delivered … delivery begins … the countdown ends … and into the world you're thrown.

Now that you're here, the identity believed to be authentic is the identity based on worldviews of religion, atheism, and agnosticism INSIDE time and space: the present. *Connecting the Dots of Identity* offers an artistic impression of the authentic identity OUTSIDE time and space—the past and the future. From this impression, three things may appear:

1) A SECURE future, a RESOLUTION of the past, and a TRUSTING present.

2) An understanding of WHY the world seems unpredictable, hopeless, and difficult.

3) A vision of God being back on the throne. A REINTRODUCTION to God.

Also, these three considerations will be addressed in the coming chapters:

THEISM – *Connecting the Dots of Identity* sufficiently separates itself from the theology of Universalism. Everyone goes to Heaven. No one goes to Hell.

AGNOSTICISM – *Connecting the Dots of Identity* may be helpful in giving agnostics reasons enough to acknowledge God can be known well enough to justify theism.

ATHEISM – *Connecting the Dots of Identity* offers atheists the possibility God may have a chance of being a reasonable explanation of reality.

CHAPTER 1

IMPROBABLE IMAGE

Free Will may truly be an illusion.

You had no control over being born.

You have no control over your death, except in suicide or self-sacrifice.

You had/have no control over being born-again (Christian Reformed theology).

Therefore, spiritually speaking, you have no control over going to Heaven or Hell.

This is actually GOOD!

How? Why? Because GOD is in control.

You probably don't have as much trust in God as you think or say. God is incomprehensible. What you know of Him is mainly from other people and the scriptures. *Connecting the Dots of Identity* introduces you to an imagery of God that introduces you to the imagery of yourself. It will be connecting dots of identity that aren't real.

The dots SIMULATE spiritual reality. As such, nonreligious people won't see the dots or the connections because of spiritual blindness. Religious people may not see them because their spiritual reality supports orthodox imagery, not unorthodox, simulated imagery.

An improbable image may help represent reality. This is *Connecting the Dots of Identity* as Modern Abstract Religious Verbal Impressionism-Roleplay Identity Array. It illuminates a SECONDARY identity that is actually the PRIMARY identity. The primary identity, the Super-Spiritual Identity (SSID) residing in Paradise before God created the world, is the AUTHENTIC identity, the real you. The "you" that is the secondary identity, the identity forced upon you by heredity, environment, and experiences, is a result of Adam and Eve's error in the Garden of Eden. This identity is INAUTHENTIC.

Who you are is a descendant of:

- Adam and Eve
- the Exceptional Eight that left the Ark after the Flood (Mister and Missus Noah and family); and
- possibly the Nephilim (angel and human female offspring)

God initiated procreation to correct The Error of Adam and Eve. A Redeemer will be born who will break the cycle of imperfection. He will be perfect. Procreation also provides a demonstration of what happens when flawless humans reject God's will for their lives and choose their own will.

No matter what humans say or do, their lives end in death. However, they all have Free Will to disbelieve God and believe in themselves. They all do so and continue to do so until their last breath unless God intercedes. When God intercedes, He changes their heart and mind to believe in Him and obey Him. Because humans are flawed by inheriting sin from Adam and Eve, they do not believe and obey Him entirely.

If God does NOT intercede, these people are the "chosen" control group proving the inability to ever choose godliness. Additionally, Satan oppresses, possesses, and accuses humans as they go about their life. Even more subtle, persons not 100 percent human—ancestors of the Nephilim—also have their role to play. Though they may not be 100 percent human beings, heredity, environment, and experience force them to also participate in the Demonstration of Free Will.

The Nephilim? What's that?

In the days of Mister and Missus Noah, we read in the Old Testament Book of Genesis that some angels, so-called sons of God, took wives of human females and created hybrid persons. These were the giants or Nephilim. The Bible further informs that the angels who left Heaven to seek human females were later imprisoned in chains of darkness. All people on earth drowned in the Flood. God drowned them as judgment—all except the eight people of Noah's family. But the Bible states there were "giants" in the earth AFTER the Flood. One solution is giants were born as a consequence of procreation from one or more of the eight persons of Noah's family.

MARVI-RPIA paints an image of less-than-100 percent human persons by way of ancestors derived from the Nephilim. Such persons may help explain how it is that people think and behave so inhumanely. We scratch our heads and say we just don't understand. *Connecting the Dots of Identity* may help. There are two aspects of identity that have never seemed connected.

1) The Pre-Life Elect identity, recognized in scripture before the world was created, is the Super-Spiritual Identity (SSID) in Paradise.

2) The less-than-100 percent human identity derived from the Nephilim.

(See Glossary of Colors and the ending chapters on Questions and Answers for more details)

These two aspects of identity were never connected, because they were never discernable. Now that MARVI-RPIA has imagery that helps create their awareness, dots of identity can be connected.

One group of people may say: So what if people are inhuman? *If the premise of Connecting the Dots of Identity* is that everyone who is 100 percent human goes to Heaven, nothing else matters. We're all safe. Another group of people, so-called inhuman people, don't care if they are less than 100 percent human. Nephilim smesphalim. I'm not human? Great. Doesn't matter what you call me. We create social groups of our own. The outrageous myths of religion and Hell don't bother us.

Roughly, this is the way people think who don't believe in God, the devil, Heaven, or Hell. Life is what you make of it. And life is what we make of it—until God intercedes and changes our identity. Until then, we are participating in the Demonstration of Free Will.

This project isn't a campaign to change your worldview. It's an attempt to share an impression of the magnificent beauty of God's Salvation Plan for every 100 percent human being. In doing so, it may convey some idea of the magnificent beauty of God.

Meanwhile, as it stands today, life seems to be losing its value. Surely, you feel dissatisfaction with the world. The world is utterly an accident waiting to happen, and accidents are happening all over at lightning speed. We know we may be in one today, next week, or next month. In fact, the whole world could end next week, next month, or next year. *Poof*! It's gone. It won't matter if it's by accident, on purpose, or by negligence.

Bad as that seems, and it is bad, a glimmer of hope, of beauty, and a chance of a much better image is possible. You decide. This is an art project. Not religion.

Art invariably implies a question. What do YOU see?

CHAPTER 2

TOO GOOD TO BE TRUE

The appearance of design is so realistic that human beings feel as if they actually have Free Will. When presented with supporting evidence pro and con, people say it doesn't matter if Free Will is an illusion or not. If I am simply responding to stimuli from the environment with no Free Will, the illusion of self-control is sufficient. If it wasn't sufficient, then it would matter.

Science tells us life began by accident, from nothing, has no purpose, and at death, goes back to nothing. There is no intelligence involved. It's all forces of nature. Our life is based on all preceding lives that resulted from a succession of unintelligent events that started with the Big Bang. A causes B, B causes C, and C causes D. As these alphabet letters branch out, they're like dominos falling. They're all mechanical, nonliving, impersonal acts. From these nonlife events came life, somehow.

We don't act. We react. A domino falls and hits you a certain way. You fall and hit another domino a certain way. It starts at conception. Who we are is based on heredity, the environment, and experiences. The thought that we don't have Free Will in our lives doesn't occur to us. Why? Because the SENSATION of freedom, liberty, and Free Will is essential for the will to live. We ignore and deny that Free Will does NOT exist to protect our sanity.

Atheists and agnostics who live as atheists aren't threatened by the absence of Free Will. If life is the result of external forces that determine thinking and behaving of live agents, we simply accept it. That life happens at all is an opportunity to make the best of a mysterious, improbable event.

Nothing at all really matters—until we accept and apply a meaningful rationale.

This atheist worldview is in response to the theists' worldview.

Theism reigned even through the infamous familial line of Cain. However, with the advantages of one language, a pristine environment, excellent health, and an exceptionally long life of a thousand years, the human intellect must have been stunningly advanced. It may be that mankind no longer worshiped God exclusively. Their worship was to themselves, objects in nature, or even evil spirits. Intellect, human and angelic, apparently became insolent, irreverent, and audacious.

The errors that caused the Flood almost matched The Error in the Garden of Eden. Additionally, we lost the ability to access Eden and pre-Flood human advancement. The worldwide Flood destroyed almost everything. This may be for our own good. The hint of this seems apparent when God reduced our lifespan from a thousand years to a hundred and twenty years. *There is now less likelihood of teaching animals to speak, as in the Garden with the Serpent, or collaborating with angels, as in producing the Nephilim.*

Gradually, as we climbed back from nothing, literacy improved, and so did science. Today, science has become the de facto religion. Science is the public default position as it aims to avoid any religious elements relative to the data. As such, it tries to be strictly objective, to not inject opinion or bias into conclusions from the research.

The scientific worldview proposes Free Will is illusionary. The brain is too complex to ascertain what conscious and subconscious dynamics are in effect that define thinking and behavior. Going further, given that the origins of life are not based on an intelligent source but an impersonal source, teleology, or purpose, is undefined.

So, human beings do not have sovereign Free Will. However, it's not only the scientific community that promotes that worldview. It's also the religious community: Christian Reformed theology. This doctrine teaches that God "elects" an individual. God has "determined" salvation for individuals BEFORE He created the world.

Now, even more specific than Christian Reformed theology, is this presentation called Connecting The Dots Of Identity. Christian Reformed theology is reimagined as Christian Reformed Impressionism (Glossary of Colors). Using the form of Modern Abstract Religious Verbal Impressionism-Roleplay Identity Array, the presentation also portrays Free Will as illusionary.

Human beings are living in a demonstration of Free Will Roleplay while governed by God. Human beings are subsequently Roleplayers, based on an Identity Array produced by heredity, environment, and experience.

A human's "Identity Array" consists of eight possibilities. One of these is a spiritual identity that is NOT Free Will. It's determined (Super Spiritual Identity-SSID). Determined is a description for predestined—before the world began. The evidence to support this is in three stages" Pre-Life, Life, and the After-Life.

PRELIFE

Pre-life is the name given to indicate a designation before the world was created. No time is passing as such since the timekeepers—sun, moon, stars, etcetera—are not yet created. Here are the Ones who are self-existent: Father, Son, and Holy Spirit. It is at this stage of pre-life that Predestination is defined. The Bible confirms certain persons are determined to be saved from damnation before the world was created (*Connecting the Dots of Identity-1*, Chapter 6, and 100 verses).

MARVI-RPIA makes use of an Identity Array model that describes eight key aspects of individual essence. An individual who is deemed an Elect Person—that is, predetermined to be saved before the world is created—will be referred to as SSID for the rest of this proposal. SSID is an acronym for Super-Spiritual Identity. SSID will be considered the first and foremost reference to a person's true identity. However, SSID persons are not alive. Their status is pre-life. The breath of life is not in them. At this point, neither are angels living.

LIFE

Life is the stage when angels, or the heavenly hosts, are created. They live but are not thought to possess the breath of life (oxygen, lungs, respiration). Initially, there is one generic class of angels. The angels abide in Heaven as ministering spirits to the Lord. They have the glorious status of existing in the presence of His Majesty. Secondly, this stage introduces God's creation of the universe, solar system, planets, Earth, sea, land, plants, and animals. Now is also when God creates humans—Adam and Eve.

AFTERLIFE

The dimension of the afterlife is in two stages. One, when death has overtaken the living person, and two, when the Demonstration of Free Will by human persons ends. At death, the judgment of where a person is to reside, Heaven or Hell, prevails. The distinction of human versus angel destination has its source in "pre-life" as well as "life" stages. In pre-life, the so-called First-Class Angels declined to exercise their Free Will to disagree with God. A Second-Class and Third-Class group of angels *did* exercise their Free Will to disagree with God.

Now, in afterlife, First-Class Angels remain in Heaven with the Lord. Second-Class Angels remain in an accusatory position toward God and human beings until Judgment Day, the end of the Demonstration of Free Will. Third-Class Angels abandoned Heaven to create offspring with human females in order to provide a redeemer for angels. They failed. God caused the Flood. The evil angels were confined to chains of darkness until Judgment Day—the end of the Free Will Demonstration.

Again, this project isn't a campaign to change your worldview. It's an attempt to share an impression of God's Salvation Plan for every 100 percent human being. In doing so, it may convey some idea of who we are, what's happening, and why.

The motto goes: If it sounds too good to be true, it ain't true.

Before reading *Connecting the Dots of Identity*, it will sound too good to be true.

After reading *Connecting the Dots of Identity*, it will sound too good to be true.

In this case, it doesn't matter if it isn't true. It's art. You like it or you don't.

CHAPTER 3

POSITION OF PATIENCE

Salvation is not a matter of knowledge. This is a very hard concept to swallow. *If it doesn't matter what you know, or how you behave, why write a book about thinking and behaving?* This book portrays how thinking and behaving, relative to salvation, serves a function in Roleplay identity. You still have a role to play. Salvation occurred before you were born. Life is about a demonstration of Free Will. It's all Roleplay.

This can be very helpful in understanding life and the quality of life. For MARVI-RPIA, Modern Abstract Religious Verbal Impressionism, the medium of art is used rather than an attempt to create another religious doctrine. As you improvise on your Roleplay identity, you may feel tempted to challenge and correct another person's worldview. If MARVI-RPIA has helped refine your worldview to the degree that it seems superior to other worldviews, you must show patience. Other people will not appreciate being told their worldview is inferior to yours. Be humble. Remember, Modern Abstract Religious Verbal Impressionism-Roleplay Identity Array is an *impression* of reality. It's not meant to convey a religious principle or doctrine.

Don't engage people. Continue to think, continue to learn. There's a lot to evaluate regarding Roleplay and identity array that MARVI-RPIA illustrates. Use it to help others, but don't preach it.

Meanwhile, life has another day, another week, and another month of newscasts, politics, and world affairs. You have limited access to the truth. You may or may not attend church services. If you do attend, churches have a point of view they expect you to follow. Other religions also have a point of view they expect you to follow. Your family, friends, and associates expect you to follow along, just as you have in the past. Do you mention Connecting The Dots Of Identity? Buy the book for others? Remain silent?

Remaining silent probably won't be very practical. You have family, friends, and neighbors. You have associates at work, at church, or on social media. You have to talk. Unfortunately, as life becomes a matter of global communication, public policies are at the forefront of our lives. As you know, the default position of public policy is secular humanism. God, or religion, is not a matter for the public. Keep God personal. However, rather than being as neutral as possible in public matters, the global position reflects pro-secular interests and anti-religious interests.

So, you must become involved in conversations and programs that support the theistic worldview, especially the Christian worldview. If you don't, or can't, secular special interest groups will continue to erode fundamental theistic rights. These include individual rights, family rights, and business rights. This doesn't mean enrollment in political science classes or law school. *This means finding out which programs preserve religious freedom and which programs oppose it. When you do, become proactive.* Write letters, make phone calls, and share information. Donate. Show up to events. Volunteer. Being silent and doing nothing is irresponsible.

Many years ago, I read that 85 percent of people don't think, 10 percent think they're thinking, and only 5 percent think. Cute, but probably not true. However, it would be that 5 percent that convey their thoughts to others that give us meaningful reference points to expand on. *Think* about that.

As *Connecting the Dots of Identity* portrays, it's so wonderful that a deformed child isn't a representation of their true identity. Though they die weeks after birth or are aborted before birth, that person's authentic identity is safe before the world was created.

Most people aren't going to understand this image of identity. I certainly did not think such an image existed before becoming a Minister of Art. Roleplayers from the theists' perspective, and also from the atheists' perspective, contributed to my understanding of how to think. I mentioned Harold Camping and R.C. Sproul in *Connecting the Dots of Identity-1*. Other people that enriched my concept of thinking include Gregory Koukl (theist), Pinecreek Doug (atheist), Christopher Hitchens (atheist), and David Hume (atheist). Christian thinkers from the distant past such as Saint Augustine, Martin Luther, Thomas Aquinas, and John Calvin are also influential. Music and art continue to have a great impact on my education. We can all make a list of public and private figures that have stimulated our growth.

Coming to realize my true identity was in Paradise helped my Roleplay identity to think. My thinking opened up. I no longer had an obligation to save myself or save others by being more intelligent or more religious than they are. Salvation is God's work. That work has been done before God created the world. Now, for me, I am to love God and my neighbor as myself. That means sacrificing my Roleplay life for the life of others.

Your church and your minister probably aren't able to endorse Connecting The Dots Of Identity. They must continue orthodox teaching. And if you support Connecting The Dots Of Identity, don't try to influence the congregation. That isn't your mandate, and it may be counterproductive. The congregation is under the doctrinal confession they agreed to when they became members of the church. For now, just be a living example of love and patience.

Meanwhile, you will be faced with teachings with which you may no longer agree. This is inevitable.

Your trusted teachers have never been taught an ontological predestined identity before the world was created. Additionally, even if they had, it's still difficult to develop how that pre-life identity relates to the flesh and blood identity after the world was created. This is the value of using art, rather than a theological doctrine, to explain this concept.

I'm thinking of the well-known, well-respected pastor who preached that Eve, in the Garden of Eden, was a sucker and a fool. When hearing this same sermon for the second time, I didn't write a letter to his church. Would it have been helpful to remind the pastor that Eve is the mother of ALL living people (Genesis 3:20)? Maybe. Would it have been helpful to remind the pastor of Commandment five—honor your mother and father (Exodus 20:12)? Maybe. Your honor is to the OFFICE of motherhood. If any mother is dishonorable, do you refer to her as a sucker and a fool? Do you attack her identity? Or do you refer to her BEHAVIOR as foolish or gullible and attack her ACTIONS? How would the pastor feel hearing someone refer to one of his female relatives as a sucker and a fool? Not her behavior, her identity.

> And Adam called his wife's name Eve; because she was the mother of all living (Genesis 3:2).
>
> Honour thy father and thy mother: that thy days may be long upon the land which the Lord thy God giveth thee (Exodus 20:12).

Additionally, most of us have heard from the pulpit that if Lucifer wasn't the first liar, then Eve was. The famous pastor mentioned above believes Eve was a liar. Eve told the Serpent that God said she was not to eat or TOUCH the tree. The pastor said God did NOT say she could not touch the tree. Therefore, it would be permissible to touch it. God only commanded Adam not to EAT from the tree. But Eve may NOT have lied to the Serpent. Perhaps Adam told her not to even touch the tree, much less eat from it. If you want to protect someone from danger, it's understandable to overemphasize precautions to minimize risk. Or, God could have told Eve not to touch the tree. How can anyone know every single word God said to Eve that is not recorded?

The position of patience should be your guide. This pastor (who will remain unnamed out of respect) is only one of many I listen to on a regular basis. Though they are a great help to my growth, I have disagreements with all such pastors. They even somewhat irritate me when I hear them speak. I may not like their accent, or their emotional delivery, or their mannerisms. Church music and many church rituals seem tedious. But I know personal likes and dislikes should not be the major factor in the quantity and quality of Christian presentations. I still listen to and support them.

Yes, it's a strange idea that what I know isn't relative to my salvation. Salvation is past tense in Paradise. For now, I'm a Roleplayer demonstrating the Free Will of fallen human beings. I must be patient that my Roleplay identity will be transformed by the Holy Spirit at or before my last breath. If not, I pray that I have a corresponding pre-life identity in Paradise that I will join in the afterlife. That prayer is in my heart no matter how my Roleplays out. That prayer may be a good prayer to practice, develop, and rely on.

OUT OF PATIENCE

Don't NOT show up for the sermon. Be there. But . . . WALK OUT … in the middle of the sermon. Now, the pastor knows WHY you're not present. Does this mean you've run out of patience? Is this disrespectful? Is this exerting your leverage on orthodoxy? Will the pastor notice or even care?

He will notice, and he should care if you do it again, and again, and finally stop attending. Unless, of course, the church is very large, or you're not a member of the church. In that case, it may not matter to the pastor. It may not matter to the congregation. You are just another person, or family, who is spiritually immature. Or maybe not even a Christian.

Recent statistics point to a decline in people who identify as Christian or attend church on a regular basis. The pastors who notice the decline in attendance or lack of growth in the Christian community may not attribute this to the fault of the church. The fault will probably be seen as losing the spiritual battle to the forces of evil.

The solution? More of the same sermons. More of the status quo. A reapplication of the orthodox message that continues to contribute tothe decline in an appreciation of the "Good News."

But . . . maybe its best you DON'T walk out in the middle of the sermon.

Connecting the Dots of Identity could be applied toward a PERSONAL promotion of the Good News. It doesn't have to be public. It doesn't have to be assertive. CD1/CD2 is an impression. It doesn't make assertions. Its leverage for assertions by others—theists, atheists, and agnostics.

You can sit back, be patient, and take notes. Or . . . you can walk out of the sermon.

Leverage. Patience.

CHAPTER 4

POSITION OF PATIENCE—POSTSCRIPT

One day, as I was listening to my usual Christian programs, Dr. X commented that Christians become angry when non-Christians attack them for specific Christian behavior. He said this was a normal reaction. But I thought, *No, that should not be normal.* A Christian should understand that the attacks on them are normal, but the Christian response should be compassion. The non-Christian can't be faulted for not understanding Christian thinking and behavior. We should feel sorry God has yet to reveal Himself to them.

So, Dr. X may have been unaware of Christian Reformed theology at that time. *It's also possible he's aware of it but may disagree with it.* This is a continuing reminder that many ministers growing up in the 1930s, 1940s, and 1950s had extremely limited access to diverse Christian voices. If your local churches didn't teach Reformed biblical doctrine, you were unlikely to hear it. Yes, in those days they had newspapers, radio, and soon television was available, but those sources were not very substantive regarding Christian representation.

Even earlier, in the 1800s, the years following Martin Luther and John Calvin, how would the aspiring minister acquire access to quality religious education? Attend the university?

Possibly. The most prestigious universities in America (and England) began with notable religious influence. Yale, Princeton, Harvard, Oxford, and Cambridge all have roots in the early climate of church and state. But if access to the university was restricted because of local obligations, finances, or disinterest, being self-taught was preferred. Just read the Bible.

Does simply reading the Bible qualify as the ability to teach Christian Reformed theology? Yes. Are any ministers on television, radio, or the internet teaching grace-versus-works as the means to salvation? Yes. However, you must ask yourself how well they understand the principles they're teaching. Do they teach these principles consistently? Are there errors in their literature? How prevalent is works, not grace, in their teaching? Have they made progress from their earlier positions on the Reformed doctrine?

Certainly, the Holy Spirit is the means to making any reader of the Bible a worthy teacher. And the truth is it isn't as important as it may seem. *No matter what time in history, no matter how gifted the minister, no matter how distant a person is from hearing the name of Jesus Christ, salvation has already been accomplished. This is what 100 verses in the Bible profess (CD-1 Chapter 6).* This is what MARVI-RPIA attempts to illustrate.

Meanwhile, you, as the star of the movie that's in progress, have no script except for one line in parentheses. Improvise. You certainly didn't audition for the part. Similar to a *Twilight Zone* television episode, somehow you find yourself onstage, expected to act.

As in real life, you have no idea when or how this drama ends. You must trust the Director and act. Remember, your character is an inauthentic identity. Your character is not your authentic identity. The stage has been set. Lights ... Camera ... Improvise!

POSITION OF PATIENCE — Post Postscript

There are two very famous ministers who hold to Christian Reformed theology. One from the east coast, and one from the west coast. One is recently deceased. In the past few months, both had programs featuring the New Testament story of the Rich Young Ruler. Virtually every Christian has heard this sermon, and virtually every minister preaches the same message. Jesus taught that the answer to the rich young ruler's question of how to obtain eternal life was WORKS, not grace. DO something to be saved.

One: *go and sell your possessions.*

Two*: give to the poor.*

Three: *follow me.*

Do these things and you're in the kingdom. Works, not grace. Stop doing that. Start doing this. You will be in the kingdom. Works, not grace.

The young man went away sorrowful because he had great possessions. The conclusion was the young man would not be able to give away all he had. He was a rich man. A few verses later, in the same chapter, Jesus comments that it's easier for a camel to go through the eye of a needle than for a rich person to be saved. This is the gist of the sermon.

The Minister of Art paints a different scenario. Not necessarily better, just another view. Jesus does NOT teach your behavior gets you into Heaven. That eliminates God's grace and His 100 percent activity in bestowing salvation. No one can get themselves saved by what they do. Here are some points to consider:

1) The young ruler came to Jesus inquiring about eternal life. He was confident he qualified for eternal life by his keeping the commandments: his works.

2) The young ruler underestimated who Jesus was. Jesus was not just a good man. Jesus was, is, God. Jesus is grace.

3) The young ruler was told his identity must no longer be known as the "rich" young ruler. He should be known as the young ruler, or the ruler. But, if he gives away all his possessions to the poor, he will then be poor like most of them are. That's irresponsible. He should be a wise steward of his riches. He should be the well-known benevolent assistant to the poor and needy.

4) *Of course, he goes away sorrowful. Do you expect him to jump for joy? Turn cartwheels?* He just now found out he may be selling his prized possessions. He must reject his old identity. He has totally misunderstood salvation. His whole life turned upside down in just a few minutes. This is all upsetting. *Being sorrowful is certainly the expectation.* That's entirely normal.

5) Mark 10:21 indicates Jesus LOVED him. That doesn't indicate the young man did not become saved. How many rich young guys keep all the commandments from their youth? The guy wasn't evil. He just thought he was a good person, deserving to go to Heaven. *How many people have the same assumption?*

However, to understand salvation by grace, such as a Pre-Life Elect inauthentic identity, our Roleplay mission is to make our life and the lives of others around us better. How? Sacrifice our life for the lives of others who do not know about salvation. The rich young ruler's life should begin to reflect the change Jesus has preached. He will begin to plan the changes. Life doesn't change overnight. Patience.

> Then Jesus beholding him loved him, and said unto him, One thing thou lackest: go thy way, sell whatsoever thou hast, and give to the poor, and thou shalt have treasure in heaven: and come, take up the cross, and follow me (Mark 10:21).

POSITION OF PATIENCE — Post Post Postscript

As we begin to plan our changes, our life should be committed to a relationship with the environment of people, not the earthly environment. PEOPLE. The benefits to the earth follow from this.

This will require patience. IMPATIENCE follows from MISTRUST in the ability to do anything meaningful to change the environment. WE are the environment. PEOPLE are the environment.

The Serpent, Eve, and Adam could have become suspicious of their responsibility in the Garden. They doubted God. They doubted who they were. They didn't see themselves as the environment they represented. *The environment is out there*, they thought, *and I'm in here. Their misapplication of Free Will led them to see themselves as separate from the environment.*

Ego-Centracism led to Ego-Skepticism (Glossary of Colors). Their inquiry into details of physical, mental, and spiritual identity could have come to an apex. They desired more. Nothing necessarily wrong with that. But HOW to get more? They thought about it. What they did know was they were forbidden to know good and evil. *Good and evil about what?* Themselves? The Garden? God? Did they trust God? Did they retain trust in God but lose trust in themselves? Exactly who were they? How far could they go without more knowledge? Is it really wrong to want to know yourself fully, good and bad?

And what about Lucifer? Lucifer may have asked, "Am I really an autonomous creature? Am I really alive? What is life? *My life or God's life through me?"* Angels don't age. Their knowledge is comprehensive at creation. Lucifer may not have been on a quest for more KNOWLEDGE, as were Adam and Eve, but for FREEDOM. Omnipotence. The power to behave as desired is paramount. Why can't God just delete unapproved behavior after the fact? He can do anything!

We all desire knowledge. We all desire freedom.

For now, at a point when God enters our life, the question becomes, *Will I still be me?*

You say, "I really don't want to be like most Christians I know. Besides, I may have family, close friends, and associates who depend on me to continue being me. Are we expected to drop our persona instantly and follow Jesus? *How can we follow someone we just recently met?"*

Patience, patience, patience.

(Matthew 19:16–30, Luke 18:18–30 and the following citation from Mark)

> And when he was gone forth into the way, there came one running, and kneeled to him, and asked him, Good Master, what shall I do that I may inherit eternal life? And Jesus said unto him, Why callest thou me good? there is none good but one, that is, God Thou knowest the commandments, Do not commit adultery, Do not kill, Do

not steal, Do not bear false witness, Defraud not, Honour thy father and mother. And he answered and said unto him, Master, all these have I observed from my youth. Then Jesus beholding him loved him, and said unto him, One thing thou lackest: go thy way, sell whatsoever thou hast, and give to the poor, and thou shalt have treasure in heaven: and come, take up the cross, and follow me. And he was sad at that saying, and went away grieved: for he had great possessions. And Jesus looked round about, and saith unto his disciples, how hardly they that have riches shall enter into the kingdom of God! And the disciples were astonished at his words. But Jesus answereth again, and saith unto them, Children, how hard is it for them that trust in riches to enter into the kingdom of God! It is easier for a camel to go through the eye of a needle, than for a rich man to enter into the kingdom of God. And they were astonished out of measure, saying among themselves, who then can be saved? And Jesus looking upon them saith, with men it is impossible, but not with God: for with God all things are possible. Then Peter began to say unto him, Lo, we have left all, and have followed thee. And Jesus answered and said, Verily I say unto you, There is no man that hath left house, or brethren, or sisters, or father, or mother, or wife, or children, or lands, for my sake, and the gospel's, But he shall receive an hundredfold now in this time, houses, and brethren, and sisters, and mothers, and children, and lands, with persecutions; and in the world to come eternal life. But many that are first shall be last; and the last first (Mark 10:17-31).

CHAPTER 5

ARTISTIC MINISTRY

Are you happy with the pastor of your church? Are you pleased with the church you attend? What if you hear of a MARVI-RPIA group meeting in your area? Would you go? Let's just say you hear of one and decide to go. The group meets on the last Friday evening and Saturday evening of the month. You arrive at the gathering, meet a few other people, and enter the building. There are refreshments, artwork, and music. You choose a seat and await the start of service.

A message for this evening regards the passage from John 8:3-11:

> And the scribes and Pharisees brought unto him a woman taken in adultery; and when they had set her in the midst, they say unto him, Master, this woman was taken in adultery, in the very act. Now Moses in the law commanded us, that such should be stoned: but what sayest thou? This they said, tempting him that they might have to accuse him. But Jesus stooped down, and with his finger wrote on the ground, as though he heard them not. So when they continued asking him, he lifted up himself, and said unto them, He that is without sin among you, let him first cast a stone at her. And again he stooped down, and wrote on the ground. And they which heard it, being convicted by their own conscience, went out one by one, beginning at the eldest, even unto the last: and Jesus was left alone, and the woman standing in the midst. When Jesus had lifted up himself, and saw none but the woman, he said unto her, Woman, where are those thine accusers? hath no man condemned thee? She said, No man, Lord. And Jesus said unto her, neither do I condemn thee: go, and sin no more (John 8:3-11).

Typically, a pastor will teach starting from verse eleven. Go and sin no more. That is the message. Jesus offers a pardon for sins, but you should stop the sin lest you be stoned. Lest you die in your sins. Jesus loves. Jesus forgives. Meet with Jesus. He is willing to give you a new life, a second chance. We are all like this guilty woman. Say yes to the Lord today. Be born-again. The opportunity is here through the Savior who loves you. God is love. Won't you say yes?

But the "Minister of Art" doesn't end with verse eleven. The Minister of Art begins speaking from the imagery of Christian Reformed Impressionism. The speech is not a sermon. Though the subject matter is religious, the speaker isn't providing a religious service. *This is an Art Appreciation Class.*

Woman: Jesus, You say go and sin no more. I will go. But how am I going to sin no more? Everyone sins! I am going to sin because I am a sinner. I may even commit adultery tonight, next week, or next month.

Jesus: Then you will probably be caught again, and you will probably be stoned to death.

Woman: I know. I am a harlot, a worthless whorish woman. Or maybe I'm being blackmailed by a wealthy man, or constantly molested by a relative. I'm a drunkard; men take advantage of me. Whatever, it doesn't matter to the authorities. I got caught. Not the man. He is not here to be stoned. I'm the one on trial. Life is so unfair. I hate everything. I hate myself. I actually want to die.

Jesus: Listen, my daughter, you are not your body. You are a Roleplayer. Don't despair. Don't feel trapped in an identity that is not really you. Who you are is an Elect Person in Paradise. Your Roleplay identity—adulteress, an alcoholic, or victim of abuse—is from heredity, the environment, and experiences of life. Adam and Eve initiated it. You were forced into a body, in this time, in this place, in history. Circumstances pushed you here from many different directions.

The person you seem to be is not really your true identity. You are the product of forces you did not permit. Your ethnicity, gender, age, height, weight, features, intelligence, and talents were all dictated. You had no knowledge of this, and no interest in being brought to life. It was all a setup. You were framed. So now what?

If you understand and accept this premise I offer to you, it will provide great freedom to you. You are not trapped in a situation with no way out. Destroying your body because you hate being you is no way out. You are not your body. You are safely in Paradise. You are in a Demonstration of Free Will. God is proving the Error of Free Will that Adam and Eve chose. Adam and Eve were given a death sentence, but also a subsequent life sentence through procreation. Their lives would be reclaimed through a Mediator, a Solution to death—Me, Jesus Christ.

However, procreation also meant sinful human beings would emerge even after Christ, the Mediator, was born. That means people like you. But people like you are not the same people whom God guarantees are saved before He created the world—the Elect in Paradise. People like you continue to be born as the Demonstration of Free Will. This must be proved with great diversity, in human bodies like Adam and Eve's, beyond any question of doubt.

Go and sin no more means you can go and be someone else. You don't have to struggle to define some identity with which you don't identify. That imposed identity isn't really you. That is a character. You were in a prison; you don't have to remain in prison. There's no lock on the door.

Your present life is not one single event. It's a middle stage between pre-life and afterlife. You're not your body.

Art Appreciation continues with another, more modern-day character:

Modern Male: But what if I'm in that demographic with the highest suicide rate among ethnic youth? I'm male, young, ethnic, poor, not well educated, unhealthy, and unskilled. My culture seems one of the worst in the world. Additionally, science tells me there is no God, no afterlife.

Jesus: Whatever you choose to do is the product of the Free Will role you find yourself in. You don't have to accept your role. By refusing to continue the role that started at birth, you don't have to commit suicide. You can accept being the Pre-Life Elect person promised by God before the world was created. Your true identity is safe in Paradise. Intuition tells you life is grossly unfair. That's why suicide is so prominent in every society. Life has no meaning. End it. It doesn't even matter. No one really cares.

This no longer has to be the case. There is another way of representing who you are—a fair way. The Pre-Life Elect person in Paradise. The true authentic you.

For now, the Elect Roleplayer living in despair, the prison door opens. Your forced inauthentic identity may look the same, live in the same place, or go to the same job, but now you have a future. You have hope. You are not your body. Your body implies a one-time chance at life. It goes away. It's just the product of a long series of lives before yours. You've been taught to accept your circumstances. Be happy, be proud, be thankful to be alive. And that may help some people. For others, it won't.

And this is why life seems great for some and horrible for others. It's just a demonstration of what happens when Free Will plays out. This is Free Will to do what YOU want; not what GOD wants. You're a character playing a role based on a long line of previous characters. It's not you—the real you.

You have no need to consider the oblivion of suicide, the escape many seek. Your escape is in the assurance that the Greatest Person who ever lived believed in the infallibility of scripture. INERRANCY, the Bible translations, isn't the essential matter. It's the fact that the scriptures are INFALLIBLE, 100 percent trustworthy. That is the issue. Jesus said they are. We can trust Jesus. He arrived as a human being to correct The Error of Adam and Eve. He lived a sinless human life. He was publicly put to death. He arose from death to guarantee eternal life.

The scriptures teach God saved you before you were born. The "you" here on earth now is just playing out the role of Free Will. Believing this is extremely helpful in making every day a better day. A day that now seems back in your own hands. Life still seems unfair, *but now the unfairness is not final.* The unfairness is the result of what all humans deserve, but God provided the Solution that resolves the unfairness.

Free Will of created living creatures is the hallmark of a flawless design. God created Adam and Eve as Roleplayers and set the Free Will Demonstration in place. What would they do? Trust God's will for themselves or pursue their own will for themselves?

Satan, the Devil, disputes the Free Will demonstration. He says Adam and Eve were a product of a flawed design. Angels are a flawed design. Flawless living creatures should have unlimited freedom of behavior. God is capable of correcting all our errors on the fly. He could do it. He won't do it. Adam and Eve chose to die rather than be limited in their knowledge of good and evil. Numerous angels risked their lives to leave Heaven and undertake a mission to create a redeemer for themselves through procreation. Why shouldn't they? God promised salvation through procreation for humans. Aren't angels as worthy? Should they express their Free Will? *A creature's objective is liberty AND equality. Otherwise, life loses meaning.*

We know many angels agree with Satan, *but the First-Class Angels did not agree.* They did not fall with Abaddon (Apollyon in Greek)) and the Third-Class Angels. They are not imprisoned in chains of darkness, as described in the account of the Flood in Genesis, 2 Peter, Jude, and Revelation. They did not fall with "Lucifer" and the Second-Class Angels. *So First-Class Angels are similar to the Pre-Life Elect persons. They are safe.*

Yes, God can correct any creature's errors on the fly. However, God is God! He is not the 24/7 on-call repairman. Flawless creatures are not children who have permission to behave like irresponsible spoiled brats. Nonetheless, God provided an arena to show the interests of flawless living creatures, both humans and angels. For humans, this is an autonomous, dynamic, life inside time and space. For angels, an autonomous, dynamic life inside and outside time and space. The expression of those interests plays out in the visible world and the invisible world.

Thanks to God that He created us—Elect Persons—before He created the earth.

> There were giants in the earth in those days; and also after that, when the sons of God came in unto the daughters of men, and they

bare children to them, the same became mighty men which were of old, men of renown (Genesis 6:4).

For if God spared not the angels that sinned, but cast them down to hell, and delivered them into chains of darkness, to be reserved unto judgment (2 Peter 2:4).

And the angels which kept not their first estate, but left their own habitation, he hath reserved in everlasting chains under darkness unto the judgment of the great day (Jude 1:6).

And they had a king over them, which is the angel of the bottomless pit, whose name in the Hebrew tongue is Abaddon, but in the Greek tongue hath his name Apollyon (Revelation 9:11).

According as he hath chosen us in him before the foundation of the world, that we should be holy and without blame before him in love (Ephesians 1:4).

CHAPTER 6

OPPORTUNITY

This chapter, "OPPORTUNITY," was initially titled "REPENT." Repent is a bit of a negative term. Repent is a spiritual word. Repent typically means a realization of error and an interest to stop what one did in error. MARVI-RPIA emphasizes that your identity is an INAUTHENTIC identity based on a construct of attributes imposed on you. Your AUTHENTIC identity is a construct in a Pre-Life Paradise awaiting the end of this Free Will Demonstration initiated by Adam and Eve.

When the Demonstration ends, your inauthentic identity will join your authentic identity, assuming you are an Elect Roleplayer. Elect Roleplayers are those 100 percent human beings who receive intervention by God (Holy Spirit Identity-HSID) after conception, in the womb, during life, or in the last seconds before death. Those persons not 100 percent human will cease to exist at death. They have no soul, no spirit. Otherwise, special circumstances may apply.

In the case of OPPORTUNITY, the idea of repentance is to recognize how detrimental it may be to ACCEPT the so-called inauthentic identity.

While reading this, you may be living in the country where you were born. As an example, let's take Japan. You were born in the last thirty years, to Japanese parents, you're female, divorced, have children, teach school, are middle-class, and living in rural Japan. Your life is better than most, worse than many. There is no real incentive to "repent." This life is not great, but it is acceptable. Or is it? Do you really like being who you are?

What about depression? Yes. Resentment? Yes. Hatred? Yes. Suicide? No.

What about slow suicide? Drinking too much. Eating too much or eating the wrong things. Drugs. No exercise. Insomnia. Stress. Lack of sunshine. Toxic friends. Toxic fun.

There's a good chance many people don't like being who they are but feel such thoughts are unhealthy. Those thoughts may even be a sign of mental illness, culminating in suicidal thoughts. Not liking who you are is also not conducive to excelling in the job market. Most of us work to earn a living. Employers seek those who are confident, capable, and work well with others. The general public shows favor to people who favor themselves.

MARVI-RPIA presents an OPPORTUNITY to repent without the usual negative connotations. Not liking who you are may manifest itself in subtle ways, in obvious ways, and in dangerous, unintentional ways. If an opportunity comes along that can show a reasonable way of not continuing to be me, I may take it. Why? Because this current "me" is not the "me" I ever really wanted or expected. How can I explore not liking myself while maintaining a positive image to others? *How can not liking myself be constructive?*

Or, how do I repent? Assuming there is a chance, an opportunity, to change my identity, how do I proceed? Everyone has so much vested in their identity that making any changes affects not just themselves, but their family, friends, and associates.

We're getting to the beauty of art. As has been said, beauty is in the eye of the beholder. Your change in identity is from a change in how you behold identity. Your intuition tells you your present identity is inauthentic. You've done bad things in your life. Bad things were done to you. You desire to do certain things but can't because of your looks, age, height, weight, intelligence, financial status, marital status, health, etcetera.

Understanding who you are as an inauthentic Free Will Roleplayer, initiated by Adam and Eve, resolved to be a Pre-Life Elect authentic identity, in Paradise, by the Person of Jesus Christ, opens a way of perceiving a new present life. *Now, I am not forced to accept my present identity.* I was forced to accept it before MARVI-RPIA because every other traditional worldview dictates we are our body. As such, we're trapped in whatever heredity, the environment, and experiences have imposed on us.

Perceiving, believing, or assuming the beauty of my Pre-Life Elect identity lifts a tremendous weight from me. Who I am now is just a temporary role of circumstances. I even have a much better definition of who I always hoped God to be but never really heard. Now, more things about life open up. *This new God I'm now exposed to, the 'One' who has saved the real me before He created the world, is the God I can believe in.* He *does* care. He *does* have a plan. The world looks much different. It's still terrible but not as hopeless as atheists and agnostics suggest.

Atheists allege there is no God. WE are God. That could be true if there is no God of the Bible. Agnostics suggest we just don't have the ability to know God or the evidence that verifies His existence. *Agnostics may go further by saying, "I don't know and neither does anyone else know. Such knowledge is unknowable."* And, until such knowledge becomes apparent to them, we see agnostics living as atheists.

By the way, they don't have a choice. *They can't evaluate both sides, atheism AND theism, because theism is unavailable to them.* God has to open their eyes to spiritual truth. We don't have the ability to open our own eyes.

So, is it God's fault agnostics and atheists aren't saved because God hasn't opened their spiritual eyes? *No. It's Adam and Eve's fault. God has already saved human beings before He created the world.* Everyone since then has been a Roleplayer, proving—with their lives, your life, and my life—the Demonstration of the Error of Free Will. Not that having 'Free Will' is error; it's exercising Free Will to disobey God. That is error.

Another way of saying we can't open our own spiritual eyes is if we could open our own eyes, we would do so. If we do so, we would recognize God as His Majesty the Blessed One Forever, amen. That would put us right back to the status Adam and Eve had in the Garden of Eden. Free Will all over again. How long does it take to become discontent with God's Will for our life? Whether as a flawless creature or a flawed creature, Ego-Skepticism and Ego-Centracism (Glossary of Colors) prompt us to again choose our own will versus continuing in the will of God. *Now, we are back to the present-day Demonstration of Free Will.*

Today, the world sees a different "good" than what theists proclaim. Orthodox teaching is the "Good News" of Jesus Christ. This news is not so great for the majority of the planet. If it was, why isn't the world a better place? Why aren't all religions the Christian religion? Why doesn't Jesus show Himself? If we have Free Will to do the right things and not do the wrong things to reach salvation, why aren't the most intelligent people all Christians? They should know what to do, and we should then follow them. What makes the most sense to almost all people? Anything? How much control do we actually have? Is control an illusion?

Can you imagine how a person might think about their present life if they felt they had their true identity waiting for them in Heaven? Everything has already been accomplished to guarantee their eternal life. Free Will is an illusion, but a temporary illusion, not a permanent illusion.

What if thinking of this present life as a temporary demonstration of Free Will helps you to visualize religion in a new way? You're an actor on stage: a temporary role of improvisation.

Your future is like getting two miraculous engagement rings for marriage! For marriage number one, you will be joined with your flawless true identity in Heaven. For marriage number two, you will be joined with Jesus Christ in a second ceremony of everlasting true love.

As you go about your day, you don't have to do anything different or say anything different. The sun shines a little brighter, the moon looks better, and the night stars have a different twinkle. Life has a new rhythm. There is a different hope. A chance there can be something other than what you've come to accept as reality.

What do you really want out of life? So far, MARVI-RPIA may have you doubting if an inauthentic identity, your Roleplay identity, is capable of determining what is best.

Let's look at that question this way: What do people generally want most for their life? What is most important to make living the best it can be? Searching the internet reveals the usual things people desire: money, happiness, love, freedom, fame, sex, health, eternal life. You could probably add some things to the list that make it more comprehensive.

Once such a list is compiled, MARVI-RPIA has more imagery to present. Think of the time when the angels had not sinned. Sin has not entered the world that God recently created. The Serpent, Adam, and Eve were enjoying a nice day in the Garden of Eden. Didn't they all have EVERYTHING? They had ongoing life with NO prospect of death. They had magnificent beauty, intelligence, health, companionship, love, shelter, sustenance, a beautiful environment, and no reason to question if any of this would ever end. This scenario includes the angels. And they were all "with the Lord" in a manner we can't quite comprehend.

Now, with MARVI-RPIA, we have the possibility of realizing a similar pre-sin time frame. As Elect Roleplayers, we will join our authentic identity, the Pre-Life Elect/SSID, in the afterlife, or when the Free Will Demonstration ends. *We already have our prayers and ultimate wishes granted. Repeat. Our prayers are already answered!* Life is waiting for us in the future, which was done in the past. We'll have a clean slate. A beautiful slate.

For now, make the most of each day. Tomorrow is not guaranteed. But there's no need to worry about anything. Why? Because there is a God. A God that does care. A God that has a plan for all of us that absolutely has to be better than the MARVI-RPIA plan. And the MARVI-RPIA plan is pretty fantastic!

Think of it. We will soon be able to come into our INHERITANCE! In an inheritance to be granted, the fortune is set. Those who are to inherit the fortune come into possession of the inheritance later. Going back to the beginning of time, the Trinity grants the inheritance which is salvation. The Super-Spiritual Identity (SSIDs) received the inheritance of salvation past tense, and we receive the inheritance as Elect-Roleplayers' future tense. For the present, we have our role to play in the Demonstration of Free Will.

This is the Great News about the Good News!

A quick review:

It seems God set determinism, which is salvation, for preexistent individual humans. This would be eternal life for flawless human beings outside time and space.

Then He created angels as ministering spirits. Angels were without determinism. They possessed Free Will.

At some point, Lucifer inquired about omnipotence—unrestricted behavior. God then constructed a Demonstration.

He created Roleplayers: the Serpent, Adam, and Eve. They were given Free Will to accept His will for their lives or reject it. Rejection was symbolized as acquiring limited omniscience in the form of the Tree of the Knowledge of Good and Evil.

The angels observed this Demonstration, as it also applied to their acceptance of God's will for their lives. Sometime earlier, the angels inquired about unrestricted omnipotence, the ability to behave as desired as God repaired or removed indiscretions.

So-called First-Class Angels vowed never to exercise such Free Will to disobey God's will for their life. Other angels (labeled later as Second-Class and Third-Class) abstained from such a vow.

However, as the Demonstration of Free Will unfolded in the Garden of Eden, the angels observed humans choose death rather than obey God. The next surprise was God's promise to provide a Redeemer through procreation, giving Adam and Eve their lives back to them in the future.

From this, Third-Class Angels left Heaven to seek a redeemer for themselves, also via procreation. Second-Class Angels remained to plead the case for angel equality with humans and denounce God's favoritism to them. Animosity grew. An angel's status as ministering spirits to God AND ministering spirits to humans may have been too much. Humans have proved unworthy to be true sons of God. Angels were the true sons of God. The only angel blemish is seeking the same fail-safe for Error that humans received:

Opportunity.

Lucifer sought Opportunity for angels to pursue unrestricted behavior. The Serpent, Eve, and Adam sought Opportunity for unrestricted knowledge. Both insist that flawless living creatures are flawless only if autonomy, ability, and OPPORTUNITY exist. Otherwise, discontent will eventually arise. Discontent leads to opposition.

However, identity can't be defined by the flawless living creature. Well, it can be, but it won't be authoritative. That must come from the One who created the flawless creature.

God.

CHAPTER 7

SEX EDUCATION—PART 1

Any comprehensive review of human identity must include sexuality. Theology doesn't address the specifics of sexuality. It's all general principles of scripture. Religion goes further to suggest how scripture applies to identity. Traditionally, popular art does not address the verbal specifics of sexuality. It's all visual until you include literature as an art form. *Connecting the Dots of Identity* will address theology, religion, and artistic specifics of sexuality. It would be irresponsible not to. We are excessively sexual beings.

Religion tries to take the lead in sex education. Unfortunately, religion has focused on what NOT to do rather than on what TO do. Parents demand the right to teach sex-ed, but all too often, they don't teach. They're too closely involved with the child to be an objective instructor. It's awkward. It's embarrassing. It's a challenge not to provide too much too soon, or too little, thus becoming totally ineffective.

Isn't it better to allow sex-ed professionals to instruct children? They're trained to know and teach the material best suited for age-appropriate children.

Yes, but that would mean sex-ed is passed on to private education or public education. Private schools are hampered by organizational and parental guidelines. This is because they are supported by individuals, religious bodies, and value-based groups. There may be NO sex education provided. Often, there is no mandate to teach it. They may teach the so-called basics such as abstinence, anatomy, contraception, disease, and procreation. They may not. There is no national policy.

Public schools lack moral objectivity, so sex-ed is a factor of what is considered normal sexual standards. This is moral subjectivity. Currently, only half of the states in the USA require sex-ed in middle or high school. The other twenty-five or so states have no sex-ed curriculum or else they include sex-ed type material within the general instruction programs. Some states notify parents that sex-ed is being featured or perhaps allow an opt-out feature. Other states make abstinence (until marriage) prominent with no complementary teaching on contraception.

Whichever situation you find yourself in, action is better than no action. We know some parents never seem to find the right time to act. Don't let that happen to you.

MARVI-RPIA's sex-ed class may seem more like scrawls and blotches than attractive, helpful religious art. And, of course, it's expected that any details that may be construed as inappropriate or offensive will not be illustrated here. This leaves room to at least highlight subjects that may initiate further exploration with the child.

What follows is an outline of topics that are beyond the "big three" concerns for almost every sex-ed plan: birth control, disease, and anatomy.

See Planned Parenthood and Center for Disease Control for comparison. Planned Parenthood (USA/Global)

MARVI-RPIA SEX-ED CURRICULUM SCENARIO – Classes 1-20:

Class 1—*PROCREATION.* Accidental, purposeful, or forceful re-creation of yourself and a second person. Should include artificial insemination.

Pursue clarifying assumptions and debunking rumors, myths, and misconceptions of how and why pregnancy occurs. Includes specific sessions regarding the impulse, motivation, and expectation of procreation.

Class 2—*UNIFICATION.* The legal and public commitment to unite with another person in marriage. Discusses why God's sanctioned plan is forming a two-person team to understand and promote love, resist exploitation, and exemplify the traditional male-female relationship.

Class 3—*PREVENTION.* Philosophy of abstaining from sexual activity until marriage. Pros and cons of marriage. Religious, cultural, and practical reasons to delay sex. Includes confinement, deterrents, threats, and coercion.

Class 4—*ELIMINATION.* Sex organs as multifunction components of sensuality, waste removal, and health indicators.

Class 5—*RECREATION.* The pursuit of enjoyment with a spouse, or alone, for fun and games, stress relief, physical, and mental health.

Class 6—*STIMULATION.* Sensual arousal via objects, self-stimulation, or stimulation by other persons. May occur by accident, on purpose, by coercion, or by force. Often initiated to evaluate mental and physical sensual attributes. Useful as a substitute for sexual events or relationships. Caution for overindulgence, carelessness, and abnormalities.

Class 7—*ATTENTION/SENSATION/EXCITATION.* Dynamics of romantic friendship, hugging, kissing, cuddling, holding hands. Acts of foreplay. Rules of safety. How five senses become over-whelmed. How the body overrules the mind. Alcohol and drug interactions. Concerns for others' feelings of rejection. Strategies for going past points of no return. Discretion in sharing intimate information with others.

Class 8A—*SIMULATION (MENTAL).* Activity for adventure, fun, stupidity, risk-reward scenarios, what-if scenarios, and recollection of past events. Compare/contrast to lust, covetousness, error, and evil intentions. Combines fantasy, education, and problem-solving.

Class 8B—*SIMULATION (PHYSICAL).* Consists of toys, machines, paraphernalia, and realistic models that may assist disadvantaged persons as well as the advantaged.

Class 9—*FUNCTION.* Details of operation, purpose, anatomy, care, maintenance, and issues that arise regarding genitalia and related anatomy to overall sexuality.

Class 10A—*PROTECTION (Emotional).* Guard against intruders, molesters, abusers, bullies, and inadvertent public exposure. Preserving modesty as a virtue. Design, develop, and maintain safety protocols that enhance stability in difficult circumstances.

Class 10B—*PROTECTION (Medical).* Applied physical techniques, resources, and objects that obstruct pregnancy, prevent disease, and offer a range of options regarding sexuality. Includes history of contraception, abstinence, celibacy, libido suppression, and useful substitutes. Incorporates home remedies, medical procedures, and drugs into the discussion.

Class 10C—*PROTECTION (Physical)*. Inappropriate sexual advancement may be met with offensive as well as defensive actions. Applies to women, the LGBTQ community, and men. Teaches strategy, tools, and awareness that may assist in the safety of the individual and loved ones.

Class 11—*ALTERATION*. Strategies that enhance or modify the body for sexual, gender, or aesthetic purposes (surgery, medicine, clothing, cosmetics, counseling, add-ons, etcetera).

Class 12—*DEVIATION*. Implications of socially unapproved behavior, cultural taboos, abnormal sexual activities. Covers acts of intent and non-intent by compulsion from trauma, rape, molestation, and abuse.

Class 13—*OCCUPATION*. Full-time/part-time risqué livelihood that is consensual or nonconsensual. Covers how to get in, how to get out, how to stay out, and how to avoid.

Class 14—*VALIDATION*. Confirmation that sex organs function properly and verification of being desirable. Provides feedback on the ability to attract suitors, acquire dates, and flirt effectively. Caution as questionable high-risk behavior to authenticate insecure identity.

Class 15—*CONTENTION*. Misuse of sexual activity manifested as resentment and defiance to protest sexual constraints in the community or society. The in-your-face rebellion that is often a consequence of unresolved identity issues or trauma.

Class 16—*OBSESSION*. A conscious and subconscious preoccupation with sex that produces significant distraction and diversion from other life activities. Addresses early signs, co-factors, worst-case scenarios, and therapy.

Class 17—*DEVASTATION*. Perceived ruination of life from a single event or multiple events characterized by past, current, or suppressed experiences. Inability to progress beyond perceived worthlessness, whether in or out of a relationship.

CLASS 18—*ABORTION*. Personal and scientific details of when, where, why, and how human conception is terminated. Arguments regarding policies based on separation of church and state. Offers discussion from theistic and atheistic points of view.

Class 19A—*RELIGION*. Affirms absence of sex in the Garden of Eden. Reasons procreation was initiated: (a) to produce the human Solution to death—which is Jesus Christ, (b) to produce Free Will Roleplayers who illustrate the error of Adam and Eve. Includes classic religious prohibitions against sex outside marriage (adultery, fornication, homosexuality, bestiality, incest, rape, pedophilia, prostitution, and etcetera).

CLASS 19B—*PREDESTINATION/ELECTION/SALVATION*. Sex-ed from the IMPRESSION of Reformed theology via MARVI-RPIA. Emphasis on the inauthentic identity as defined by heredity, environment, and experiences and the contrast with authentic identity defined by scripture as Election-Predestination. Features Godly Marriage Material, Team Companion, Single-Persons Champion, and Team Player.

CLASS 20—*CONVERSATION*. Important sex-ed method with the potential to do the most good. One-on-one discussions. Group discussions. Simulated discussions. Observed discussions.

Proposing to speak with children on these topics helps them to understand that you're willing to communicate. If children show no interest in discussion, be sure to locate a resource you trust that covers a comprehensive approach to sexuality. If parents aren't involved, children are resourceful. Their resources are often not trustworthy, ill-advised, or tragic.

Communication is the surest chance of gaining and maintaining trust with your child. When this is in place, you can't be faulted for negligence in educating the child. Don't overlook the importance of listening. Education is not all monologues. Learn to listen, even listen to what is NOT being said. Be open-minded. Be patient. Hear with your heart. Trust your intuition. Face your fears.

Like many of you, MARVI-RPIA would prefer to stay out of such an intimate personal matter. But wouldn't that be apathy? Irresponsibility? Are you aware of what is being taught in public schools? Are you aware of which organizations provide the curriculum? Find out. *You will discover how woefully inadequate children are prepared to manage sexuality.* If you care, you must be involved. If you won't be involved, the sex-ed job continues to be managed by bureaucracy—and the internet.

Sex education by bureaucracy means individual rights and family rights are gradually replaced by the government. Don't be intimidated by the task of parenting. Find help. Be a helper. Keep the government at bay.

Sex-ed by the internet means … well, anything goes. And goes. And that means ANYTHING!

You don't have children? You can still be involved. It's never too late to learn about sexuality, gender, and identity. There's a big difference between science, belief, and misinformation. What you think is true may not be. How you feel about an issue may hinder your understanding of it. You may be emotionally biased. Your subjective ideas can cloud the objective view. You may be influenced by the larger group you have an allegiance to. Their view is the trusted view. You follow them. “Trust but verify” as the motto goes from the deceased ex-president.

Think for yourself. Don't concede your Roleplay character. You're not forced to if you understand the Roleplay and identity array painted by MARVI-RPIA. Maybe you could influence others to do likewise. Admittedly, this is a bit much to expect. Life is a bit much to expect.

Another aspect of sex education is counseling and therapy. *Adult relationships suffer to a great degree from poor sex education or no sex education.* Once again, the church's role is not at the forefront. The brunt of the counseling may fall to the pastor. The pastor may or may not be qualified for the position. Professional therapists may not have a Christian background. As daunting as sex-ed proves to be, Connecting The Dots Of Identity intends to be a factor in this challenge. How this factor is played out remains to be seen. Meanwhile, we need all the help we can get.

The last sex-ed point regards acceptance of LGBTQ rights. Christians specify common graces, or rights, which should be extended to people regardless of their sexual orientation. The LGBTQ community disagrees. They suggest Christians seek to withhold, restrict, and deny the same basic rights heterosexuals enjoy. These rights include marriage, access to medicine, surgery, hormone therapy, sports, military, and certain church services. In the Christian's defense, they point out that many so-called LGBTQ "rights" are not Christian—they are anti-religious. Therefore, they are not condoned.

Christians do not tolerate bullying, abuse, or harassment against the gay community. No "true" Christian supports violence, persecution, or advocates the death penalty for gay people. Discrimination in housing, employment, and education is against Christian principles.

Meanwhile, as non-Christian entities create legislation that mandates Christian compliance or restricts Christian opposition, tension grows and sex-ed suffers. *This is especially the case where legislation mandates the church not only comply with the gay community but demands celebration, participation, and advancement for it.*

Somehow, compromises must be introduced. How can male/female restroom accommodations include LGBTQ persons? How can marriage rights include gay couples throughout the nation? Transgender athletes await approval to participate with women. Adoption agencies evaluate same-sex couple applications. The military must adopt protocols that address scenarios outside the conventional male/female roles.

MARVI-RPIA's Roleplay imagery seeks to help the Christian Roleplayer see past the temporary position of heterosexual/homosexual. The hope is that non-Christians benefit also. We must get better at how to think about sex—not just talk about sex.

Male and female Roleplay is increasingly redefined by nonreligious subjective standards. Religious standards are being vilified as illegitimate and unrealistic by nonreligious groups. Religion professes strict male and female guidelines for behavior. Your thoughts are private, but your behavior must adhere to biblical principles of opposite-sex behavior.

Secular opposition to religious doctrine refutes restrictions on male and female expression. *This is on the basis that thinking and behaving are a function of heredity, the environment, and experiences. Identity is not a choice. This is Biology 101.*

Imagine converting from one sexual orientation to the other. One way it's done is through spiritual intercession (HSID). Otherwise, converting from one sexual orientation to the other requires open and honest communication regarding gender identity, gender expectation, and gender expression. Is it possible to be truly open and honest with yourself, open and honest with others trying to "convert" you, and finally, to be open and honest with God?

Do you know yourself well enough to be open and honest? Honest with a "self" that is the product of heredity, the environment, and experiences? A self that was forced upon you without your knowledge, permission, or interest?

SEX EDUCATION 1—POSTSCRIPT

Q & A sessions often get heated during discussions of sexual identity. This is especially true when the participants are young and speak from emotion rather than reason. They shouldn't be blamed when we realize how their sex education has been acquired.

Well-meaning Christians don't necessarily have the forthrightness to discuss sexual matters in a setting that may require it. Instead, the nuances of sex are met with overall principles that don't address the specifics of what makes sex so bad, so unspeakable.

The youngsters ask: *What's wrong with two men or two women having sex? What's wrong with group sex? What's bad about oral, anal, and vaginal sex? Bestiality, pedophilia, and rape are wrong, but tell us exactly WHY they're wrong.* Is it because God says so? The law says so? Culture says so? Please define "wrong"!

We get nice answers. We get standard answers. We get legal answers. And we get answers from the world. *The world that not only gives the most direct, gruesome, and crude answers, but answers that mislead, traumatize, and confound the inquirer.* The inquirer may come away not one bit wiser. More information, yes. But wisdom? Not likely. In such cases, they could come away with a sexual maturity they may not have expected, though it came necessarily with the exposure. The knowledge of good and evil, as it were.

No parent or educator wants to give sex a negative image. Unfortunately, in the absence of quality sex education, all the positive imagery of sexuality cannot overcome the consequence of sexual negativity.

We are dependent on the legal system to help manage the sexual adversity we suffer. However, as laws are overlooked, circumvented, or rewritten, the future appears mostly bleak.

A case in point is the current situation with gender identity. When gender is discussed, Christians oppose the assumption that a person can change their gender. They say it's impossible. A male born as a male will always be a male, and a female born female will always be a female. No gender transition from male to female or female to male can be achieved.

However, gender EXPRESSION is possibly where the contention arises. Miscommunication between Christians and the LGBTQ community often causes much of the conflict. The Christian declares to the young man: You can never be a girl. You were born a boy. The young man declares—I can certainly express myself as a girl as long as people like you don't prohibit me. My expression is what matters. It doesn't matter what label or category or misconception applies to me. I fight for my right to self-expression. As an infant, I had no choice. As an adult, I do.

CHAPTER 8

SEX EDUCATION—PART 2

Sex-ed doesn't end with communicating principles to children and young adults. Adults also benefit by reviewing the twenty MARVI-RPIA sex-ed classes. Sex-ed essentials are appropriate to guide adults in their thinking and behavior. This includes married adults.

Connecting the Dots of Identity is meant to enhance the lives of everyone exposed to it. As the time comes to discuss sex education, the focus centers on children and young adults. The overall image is intended to convey how sex-ed ties into navigating identity in the formative years. These years usually cover the time a person is still living at home, under their parents' supervision. At this time, the most prominent influences include home life, school life, peer pressure, and internet access.

Today is an opportune time for exposure to an identity model that features a foundation young people can appreciate. *Appreciate, not necessarily believe in. As art, MARVI-RPIA is an impression. It's an alternative perspective to the worldviews in place.*

The absence of sex-ed, the presence of limited sex-ed, and a multitude of inadequate sex-ed sessions have contributed to the ruin of many young lives. Kids get married too soon, get pregnant, and get fixated on sex. How in the world can any program slow down raging youthful hormones? You can't. Well, you can, but it doesn't last very long. One strategy that may channel some of that energy is a focus on identity.

Imagine yourself as an Elect Roleplayer participating in a Demonstration of Free Will. Then, as you finally come of age to say what you want and do what you want, there are still a lot of rules to follow. Not only that, but you must also earn a living. One of the enticing distractions away from adult responsibility is sensual pleasure. Religion teaches not to engage in sensual exploration until marriage. The rest of the world says sensual exploration is natural. Have fun; just be careful. So, a large percentage of youth get married. They have fun—for a while.

By accepting identity as the Free Will Demonstration painted by MARVI-RPIA, who you are is not fixed in the present. Who you are is fixed in the future. The pressure to achieve pleasure, happiness, excitement, romance, and self-esteem becomes less pressing. The belief you've only got one chance at life may not be the whole story. Who you think you are may not be the whole story.

It makes sense to recognize your identity as a composite of all your ancestors, going all the way back to Mister and Missus Noah, and even further to Adam and Eve. The angels who created offspring through human females may also be involved in our ancestral line. Who you are is not just your parent's child, not just where you grew up, not just your education, life experiences, or role models.

You may have a counterpart in Paradise. The urgency to get all life has to offer here and now is less urgent if a better life is in the future. The future as guaranteed by the One who cannot lie: Jesus Christ.

With that in mind, one of the first issues in living as a Roleplayer in the Demonstration of Free Will is whether to continue as a Roleplayer or become a Team Player. You are no longer a Roleplayer if you become married. You are now committed to another Roleplayer. Your identity is now a dual identity. You become a team.

As a team, in a traditional two-person marriage, you relinquish individual rights to your individual identity. You acquire rights to your spouse's identity and vice versa. This is ideal to assure a marriage bond holds through all difficulties a marriage entails. The team-player analogy continues if children arrive. The child is also a Team Player. The role of Team Player as a child is forced. They are on their parents' team whether they want it or not. A child's Roleplayer status remains subservient until adulthood.

Outside of the Christian moral standard, unmarried Team Players lack a commitment to the team concept. They are still free agent Roleplayers, insincere Team Players unwilling to commit their lives to building a team. Why should they? Life is short. Life is unpredictable. Be flexible.

Unless there is 100 percent dedication to the team identity—not individual identities disguised as Team Players to seek advantage—the team will be dysfunctional. It'll still work, but not well.

Are both individuals Christians? How do they define Christianity? Have both individuals understood Christian principles well enough to remain celibate during their dating experience? If so, this means high pressure to abstain from sex—or else get married.

Communication with a potential Team Player with limited identity awareness is possible. The influences on identity now come up for evaluation. Yes, my family has a great influence. Yes, my culture, where I grew up, and my education have a great influence. Yes, the things that have happened to me have had a great influence on how I see myself. Now, am I willing to reprogram myself? Yes. Do I accept my past as inauthentic Roleplay, simply reacting to heredity, environment, and experiences? Yes. Is living my life based on Christian Reformed Impressionism a life worth living? Yes. Can I do it? Maybe.

How well do you communicate? Are you able to tell a potential spouse, or a Team Player, what you think? Do you trust them with intimate details? Can you articulate influences that shaped your character? Why do you want to be married? Have you ever been engaged? Do you hate being single? Do you hate yourself? Who are you?

Assuming you have no sexual experience, how can you communicate compatibility? Turn-ons? Turn-offs? Libido? Insecurities? Fears? If you have sexual experience, what were the circumstances? How important is having children? Why have children? How long have you been a Christian? Which denomination do you belong to? Do you read the Bible? Do you attend church on a regular basis? Do you like church?

When you have no idea how you will change in the future, and your libido is sky-high, what do you do? It would be great to meet the right person and get married, but that may not happen right away. You certainly don't want to marry the wrong person just to escape the confines of celibacy.

Meanwhile, the Church seems to always preach the same frustrating message: Be patient. Hang on. Being single is a gift of God (1 Corinthians 7:7). Appreciate the wonderful time you have to focus on the things of the Lord. Yeah. *Meanwhile, 99.9 percent of them are married. Singleness is no gift to them. No. They didn't want their gift. That's because being single is NOT a gift.* But First Corinthians say it *is* a gift!

> For I would that all men were even as I myself. But every man hath his proper gift of God, one after this manner, and another after that (1 Corinthians 7:7).
>
> (The rest of 1 Corinthians follows at the end of this chapter)

If God grants each one his own gift, one of one kind and one of another kind, you would think of such gifts as singing, public speaking, and cooking. You would think of hospitality, clerical skills, or teaching children. Something worthwhile, something desirable. But being single? That's a gift?

Who wants to be single all their life? Raise your hand, please. Who doesn't want love, romance, intimacy, companionship, or a helper? Not many hands are going up. No. Most everyone wants these things. Why would I desire to be single? I'm the author of *Connecting The Dots Of Identity*. I'm single, never married. I have never, ever considered it to be a gift. If there is a gift in singleness, it has to be not marrying the wrong person. *That is a gift.* I'm stupid enough to have made that wrong choice many times. I have no idea why I'm not married.

It seems that the person who is single and committed to celibacy is doing so in the interest of honoring Christian values. *There is no vow to REMAIN single. There is no OBLIGATION to singleness.* The obligation is to be patient, not force the issue, and be strong in remaining celibate. You want GOD'S WILL to be done, not yours. This is also a gift. *Think and live to put God first. Not a spouse. Not children. Not family.* But you remain open to the possibility of meeting someone and becoming a potential Team Player. You always have the option. That means there is always hope. Mister or Missus Right may come along tomorrow. Nothing wrong with being ready to put your "gift" in the dumpster. Yaaaaay! Goodbye gift!

The end.

Hold on just a minute. Let's not end the chapter here. Let's face THE big fact. *Sex drive.* It's a monster. Religious concepts are great, but how do you compete against an incessant sex drive? It just can't be done. It always comes back, and it comes back strong.

No. Wrong. You *can* compete. *Sex drive is a monster,* but it can be managed. You can't go into the challenge thinking religious concepts have no chance. Are you really a Christian?

You might ask:

How can a spirit compete against flesh and blood? God is a spirit.

Can a spirit hug me, kiss me, and give me physical pleasure? Can a spirit light up my apartment with well-set hair, perfume, and a sensual voice? How does the Spirit compensate for all the things that are female?

Can a spirit press me with his weight, lift me in his arms, or kiss me through the night? Can a spirit light up my apartment with his confidence, an angular image, and a sensual voice? How does the Spirit compensate for all the things that are male?

It's reasonable to think that if you commit to giving the Spirit of God time to compete, He can compete! You just have to be patient and trust Him. Give Him an honest chance to be significant to you. No, nothing is the same as flesh and blood. But nothing is the same as the Spirit of God either.

You still have doubts. Could this really work?

God: Are you going to give Me a chance?

You: Well, I really don't want to take a chance on You. I want the real thing: a guy, a girl.

God: Of course you do. It doesn't mean you will never have the real thing: a guy, a girl. I just want to show you what I can do.

You: Well...

God: You have to give Me a chance though. A real chance.

You: Well … hmmm … (sigh).

> And I say unto you, whosoever shall put away his wife, except it be for fornication, and shall marry another, committeth adultery: and whoso marrieth her which is put away doth commit adultery. His disciples say unto him, if the case of the man be so with his wife, it is not good to marry. But he said unto them, all men cannot receive this saying, save they to whom it is given. For there are some eunuchs, which were so born from their mother's womb: and there are some eunuchs, which were made eunuchs of men: and there be eunuchs, which have made themselves eunuchs for the kingdom of heaven's sake. He that is able to receive it, let him receive it (Matthew 19:9-12).

> Now concerning the things whereof ye wrote unto me: It is good for a man not to touch a woman. Nevertheless, to avoid fornication, let every man have his own wife, and let every woman have her own husband. Let the husband render unto the wife due benevolence: and likewise, also the wife unto the husband. The wife hath not power of her own body, but the husband: and likewise, also the husband hath not power of his own body, but the wife. Defraud ye not one the other, except it be with consent for a time, that ye may give yourselves to fasting and prayer; and come together again, that Satan tempt you not for your incontinency. But I speak this by permission, and not of commandment. For I would that all men were even as I myself.

But every man hath his proper gift of God, one after this manner, and another after that. I say therefore to the unmarried and widows, it is good for them if they abide even as I. But if they cannot contain, let them marry: for it is better to marry than to burn.

And unto the married I command, yet not I, but the Lord, Let not the wife depart from her husband: But and if she depart, let her remain unmarried or be reconciled to her husband: and let not the husband put away his wife. But to the rest speak I, not the Lord: If any brother hath a wife that believeth not, and she be pleased to dwell with him, let him not put her away.

And the woman which hath a husband that believeth not, and if he be pleased to dwell with her, let her not leave him. For the unbelieving husband is sanctified by the wife, and the unbelieving wife is sanctified by the husband: else were your children unclean; but now are they holy . . . Now concerning virgins I have no commandment of the Lord: yet I give my judgment, as one that hath obtained mercy of the Lord to be faithful. I suppose therefore that this is good for the present distress, I say, and that it is good for a man so to be. Art thou bound unto a wife? Seek not to be loosed. Art thou loosed from a wife? Seek not a wife. But and if thou marry, thou hast not sinned; and if a virgin marry, she hath not sinned. Nevertheless, such shall have trouble in the flesh: but I spare you. But this I say, brethren, the time is short: it remaineth, that both they that have wives be as though they had none . . . But I would have you without carefulness. He that is unmarried careth for the things that belong to the Lord, how he may please the Lord. But he that is married careth for the things that are of the world, how he may please his wife. There is difference also between a wife and a virgin. The unmarried woman careth for the things of the Lord, that she may be holy both in body and in spirit: but she that is married careth for the things of the world, how she may please her husband. And this I speak for your own profit; not that I may cast a snare upon you, but for that which is comely, and that ye may attend upon the Lord without distraction. But if any man think that he behaveth himself uncomely toward his virgin, if she pass the flower of her age, and need so require, let him do what he will, he sinneth not: let them marry. Nevertheless he that standeth stedfast in his heart, having no necessity, but hath power over his own will, and hath so decreed in his heart that he will keep his virgin, doeth well. So then he that giveth her in marriage doeth well; but he that giveth her not in marriage doeth better. The wife is bound by the law as long as her husband liveth; but if her husband be dead, she is at liberty to be married to whom she will; only in the Lord. But she is happier if she so abide, after my judgment: and I think also that I have the Spirit of God (1 Corinthians 7:1-14; 25-29; 32-40).

SEX EDUCATION 2—POSTSCRIPT

Boo-hoo. Nobody loves me.

This isn't just about sex and celibacy. I want to be a mom. I want to be a dad. I want children. Sex is important, but not that important. Nobody appreciates my attributes, physical AND mental. How can I find the best match for my identity, someone who wants what I want?

As you think back and think forward about your feelings, you can admit your focus has been on other people to confirm your value. If there is no one to appreciate you, you are not appreciating yourself. If no one is there, do you really matter? If you don't really matter to others, isn't that an identity disaster?

Not necessarily. Not if you have access to tools that redefine inauthentic and authentic identity.

An inauthentic identity is often thought of as delusional, psychotic, or mental impairment of some kind. But what if INAUTHENTIC identity is derived from heredity, environment, and experiences, the most commonly accepted AUTHENTIC identity? In this case, the commonly held inauthentic identity must have a replacement identity that has enough substance to represent authenticity.

This is why Connecting The Dots Of Identity is being presented. Does it help you see your efforts to find self-worth in an identity that is dependent on other identities are flawed? Your self-worth's real value should be based on God's identity. Of course, God has to be defined and has to be known before you can put your trust in Him.

Connecting the Dots of Identity uses the Modern Abstract Religious Verbal Impressionism-Roleplay Identity Array model to illustrate God. This is the God derived from orthodox religion, by way of impressions, or artistic expression to convey the image. The examples from General Revelation (God in the environment), Special Revelation (scripture), teachers, experiences, and intuition form the impressions. This book project is sharing those images.

Boo-hoo. Nobody loves ME, I said.

But this life is not about you. This life is about your role. This life is the opportunity to prove the limitation of Free Will refused by the Serpent, Adam, Eve, and Lucifer. God's will for your life versus your will for your life. The Demonstration of Free Will.

Will you give God a chance to show you love? A real chance? Real love?

God loves you. The authentic Super-Spiritual Identity (SSID) you. The Roleplay you are temporary. It will end. The SSID you never end.

God: Always was. Always is. Always will be.

You: Super-Spiritual Identity (SSID). Always is. Always will be.

Boo-hoo. AGAIN. I say... nobody ... loves ... me.

I'm lonely! It's not that easy to explain. I'm a Christian. I still feel alone. It's not about sex. I can manage that. And I'm not so much interested in marriage and children. A second income from a partner would be nice, and there's security and safety in a companion. But the real problem that makes me feel boo-hoo like is LONELINESS! I fear being alone my entire life! I'm a PEOPLE person. I'm VERY social.

What if I'm made to serve a spouse? What if I simply love to share things? Who's going to help me if I'm ill, afraid to go out alone, or care for me when I'm older?

Even if I have to buy a pet, a toy, or a game, I have to be occupied with something. I depend on the TV, movies, my phone, and my computer to keep me company. The next level of defense is the people I keep close to me. But friends become lovers. Friends become users. Friends become fiends. My relatives count, but don't. They're a captive group. The same can be said about the church. They're a captive group. They HAVE to be there for me.

Being single should not be scary for a Christian. God is our Companion Extraordinaire. "What a Friend We Have in Jesus." You know the song. The shameful truth is we just don't trust God to manage our loneliness. God is spirit. We are flesh and blood. How can He help me? He can't. He really isn't supposed to, not in this area. We have to manage it ourselves via other people.

It seems that almost all people of God are married, praying to be married, or are divorced and seeking remarriage. All the blessings of God are toward the people who advocate marriage. Second-tier blessings, or blessings left over from the matrimony crowd, are given to single people. At least, that's how it feels.

We always hear that in the Book of Genesis, God made Eve for Adam so Adam wouldn't be alone. It's NOT GOOD to be alone.

> And the Lord God said, It is not good that the man should be alone; I will make him a help meet for him (Genesis 2:18).

In *Connecting the Dots of Identity-1*, Chapter 21, "Adam and Eve," the following citation may help regarding loneliness:

From the Book of Genesis, we follow the creation process to arrive at Adam and Eve. Slightly before Adam is created, animals are created. The Serpent is especially singled out to be cunning above the animals of the field. Then, as Adam is alone, God says that is not good. Why? Being alone could not be the condition of being lonely. God is omnipresent. His presence certainly overcomes any aspect of loneliness. And, there is a numerous assortment of other living creatures around Eden. Adam is in a beautiful relationship with God and with all of God's magnificent creatures. Adam could not possibly be lonely. But Adam was considered alone.

Why was that not good?

It's not good if Adam exercised Free Will to disobey God. That would bring death. The human race ends. That would not be good. Adam being alone meant a one-person Demonstration of Free Will. There should be more than one person. A team of persons provides collaboration and perspective, future proofing.

Angels were a large sample size to determine Free Will. Humans need not be. That could be done through procreation if necessary. Procreation could be used in lieu of a large sample of human beings. Procreation could also serve as a fail-safe. Fail-safe? Fail-safe for what? A flawless human should ever become flawed. END.

Boo-hoo. Nobody loves me, I say again, again, and again. Help!

We are just not cut out to be single. We can deal with it for a while, under quiet protest, but we don't like it. God didn't make us this way. We are made to be married. Period.

Connecting the Dots of Identity applies the MARVI-RPIA concept to question whether God makes anyone the way they are. Heredity, environment, and experiences make you the way you are. This appears as your inauthentic identity. God made your authentic identity, which is in Paradise, awaiting the end of the Demonstration of Free Will.

It's not unreasonable to assume people fear being alone because they sense *they are NOT alone.* There are evil spirits everywhere, from humans and those less than 100 percent human. They said of themselves that they are legion! Bible verses indicate there are a vast number of angels, good and bad.

> For he said unto him, Come out of the man, thou unclean spirit. And he asked him, what is thy name? And he answered, saying, my name is Legion: for we are many (Mark 5:8-9).

That's bad enough, but people also fear their own thoughts. Being alone means time spent thinking. *Thinking brings up thoughts that are very pleasant, but also thoughts that are very, very UNPLEASANT. Thoughts that are way past unpleasant.* Gruesome, terrifying, and heart-wrenching thoughts. Embarrassing, crude, and forgotten thoughts. Suppressed and repressed thoughts you dread may inadvertently arise. You just don't want to expose yourself to time spent thinking of the past. If there are things to be done that protect and distract from your idle thoughts, they must be done.

As a Christian, it does sound like a lack of faith in God. Sorry, but that's what it sounds like.

Yes. That speaks for Christians worldwide. It's why Connecting The Dots Of Identity makes use of MARVI-RPIA to reintroduce God as He may be seen. No, it's not meant to persuade you to adopt art as theology. It's meant to give you a reason to trust God is wiser, stronger, and more beautiful than we imagined. He actually thought of everything.

CHAPTER 9

SEX EDUCATION—PART 3

You've heard that science contends homosexuality is no longer abnormal behavior. Psychiatric, psychological, and biological experts support data that suggests homosexuality is neither a positive nor negative form of human diversity. It is what it is, be that hereditary, environmental, or experiential causes. Of course, there's no mention of sin. Sin is not a scientific term. Science doesn't include God in its assessment of reality.

Theology describes sin as thinking and behaving in opposition to God's will. God's will is outlined in General Revelation and Special Revelation—natural order and scripture. MARVI-RPIA comes along as a mural on the building of the church. MARVI-RPIA is not trying to replace the building, just adding a little "artwork" to the architecture. This includes images of sex.

Science has a good point in removing the "mental disorder" classification from same-sex behavior. Any deviation from a broad category of social behavior could be labeled a mental disorder, or abnormal. *However, the number of people who engage in any behavior should not be the standard of a mental disorder. What is normal shouldn't be what is socially acceptable.* What seemingly has happened is public awareness of same-gender relationships has increased its acceptability. As awareness grows of impediments to the progress of marginalized groups, their perceived stature also increases.

Christians assume the task of proving homosexuality is not normal. The Bible says homosexuality is an abomination, accursed by God. God made Adam and Eve: male and female. There are two genders, not less, not more. There can be no option to choose whatever you wish and become something other than male or female. That's the standard Christian position, though in some religious circles that's coming under review and modification.

Science says we have hard data. These are rational people who declare their status as gay people. They aren't choosing their status. They have no choice. They should know who they are, not us. This behavior is noted in history, though broadly held in discretion and guardedness.

Conversely, Christians say the LGBTQ community is confused. They are confused by science and society. People do disavow and change their gay behavior with patience and counseling. Otherwise, we continue to see people suffer depression, anxiety, and suicide because they are confused and aren't receiving adequate help. And the gay people that seem happy? Christians assume they are in denial of their misery or victims of a corrupted, disillusioned conscience.

MARVI-RPIA takes the position that religion, science, and society miss the mark. Religion misses because it teaches God made Adam and Eve to continue heterosexual behavior throughout creation. *Generally speaking, religion doesn't place the blame for homosexuality on Adam and Eve, where it belongs.* God made the human being's blueprint. It was male and female. It was pristine. When Adam and Eve sinned, they altered that blueprint. Not only was the hereditary blueprint altered, but the environment was also altered. Environmental factors absolutely affect a human being's blueprint from conception through maturity. We might call them "birth defects of the overall sin nature." Additionally, experiences contribute significantly to the configuration of identity.

Science and society say as much without the moral aspects of thinking and behavior. Science observes behavior and explains it in terms of voluntary and involuntary responses to stimuli. Forces acting on the agent remove a level of responsibility from the agent. The agent simply responds to the environment based on the resources it possesses to maintain or continue life. There is no such thing as good behavior or bad behavior, just behavior. Advances in civilization only mean social contracts to abide by subjective standards. Still, no moral objectivity prevails. No transcendent standard applies to everyone.

MINISTER OF ART PROPOSES MARRIAGE?

The imagery of MARVI-RPIA welcomes all LGBTQ persons. *The Minister of Art, CD1/CD2 author, admits he could marry such a person.* What? How is this so? Questions and Answers, Chapter 33, 48A and 48B may help.

A mature Christian, in good standing with the Orthodox Church, affirms marriage is between two confessing Christians—male and female. Yes. Agree. The person the Minister of Art COULD marry, not necessarily WOULD marry, must convince him the bride-to-be is definitively female. No matter the birth records. No matter the transition path. The issue is:

a) *How Christianity is defined.*

b) *How gender is defined.*

c) *Expectation of the assumed gender role.*

The marriage progression begins with an introduction to a person and the initial evaluation. From there to physical attraction, and then, mental attraction. Following the physical and mental attraction is the assessment of spiritual attraction. From a Christian perspective, this stage includes gender identity discussions. From here, the line is drawn on how much further friendship can go.

A same-sex relationship should progress no further than friendship. The Bible sets the standard for this. *To progress beyond friendship—all the way to marriage—means one person convinces the other person this is NOT a same-sex friendship.*

Is this a reasonable scenario for a sex education session?

To review, the prohibition of same-sex marriage is unmistakable in scripture. Both parties must be assured one is “as a” male, and one is “as a” female. This is regardless of how they were born, how they were raised, or how they look. “As is” means essentially, effectively, and substantially that the specific male or female gender is de facto. Also, sexual activity other than male-female activity is an affront to God. It is sinful.

If you can't or won't heed the Bible's admonishment to refrain from same-sex sexual activity, you’re going against a preponderance of scriptural principles. Opposite-sex sexual activity is the biblically sanctioned relationship—male with female, boy with girl, man with woman.

The other matter to consider is IDENTITY is not necessarily constant. No doctor, no parent, no culture, and no society should be able to dictate personhood. *We know that identity is not 100 percent physical.* Under examination, a doctor who assures the parent(s) you are a boy or girl isn't foolproof. *Yes, there are medical protocols in place that verify gender, but even then, the medical model can't measure nonphysical aspects of identity.* They can’t measure the brain or the mind. Human anatomy and physiology are extremely complex. XX, XY genetic material or genitalia can’t be the whole story.

It shouldn't be unreasonable to explore sexuality and gender as people are more open to discussing such things. And worldwide research and communication make it easier to collaborate and corroborate data regarding ongoing developments. Currently, there is no one gene associated with homosexuality. Therefore, science confirms homosexuality isn't congenital. It isn't locked in at birth.

Christians agree. Otherwise, it would mean God is responsible for people being born gay. Is He responsible? The Glossary of Colors includes Creationism, Designationism, and Traducianism. These concepts help explain how, when, and by whom the soul or spirit is created. *Is the creation of the soul before conception, at conception, or after conception, and is it created by the parents or by God?*

Is it safe to say that an undiscovered combination of heredity, environment, and experiences influence sexuality? How much more will be known in 100 years? A thousand years?

Once a person becomes convinced of their inauthentic identity Roleplay gender, they have a right to pursue it. However, they must be absolutely consistent, persistent, and insistent in that gender pursuit. This must be indisputable. Otherwise, doubt will undermine their identity. This opens the door to confusion, depression, anxiety, self-harm, and even suicide. Doubt also leads to questions of Christian identity. There will be uncertainty on top of uncertainty.

Remember, as Free Will Roleplayers, gay people are not their physical identity (PID) or their mental identity (MID). Who they are is an identity array of eight potential identities, as mentioned in the Glossary of Colors (SSID, HSID, SID, PID, MID, CID, DID, ESID). The dynamics of sexuality are not confined to only the physical properties of anatomy. The saying goes: sex is mainly between the ears (MID), not the legs (PID). *The insistence on physiology to determine gender identity and sexuality undermines the principle Jesus taught. We are spiritual creatures in physical bodies. Overthrow the tyranny of physicalism.* God will help you. Live for the afterlife of your spiritual identity. Your physical identity isn't real. It's temporary. Spiritual life is reality. It's eternal.

THOUGHTS OF SEX

Christian teaching includes the admonition that to even think about sex outside marriage is adultery (Matthew 5:28). We should know that is not to be taken literally. Homosexual and heterosexual thoughts may be constructive in simulating situations that may occur. Fantasy, simulation, and what-ifs are mental techniques that avoid physical acts.

That you think about sex can never be practically forbidden as a sin. Sexuality includes mental imagery, and thoughts. It's much more than behavior. This is anticipation, expectation, suggestion, experimentation, and communication. It's a proactive responsibility. When a guy and a girl consider marriage to each other, God expects them to communicate. *Communication includes sexual language.* Even an arranged marriage decreases its chance of remaining intact if the dominant person doesn't find a level of attraction to the recessive person. Attraction is mental. It's thoughts of matrimonial responsibility. It's a function of presenting the identity being offered for consideration. This is the time to share with each other possibilities, repercussions, complications, or implications going forward.

What dynamics were involved when the good man Joseph chose the Virgin Mary over any of the other females available to him? Even if he had no knowledge of Mary's physical qualities, knowing her other attributes was enough for him to accept her. His acceptance factored in psychology. *Females other than Mary were excluded. This meant mental scenarios with the other potential females. Nothing wrong with that. It's an obligation. Divorce should not be an option.* Communication means discussion of compatibility, an obligation to compromise, and confidence of trust. Once these things were discussed, Joseph and Mary knew enough about sex-ed to understand sexuality would be part of their marriage agreement.

Every person does not have an equal opportunity for marriage. Being celibate involves maneuvering through sensual situations and not being naive about sexuality. Graphic imagery comes with the territory. *The issue comes back to context. Not what you are thinking, but why.* Where is motivation, intent, opportunity, enlightenment, and rationale featured? These are factors relevant to simulation scenarios and avoidance/mitigation techniques.

Never hide sexuality from God. Share everything with God—not just your friend or counselor. Shame may be healthy as it reflects discomfort from pressing inquiry. Questions are good therapy. God created sexuality. *Your strong sexual preferences are not evil. They are simply a feature of the body and mind you occupy. This is not who you are. It's simply a role dumped in your lap.* Once you understand that, it isn't as difficult a struggle to admit you're a sexual being with natural proclivities. This is a facet of your unique Roleplay identity.

Being homosexual, thinking homosexual, and appreciating homosexuality doesn't make you a sinner. We are all sinners, especially heterosexuals, because there are more of us to sin. The issue is ENACTMENT:

a) Engaging in same-sex activity

b) Engaging in same-sex marriage

You may be gay. Scripture forbids sexual enactment. Your mind is the only sinless option. Or, if you absolutely must marry, one of the partners must be the opposite sex, and both should be Christians.

And as a Christian, the idea of "imitating" an opposite-sex identity for the purposes of marriage isn't legitimate. Roleplaying is not the authentic identity. You aren't obligated to assume your imposed identity because no other recourse exists. There is at least one recourse: MARVI-RPIA, the imagery of an authentic identity.

You may object, thinking: What does it matter? Isn't Roleplay of gender the same as a heterosexual male or heterosexual female? They have God's permission to marry, even though their gender role is also dumped on them at birth.

The difference is the standard set by God's principles for continuity in families, society, and government. Confidence in gender roles CONTRIBUTES to overall mental health and REDUCES social tension. Misunderstanding gender expression DETRACTS from mental health and INCREASES social tension. The teaching of scripture is to improve mental health and elevate society.

Unfortunately, the average young person does not receive dependable sex education. The very people who should speak loudest and most often about sex—Christians—are the quietest and most reluctant to speak. When they do speak, they are so careful not to offend that the use of euphemisms and awkwardness undermines their effectiveness. It's understandable they must avoid pornographic realism, but realism is imperative, no matter who or where it comes from.

On the other hand, Christianity is about the GUIDELINES for sexual intercourse. It isn't about sexual intercourse. Sexual intercourse is a commitment in marriage regarding procreation, recreation, and communication of love. Christian commitment to never divorce strengthens the meaning of love to ensure marriages last and provides a model that enhances the community, the nation, and the world. Otherwise, love, marriage, and sexual intercourse devolve into subjective standards. That means no objective standard, as modeled in Christian morality. The result is whatever is acceptable is normal. Normal is redefined as individuals organize to represent subjective interests.

What is right? What is wrong? Whatever you define it to be. Not what God, any religion, or society dictates? Everyone should have the right to represent who they are … what they want. So what if science proves I was born male? So what if I'm legally male? I'm a girl. My body doesn't run the show; my mind runs the show! If enough people agree, we can change the laws. We can change society. Discrimination is wrong. Sex, gender, and identity are personal matters. Who are you to force your standards on me?

This is what sex education is up against. An objective standard or a subjective standard. A loving context or a context defined by feelings. Realism or euphemisms. The big picture or vignettes.

Meanwhile, tension rises as social policy attempts to preserve traditional values while advancing contemporary values at an ever-increasing pace.

Ye have heard that it was said by them of old time, Thou shalt not commit adultery: But I say unto you, that whosoever looketh on a woman to lust after her hath committed adultery with her already in his heart (Matthew 5:27-28).

CHAPTER 10

SEX EDUCATION—PART 4

I'm gay. God made me the way I am. This is natural.

People say this all the time. Alternately, you are born a gay person because of Adam and Eve, not God. God allows it but does not cause it or permit it. People wonder: Why is it a sin for gay people to express love and become married? It's normal. It's natural.

According to MARVI-RPIA imagery, your Free Will Roleplay identity was forced upon you. It is natural. It is normal. *Being gay is not your choice. It's who you are. However, it is NOT who you are. Being heterosexual is NOT who you are either. So, who are you? A sexual being.* Heterosexuals may feel a twinge at the implication. They might be bisexual, or even homosexual.

Being heterosexual is part of the Roleplay Identity Array (RPIA) image. *Your mental identity (MID), for the most part, guides your sexual orientation.* The sexual cues come from your five senses: sight, sound, taste, touch, and smell. *If you remove all but touch, the touch indicator of sexual preference becomes indifferent.* All that matters with touch is that it achieves the objective—happiness, or a "happy ending."

Think of the Four Senses Dark Room experiment. You're in a darkened room with sight, sound, taste, and smell prevented. You can be touched by another person's hands, mouth, or body parts. Since your other four senses are unavailable, touch is all that influences your response to the stimulation. A lot of people will smile and say, "No thanks, can't participate. Probably out of town that day." They know their body will "betray" their mind.

Okay. Maybe we can find some "brave" ones who will contribute to "science."

Begin. You're placed in the darkened room and told to lay back and relax. People will be with you presently. People? Yes, someone within the group will come close to you and stimulate you. One person at a time, that is. Just act normal. Enjoy.

It's reasonable to assume your body won't know which gender is stimulating you, and your body probably won't care. It just wants to be "happy." Does that make you bisexual or a closet homosexual? No. *All that means is your mind dictates the interest, arousal, and satisfaction derived from another person. Your mind assigns sexual expression to a gender role.* You accept or reject sexual expression based on heredity, environment, and experiences.

Your body could be just as happy from male or female stimulation. *It may be that most people abhor homosexuality only because they believe society or God abhors it.*

Atheists may abhor same-gender relationships as an obstacle to the advancement of the human species. Even with advancements in reproductive science, people pursue vicarious immortality through procreation. It's the crown jewel of progress. Procreation is the pathway for ensuring the human race lives long enough to achieve immortality.

Your sexual preference for a person of the male or female gender is a factor of your Identity Array. Your physical identity (PID), mental identity (MID), and childhood identity (CID) are a consequence of heredity, environment, and experience. You may encounter salvation (HSID) and be born-again into a new identity. Your sexual preferences may continue to be for the same sex, but as a new Christian identity, your commitment is now to celibacy or heterosexuality.

Your authentic identity, Super-Spiritual Identity (SSID), your pre-life identity before the world was created, is not male or female, gay or straight. Heterosexuality is the sexuality of Adam and Eve. This acts as a built-in fail-safe for procreation should they ever exercise Free Will to disobey God.

As a toddler, you had no idea your genitalia could be used for procreation. You barely knew you even had genitalia. *Adam and Eve would have been in a similar state of innocence, especially considering there was no need for the excretion of waste.* No waste was produced in the Garden.

Once Adam and Eve disobeyed God, however, their flawless human blueprint became corrupted. The result was offspring that replicated and further produced corrupted offspring. That corruption is manifested in physical and mental attributes. Additionally, the environment was cursed. The environment also has a significant impact on the conception and development of offspring.

As a gay person, it's understandable you want to behave naturally. You don't want to attempt to be someone you aren't. Would a heterosexual person want to be told they must engage in homosexual behavior or be denounced, punished, and ostracized? Would heterosexuals patiently endure ridicule, embarrassment, humiliation, bullying, assault, and murder?

Why can't LGBTQs experience sexual intimacy and marry?

God forbids it. Why? *The sin of homosexuality, the curse, was the opposite of the blessing—procreation. Homosexual activity meant a diversion from the "divine mandate": namely, produce the Child that may redeem the world. No children meant no opportunity for salvation from the cycle of death. Homosexuality was rebellion, selfishness, and genocide against the rest of society. It was a mental illness.* Homosexuality was, therefore, "unnatural."

The nation of Israel was taught commands and rituals to separate them from the world. Meanwhile, the world pursued its own standards. Sexuality remained primarily for procreation, but other pursuits ensued. Recreation, remuneration, and self-stimulation progressed throughout the nations. Worship of sex, rituals of sex, the atrocity of sex, tragedy of sex, and diseases from sex devastated otherwise ordinary communities. They weren't ostensibly evil, just exercising their Free Will.

Christians will point out that homosexual activity is "against nature" (Romans 1:26-27). A quick, crude study on sexual activity reveals *the THREE most frequent sexual acts can't be unnatural, judging by how commonplace they are "in nature."* Going further, reviews from internet articles found *what has been considered "against nature" for centuries could be BIRTH CONTROL.* Any sexual or parasexual activity that doesn't permit, or aid procreation, is against nature—unnatural. A woman behaving "unnaturally" may not be lesbian behavior. She's just using birth control. A man behaving unnaturally may not be homosexual behavior. He's just avoiding the possibility of childbirth.

Same-gender relationships have another objection regarding the model of "natural use." *Anatomical parts don't "fit together." That tells you it's unnatural sex.* Are you serious? That's a naïve point of view if you're speaking to adults. The Bible says be babes in evil (1 Corinthians 14), but to what extent are you babes? You never want to expose yourself unnecessarily to despicable matters, but ignorance of details is counterproductive.

All same-sex parts fit together just fine for the purposes intended. Participants are content with intimacy, sensuality, and eroticism. Labels by society don't matter. "Happy endings," no pregnancies, and innovation matter much more. So, an appeal to nature may not be a suitable argument against LGBTQ activity.

Remember, the Bible is not against the person. The Bible is against the activity. The person feels they must act out their identity because it's the only identity they've been taught. *Connecting the Dots of Identity* suggests a second identity that subordinates the first identity. Don't act on your feelings. They are inauthentic. Awareness of an authentic identity helps expose the limitations of living an inauthentic life. That inauthentic life is not you.

God is not condemning you. He condemns the Roleplayer's behavior. You are safe in Paradise. Don't let Roleplay dictate who you think you are. Its deceit, coercion, and manipulation. There are forces directing you to accept heredity, environment, and experiences as your ONLY identity. It isn't, necessarily.

If you don't think you could ever be attracted to someone of the opposite sex, think again. It's not that hard to find someone of the opposite sex who has many of the attributes of your same sex. *We've all seen guys who look like girls and girls who look like guys.* Physical attributes as well as other attributes are malleable. There's great diversity in Roleplayer choices.

The point is the best relationship you could have is with someone who is a 100 percent Team Player. *They do what it takes to make two people the best they can be in all areas—especially sex.* They figure out what it takes if sex is five times a day, once a week, once a month, or once a year. If there is NO sex, they work out a plan. Where there's integrity from objective morality, there's trust. There's patience. There's forgiveness. *With the right person, ANYTHING can work. You FIND a way. You MAKE it work.*

If you are a "true" Christian, you may come to understand your relationship with God, Jesus, the Holy Spirit, is worth EVERYTHING to you because THEY are the ultimate Team Players.

If you are a Christian, you are a child of the King. You're ROYALTY. If you do marry, you should marry royalty. Your potential children deserve royal heritage—starting with YOU. Think like royalty. Act like royalty. If you meet a Team Player worthy of marriage, they absolutely, positively must be of royal Christian birth: born-again. Never settle for less. Never.

> So God created man in his own image, in the image of God created he him; male and female created he them (Genesis 1:27).

> And he answered and said unto them, Have ye not read, that he which made them at the beginning made them male and female (Matthew 19:4).

For this cause God gave them up unto vile affections: for even their women did change the natural use into that which is against nature: And likewise also the men, leaving the natural use of the woman, burned in their lust one toward another; men with men working that which is unseemly, and receiving in themselves that recompence of their error which was meet (Romans 1:26-27).

Thou shalt not lie with mankind, as with womankind: it is abomination (Leviticus 18:22).

If a man also lie with mankind, as he lieth with a woman, both of them have committed an abomination: they shall surely be put to death; their blood shall be upon them (Leviticus 20:13).

Know ye not that the unrighteous shall not inherit the kingdom of God? Be not deceived: neither fornicators, nor idolaters, nor adulterers, nor effeminate, nor abusers of themselves with mankind (1 Corinthians 6:9).

Brethren, be not children in understanding: howbeit in malice be ye children, but in understanding be men (1 Corinthians 14:20).

And Er, Judah's firstborn, was wicked in the sight of the Lord; and the Lord slew him. And Judah said unto Onan, Go in unto thy brother's wife, and marry her, and raise up seed to thy brother. And Onan knew that the seed should not be his; and it came to pass, when he went in unto his brother's wife, that he spilled it on the ground, lest that he should give seed to his brother. And the thing which he did displeased the Lord: wherefore he slew him also (Genesis 38:7-10).

CHAPTER 11

SEX EDUCATION 4—POSTSCRIPT

One of the best Christian apologists has a popular call-in question-and-answer program. One of the questions came from a caller whose adult brother recently came out as trans-boy-to-girl. The family thought it best to let the situation resolve itself, thinking the older brother may realize his mistake. The caller, the younger brother, disagreed with the family. He wanted to talk to his older brother, transitioning now to be his sister. What should he say?

The host counseled that the younger brother (let's call him Jack) should refer to his brother by his brother's chosen new name—let's say, Karla. However, he should not affirm that Karla is now female. He can never be female. *His body, his physical identity, will always be male, no matter how he modifies it. It is a perfect male body. The problem is his mental identity. His mind is imperfect, confused.* If the family supports Karla's new lifestyle, then you must disagree with the family. The Christian position is to affirm male-female gender-sexual relationships and oppose same-sex gender-sexual relationships. The goal of humankind flourishing has always been the natural order of male-female relationships to advance the human species. Same-sex relationships oppose the natural order.

The implication from the host was same-sex relationships decrease birth rates. Fewer births increase the likelihood that catastrophic events and unforeseen circumstances decimate the population. Human flourishing would be curtailed, initially on a minuscule scale.

From here, the host reminded Jack that LGBTQ suicide rates tell you all you need to know. The unhealthy transgender mental imagery simply doesn't suffice to support a long life. They end their life at rates disproportional to society.

Now, how does the Minister of Art answer the caller's question?

The first thing to say is neither the caller nor his parents are responsible for Karla's salvation. God has taken care of that. They should be neutral but ready to communicate Christian principles. Karla may reply he knows Christian principles and that he is pursuing his life as God made him.

As a person grows up, parents or guardians assist in gender identity development. This is in combination with all the identity components of heredity, environment, and experiences. If there are no conflicting forces to the contrary, gender identity conforms to the assigned identity from birth.

Where there is nonconformity in gender assignment, the issue relates to the degree of nonconformity. *If the level shows a consistent, persistent, and insistent degree of nonconformity, the parent or guardian applies theistic, atheistic, or agnostic principles of conduct to the child.*

Religion maps over gender and sexuality to convey the direction God wants us to follow. Nonreligious standards put the direction back in the hands of the individuals. Individuals decide what's best, not God, whomever God is.

And, as Reformed Theology suggests, Free Will reigns unless God intercedes to overrun Free Will.

If Jack's brother, Karla, becomes so sure he can no longer live as a male, he may become suicidal if pressured to remain male. If Karla transitions to female and comes to believe he can never be sufficiently female, he may become suicidal.

What if Karla asks can he still be a Christian if he removes his penis, takes hormones, and enters therapy? Karla explains that the transition is only to return to being female as a consequence of being misassigned as a child.

If any male comes to the point of no return to remove his penis, take hormones, and enter therapy to reclaim a misappropriated female identity, he is no longer male. A male might go to therapy, and a male might take hormones. But no male is going to remove his penis. To do so would indicate a 100 percent commitment to renouncing masculinity, no matter what degree of femininity is achieved. To do so also means accepting the possibility of mental impairment—fatal mental impairment.

The same applies to females. No female is going to remove her breasts, take hormones, and go to transition therapy. She won't pursue genital transition surgery. *To do these things is to repudiate femininity. She's no longer a female Roleplayer.*

These examples don't mean the transition person now becomes the opposite gender. It just means they no longer identify as the former gender. So, what are they now? They are a *presumed* identity, seeking to *emulate* gender. The goal isn't necessarily 100 percent male or 100 percent female. Eighty percent may be good enough. Sixty percent or less may even be good enough. Now there is an additional inauthentic role to play. The goal is to recover the lost gender identity. *However, a gradual realization that identity is not gender related may prove to be devastating. So devastating that life eventually loses its meaning.*

And what of people who have the misfortune to have their "gender markers" removed by force, illness, or by accident? Their body (PID), the former gender identity, doesn't become illegitimate. They still identify as their former gender identity. *But physical identity doesn't dictate gender terms; mental identity (MID) does.* You still THINK of yourself as your gender identity before the loss of gender markers.

The point is that male-female gender terms shouldn't refer to GENDER identity. *The terms should refer to ROLEPLAY identity.* The loss of gender markers would call for a revision of male-female Roleplay. You have to rethink gender.

The Bible lays out the terms of gender Roleplay, not gender identity. You are to BEHAVE as close as possible to opposite-sex relationships, especially sexual relationships. You must overrule the urges of the body and of the mind. You can't do it by yourself. God has to help you. He will help you.

Otherwise, male-female Roleplay will be described by society, the culture, and the individual. You may behave as you feel. What does your BODY tell you? What does your MIND think is right? YOU are the captain of the ship. Right-wing Christians are not.

You should understand WHY Christians object to gender transition and same-sex acts. They don't hate the LGBTQ community. They don't hate sexual intercourse between consenting adults. *They are simply advancing the principles the Bible proclaims. God created discrete gender differentiation to protect the integrity of marriage, procreation, and sexual activity.* If left to the individuals, there would be no principles. Everyone would define gender as they saw fit.

This is what we see when non-Christians define gender. They advance the notion that gender has no specific meaning. Marriage, children, and sex are no longer illegal for same-sex partners. Marriages are now legal, adoption is possible, and arcane laws regarding homosexuality only apply in the most backward of societies.

Of course, it had to come to this because, generally, the Bible is not respected by atheists, agnostics, and non-Christians. The other factor is Adam and Eve's compromised male-female Roleplay. Instead of true love, a team mission, and companionship with God, a warped male-female relationship arises after they left the Garden. The new relationship now includes an obligation to produce the Redeemer through procreation. However, sexual activity devolved into recreation, coercion, and seduction. Even worse, sexual activity progressed to prostitution, molestation, and further acts of violation.

Now that we are in a time when people feel it's their right to be free of gender labels, it underscores the lifestyle of other segments of society. Decisions to follow your goals and dreams lead to life-or-death decisions. Risking your life to express your identity is what we see today.

People risk their lives to pursue risky occupations, hobbies, and relationships. They know it could cost them their lives. They pursue them anyway. People live a life of crime, live in dangerous neighborhoods, and take chances with the lives of their families. People take drugs, smoke cigarettes, and overindulge alcohol. Who they are, their identity, is obscured.

That high suicide rates are attributed to the LGBTQ community depend on how any death is reported and how deaths are classified. Death is death, no matter by intent, accident, malice, or age. Until death makes its claim on us, our quality of life seems a high priority. Theists offer high-quality life expectations. Atheists and agnostics offer high-quality life expectations.

However, which group has the higher respect for life?

Consider one group that touts the following philosophy as science, as reality: Life is created from nothing, as an accident, with no purpose, and goes back to nothing.

Consider another group's philosophy as theology, as reality: Everything, including living creatures, was created by God to glorify Him. Jesus, as God, redeemed man's sins to join Him forever in Heaven. Those who don't glorify Him suffer damnation forever.

Consider this last group's philosophy as art, as an impression of reality: LGBTQ persons were saved before they were born. Atheists, agnostics, and theists were saved before they were born. All 100 percent human beings were guaranteed salvation before the world was created. None go to Hell.

Which group has a higher respect for life? If no answer is obvious, blessings to you as you follow your intuition regarding the highest respect of life.

GENDER FLUIDITY

One of the best Christian apologists had another call regarding sexuality.

The Caller: How does a person afflicted with hermaphroditism manage their life? Would they be considered transgendered?

The Host: Even though the rare case of hermaphroditism exists, the responsible moral position is to choose and subsequently assume the male or female gender. Any future sexual relationship should be based on an opposite-sex relationship. That's the orthodox Christian response. Babies are defined as male or female when they come into the world. That cannot be changed no matter what physical or mental techniques are applied.

END.

In most cases, gender determination is by genitalia. Other determinants are dependent on whether further investigation is warranted. If so, various methods are available for verification. *However, genital observation is 99 percent reliable for the most relevant assignment of gender roles by parents or guardians.* In extremely rare cases where gender is ambiguous, medical professionals set the precedent.

This Christian apologist host is A-rated and works at a fabulous organization. However, the Minister of Art doesn't agree with this answer.

A person does not CHOOSE to be male or female. A person does not CHOOSE their body or brain. They are ASSIGNED a ROLE of GENDER EXPRESSION by heredity and the environment. They are a Roleplayer of Free Will.

Before birth, there is a range of influences affecting gender formulation. Some are known. Some are unknown. This would have to include *mental* as well as physical formulation. From what we observe in human sexuality, sexual expression may be *neutral*. Emphasis has been placed on heterosexuality for two essential reasons.

One, to produce the Antidote to Adam and Eve's error in the Garden of Eden, Jesus Christ.

Two, to produce human Roleplayers for the Demonstration of Free Will that proves the error Eve and Adam made as flawless creatures disobeying God.

Therefore, homosexuality has the scourge of defiance toward God's precepts which, from the distant past, promoted sustained levels of procreation. With no reliance on the advanced medical protocols of today, the doctor, or persons assisting in delivery, made a PHYSICAL determination of gender. *Then, gender expression is ASSIGNED as masculine or feminine depending on genital observation, medical personnel, parent/guardian upbringing, and culture*. This continues today, although people disapprove of rigid male-female expectations.

In the case of hermaphroditism, the attending medical professional, in consultation with the parents, decides on which gender seems most dominant. If this is inconclusive, a decision is made on which gender to pursue. Depending on how appropriate surgery or other techniques are, *the child is assigned a gender direction that is expected to last a lifetime.*

Considering a child is the culmination of heredity, environment, and experience to the point of young adulthood, their physical identity (PID) is only part of their overall identity. *Gradually, their mental identity (MID) begins to evaluate the feedback from their physical identity. Expression or suppression of the feedback is largely influenced by the environment of family, culture, and society.* Along with experiences in life, the person acts out the assigned identity. CD1/CD2 illustrates the identity via MARVI-RPIA.

The well-known Christian apologist apparently meant that gender isn't chosen at the EARLY stage of life. Gender is chosen LATER as a method of unassigning the incorrectly assigned gender identity imposed upon them.

The apologist went on to assert that the BODY is ALWAYS the determining factor in gender. The MIND that questions the initial gender assignment role is always in error, not the other way around, as transgender persons believe. They believe they are in the wrong body and seek to change the body. No, don't do that. Your body knows best. Don't mutilate a perfectly good body. The body has the wrong mind. Change the mind. Leave the body alone.

Perfectly good body. Really? Says who?

By contrast, the imagery' *Connecting the Dots of Identity'* paints is the following:

1) A perfectly good body is neither perfect nor good. It is subject to HEREDITY from the vast number of bodies descending from Adam and Eve, through the ENVIRONMENTAL factors of the pre- and post-Flood world, to finally emerge in the present day after nine months in the womb. Being born in sin guarantees widespread birth defects of every kind. Life EXPERIENCES further confirm the ongoing conflict between mind and body. You're given a body you did not request. You're given a mind you did not request. Make the best of it or give up and die, slowly or abruptly.

2) *There's also no such thing as a perfectly good mind in the same way as there's no perfectly good body.* Both are corrupted by sin and only partially recover when the Holy Spirit intervenes.

3) The choice of gender is assigned to children based on the identity of parents, guardians, or medical professionals who may be *sane, unsane, or even insane.*

4) Refusal to accept the assigned gender, pursue opposite-sex expression, or attempt to change gender identity should not be undertaken until reaching the stage of young adulthood. *Caution: extreme danger to the individual, family, and society.*

5*) Gender identity and gender expression are defined differently by sane and unsane persons.* There will always be tension as each side struggles to prevent the other from preeminence.

After the Garden of Eden, and after the Flood, human sexuality continued the mission to produce the Redeemer for mankind. The secondary mission was to produce human Roleplayers who would demonstrate the Error of Free Will initiated by flawless Adam and Eve.

Before the Flood, the overall violation of God's natural order regarding angel and human-induced procreation may have diminished the status of procreation. *Now in the days after the Flood, with man's lifespan reduced from 1,000 years to 100 years, procreation as sexual expression drastically changed.* Now what? Its 1500-2000 years after Adam and Eve left the Garden and still no Redeemer. High effort, no result. There was no sexual dysfunction or infertility in the population. What was the problem?

Every female was able to conceive. But … at what age does sexual activity begin? Ten, twelve, thirteen? Were children having sex with other children? Was children and adult sex okay? The end justifies the means. The Redeemer must be born! It was a worldwide emergency.

Years later, procreation was still held as the standard for sexual expression but became less and less a priority. *This became so much the case that even after the Redeemer arrived, procreation had long since been downgraded to a lower status. Procreation today is just another category of sex.* Sex is now big business, money, power, looks, politics, strategy, responsibility, expectation, escapism, adventure, occupation, crime, and IDENTITY.

As Free Will Roleplayers, sexuality highlights only one of the many freedoms God allows. He requires adherence to His standards of right and wrong, good and bad, but only intervenes in Free Will to verify Election-Predestination. Until He intervenes, God requires people to disavow their sexual identity imposed by heredity, environment, and experience. You are to follow His words in scripture regardless of circumstances. He will help you.

Meanwhile, being spiritually blind until the Holy Spirit arrives means your gender identity is YOUR province, not God's. *This comes to mean opposite-sex relationships are not fixed; they are fluid.*

Therefore, when the religious person objects to fluidity, stating that gender and sexuality are fixed, *ask them if they would still be 100 percent heterosexual if they were not religious.* How could they know? They're captured by religion—as in Election/Predestination, compulsion, coercion, or subversion. LGBTQ persons are not captured by religion; thus, they are free to express sexuality as dictated by heredity, environment, and experience.

The LGBTQ community champions the flexibility of gender expression. This continues until they meet the Holy Spirit. It may continue after meeting the Holy Spirit but only as the old creature dies and the new creature lives.

CHAPTER 12

SEX EDUCATION 4—POST POSTSCRIPT

Knock, knock.

Yes. Who's there?

Me. Same-Sex Marriage.

Okay. What can we do for you?

Well, now that same-sex marriage is approved worldwide, it has become obvious that there are still artificial limits on marriage that are discriminatory and support hate. An initiative for marriage INDEMNITY is forthcoming. It seeks to remove impediments and provide protection regarding the GENDER of spouses, the NUMBER of spouses, the AGE of spouses, the SPECIES of spouses, and the CATEGORIES of spouses.

Love and marriage are synonymous. Love of an animate being or an inanimate object is a personal expression. Therefore, an absolute right exists to define and pursue this expression that culminates in marriage, a solemn public commitment protected by the government.

Society says, "Oh no." It will never go that far. Go knock on some other nation's door.

–Male marriage to more than one male? No.

–Female marriage to more than one female? No.

–Adult marriage to one or more underage children? No, never.

–Underage children marriage to underage children? No, never.

–Adult marriage to animate objects? No.

–Adult marriage to inanimate objects? No.

None of these ideas would ever be tolerated. Oh, really? How naive can you be? Just look at how far, or how low, we've "progressed" in the last 100 years. It won't take long before you realize what was against the law in the past 100 years is now perfectly acceptable, and efforts are always ongoing to further push the agenda of personal freedom. A hundred years from today will see even fewer restrictions. It's the nature of progressive individuality.

Same-sex marriage on its face is not a threat to opposite-sex marriage. Same-sex unions are recognized and have legal standing. Public declaration of love and commitment to partnership is not prohibited in most nations of the world. What religious organizations object to is coercion to endorse, participate, and celebrate same-sex marriage.

Along with religious freedom comes a concern for individual freedom, business freedom, and parental freedom. *If governments mandate conformity to promote and participate in the gay lifestyle evolution, exercising religious rights will be criminalized. You may be individually prosecuted for opposing gay activities. Your business may be prosecuted for not participating in gay activities. Your parental right to raise your child the way you think best may be prohibited and cause your children to be removed from your care.*

But why would governments be so inclined to become involved in the LGBTQ community? The most obvious answer is POWER. Governments led by people who lack integrity seek power. *Removing power from the individual, from businesses, from parents TO the government, BY the government, is the goal. Where there is no organized resistance to governmental intrusion, the incessant erosion of rights will continue.*

On second thought, you may be right. Marriage probably won't ever degenerate to the levels mentioned earlier. The reason? We'll destroy ourselves before we get there. Or maybe God will intercede. Again. Not with water, like the Flood in Genesis, but this time with FIRE!

> And I will establish my covenant with you, neither shall all flesh be cut off any more by the waters of a flood; neither shall there anymore be a flood to destroy the earth (Genesis 9:11).

> But the day of the Lord will come as a thief in the night; in which the heavens shall pass away with a great noise, and the elements shall melt with fervent heat, the earth also and the works that are therein shall be burned up. Seeing then that all these things shall be dissolved, what manner of persons ought ye to be in all holy conversation and godliness, looking for and hasting unto the coming of the day of God, wherein the heavens being on fire shall be dissolved, and the elements shall melt with fervent heat? Nevertheless we, according to his promise, look for new heavens and a new earth, wherein dwelleth righteousness (2 Peter 3:10-13).

As long as Ego-Skepticism, getting married, and having children drives thinking and behaving, distortion of marriage, procreation, and identity will advance. It's human nature to be free, unencumbered by rules. Otherwise, why ignore the rules, change the rules, or break the rules? Because it's okay to do so. It's the advancement of individual freedom.

Connecting the Dots of Identity strives to be the imagery that offers the possibility of an authentic identity. By doing so, the caricature of the inauthentic identity loses its significance of Ego-Skepticism, insistence on marriage, and persistence in recreating further inauthentic identities.

The Minister of Art is not AGAINST marriage and children. The Minister of Art is not FOR marriage and children. The Minister of Art is for a Single-Persons Champion, Team Companions, and Team Players.

SINGLE-PERSONS CHAMPION

Until another Roleplayer presents themselves as the Team Player, the Helpmeet, to cultivate the garden of people, be a Single-Persons Champion. Good Roleplayers, loving Roleplayers, and godly Roleplayers are so conditioned for marriage and children that they frequently compromise their Team Player potential. You must be 100 percent committed to the "game," to the"mission," in order to be a world-class team. Otherwise, it's easy to plug in any Roleplayer and be an effective team. There are many good-to-very-good Christian teams. There are NOT that many great or super teams. If there were, we would know them.

You should want to be in a position where you are effective as a Single-Persons Champion. Marriage may not happen. Your potential Team Player must convince YOU that THEY are the consummate, indispensable, essential person to build a team on. It's not your job to convince them to join you. If a team is to be built, you will know when the two of you become INSEPARABLE! Force yourself to stay away as long as you can. Don't let your heart run the show. Hearts are easily broken. Feelings are easily hurt. Misunderstandings occur.

There are hundreds of Roleplayers who qualify as a teammate. All ages, shapes, sizes, colors, and backgrounds. *God, Jesus Christ, and the Holy*

Spirit will fill in until the right person comes along. The clock is NOT ticking. It already ticked before the foundation of the world. Your life awaits in the future. For now, it would be wonderful if you could sacrifice yourself to bring beauty to others.

Sacrifice my life? A spouse, children, a career? Why should I? I don't have to find a teammate who can score as well as I can. I don't need a copilot who can also fly the plane as well as I do. I work best with an audience in the arena, cheerleaders on the sidelines, and fans. Two leaders don't always work out so well. Besides, I know I'm cut out to be a dad, not a role model. I'm cut out to be a mom, not a role model.

Okay. Some 40 percent of you, 50 percent of you, all the way to 75 percent of you will say as much. You MUST get married. But 95 percent of you? Apparently, EVERYBODY thinks it's asking too much to sacrifice your life FIRST and WAIT to see IF the right person comes along. *God, Jesus Christ, and Holy Spirit are woefully insufficient to keep you company.* This must be the case.

Or, how about this? Christian Roleplayers do a lousy job of expressing the HONOR and the OPPORTUNITY of being a Christian single person. Maybe that's the problem. Being single isn't a gift. It may be a gift. It's not permanent. It may be permanent. Do people pray for gifts? Request gifts? Seek gifts? The only people who pray for the gift to be single are married people. (You're supposed to smile).

You may say: What about the planet? What about the human race? What about God's mandate to be fruitful and multiply?

The "be fruitful and multiply" mandate was to establish Free Will Roleplayers, fulfill prophecy, and produce the Redeemer—Jesus Christ.

The Demonstration of Free Will continues afterward to prove the error of Adam and Eve. Then comes the responsibility for HSID Roleplayers to care for the environment of other Roleplayers.

Godly Marriage Material (dating): *Bronze.*

Team Companion (friend/not marriage material): *Silver.*

Single-Persons Champion (unattached/not dating): *Gold.*

Team Player (engaged/married): *Gold.*

GODLY MARRIAGE MATERIAL

The person who accepts who they are as the inauthentic identity imposed by heredity, environment, and experience gives themselves an opportunity to redefine identity based on a new, exciting worldview. If their authentic identity is recognized by God, who granted salvation before the foundation of the world, life is now a responsibility to assist the Holy Spirit in healing spiritual blindness in the world. The secondary responsibility is addressing intentional and unintentional blindness as defined by the Blind Eyes Chart. In the interim, every effort is made to overcome the effects of identity flaws that inhibit the attractiveness to bond with others who follow *Connecting the Dots of Identity.*

TEAM COMPANION

As a Single-Persons Champion, it would seem fitting that, by virtue of your temporary commitment to chastity, *you may meet a qualified Team*

Player but prefer not to marry. So, what's stopping you from continuing in a Team Player relationship? Marriage may NOT be necessary, compelling, or unavoidable. *In this case, companionship, networking, or a partnership should be worth cultivating.*

Or, instead of acquiring a once-in-a-lifetime marriage partner, perhaps one, two, three, or more team companions will be better. It makes sense that any person who qualifies as a potential Team Player should be retained in your circle of companions—especially if they are pleased to continue as a non-married partner.

How would the Minister of Art feel about finally meeting Missus Right who prefers not to marry? She would be pleased to have the Minister of Art as one of her five other companions. Is that acceptable?

Absolutely! I would be honored to be a teammate of any potential Team Player who did not desire to marry me, for whatever reason. I may be too old, too dark, too poor, too short, too uneducated, too worldly, too quirky, or too antisocial. It's all up to the attributes and standards she feels are essential.

Of course, this does not factor in the insanity of what people describe as "falling in love." Apparently, when this happens, self-control is no longer reliable. You are in a twilight zone of emotion. If that occurs, well, you just have to go through it.

TEAM PLAYER

If you come to accept some of the tenets of MARVI-RPIA, you should be in the process of becoming Godly Marriage Material. The next step is being a suitable Team Companion to a Single-Persons Champion. The steps to take begin with being the best single person you can be. As you evaluate the effects of heredity, environment, and experience that formed what could be considered your inauthentic identity, *you realize you're not limited by your appearance, your intellect, or your experiences.*

Temporarily, you are a Roleplayer assigned to this time and space. You had no choice in the matter. The decision to refuse the identity imposed upon you and accept the identity described in scripture opens up new meanings of how to live. Life is not about MY circumstances. Life is about making the Earth a better place by cultivating the environment of people. Cultivation begins with cultivating the self. It's improving the soil of growth, removing impaired attachments, and pursuing the source of life. Circumstances don't control you. You control definitions and reactions to circumstances.

With an improved focus on identity, you are able to convey a positive effect on other people. They are not threatened by your ego because your intentions are directed toward their well-being, not your own. *Also, you don't need them. You aren't insecure. Your identity isn't based on what they think of you. You aren't you. You are just a temporary Roleplayer. Who you are is safe with God in Paradise—your authentic identity.*

You should soon see that the people who perceive your heart will speak to your heart. Your gender, your race, your intellect, your wealth, and your appearance won't matter. Your heart matters to them. *If not, your hearts don't match at this time. Move on.*

The progression from Godly Marriage Material to Team Companion to Single-Persons Champion, to Team Player, takes time and patience. But once you get there, or get close, it's worth your sacrifices. You may have to sacrifice not only time and patience but people. Your family, friends, and associates may not have access to you. Don't be intimidated. Manage your time. Be assertive. Make *forward* progress.

Being a Team Player to a Single-Persons Champion is an artistic way of saying if enough people follow the impression of CD1/CD2, your likelihood of contact with high-quality people increases. Even if marriage doesn’t happen, Team Companionship may. If Team Companionship is delayed, at least you should be in the stages of Godly Marriage Material. Be patient. Be optimistic. You can’t lose. You’ve already won.

CHAPTER 13

SEX EDUCATION—PART 5

Have you ever wondered about the examples in the Old Testament of God killing thousands because of homosexuality? This is what Orthodox Church leaders teach.

The reference is to the passages in Genesis 14 (Sodom, Gomorrah, and nearby locations), and Judges 19 (Gibeah/Jabesh-Gilead). The two accounts document groups of men who come to a dwelling demanding a meeting with the male occupant(s). The implication is for sex. By refusing to comply with the antagonists' request, great destruction of the antagonists and others follow.

MARVI-RPIA displays these two biblical scenes in the spirit of INHOSPITALITY rather than the spirit of HOMOSEXUALITY. The conservative view citing homosexuality is held by some of the most brilliant and well-known Bible teachers. Conversely, inhospitality suggests a larger, more "natural" view. Hospitality in those ancient times was a matter of life and death. Your life depended on food, water, and lodging. Who you know in any given location or destination may not be known except through direct kinship, adoptive kinship, or cultural kinship.

There were cities and countries, but there were no "common decency" standards across the lands. Only the Lord's people, Israel, were held to godly standards. Strict standards. Conversely, for the general populations of that time, there were no top-down, ritually pure standards. To travel any significant distance puts you at risk of uncleanliness in all its forms.

There were no police, no motels/hotels, no restaurants, hospitals, or public transportation. No restrooms (of any kind, much less male/female), Laundromats, or banks. When you traveled, you had to plan everything. If there were no reliable sources in other locations, your life, and the life of your party, would be in jeopardy.

People who did not know the Lord were themselves the law. They did that which was right in their own eyes. Morals were totally subjective; there was no overall "right" that everyone was entitled to that was above individual rights. Individual rights ruled.

SODOM AND GOMORRAH

In the case of Sodom and Gomorrah and nearby locales, the decision to destroy this area was already made before the angels arrived in town (Genesis 18). What transpired afterward wasn't so pertinent, even though Abraham pleaded with God for their mercy. But the story goes that the men of Sodom, old and young, and all the people of every quarter, came to Lot's house demanding the "men," who are the angels, come out so they might "know" them.

So, this town, and the towns nearby, were already marked for destruction BEFORE the angels arrived. *The countdown had begun before any so-called homosexual scenario took place.*

From the story, the implication is that the demanding group calling to "know" the angels were all homosexuals, or those persons in support of homosexuals. They wanted to engage in homosexual behavior with the strangers in town—or promote homosexual behavior.

Aside from the fact that God had previously marked the towns for destruction, MARVI-RPIA takes the position that the city was corrupt because of their refusal and opposition to HOSPITALITY. *How could the whole town be engaged in homosexuality, from the youngest to the eldest?* They may have all been exceedingly rude, belligerent, and uncivilized. They were certainly accomplices in whatever transgressions marked them for destruction. *But it's highly suspect that towns in any era in history could be 50 percent to 100 percent homosexual. Bisexual perhaps? Also, not at all likely.*

Were there not fifty heterosexuals (righteous) in the towns? Not forty, thirty, twenty, ten? Not in the whole town? Not even ten heterosexuals (see Genesis 18)? *Only Lot, his wife, and two daughters were heterosexual? If all the homosexuals in the towns engaged in heterosexuality just to create children, did that make them at least bisexual?*

Were all the other cities in the world escaping destruction by keeping homosexuality in the closet? *Does this mean all the other sins people were engaging in were not as bad as homosexuality? Bestiality was okay? Murder was okay? Idolatry was okay? Sorcery, witchcraft, or divination was okay? What about child sacrifice? Rape? Robbery? Theft? Pedophilia? Abortion?*

We read in the Bible God did destroy other cities because of evil. God even destroyed thousands of His own people for the evil they committed.

The argument could be made that the only real crime against homosexuality in the Old Testament was the prevention of procreation. Procreation was the method God designed to bring about the Redeemer of mankind. *Preventing procreation was preventing the Messiah from arriving on the scene. This is apparently why God was so against homosexuality.* And nowadays, after the era of the Messiah, homosexuality is still reprehensible but not as irreverent and ungodly.

But this is not the teaching of the church. They teach God destroyed the cities around Sodom and Gomorrah because they were engaging in same-sex behavior. Period. God winked at almost everything else the world was doing—for a season. Some situations immediately called for acts of God. Others were specific to God's people for edification or for generations forthcoming.

Inhospitality includes a wider range of sins than homosexuality. Homosexuality was a capital offense for God's people. Other nations did not have the standards of morality, law, and cleanliness observed by Israel.

Furthermore, homosexuality is a practice of mutual sexual consent. If no consent, it's not sex. It's assault. It's rape. Ask any woman who has been raped if the act was a sexual act. Rape is an act of violence, assault, mayhem, molestation, abuse, coercion, or force.

People may assume that the Sodomites used their own bodies to have sex with or assault other men. Not at all. You can assault someone with objects. Assault with objects is a further act of humiliation. *The Sodomites may not have been about sex. It could have been bullying, ridicule, extortion, sport, or even some demonic ritual. They didn't have to physically touch the innocent party at all with their own masculine parts. The use of inanimate objects, or even animate objects, is sufficient. Even the threat of use is grounds for great violation.*

You demand the strangers come out. You threaten, intimidate, and extort them. Then "know" them by removing their clothing. Nakedness is also a form of knowing someone. They humiliate them and then kidnap them by parading them through the town down to the arena. There you make sport, experiment, and perform wicked rituals that may involve animals, objects, drugs, alcohol, sorcery, and etcetera.

The argument goes that the aggressors were offered the host's maiden daughter(s). The aggressors declined. That isn't necessarily proof of homosexuality. Women and girls represented treasure, barter, or financial value for the homeowner. But the aggressors probably knew the girls. The aggressors wanted foreigners, or strange flesh. They wanted sport.

When noteworthy strangers came to town, they may have promoted or enacted new laws, threatening the perverse law of the land. Maybe the strangers were spies from another government. Make them disclose their mission. There are ways of making people talk.

How did Lot avoid the hostile stranger treatment in the preceding years? Maybe Lot had a very low profile or special skills the city deemed essential. Perhaps his wife or wife's relatives excused Lot, assuming Lot married a woman of Sodom. As the city became worse and worse, maybe his sons-in-law spoke up for him. They were betrothed to his daughters, who were still maidens until marriage.

And then ... the end is near. Inhospitable behavior from the people in cities around that area had escalated to the point the spillover was affecting many people of God. The angels go forward to warn Lot and entreat him to gather his family. Lot's sons-in-law do not heed the warning to leave. Lot's wife doesn't escape the destruction. Lot's daughters not only suffered from the loss of their mother and husbands but bore children from their own father. The daughters were not blessed (figuratively), and their children were not blessed (figuratively). The children were Moab and Benammi.

GIBEAH

In the matter of the Levite and his concubine in Gibeah (Judges 19), we see, again, men coming to a dwelling, demanding to know the man inside.

For sex? That's the popular conservative view backed up by Sodom and Gomorrah. MARVI-RPIA again paints a different scene. *Coercion, extortion, and intimidation, rather than homosexuality, is the crime.* The men expect to bully, humiliate, rob, and exploit strangers for personal gain and preserve the immoral law of the land. The men are the local law of the land. Some are good, some are bad. These men are from the honorable tribe of Benjamin, though this particular group are the sons of Belial.

Benjamin is one of the revered twelve tribes from Jacob—who is Israel. They are NOT known for homosexuality. *Homosexuality is strictly forbidden by the people of Israel. Capital punishment is the penalty. Homosexuality is a secret, behind-closed-doors type of sin.*

The Levite refuses to go out to the men. The host of the dwelling offers his maiden daughter, but the Levite sends out his concubine instead of himself or the host's daughter. The men do not accept the offer. They assault and abuse the concubine and leave her for dead. The next day the Levite doesn't arouse her. Perhaps she is drugged, or maybe in a coma. Maybe she's dead. He takes her, leaves town, and goes home. When home, he dissects her body and sends her parts to the tribes of Israel.

HOMOSEXUALITY VERSUS INHOSPITALITY

Whatever may be said of same-gender relationships, once the Messiah arrives on the scene of history, same-sex relationships loses most of its compelling significance. We have achieved the mandate. Sex between men and men or women and women no longer have the same stigma it once had, relative to procreation. *Procreation is no longer the dominant sexual goal of mankind.*

In looking at the hierarchy of evils regarding sexuality and its counterpart, inhospitality, what can we draw from this?

Consider this list in degrees of "bad" to "worst":

SEXUALITY (BAD-case examples to WORST-case examples)

Man and a woman (fornication/adultery/polygamy/incest).

Man and a man/woman and a woman (homosexuality/lesbianism).

Man and child or animal or dead person (pedophilia/bestiality/necrophilia).

Woman and evil spirit (Nephilim).

INHOSPITALITY (BAD-case examples to WORST-case examples)

Don't accept strangers/ignore strangers.

Bully/harass/humiliate strangers.

Rob/assault strangers.

Kidnap/make sport/experiment on strangers.

Sorcery, witchcraft, necromancy.

Kill strangers.

Inhospitality may be in view regarding the verses Matthew 10.

> And when ye come into a house, salute it. And if the house be worthy, let your peace come upon it: but if it be not worthy, let your peace return to you. And whosoever shall not receive you, nor hear your words, when ye depart out of that house or city, shake off the dust of your feet. Verily I say unto you, It shall be

> more tolerable for the land of Sodom and Gomorrha in the day of judgment, than for that city.

The case for homosexuality, as in Sodom and Gibeah, as the reason God destroys thousands, only covers the first two of the worst-case examples named above. *It would seem God's anger would be stirred more by sex with children, animals, and evil spirits than men with men or women with women.* Maybe God's reason to destroy Sodom and Gomorrah was because of all four bad-to-worst case examples. God's decision was made before the angels arrived, so the main sin is not obvious.

The case for inhospitality as a reason God would destroy thousands covers all six reasons. *Whereas both forms of behavior exist, the average person would probably prefer a gay person who lives next door, or in their city, than a person who is hostile to the point of murdering strangers in the community.*

One of the leading apologists, a Master of Philosophy, has pointed out that homosexuality is the only obvious reason for Sodom and Gibeah. His case is quite persuasive. He cites all the usual anti-homosexual verses. He then adds two other not-so-familiar verses from 2 Peter and Jude. They both refer to the sin of Sodom and Gomorrah. When reading beyond the verses he gives to prove HOMOSEXUALITY, the remaining verses yield a secondary meaning of INHOSPITALITY. This secondary meaning is MARVI-RPIA's choice.

> And turning the cities of Sodom and Gomorrha into ashes condemned them with an overthrow, making them an ensample unto those that after should live ungodly. And delivered just Lot, vexed with the filthy conversation of the wicked For that righteous man dwelling among them, in seeing and hearing, vexed his

> righteous soul from day to day with their unlawful deeds (2 Peter 2:6-8).

Here are excluded verses that could be included as inhospitality:

> But chiefly them that walk after the flesh in the lust of uncleanness, and despise government. Presumptuous are they, selfwilled, they are not afraid to speak evil of dignities. Whereas angels, which are greater in power and might, bring not railing accusation against them before the Lord. But these, as natural brute beasts, made to be taken and destroyed, speak evil of the things that they understand not; and shall utterly perish in their own corruption. And shall receive the reward of unrighteousness, as they that count it pleasure to riot in the day time. Spots they are and blemishes, sporting themselves with their own deceiving while they feast with you. Having eyes full of adultery, and that cannot cease from sin; beguiling unstable souls: a heart they have exercised with covetous practices; cursed children. Which have forsaken the right way, and are gone astray, following the way of Balaam the son of Bosor, who loved the wages of unrighteousness. But was rebuked for his iniquity: the dumb ass speaking with man's voice forbad the madness of the prophet. These are wells without water, clouds that are carried with a tempest; to whom the mist of darkness is reserved for ever. For when they speak great swelling words of vanity, they allure through the lusts of the flesh, through much wantonness, those that were clean escaped from them who live in error. While they promise them liberty, they themselves are the servants of corruption: for of whom a man is overcome, of the same is he brought in bondage (2 Peter 2: 10, 14-15, 18-19).

And here are the Bible scholar's verses helping prove homosexuality as a "crime" of the ages, second only to the crime causing the Flood:

> And the angels which kept not their first estate, but left their own habitation, he hath reserved in everlasting chains under darkness unto the judgment of the great day. Even as Sodom and Gomorrha, and the cities about them in like manner, giving themselves over to fornication, and going after strange flesh, are set forth for an example, suffering the vengeance of eternal fire (Jude 1:6-7).

Another piece of the sodomite puzzle may come from the book of Ezekiel:

> And thine elder sister is Samaria, she and her daughters that dwell at thy left hand: and thy younger sister that dwelled at thy right hand is Sodom and her daughters. Yet hast thou not walked after their ways, nor done after their abominations: but, as if that were a very little thing, thou wast corrupted more than they in all thy ways. As I live, said the Lord God, Sodom thy sister hath not done, her nor her daughters, as thou hast done, thou and thy daughters. Behold, this was the iniquity of thy sister Sodom, pride, fullness of bread, and abundance of idleness was in her and in her daughters, neither did she strengthen the hand of the poor and needy. And they were haughty, and committed abomination before me: therefore I took them away as I saw good (Ezekiel 16:46-50).

From this, we may see Sodom as an image of pride, leisure, unconcern for retribution, a lack of empathy, corrupt, and no regard for God or man.

Deuteronomy generally teaches principles and order of conduct: There shall be no whore of the daughters of Israel, nor a sodomite of the sons of Israel (Deuteronomy 23:17).

Daughters and sons of Israel were to be chaste and hospitable. Boys and men were instructed to honor themselves, others, the congregation, the house of God, and God Himself.

Consider the word Sodom: Sodomites. This is universally a term for the homosexual act. That may be true. *However, consider the current, crude, universal term "motherf----."* Initially, there was no term for this act (1 Corinthians 5:1). It is a literal term and a universal term. The sexual act has no literal relationship to what it means today. The word sodomite may be a similar term, a word to symbolize crudeness, lewdness, strange and unusual acts, stunts, exhibitionism, and extortion.

Deuteronomy speaks of female and male sexually immoral behavior. From various translations, the meaning may refer to whore and whoremonger, prostitute and pimp, abused and abuser, or immodest female and aggressive male. Sodomite could refer to something other than male-to-male sex acts.

The man Lot, his wife, and his daughters were *citizens of Sodom—Sodomites.*

Just thoughts. Just colors of the MARVI-RPIA verbal palette.

Here are supporting verses:

There shall be no whore of the daughters of Israel, nor a sodomite of the sons of Israel (Deuteronomy 23:17).

It is reported commonly that there is fornication among you, and such fornication as is not so much as named among the Gentiles, that one should have his father's wife (1 Corinthians 5:1).

And the Lord said, because the cry of Sodom and Gomorrah is great, and because their sin is very grievous. I will go down now, and see whether they have done altogether according to the cry of it, which is come unto me; and if not, I will know. And the men turned their faces from thence, and went toward Sodom: but Abraham stood yet before the Lord. And Abraham drew near, and said, Will thou also destroy the righteous with the wicked? Peradventure there be fifty righteous within the city: wilt thou also destroy and not spare the place for the fifty righteous that are therein? (Genesis 18:20-24).

And he said, Oh let not the Lord be angry, and I will speak yet but this once: Peradventure ten shall be found there. And he said, I will not destroy it for ten's sake (Genesis 18:32).

But before they lay down, the men of the city, even the men of Sodom, compassed the house round, both old and young, all the people from every quarter: And they called unto Lot, and said unto him, where are the men which came in to thee this night? Bring them out unto us, that we may know them. And Lot went out at the door unto them, and shut the door after him, And said, I pray you, brethren, do not so wickedly. Behold now, I have two daughters which have not known man; let me, I pray you, bring them out unto you, and do ye to them as is good in your eyes: only unto these men do nothing; for therefore came they under the shadow of my roof. And they said, Stand back. And they said again, this one fellow came in to sojourn, and he will needs be a judge: now will we deal worse with thee, than with them. And they pressed sore upon the man, even Lot, and came near to break the door. But the men put forth their hand, and pulled Lot into the house to them, and shut to the door. And they smote the men that were at the door of the house with blindness, both small and great: so that they wearied themselves to find the door (Genesis 19:4-11).

Thus were both the daughters of Lot with child by their father. And the first born bare a son, and called his name Moab: the same is the father of the Moabites unto this day. And the younger, she also bare a son, and called his name Benammi: the same is the father of the children of Ammon unto this day (Genesis 19:36-38).

Now as they were making their hearts merry, behold, the men of the city, certain sons of Belial, beset the house round about, and beat at the door, and spake to the master of the house, the old man, saying, Bring forth the man that came into thine house, that we may know him. And the man, the master of the house, went out unto them, and said unto them, Nay, my brethren, nay, I pray you, do not so wickedly; seeing that this man is come into mine house, do not this folly. Behold, here is my daughter a maiden, and his concubine; them I will bring out now, and humble ye them, and do with them what seemeth good unto you: but unto this man do not so vile a thing. But the men would not hearken to him: so the man took his concubine, and brought her forth unto them; and they knew her, and abused her all the night until the morning: and when the day began to spring, they let her go. Then came the woman in the dawning of the day, and fell down at the door of the man's house where her lord was, till it was light. And her lord rose up in the morning, and opened the doors of the house, and went out to go his way: and, behold, the woman his concubine was fallen down at the door of the house, and her hands were upon the threshold. And he said unto her, Up, and let us be going. But none answered. Then the man took her up upon an ass, and the man rose up, and gat him unto his place. And when he was come into his house, he took a knife, and laid hold on his concubine, and divided her, together with her bones, into twelve pieces, and sent her into all the coasts of Israel (Judges 19:22-29).

CHAPTER 14

SEX EDUCATION — PART 6

A parent notices their young child is not following traditional gender Roleplay. After a few prompts to ascertain whether the child prefers articles of the same sex or the opposite sex, the parent becomes convinced the child may be transsexual. Transsexual in the sense that the child is not conforming to the assigned gender the parent has assumed and guided. Now, what to do?

One of the first questions the parent addresses is: Does the child have the ability to know their gender is incorrectly assigned?

Answer: Yes. The mural MARVI-RPIA paints onto the architecture of the Bible includes young children. There is a huge problem with sex education in almost every country. *Probably half of all children receive mediocre or no useful sexual education. It is not so much the fault of the parent(s) as it is of the preceding line of parents, the culture, and restrictions placed on public and private schools.* Is there a method of informing children of sexual details in a comprehensive and responsible way? Does it avoid the pornographic correlation? If so, can such a method garner the consent of the parent(s) or guardians?

MARVI-RPIA has an image of the child's identity that helps the child understand their gender role is a temporary compilation of who they appear to be but actually aren't. Whatever role they are thrust into is made up of forces they had nothing to do with.

These forces act upon the body and the mind. Some forces begin at conception, some in the womb, and some after birth. Some forces are temporary, and some last a lifetime. Parents are very influential. The worldview of parents and parenting skills are also determining factors in how children perceive identity.

A child's true identity is in Paradise, created before the world was created. Any role they are forced into now doesn't represent who they are. It's just a role. Its circumstances.

If a child is able to bear the misery and distress of their currently assigned role until the age of young adulthood—eighteen years old or so—the parent(s) should learn to be adept at managing the hardship. After adulthood, the child assumes responsibility. In the interim, the parent(s) is responsible for guidance in development. A child isn't mentally mature enough to communicate matters of identity as complex as gender assignment and expression, sexual expectation, puberty, and procreation. *Adults must communicate that they understand the child's preferences, but the child must respect the parent(s) role to responsibly guide and instruct them.*

It may be helpful to review some of the age restrictions currently in place. The parent and the child should be reminded that safeguards exist for the benefit of underage persons, parents, and society.

Children are protected from exposure, participation, and responsibility in the following examples: pornography, profanity, nudity, sexual intercourse, marriage, alcohol use, tobacco use, marijuana use, voting, gambling, sports activities, employment, owning firearms, operating vehicles, and criminal liability.

It seems gender has been overemphasized. Gender serves two purposes:

1) To facilitate procreation that arrives at the Redeemer who provides the remedy for the Error committed by Adam and Eve.

2) To facilitate the number of lives needed to prove the Error of Free Will by using living human Roleplayers descending from the original Roleplayers—Adam and Eve.

Your true identity, Pre-Life Elect person in Paradise has no gender role to play. They may assume gender, as the angels have. Some angels served as ministers of the Lord doing good. Other angels, as sons of God, committed evil. Or gender may become a selective feature of the past life on Earth. It won't be a randomly imposed assignment. It won't be a countermeasure to error.

How these concepts are communicated, and how these concepts are understood by the child, will determine how well gender roles are accepted by young children. The young child is simply a Roleplayer. The parent(s) is a Roleplayer. *Parents probably have limited sex-ed training, and their parents probably had limited sex-ed training.* Children of past generations assumed gender assignment based on the most rudimentary evidence available: observation. Physical characteristics were all they had to go on. The social structure of the day determined male and female expectations. Aberrant thinking and behavior certainly existed, but it was behind the scenes. *Rejection of traditional male/female gender assignment was morally offensive to people, obscene, and even unlawful for countless generations.* It's only in the recent past has this changed.

The expectation of gender identity as male or female carries with it specific responsibilities. As mentioned earlier, the label of "unnatural sex acts" isn't necessarily confined to same-sex activity. If a man leaves off the natural use of a woman and the woman abandons the natural role of a woman, *it's assumed that "natural use" is procreation centered.* Natural use means male/female activity leading to procreation. That eliminates male-to-male and female-to-female interaction.

However, a lack of participation in gender "natural use" may also be a definition of Planned Parenthood or non-procreation sexual activity. The label of "unnatural" sex in this case as a secondary meaning may be inappropriate.

STORYTIME

One day, while listening to the Bible being read, the reader came to Genesis 38. Judah has a son named Er. The story continues through the rest of the chapter.

Wait a minute. *God killed Judah's son, Er, and God also killed Judah's second son, Onan.* Judah's third son still lived. Let's go back and see what that was all about.

Judah chose a wife for his son Er. Her name was Tamar. Er did wickedly in the sight of God. God killed him. What was the wickedness? We aren't told. Judah told Er's brother Onan to marry Tamar and raise children for his brother. Onan married her but knew his children with Tamar would be his brother's children. Onan aborted his mission by spilling his seed on the ground rather than with Tamar. This displeased the Lord. The Lord slew Onan.

Whatever Er did that was so wicked to cause God to suddenly kill him could have been anything. However, Er and Tamar had no children. Was Er displeased with his father, Judah, choosing Tamar for his wife? Was Er impotent? Did Er have his heart set on some other woman? Was Er gay? That sounds a bit funny, but it's actually serious.

Okay, here's the point. It seems that Tamar was not barren. We know this from the rest of the narrative.

Tamar tricked her father-in-law, Judah, into impregnating her. Tamar became pregnant with twin boys right away. Earlier, Judah promised Tamar he would give her his third son, Shelah, for a husband, since both Er and Onan were killed. But he didn't do so. After Judah's wife died, he was out and about and saw his daughter-in-law, Tamar, now disguised as a "harlot," and took her.

In this story, procreation plays a major role. For Er and Onan to not produce children is quite significant. It would seem quite UNNATURAL for the two boys to have NO children, especially considering Tamar was willing and not barren. The question about Er being gay is unlikely. The penalty for homosexuality meant banishment from the community and could be fatal, depending on the mercy of the judges. However, Er being gay is still a slight possibility.

And one other detail has to come up. This is the "bloodline" of Jesus Christ. Er and Onan did not do what would have been "natural" for them with Tamar. Shelah was too young. That leaves Judah. Yes, God could have done things other ways, but this gives us a highly dramatic scenario.

The arrival of Jesus Christ via male-female "natural use" underscores the importance of gender Roleplay *regardless of gender identity presumptions or marital individualism.* The law of capital punishment was not unjustified.

And it came to pass at that time that Judah went down from his brethren, and turned in to a certain Adullamite, whose name was Hirah. And Judah saw there a daughter of a certain Canaanite, whose name was Shuah; and he took her, and went in unto her. And she conceived, and bare a son; and he called his name Er. And she conceived again, and bare a son; and she called his name Onan. And she yet again conceived, and bare a son; and called his name Shelah: and he was at Chezib, when she bare him. And Judah took a wife for Er his firstborn, whose name was Tamar. And Er, Judah's firstborn, was wicked in the sight of the Lord; and the Lord slew him. And Judah said unto Onan, Go in unto thy brother's wife, and marry her, and raise up seed to thy brother. And Onan knew that the seed should not be his; and it came to pass, when he went in unto his brother's wife, that he spilled it on the ground, lest that he should give seed to his brother. And the thing which he did displeased the Lord: wherefore he slew him also. Then said Judah to Tamar his daughter in law, Remain a widow at thy father's house, till Shelah my son be grown: for he said, lest peradventure he die also, as his brethren did. And Tamar went and dwelt in her father's house. And in process of time the daughter of Shuah Judah's wife died; and Judah was comforted, and went up unto his sheepshearers to Timnath, he and his friend Hirah the Adullamite.

And it was told Tamar, saying, Behold thy father in law goes up to Timnath to shear his sheep. And she put her widow's garments off from her, and covered her with a vail, and wrapped herself, and sat in an open place, which is by the way to Timnath; for she saw that Shelah was grown, and she was not given unto him to wife. When Judah saw her, he thought her to be a harlot; because she had covered her face. And he turned unto her by the way, and said, Go to, I pray thee, let me come in unto thee; (for he knew not that she was his daughter in law.) And she said, what wilt thou give me, that thou mayest come in unto me? And he said, I will send thee a kid from the flock. And she said, Wilt thou give me a pledge, till thou send it? And he said, what pledge shall I give thee? And she said, Thy signet, and thy bracelets, and thy staff that is in thine hand. And he gave it her, and came in unto her, and she conceived by him. And she arose, and went away, and laid by her vail from her, and put on the garments of her widowhood. And Judah sent the kid by the hand of his friend the Adullamite, to receive his pledge from the woman's hand: but he found her not. Then he asked the men of that place, saying, where is the harlot, that was openly by the way side? And they said, there was no harlot in this place. And he returned to Judah, and said, I cannot find her; and also the men of the place said, that there was no harlot in this place. And Judah said, Let her take it to her, lest we be shamed: behold, I sent this kid, and thou hast not found her. And it came to pass about three months after, that it was told Judah, saying, Tamar thy daughter in law hath played the harlot; and also, behold, she is with child by whoredom. And Judah said, bring her forth, and let her be burnt. When she was brought forth, she sent to her father in law, saying, By the man, whose these are, am I with child: and she said, Discern, I pray thee, whose are these, the signet, and bracelets, and staff. And Judah acknowledged them, and said, She hath been more righteous than I; because that I gave her not to Shelah my son. And he knew her again no more. And it came to pass in the time of her travail that, behold, twins were in her womb. And it came to pass, when she travailed, that the one put out his hand: and the midwife took and bound upon his hand a scarlet thread, saying, this came out first. And it came to pass, as he drew back his hand that, behold, his brother came out: and she said, how hast thou broken forth? This breach be upon thee: therefore his name was called Pharez. And afterward came out his brother that had the scarlet thread upon his hand: and his name was called Zarah (Genesis 38: 1-30).

The book of the generation of Jesus Christ, the son of David, the son of Abraham. Abraham begat Isaac; and Isaac begat Jacob; and Jacob begat Judas and his brethren. And Judas begat Phares and Zara of Thamar; and Phares begat Esrom; and Esrom begat Aram. And Aram begat Aminadab; and Aminadab begat Naasson; and Naasson begat Salmon. And Salmon begat Booz of Rachab; and Booz begat Obed of Ruth; and Obed begat Jesse. And Jesse begat David the king; and David the king begat Solomon of her that had been the wife of Urias. And Solomon begat Roboam; and Roboam begat Abia; and Abia begat Asa. And Asa begat Josaphat; and Josaphat begat Joram; and Joram begat Ozias. And Ozias begat Joatham; and Joatham begat Achaz; and Achaz begat Ezekias. And Ezekias begat Manasses; and Manasses begat Amon; and Amon begat Josias. And Josias begat Jechonias and his brethren, about the time they were carried away to Babylon. And after they were brought to Babylon, Jechonias begat Salathiel; and Salathiel begat Zorobabel. And Zorobabel begat Abiud; and Abiud begat Eliakim; and Eliakim begat Azor. And Azor begat Sadoc; and Sadoc begat Achim; and Achim begat Eliud. And Eliud begat Eleazar; and Eleazar begat Matthan; and Matthan begat Jacob. And Jacob begat Joseph the husband of Mary, of whom was born Jesus, who is called Christ (Matthew 1:1-16).

EFFEMINATE

What about 1 Corinthians 6:9? Doesn't this imply being born effeminate is a sin?

Know ye not that the unrighteous shall not inherit the kingdom of God? Be not deceived: neither fornicators, nor idolaters, nor adulterers, nor effeminate, nor abusers of themselves with mankind (1 Corinthians 6:9).

As you might admit, we are all born in sin. The verse mentioned, and other similar verses, point out "conditions" that prohibit entry into Heaven. These include the alcoholic, adulterer, thief, idolater, and etcetera. The issue is that the other vices are a part of life. These people can change; they can go to Heaven. But effeminate persons are born that way. They can't change their physiology. Are they doomed to Hell?

MARVI-RPIA paints the picture of a Pre-Life Elect identity. Effeminate persons are born into an inauthentic identity. It's just a role imposed by heredity, the environment, and experiences. Their authentic identity, saved before the world was created, abides with God in Paradise.

For now, effeminate Roleplayers participate in a Demonstration of Free Will began by way of Adam and Eve. *An appreciation of this image should comfort effeminate persons, for they are not locked into the identity imposed on them. It's not the only chance at life they'll ever have.* They may be born this way but aren't compelled to pursue the consequences of this body type. It's not their only chance to live. Life is NOT a freak accident of being something, then a return to nothing.

There is an afterlife. The greatest Person who ever lived told us so. He was perfect. He can't lie.

Additionally, effeminate isn't necessarily a derogatory term applied to the physical characteristics of males. *Effeminate men may refer to those males who abdicated their masculine role.* They relinquish their obligations. When this happens, females and adolescents often attempt to replace them. God ordains government, that is, the assignment of leadership to serve order. The standard order is fathers and mothers, police officers and citizens, managers and employees. This follows even though the mother may be more qualified than the father, the citizen than the police, and the employee than the manager.

As a side note, only males qualify as pastors, not females. As pastor Alistair Begg teaches, the Apostle Paul wasn't referring to a CULTURAL principle of women being silent in the congregation. Paul spoke of the SCRIPTURAL principle by quoting from the Book of Genesis. God made them male and female. Male first, then female. An order. A hierarchy.

This has nothing to do with status or worthiness. This is simply government—assignment of responsibility. Unfortunately, Adam was irresponsible in relinquishing leadership to Eve. Males have responsibility for spiritual leadership. *Only when they are absent should females assume authority.* Otherwise, females may assist males in leadership until males qualify.

What if no male and no female assume leadership? *Then children (immature adults), animals (like the Serpent), or persons less than 100 percent human assume leadership. Even further, artificial intelligence is poised for leadership.*

> For God is not the author of confusion, but of peace, as in all churches of the saints. Let your women keep silence in the churches: for it is not permitted unto them to speak; but they are commanded to be under obedience as also saith the law. And if they will learn anything, let them ask their husbands at home: for it is a shame for women to speak in the church (1 Corinthians 14:33-35).

> Let the woman learn in silence with all subjection. But I suffer not a woman to teach, nor to usurp authority over the man, but to be in silence. For Adam was first formed, then Eve. And Adam was

> not deceived, but the woman being deceived was in the transgression (1 Timothy 2:11-14).

Men who won't serve in leadership roles, preferring to pursue other interests, or can't serve in leadership roles because of their passive disposition, *disrupt government. That could be considered effeminate.* Those not endowed with mature masculine skills to lead may attempt to lead but can't. They may not possess the attributes necessary to lead. That isn't necessarily effeminate. That could be trying but failing.

Men aren't leaders in every matter. Women lead also. But in matters of high levels of responsibility, men have a Christian obligation to be at the forefront. Yes, women can lead, but that's often because no men do so. *And misinformed or corrupt people often place women and immature individuals in leadership roles.* They reject Christian values. They reject fair, neutral policies that represent the community. "Control of the leaders" is their strategy for illegitimate governance.

Finally, masculinity does not, and cannot, be a guarantee to Heaven. Being virile, strong, and aggressive may be the opposite of femininity but not necessarily a virtue. The real virtue comes as men and women apply Christian values to gender roles.

And on the other side of the coin are females born with masculine attributes. Most of us are familiar with young girls who look or behave like one of the boys. It's not so unusual, even looking back over generations. The difference between times past and today is girls are more likely to remain in masculine roles longer than before. Girls have more examples to compare themselves with, and society is more accepting of reassigned gender roles. As always, parents have a major impact on how a girl develops and how her physical qualities match expectations.

Parental influence is doubtless the major factor in the formative years of adolescence. But as the child grows older, the factors of heredity, the environment, and experiences strongly effect the girl's identity. In the distant past, cultural factions in society, along with family, obstructed women's rights to self-identify and pursuit of personal interests. That is no longer the case.

As the girl becomes a woman, the nonreligious, secular, default position is to just be yourself. If you want to be a male, be male. If you want to remain female, be female. Don't let your family, culture, society, or religion dictate your identity.

Connecting the Dots of Identity has a similar message. But first, you must know that who you are is not simply choosing a gender as you may. *Your gender has little to do with who you are. You didn't choose it. It chooses you.*

If your gender was assigned improperly, that is a specific case that may or may not be determined. It only matters in the areas of marriage, children, and sex. Otherwise, it's a designation for relationships with people, the legal system, and the religious system.

We've all seen females who were mostly male, and we've seen males who were mostly female. Some may have been exaggerating, but others seemed as if there was nothing they could do about it. Their look, their walk, body language, athletic ability, and so forth appeared set. And you hear people say homosexuals are not born. They have a choice to be gay or straight.

Really? Do we know enough about the dynamics involved in biology to affirm that statement? The adage goes nature or nurture. Does nature (heredity) determine identity, or does nurture (environment/experiences) determine identity? It ends up being answered as both determine identity, one or the other having a dominant effect depending on a multitude of factors.

Your gender IDENTITY is female, but you are in a male's body (or male in a female's body).

What does the Minister of Art say?

Of course, you can be anyone or anything you want within the confines of resources, ability, and interest.

Spiritually, your mandate is the gender EXPRESSION of a male. God doesn't care about your feelings. They're inauthentic. ROLEPLAY matters—the expression of identity that's based on factors of heredity, environment, and experience. You only have limited control. God wants you to realize your authentic identity is safe in paradise before you were born. For now, *He will assist you in exemplifying moral objectivity—the standard of right and wrong. In this case, it's the sexual expression of the male gender, regardless of a female identity character.*

However, if you come to KNOW your gender ASSIGNMENT was done in error, you have a right to challenge that. The integrity of the evaluation of the error determines the validity of the error. The insistent, persistent, consistent pursuit of gender inquiry should help verify whether the pursuit is justified. You're betting your life on this gender path. People bet their lives on all manner of pursuits. Many fail. Many are ill-advised.

In the meantime, your expression should be the public image of a masculine person. Privately, you have liberty. Publicly, in the matter of marriage or sexuality, again the expression is to be that of a masculine person.

Bisexuality in the population is certainly prominent. Some people will deny it. Some people admit it but would never act on it. Same with homosexuality. Some deny, some admit but would never act. Other people have no idea and avoid all serious thoughts about sexuality that is not heterosexual. But, just like everyone else, their perspective is based on heredity, environment, and experience until they meet the Holy Spirit.

CD1/CD2 hopes to provide an introduction to meeting the Holy Spirit.

A follow-through question is: Why does it all matter if predestination is true? I was saved before the foundation of the world. Even further, if Connecting The Dots Of Identity is truly as beautiful as it appears to be, whatever role I play doesn't matter. It's just a role. It's an inauthentic me, not the real me. The real me, the authentic me, is in Paradise, awaiting the end of the Demonstration of Free Will. *Therefore, I have freedom of gender identity and gender expression.*

Yes, so it does appear. However, when a Christian is REBORN, they're a new creature (2 Corinthians). The identity goes from Elect Roleplayer to Holy Spirit Identity (HSID). But what if you are a Non-Elect Roleplayer—not 100 percent human? What if you descended from a long line of ancestors that began with the Nephilim in the Book of Genesis? How would you know? You couldn't, except the Holy Spirit witnessing with your spirit, you are a child of God (2 Corinthians).

And remember, Connecting The Dots Of Identity is sharing with you an impression of spirituality. It is not the Bible. *It's art. Don't be tempted to live as you please, thinking the afterlife is a foregone conclusion.*

> Therefore if any man be in Christ, he is a new creature: old things are passed away; behold, all things are become new (2 Corinthians 5:17).

> The Spirit itself beareth witness with our spirit, that we are the children of God (Romans 8:16).

> Know ye not that the unrighteous shall not inherit the kingdom of God? Be not deceived: neither fornicators, nor idolaters, nor adulterers, nor effeminate, nor abusers of themselves with mankind (1 Corinthians 6:9).

> As for my people, children are their oppressors, and women rule over them. O my people, they which lead thee cause thee to err, and destroy the way of thy paths (Isaiah 3:12).

SEX EDUCATION 6—POSTSCRIPT

You may be aware of the controversy regarding the possibility of men becoming pregnant. How this is a question considering no male has ever achieved pregnancy, let alone delivered a baby?

Uncertainty may come from two viewpoints:

1. Hypnosis: The principle of hypnosis is a trusted source that prepares and presents suggestions to willing and suggestible participants. In this case, the trusted source is liberal news, social media, academics,

big business, and peer pressure. A segment of the population will believe almost anything.

2. The Medical Model: A hundred years ago, the characteristics of males and females were much more obvious and defined. Today, with advances in medicine, surgical procedures, and gender-defining techniques, a sex change may still be impossible, but it's close enough not to matter. Simulation of the desired gender is capable of offering an acceptable experience.

If a male can be physically modified with the essential female components to facilitate pregnancy and birth, then the science of gender has new definitions.

Do you get any sense of dread from imagining such an idea: A male giving birth to a baby?

Do you get any sense of déjà vu? What may have transpired in the days of Noah? The violence spoken of in the Old Testament Book of Genesis may refer to violations of God's natural procreation process. A man giving birth cannot be any less a violation of God's natural order.

People laugh and say how utterly ridiculous. A man giving birth? No, never.

And they say the same about angels and human females producing offspring—the Nephilim.

The obstacles to “advancements” in medicine and biology may only be restricted by legal and moral considerations. These considerations change over time. *Not only do they change, but they are also circumvented in the interest of "progress" by those operating outside the rules in secrecy.* You can be sure research and development are ongoing and being funded by the usual suspects.

If we were to commission a top-rated bookmaker to offer propositions on male pregnancy odds, would they receive significant action? For example, the odds of male pregnancy occurrence by the year 2027, 2028, or 2029.

Assuming the science of male pregnancy advances to the stage of being possible, would it be medically ethical? Would objections relegate the process to operate outside the law? Would the laws apply across the nation? The world? We see clearly that there are people in positions of authority who simply ignore the laws in place or do not respect the laws in place. The Demonstration of Free Will is playing out in the lives of those who are unsane—people who hold a derisive, contemptible, antagonistic view of moral objectivity. The only morality is subjective—driven by individual values—not transcendent values of God.

Therefore, human males give birth to human offspring. Human females give birth to human offspring. Will the next hurdle be other living primates or nonliving primates acquiring the ability to conceive human offspring? Where does it end?

Speaking of the end, the Nephilim exploitation of procreation allegedly brought about the end of the world. Could male pregnancy be a sign of the next World End?

The lifespan of the population in Noah's day approached a thousand years. Our lifespan is greatly reduced to roughly one hundred years. *Has the cumulative effect of knowledge since Noah left the ark reached the level of a thousand-year lifespan?* If so, the intrusion of angels into human procreation processes may not be necessary to duplicate pre-Flood violence. We have sufficient human (and less than 100 percent human) agents who violate the procreation process of God. Meanwhile, in the background, Satan and his rogue angels continue to instigate evil.

The End of the World, Judgment Day, could be brought about when the last Roleplayer is conceived. God has fulfilled the perfect number of lives for the Demonstration of Free Will. There's no need to continue another day to prove God's Determined Will for human beings is superior to a human's Free Will for their own life.

But … the world may become so filled with violations of God's natural order, the perfect number of Free Will Roleplayers may be defined by a final transgression, a final infringement, a final unforgivable encroachment. *The height of human intelligence, artificial intelligence, and scientific discovery hasn't been made public. The details are too controversial.* So, people have no idea how proficient mankind has become in these areas. These pursuits may not be legal, moral, or authorized for public knowledge. And so the world continues another day, another week, and another month.

Suddenly: The End! Jesus Returns!

Yes, this is all far-fetched, and perhaps much ado about nothing. However, as a Minister of Art, the mission is to share the potential of spiritual reality. The language may be too vivid, too melodramatic, and too unorthodox to accept.

Okay. Don't accept it.

CHAPTER 15

SEX EDUCATION—PART 7

ANOTHER chapter on sex? Why so many?

Because sex permeates society. Sex is right in the middle of the leading issues we face. Unplanned Children. Abortion. Homicide. Adultery. Pornography. Sex-related crime. Cheating.

As a sane person, one who ascribes to objective morality, you will be strongly encouraged to seek love, get married, and have children as soon as possible. One of the reasons for this is to counter a subjective amoral position of non-marriage and no children. The concern is that without the sanctity of marriage coupled with decreasing birth rates, society will be at risk of abnormal sexual relationships and worldwide economic downfall from low population rates.

Connecting the Dots of Identity strives to produce new relationships based on Roleplayers who deemphasize their inauthentic identity. In doing so, you are no longer content to clear a space in the overrun world-garden for your own little world. Your own little world of spouse, children, and shelter. Your own little world of entertainment, sex, and financial regularity. You come to realize care of the environment has a priority if your personal space is to remain inviolate. You feel responsible to help others understand how they may contribute to caring for the environment of humanity.

Being a MARVI Single Person and meeting another MARVI Single Person has the potential to produce relationships never seen. Concepts of sexuality, romance, commitment, children, and love could have new meanings. Compare the inauthentic identity to the authentic identity. The focus on this present life is no longer so immediate that it disassociates from the afterlife. An association with an afterlife identity changes your perspective. You learn about patience, trust, and possibility. You discover peacefulness and purpose in your inauthentic identity. It no longer holds its primary, immediate, insecure status.

Why search for love? Why get married? Why have children? If it happens, that's being open to God's will. If it doesn't happen, that's being open to God's will. *The most important thing is to help other people see a possibility of beauty in the Demonstration of Free Will, and the authentic identity God has reserved in Paradise.*

So, as well-meaning Christian leaders push hard for young people to find love, marry, and produce the next generation of Christians, this strategy leaves out good reasons NOT to marry and create more people. Finding love and having romantic adventures is fun, therapeutic, and builds networks. However, think about why young people marry.

People fear being alone. People desire financial support, social status, and responsible sexual partnerships. People marry for looks, to please their families, and to alleviate peer pressure. There are cultural and religious expectations involved. The list isn't meant to be exhaustive. It's an indication of why marriage and children take precedence over character development. Character development is what Connecting The Dots Of Identity illustrates by making use of MARVI-RPIA. Your character is largely dictated by heredity, environment, and experiences.

As your spiritual identity moves from neutral to negative or neutral to positive in your formative years, the appeal to theistic and atheistic ideals forms. A part of that formation is based on how God is presented to you. Atheists say, "What God? If this life is the best God can do, it's so obvious He does not exist." And that is not an unreasonable conclusion. This life is unfair, unpredictable, and fragile.

Theists say, "God is doing the best He can without direct and obvious intervention. That would undermine and overrun our Free Will. Don't you want Free Will? Oh, you do want Free Will, just without all the bad stuff? What bad stuff?"

How would you eliminate evil? Eliminate murder? Eliminate theft? Eliminate illness? Eliminate weather? Eliminate accidents? Okay . . . poof! They're all gone! Now what? Start over in the Garden of Eden? Wouldn't the same things happen all over? No. They say God should make things PERFECT! *No devil, no serpent, no tree of temptation.*

Yes. That's what Election-Predestination is about. *Perfection is already established.* God elected individuals before the foundation of the earth.

And now we're back to why Connecting The Dots Of Identity was written. It's somewhat of a middle ground between theism and atheism that paints a picture of how God may have arranged reality. When we consider how hopeless large segments of life have become, an art event like MARVI-RPIA could literally save lives. Despair and depression are killers. Suicide is an epidemic. Cynicism and skepticism contribute to an apathetic attitude about the present and the future. It's already too late to save the world. Nothing matters, and if it does, it can't be controlled.

The Good News of Jesus Christ is meaningless if God is misrepresented. The Holy Spirit is virtually unknown. However, we are given what they, the Trinity, want us to know. We make the best of this. They help us, but the Demonstration of Free Will must play out. It's not too late to save the world. It's already saved.

SEX EDUCATION 7 — POSTSCRIPT EXTENDED

What if we had a Single-Persons Champion? Someone who never married, who is divorced, or who is widowed (Glossary of Colors). There really is no such person today. Why not?

Why don't we have a great champion that represents people who appreciate and exalt the single-person position? Is it ever really considered worthy to elevate and praise? Isn't being single a rather uncomfortable situation to bear until finding that certain someone to fill the void? We may think of the Bible right away. No, don't think of the Bible. Think of a single person. Do we have a Single-Persons Champion from recent history?

We do have them? From RECENT history? Yes, of course. They must *always* be present.

Then why is it that they are not well-known? The only Christian we ever hear of is the Apostle Paul. Nobody comes to mind from the recent past. When we do find names of the recent past, most likely what comes up is Hollywood celebrities, artists, or musicians. Famous single people are all lumped together. We don't necessarily hear of any Christian singles.

Okay. Let's look at the most obvious person anyway—Apostle Paul.

No. He likely doesn't qualify. Huh? Apostle Paul of the New Testament? Right. Here's what was heard a few months ago …

Well-known pastor Alastair Begg says Paul was probably married, due to Jewish custom in those days for men in his position. His wife either died or left him after his encounter with Jesus Christ on the road to Damascus. Paul was no longer living in the tradition of Jewish doctrine. He was now Christian. (Alister Begg. "Truth for Life". Cleveland, Ohio).

Very well. It seems that before Apostle Paul met the Holy Spirit, he was a married man named Saul. Could be. No problem. Then, for the rest of his Christian life, the Apostle Paul taught the principles of the Christian single life.

So, now what? The problem may be that we can name famous Christians, but we aren't generally aware of their marital status. The suspicion is 90 percent will be married.

Then, will YOU be the Champion of Single Persons?

If you do, it should NOT be because you took a vow of singleness. To take such a vow may mean a disregard for God's will for your life. A maturing Christian will recognize being open to God's will for their lives and not their own will. But what if being single is the 100 percent commitment to honor God? Great, but being single and staying single are too different things.

Be single. Don't pursue marriage. Don't avoid marriage. Make the best of being single until meeting that certain someone who turns your life upside down. Even then, it doesn't mean you have to marry that person. Don't fear and faint at the prospect of no spouse, no sex, no children. God is the ultimate companion. *Sex is a monster, but God can tame ANY monster.* Children are not necessarily unavailable. There are options to obtain children.

So, there can be no Champion of Singleness?

There can be. He or she goes after the title until God sends someone to take them down in marriage. But the title Single-Persons Champion should be once a year like in sports, beauty contests, or other award shows. Single

Man or Woman of the Year has a nice ring to it. Single Christian Man or Single Christian Woman of the Year has a nicer ring to it. If you win multiple times, you then become known as the Single-Persons Champion of honor, of renown, or of all time.

As for qualifications, a Single-Persons Champion of the Year should not have been in a romantic relationship for twelve consecutive months. Dating different people once is okay, just not the same person more than three times. Three-strike rule. Dates that are not romantic don't count. Of course, this is on the honor system. If you don't qualify but want to represent singleness, go ahead. Be a Single Champ of the Year. *Help other people become better people BEFORE they get into a relationship or get married. WE NEED YOU.*

And then, who keeps score? Who crowns the champions? Where does recognition occur? The churches! Make the pastors pay attention. Yes, they're all married, but push the agenda. Speak up for singles! Make it fun. Make it serious. Just make it.

MONSTROSITY

As noted, sex is a monster. God can tame any monster...

But can God tame, whip, and defeat the monster EVERY day? This isn't a defeat-the-monster-once-and-it's-over kind of fight. This sex monster is … a monster! When it's thrown to the ground, stomped on, and beheaded, it rises again the next day.

Then you fight again. Round one, round two, round three. You may win by points, round by round. It may not be a knockout for each fight. If YOU'RE knocked out, spiritual help comes in to pick you up, revive you, give you encouragement, and send you back to fight.

When God's people reached the Promise Land, the representatives of the people said, “The land is full of giants. We cannot defeat them” (Numbers 13). The people were not confident God would help them. Same with sex. Sex is too hard for us to defeat. We are like grasshoppers in the sight of the giant sex monster.

But two of the people sent out as scouts—only two—said “God is with us.” Joshua and Caleb. They said, “God will win the battle for us. We can take the land from the giants.” So, the fearful people were not allowed to enter the Promised Land. They died out before the day came to enter.

> And they brought up an evil report of the land which they had searched unto the children of Israel, saying, The land, through which we have gone to search it, is a land that eateth up the inhabitants thereof; and all the people that we saw in it are men of a great stature. And there we saw the giants, the sons of Anak, which come of the giants: and we were in our own sight as grasshoppers, and so we were in their sight (Numbers 13:32-33).

> And the men, which Moses sent to search the land, who returned, and made all the congregation to murmur against him, by bringing up a slander upon the land. Even those men that did bring up the evil report upon the land, died by the plague before the Lord (Number 14:36-37).

Of course, singleness is not just abstaining from sex. Children and marriage are still a possibility. But being open to sex has developed into unplanned children and coerced marriages worldwide. Sex sells in more ways than we can name. It’s unavoidable wherever we may be. So, any interest in being single will include sexual tension. It also includes the possibility of marriage AND children (stepchildren, adopted children, or biological children). You are open to the will of the Lord.

HUMAN TORCH

Apostle Paul preached it is better to marry than to burn.

> I say therefore to the unmarried and widows, it is good for them if they abide even as I. But if they cannot contain, let them marry: for it is better to marry than to burn (1 Corinthians 7:8-9).

It's better to marry than burn—burn away your spiritual integrity and degrade your spiritual commitment. Marriage in this case becomes sexual defense. Hormones rage most when we are young, so marriages occur frequently in the late teen years and early twenties.

Besides hormonal reasons, one of the major reasons people have so little self-control in their teens and early twenties is that so few people teach sexual self-control. And this is because *most teachers don't have sensual self-control themselves. That's why most of the teachers are married!*

As the author of Connecting The Dots Of Identity, I assure you I have a very high libido. I have never been engaged to be married, nor have I ever married. I am heterosexual. I would even consider a relationship with a transgender person if assured they were female and assured they were Christian. It's not up to me. It's up to God. It's up to the person who convinces me they are the only one for me.

Meanwhile, I am not against marriage. I'm not for marriage.

Relationship with a transgender person? *The Minister of Art could marry a trans-person?* What kind of relationship can a single, high-libido, Christian male have with a transgender female?

I don't know. Maybe none. Maybe a very limited one. Perhaps a slight chance of marriage, although extremely unlikely. Marriage to anyone, in my case, at this stage in life, is extremely unlikely. But—I should be honest—it's still possible.

As I have gone through life, there have been sensual indiscretions. As I developed in Christian maturity, the sensual indiscretions became apparent before they actually happened. Yes, there was a strong sexual desire, but it wasn't as out of control as it was in my youth. As I implied earlier, youthful sexual desire has a secondary factor beyond chronological age. It's the sexual education factor—mental age.

If sex-ed had more dedicated, mature, Christian singles communicating how to handle sexual burning, more young people would burn less, because they would have more tools to put out the fires, so to speak, or to at least minimize the blazes. There will always be smoke, sparks, and burning embers in healthy individuals. The severe burns and lethal fires don't have to claim so many lives to marriage, unplanned children, or abortions. Sexual identity doesn't have to include sexual crimes, sexual diseases, and sex occupation professionals.

Even being consistently preoccupied with sexual thoughts isn't necessarily a bad thing, especially if it's balanced with spiritually mature imagery. We don't have much spiritual maturity in the world that can handle real-world sexuality. This includes parents, the education system, and the church. Sex is less taboo, less offensive, and not as disrespectful as in the past, but it's still disconcerting.

It's okay to burn sexually. You won't die if you don't have sex. You won't die if you don't get married. You won't die if you don't have children. Burning is normal. You don't have to completely put out the fires. And you certainly know that, once you have a lover, a spouse, or a child, your sexual burning may not be quenched. It may even escalate. The perfect partner is hard to acquire. Wrong guesses happen every single day.

And now that we have dating sites, how can it be any easier to find that certain someone? You can almost custom-tailor the kind of person you want or at least interview/date 100 of them until the right combination clicks on the winner. *I could have done that. I didn't. I wanted to do that. I didn't. Why not? YOU!*

You're more important than I am. I couldn't NOT pursue world answers, as I see the world devolving to the point of no return. People are hurting. Problems are everywhere. There are a lot of great answers that do help. But I always wondered if I could just push a little harder, would I ever see better world answers?

This would mean, at least for me, no wife, no kids, no pets, no friends, no hobbies, no adventure travels, and no vacations. Mental breaks, yes. Controlled distraction time, yes. Otherwise, the constant, incessant, continual pursuit of answers—COMPREHENSIVE answers.

By the way, there was no guarantee I would ever find the right answers. I may have to be content with what was being offered as almost right answers. In this case, I would have thrown my life away trying to solve something that's already been solved.

Even now, having finished Connecting The Dots Of Identity 1 and 2, there is a slight nudge to celebrate the project as finished. Now, I can finally spend some time on ME. Find romance, finish piano lessons, catch up on movies, and travel. Why not? This should be good therapy for me.

But the words of Uriah the Hittite often remind me I'm in a war. Around the year 1994, I learned *150,000 people die every day, worldwide.* What am I doing to help them? Why am I here? For my own enjoyment? How can I leave the battle to pursue hugs, kisses, a wife, a family? That's okay for most people. But I'm not most people. I should do what I'm here to do.

> And Uriah said unto David, The ark, and Israel, and Judah, abide in tents; and my lord Joab, and the servants of my lord, are encamped in the open fields; shall I then go into mine house, to eat and to drink, and to lie with my wife? as thou livest, and as thy soul liveth, I will not do this thing . . . And it came to pass in the morning, that David wrote a letter to Joab, and sent it by the hand of Uriah. And he wrote in the letter, saying, Set ye Uriah in the forefront of the hottest battle, and retire ye from him, that he may be smitten, and die (2 Samuel 11: 11, 14-15).

Anyway, getting back to the monster. You can stand the heat. Don't be afraid. The sex monster can be defeated. God is God. How can you be so fearful if you believe there is a God who can do anything?

God can do anything, but will He do it for me? Who are you? Are you a temporary Roleplayer who already has everything waiting in Paradise? Why are you so fearful?

What can a spiritually mature Christian offer as ways God helps you fight the sex monster?

Let’s imagine: Weapons against the Sex Monster…

WEAPONS

Here are fifteen weapons. As you become adept at using them, devise more of your own.

1. Minimize being alone with your person of interest. Interact in public places.

2. When you are alone together, don't consume alcohol.

3. If you have alcohol with meals, minimize hugging, kissing, and close contact.

4. Avoid overnight sleepovers, or else maintain separate sleeping areas.

5. Communicate celibacy in no uncertain terms. Be emphatic.

6. Have fun but don't tease. If you like to tease, give notice, and find where the limits are.

7. Communicate flirting, fun, and romance, but be aware and denounce seduction habits.

8. Communicate adventure of romance for the sake of romance rather than sex.

9. Don't act. Be brutally honest. It's the best relationship policy.

10. Don't assume body and emotional mastery in the moment. You both will be at high risk.

11. Avoid various indiscretions before they occur. Anticipate awkward sexual scenarios.

12. Practice “no means no” to yourself frequently. Be in charge. No is okay. A REAL no.

13. Don't relive past mistakes. That was not you. You are now a new creature.

14. Keep good angels nearby, bad angels away. Pray. You may be rescued from going too far.

15. Self-stimulation is healthy. Don't abuse it. God gave it to us. Thank Him. Don't avoid Him.

Screenshot these weapons, rewrite these weapons, or make your own weapons. Keep them in your smart device. Give them to your romantic interest. This may help communicate what's hard to put into words in the times needed.

Okay. The fifteen Sex Monster Weapons are helpful in controlling romantic adventures.

But there comes a time when things somehow become uncontrollable. You can't stop it. Then what? Run away? Fight? Suggest you have an STD?

Unfortunately, there are NO good answers! However...

Warning! A Sex Talk! Explicit content!

CD2/Chapter 7 implied puberty, menstruation, breasts, testicles, hormones, wet dreams, STDs, homosexuality, lesbianism, pornography, hygiene, erection, orgasms, molestation, voyeurism . . . and . . . ORAL SEX.

If you absolutely, positively MUST have premarital sex—it seems UNAVOIDABLE—then make it *oral sex only.* NEVER vaginal. Even anal is second place to oral. NO vaginal. NO accidental or unwanted pregnancies. NO abortions. NO disruption-of-life event. *Not saying that oral sex is okay BEFORE marriage. It isn't.* God doesn't like it. The Minister of Art doesn't like it. It's just better than the other scenarios when sex is about to happen. You must protect yourself and protect others until you're married. Never let the present blow up your future.

Think how CD1/CD2 sex-ed. compares to that of your parents, friends, school, or church. You may get an oral-sex sex-ed. strategy, but you won't get the CD1/CD2 comprehensive Christian principles that come with it. This is critical to integrity and success. We are a family. We are a team. CD1/CD2 loves you. The real you. Your authentic identity.

Now, two other sex-ed. issues that you may not hear much about:

1) Be aware that a penis is like playing with a loaded gun. Male genitalia secretions may contain living sperm cells. Don't allow this substance to come in contact with her vagina. This means clothing, bedding, objects, or other body parts. Pregnancy is unlikely but certainly possible.

2) Females intent on becoming pregnant may acquire a used condom surreptitiously. Don't assume. Discard condoms with the utmost care. The legal issues involving male rights are convoluted.

SENSUOUS SIMULATION

But what about Sex Monster Weapons Number fifteen: self-stimulation? Doesn't the Bible suggest an admonition against it?

> Ye have heard that it was said by them of old time, Thou shalt not commit adultery: But I say unto you, that whosoever looked on a

> woman to lust after her hath committed adultery with her already in his heart (Matthew 5: 27-28).

> But every man is tempted, when he is drawn away of his own lust, and enticed. Then when lust hath conceived, it bringeth forth sin: and sin, when it is finished, bringeth forth death. Do not err, my beloved brethren (James 1: 14-16).

As *Connecting the Dots of Identity* portrays, your Mental Identity (MID) is not you. Your thoughts, your fantasies, and your imagery is not your identity. Your mind is the mechanism to process information, simulate what-ifs, and keep you healthy. It's okay to simulate sex in your mind or with your body. It's a simulation. It's not actual sex with another person. The simulation is possibly a same-sex session, multiple-partner event, or even underage sexual activity. A simulation could feature violent sex, a fantasy marriage, or any number of unmentionables.

This is all between you and the Lord. This is what your mind is for. Fun and games. Stupidity and impossibility. Disgust and humiliation. Illegal and shameful. *It doesn't matter because it's not anything you really want. You have no desire to engage in sinful behavior. It's make-believe. It's not an indication of who you are.* These scenarios are similar to your dream identity (DID). It seems like you—it's your first-person perspective—but it's not you. You're safe in bed.

Or think of when you watch TV, movies, and play games. When you imagine another occupation, enjoying recreation, or engaging in extremely dangerous behavior, it's all mental experiences. They are not meant to be necessarily desirable, of interest, or practical. It's entertainment. An adventure.

It may be interesting to be a king with a fabulous harem, or a secret agent paid to kill bad people, or a mother of six children who becomes the world's best computer hacker amassing trillions of dollars illegally. Lusting after these things, or contemplating them in your heart, implies insidious planning, seeking illicit opportunity, or a disregard for the moral boundary. People who regard objective morality as the standard for their life submit to that standard. Amoral behavior is not in their heart or their physical identity, even though it's in their thoughts and mental identity. Their heart has been changed to the Holy Spirit identity. There's now a commitment to Christian principles.

"Objection!" you say. "How is it that my thoughts are so obsessed with revolting, ghastly, and lurid imagery? I'm embarrassed to reveal this to my spouse, my children, or my friends. I certainly couldn't disclose this pastime to my pastor. I even feel guilty when I'm in church. *If I'm supposed to share everything with the Lord, what does He think of me in this regard?*"

The Lord understands you are a product of heredity, environment, and experiences. You didn't create yourself, and God didn't create you as you are. The nature of sin in every human being manifests itself according to your life factors. That may be drugs, sex, gluttony, alcohol, crime, gambling, money, or any number of attractions based on your proclivities. Additionally, it takes time to mature in spiritual life. Be patient. Carefully choose the people in your life. The most important point is the commitment to objective morality. God is worthy of setting the standard. It's the people who don't believe God is any more moral than they are that corrupt society.

As restrictive and unappealing thoughts of limitation and composure sound, finding a partner who agrees with similar boundaries gives a relationship the trust it needs for advancement. Advancement means a richer quality of life for both parties AND a higher quality partner who lives by such guidelines.

Don't be discouraged. You may think, “This is my ONLY chance at companionship, sex, and children.” No, it isn't. It may feel this way when you accept ONE chance at life and NO afterlife. If you trust Jesus Christ, He guaranteed the afterlife. You will have more companionship, more sex, and more children BEYOND what you could ever imagine.

And don’t forget. There may be people who love the impressions Connecting the Dots of Identity paints. They may communicate and form groups. Those groups produce relationships among the members. The members should exemplify high-quality prospects for friendships, companions, and serious relationships. Who knows? Start a group in your city.

Until then, your thoughts on all matters of interest are only bounded by purity of heart. This is a spiritual principle. Do you know it?

CHAPTER 16

SUICIDE—PART 1

We know homicide is terrible. There's been a murder. Someone kills someone else. This occurs around 400,000 times each year around the world. But what about this: suicide occurs 800,000 times a year! Twice the number of homicides. This is a LOT of people killing themselves. Did you know this?

Just review such organizations as the World Health Organization, National Institute of Mental Health, and Our World in Data. The numbers are gut-wrenching.

Why don't most of us know this?

Probably because suicide is such a depressing topic. Additionally, suicide may be the epitome of mental illness. *We don't know enough about mental illness to prevent slow suicide (alcoholism, smoking, drugs, gluttony, or crime), much less sudden suicide.*

You may wonder if murder-suicide, or suicide-by-cop, are included in the suicide statistics. Even if they aren't included, what can we learn by exploring suicide?

This is the second of three topics I dreaded painting. First came sex-ed, now suicide, and third is abortion. When I retired from employment in 2009, I expected many of the things retirement brings. Sleeping late, enjoying hobbies, traveling, playing video games, romancing the girls . . . but no. Even in the few years leading up to retirement, I was working on spiritual projects. Now that I had much more free time, more time was spent on those spiritual projects. In the ten years from 2009 to 2019, I had a substantial amount of material to consider sharing.

The suicide material was particularly distressing. *It's a gruesome reality of the inauthentic identity.* Why would a person put a loaded gun to their head and pull the trigger? Why do they hang themselves, jump in front of trains, and throw themselves down from tall buildings? The overall answer is insanity. Insanity has come to be a euphemism for "it doesn't make sense." The legal term for insanity advances a definition regarding some level of individual responsibility. In the case of suicide, individual responsibility no longer matters.

The suicidal inauthentic identity MARVI-RPIA portrays is the person who resents themselves. They're trapped in a body. There doesn't seem to be anyone who can help. Every solution is no solution. People don't understand. Family and friends fear speaking of death. Social service professionals often allocate limited access to their services. Limited and untimely access to professional help only prolongs the misery of life.

Accepting the inauthentic identity of heredity, environment, and life experiences imprisons you in the circumstances of life. This accepted personality is a constant reminder that you had nothing to do with being brought to life. We're all supposed to make a great life and love each other. Make the best of the circumstances. But it's not that easy. Circumstances dictate that life is unfair. Life is unpredictable. You may be dead tomorrow, next week, or next year. You get no warning. This may occur even if you happen to be one of the fortunate ones to have beauty, fame, and riches. It doesn't matter. Good fortune may be here today, gone tomorrow.

Since this INAUTHENTIC identity is the widely held AUTHENTIC identity, suicide prevails as a popular option. *MARVI-RPIA says DON'T!* Your life is a Demonstration of Free Will instigated by Adam and Eve. This is an inauthentic version of who you are. God has set a Demonstration of Free Will via the offspring of Adam and Eve. This is to prove the error of exercising human Free Will rather than accepting God's will for your life. The error is so insidious that unless God intervenes no one—under a trillion circumstances—accepts God's will. This Demonstration is fundamental to the whole reason God created flawless living creatures. Autonomy.

This inauthentic Roleplay of who you are is simply the result of heredity, the environment, and experiences. *It's a role. It's not really you.* You had no say in being born. You suddenly materialize and must accept what the situation dictates. But recognizing life is only a temporary role to play and not a definition of who you are gets you out of solitary confinement to your body. *You're not trapped in time and space.*

Your true authentic identity is a Pre-Life Elect person residing in Paradise. At death or the End of the Demonstration, your inauthentic Roleplay identity ends.

The afterlife? You, the real you, are already in Heaven. Hell is created for the Devil and his evil angels. Roleplayers, assuming they are 100 percent human beings, will receive the Holy Spirit at or before death. If no Holy Spirit Identity (HSID) arrives, it still doesn't mean damnation. It simply demonstrates that unless the Holy Spirit intercedes, no one will ever choose God. He has to choose you.

Otherwise, there is no Pre-Life Elect counterpart in Paradise. This means that life will be explicitly discarded as waste. Disposed. That person was likely less than 100 percent human, compromised by evil spirit immaterialism. However, the Bible indicates that some persons compromised by evil spirits did overcome that situation.

Would you recognize evil spirits as a reason why people do what they do? The de facto positions of science, the media, and public policy are secular, meaning that, to them, evil spirits do not exist. Good spirits do not exist. The inauthentic identities MARVI-RPIA paints do not exist.

Therefore, the reason people do “abnormal” things is because abnormal isn't abnormal. It's just normal behavior. They do what they're able to get away with. What do they have to lose? Life is an accident. Once life ends, there is nothing more. To continue procreating means continuing life only to have a random end. On top of this, the time has come when mankind has the ability to annihilate every human on the planet. Life is fragile. Tomorrow is never a guarantee. The only value life has is the value you give it.

AMERICAN INDIAN

Connecting the Dots of Identity expects to be of value. It seeks to be one of the explicit reasons suicide rates fall. A quote will soon follow that makes mention of the Native American youth suicide rate. Why youth? Why Native Americans? As suggested, a factor might be because people accept an inauthentic identity. They despise the ethnic identity forced upon them. But to object is to reject who they are, including their family, friends, and ancestors. How can you reject something you obviously are? You're Indian! You can't be anyone else.

But that's not necessarily true. You don't have to be Indian, Asian, Latin, Black, or White. The inauthentic identity of the culture or race you're born into has nothing to do with your authentic identity residing in Paradise. You don't have to be proud of your ancestral line.

However, you're told you MUST be proud. Otherwise, it is self-hatred about who you are. No, not true. *Self-hatred is being forced to assume an identity that is NOT you.* That seems a reasonable conclusion as to why people commit suicide. If there are only two choices—inauthentic identity or no identity—many people choose no identity. They delete themselves. Exit. Flee. Vacate. Suicide.

Imagine being forced to represent a race of people who have been victimized for hundreds of years. You are severely underprivileged. The opportunity to participate in government, education, sports, the arts, and high society is limited. Your land has been seized, your people relocated, and your natural resources exploited all because you happened to be born to the wrong people at the wrong point in history. But you must be proud of yourself: embrace ethnicity. Ethnic pride! Be proud of being born? Be proud of ethnicity crammed down your throat? Be proud of your physical appearance, which is NOT really you? No!

MARVI-RPIA opens a door previously not known to exist. You are not trapped being someone forced upon you. That someone is only a role. It isn't you. That means you can continue in the role, but now, realizing it's just a role, you have confidence in an authentic identity in the future.

You have hope. You can bear the present. It's temporary.

My Native American friends, you are not Native American. *You are human beings. Roleplayers.* Your identity is not the ethnicity your birth requires you to applaud. You feel guilty for not wanting to be Native American, adopting and carrying forward the traditions of your family, your forefathers, or contributing to Native pride projects.

This doesn't mean you want to be Caucasian, Negro, or Asian. It means you detest the obligation to be on an ethnic "team." *"Team ethnicity" removes individual identity and replaces it with "team identity."* In most cases, the body you're born into dictates ethnic identity. No escape, except in death.

You hate being Native American. You would also hate being Black American, Latino, or White. *You hate not having a choice. You hate having to pretend you love your race. You don't love it.*

You don't want to be compelled to be of ANY ethnicity. You are not like "them." You don't want to be them. *But you can never say this. You must love your race.* That is, until *Connecting the Dots of Identity.* Now you realize racial identity is just a temporary role. Not permanent. Not you.

MENTAL HEALTH POINTS

Perhaps all this doesn't mean a lot right now. However, there is a time coming when world calamity is so dire that suicide dramatically increases. The frequency and reporting of the incidence of suicide may influence further suicide. Underneath reports of suicide are non-reported suicides. We don't hear of all the deaths that occur from activities, or in-activities, resulting in self-fatalities. These people indicate they lost the will to live. In many cases, their death is labeled as an accidental injury, carelessness, or negligence. Maybe they just don't care if they die or not. *They've already taken their life—the exact day finally catches up.*

The global community is increasingly interwoven. Country A affects what happens in Country B. The global economy is fragile. Political diplomacy is fragile. There's unrest across the world. Tomorrow's headlines may signal the beginning of you-know-what.

As bad as things may seem, and they may become significantly worse in the coming months, don't lose sight of life's purpose. We are all here to fulfill a role. Our identity is inauthentic but necessary to demonstrate the Free Will of human creatures. Suicide is not a solution to escape being who you are. You can continue your Roleplay assignment, just temporarily go through the motions. Your life may seem unbearable, but that is only because you feel it's the only life you may ever experience. It isn't.

The Book of Corinthians mentions God is mindful of your "unbearable" situation. It is the situation that is representative of being human. It is not more than you are able to bear.

> There hath no temptation taken you but such as is common to man: but God is faithful, who will not suffer you to be tempted above that ye are able; but will with the temptation also make a way to escape, that ye may be able to bear it (1 Corinthians 10:13).

Hold on. Stop. It is NOT unbearable? Really? Then why did my child commit suicide? My spouse commit suicide? The entertainer, the musician, the military veteran. They all committed suicide. Wasn't their life more than they could bear?

Not necessarily. Scripture indicates there is a way of escape. An escape route exists so that you may bear temptation—bear provocation, error, urge, and impulse. *Making the escape routes ACCESSIBLE is part of the mission of the church, ministers, and teachers.* Other agents such as philosophers, scientists, and governments have realized the responsibility to assist, but suicides reach crisis status day after day. Who of us is making the escape route visible and attractive to the suicide prospect?

It's reasonable to have extreme resentment and rage at being forced into adulthood from childhood and adolescence. You're under strict rules and regulations at home and at school. You are finding out about death, old age, pregnancy, sickness, war, religion, and work. You have to prepare for a future of working to earn money to make a living. Do you have the intelligence, the looks, and the talent to succeed? Meanwhile, there's fear of failure, fear of accidents, fear of embarrassment, and fear of life.

Where is my escape route? Who's making it visible? There is escapism in drugs, sex, and alcohol. Escape into video games, television, or the internet. Those escape routes grow more popular each year. Where else is there hope?

Before MARVI-RPIA, I also disliked being me. Now, I understand the "me" I didn't like was the Roleplayer me—the inauthentic me. That was a contrived me from all the components that shaped that identity. The Holy Spirit opened my eyes, and I no longer had to accept that previous Roleplay identity. I'm not locked into being that person. I have an identity that God knows as the authentic me that is waiting in Paradise. One day, the Demonstration of Free Will ends. I can be my true self. In the meantime, I just have to practice patience, one day at a time. I have to see the big picture.

Think about this. Help your mind to protect your body. As you think about the worst, dark, deadly things to escape from reality, you lose Mental Health Points. For example:

- I'm in the wrong ethnic body: 1,000 points drained from mental health.
- I was bullied: 1,000 points drained.
- I was molested: 1,000 points drained.
- My dad ruined my childhood: 1,000 points drained.

- My spouse divorced me: 1,000 points drained.
- I'm very unattractive: 1,000 points drained.
- I have many medical problems: 1,000 points drained.
- I'm poor: 1,000 points drained.
- I'm depressed: 1,000 points drained.
- I hate myself; I hate God, I hate everything: 100,000 points drained.

As the example goes, thoughts of different events drain your mental health. The assigned number of negative points may be from one hundred to one million. How you perceive the event is how devastating it is to your mental health. One million may be the point of suicide. A hundred thousand may be the point of suicide. One thousand may be all the mental health points needed to end your life.

You may feel justified in the magnitude of your negative thoughts. But CD1/CD2 could be justification for positive thoughts—artistic thoughts. Protect your mind. Do whatever it takes. CD1/CD2 isn't real. It isn't a legitimate worldview. But it's something that isn't so far removed from everything else available.

WATER OFF A DUCK'S BACK

Connecting the Dots of Identity tries to envision an identity that was saved before the foundation of the world. That is your authentic identity. Who you are now is inauthentic. Your identity demonstrates the error of Adam and Eve's choice to disobey God's will for their lives. The penalty was death. God chose procreation to produce the Perfect Human that corrects their error. Procreation also proves the GRACE versus WORKS principle.

Grace is God's salvation plan of saving the people he elected before the foundation of the world. A hundred verses in scripture attest to this (CD1-

Chapter 6). Works is the opposite of grace; a person is capable of acquiring salvation by their own means or with the assistance of other persons. God is not the agent. Humans are the agents.

Since God has saved all His elect, why does life continue?

Life continues to prove the consequences of Free Will. If a FLAWLESS creature chooses to disobey God, *that is exceptionally significant.*

The Serpent was flawless. He had Free Will. Ego-Skepticism and Ego-Centracism undermined his Free Will Roleplay character. He had everything, then lost everything—including his life.

Adam and Eve were flawless. Ego-Skepticism and Ego-Centracism undermined their Free Will Roleplay. They had everything, then lost everything, including the whole world.

Though the penalty for disobedience was death, they didn't drop dead suddenly. That would not be instructive if no one else is alive. Yes, there would be animals, birds, fish, plants, trees, and etcetera. Yes, there were angels. The Heavenly Hosts were alive. But there must be flawless human beings, made in the image of God. They must be autonomous. They must Demonstrate Free Will.

God's amazing mercy is to prolong Adam and Eve's death and correct their death by arranging a Redeemer via procreation. So, life continues in the interest of producing Jesus Christ. The secondary provision is the Demonstration of Free. We are all going through 2,000 years since Jesus arrived. His Second Coming will end the Demonstration.

In the meantime, get over it. Please. You feel your life is worthless? Of course. So what? That is not YOU. It's a Roleplay you. This life is a temporary event. It's not the only life you have. Don't let negative mental health points overrun your mental health. They're water off a duck's back. You are not soaked through with water, mud, tar, glass, corrosives, or parasites. They may disrupt but they are not permanent. They are part of a temporary inauthentic role you play. *Don't hate yourself. Don't hate the other Roleplayers. Don't hate God. You are safe in Paradise.*

There is an afterlife. Jesus Christ guaranteed this. Jesus was 100 percent human. He led a sinless life. He qualifies as the Redeemer for Roleplayers. His words were all 100 percent accurate. He confirmed the Bible as infallible. No one—and that means NO ONE—is more trustworthy than Jesus.

Dry your tears. Jesus is omnipresent. He's with you. If it doesn't feel like He is, that's probably because you're deeply entrenched in your inauthentic Roleplayer character. Let that be like water off a duck's back.

You Are Not Alone: 1-800-273-8255 24/7 (National Suicide Hotline).

988 is the 3-digit 24/7 National Suicide & Crisis Lifeline.

According to the Center for Native American Youth: "In the United States, Native American communities experience higher rates of suicide than any other ethnic group. Suicide is the second leading cause of death for Native American youth ages ten to twenty-four, and Native youth teen suicide rates are nearly 3.5 times higher than the national average." Accessed April 2022.

CHAPTER 17

SUICIDE—PART 2

The MARVI-RPIA suicide model absolutely, positively has to work. It treats the root of suicide, not the symptoms of suicide.

You shouldn't hate yourself. You shouldn't hate other Roleplayers. You shouldn't hate God.

If you do hate yourself, don't freak out. It's really not you that you hate. It's your inauthentic identity that's hateful. Circumstances created that identity. No reason to kill it. Ride it out. Improvise. This life is temporary. The real you await in Paradise. Jesus guaranteed it. No one is more trustworthy than Jesus Christ. He will help you.

You shouldn't hate other Roleplayers. They are like you, acting out factors dictated by heredity, environment, and experiences. They don't understand life until the Holy Spirit meets them.

You shouldn't hate God. God sent the second Person of the Trinity to save you—Jesus Christ. The things you've heard about God that you hate are not valid. God actually is love. He actually does care. He does not send people to Hell just because they don't love Him, never heard of Him, or disagree with Him on how to live their life. You, the real you, are safe in Paradise.

Don't hate life. Yes, it does seem very unfair. It does seem very harsh. It does seem so tenuous that it may end by this time tomorrow. Life has to seem unpredictable because it's Free Will. Otherwise, God would have started with human puppets, robots, or automatons. Life is an experience of people doing what is right in their own eyes and reaping all the consequences. Consequences like death in the womb, death as a child, death as an accident, death by homicide, and death by suicide.

Now let's back away from the people who have the ability to appreciate the artistry of MARVI-RPIA. You're probably all sane people or will become sane. But how do you communicate with insane people? We know suicide is insanity.

It may be helpful to put up the insanity chart right now. Huh? What? You're thinking there is no such thing as an insanity chart. You're right. This is a quick and dirty sketch from a *Connecting the Dots of Identity* rough draft. It may help to separate a segment of people MARVI-RPIA may influence from the ones MARVI-RPIA may not influence. Consider the chart when thinking of how to communicate with difficult people.

Also, see the Blind Eyes Chart at the end of the chapter.

INSANITY CHART

SANE

The status of Pre-Life Elect individuals (Holy Spirit Identity-HSID) who possess a Christian worldview while continuing the Demonstration of Free Will through heredity, environment, and experience. They affirm objective morality as the standard of thinking and behaving based on the transcendent, universal, top-down imperative from God of the Bible. The sane include people who are Holy Spirit immature, spiritually minded people who have yet to receive the Holy Spirit, and people whose mental impairment prevents them from consistent Christian participation.

UNSANE

People who ascribe to atheists, agnostics, and non-Christian worldviews. They are spiritually blind but broadly mentally competent. Their profile is a cynical, derisive, contemptible view of objective morality. They reject the standard of thinking and behaving based on the transcendent, universal, top-down imperative from God of the Bible. They are against godliness unless God overrides their Free Will. They portray the Demonstration of Free Will through heredity, environment, and experience. (See Blind Eyes Chart)

INSANE

Group A: The group of people who are 100 percent human that suffers mental impairment from heredity, environment, and experience. They may be sane, adult Christians but, in general, are mentally irresponsible. Additionally, the unsane also may suffer insanity from the effects of heredity, environment, and experience.

Group B: The group of people who are less than 100 percent human. Their mental identity also suffers the effects of heredity, environment, and experience. These are most likely ancestors of the Nephilim.

INSANITY LEVELS ON THE SANENESS SCALE:

Level 0: Inconclusive.

Level 1: Those who show poor judgment on many issues though they share agreement with sane persons on particular issues.

Level 2: Delusional. Persons who are conniving, untrustworthy, and immoral. Showing limited empathy for anyone but themselves or their group. Risk of danger.

Level 3: The simpleminded, slow, and easily influenced. They exercise poor judgment. Risk of danger.

Level 4: Unless they are medicated, they don't cope well with reality. Poor social skills. Risk of danger.

Level 5: People who have limited freedom, under guardianship, or care of a responsible person. Danger.

Level 6: Institutionalized. Those with limited self-awareness who can't discern right from wrong. Danger.

Level 7: Dangerous to their own person and others. Moody. Irrational. Unstable. High risk of danger.

Level 8: Attempted suicide. Suicide prone. On life support/coma. High risk of danger.

Level 9: Committed suicide.

Level 10: Nephilim ancestor. Their thoughts and actions are characteristic of inhuman behavior. Not 100 percent human. High risk of danger.

You may begin to realize why there is no such thing as an insanity chart. Everybody would be on one. People are crazy. Some crazy is okay. Other crazy is absolutely not okay. We know this. However, it's presumptive to point out who they are by defining mental competence by its relationship to Christian identity.

Going further, a sane person may be TEMPORARILY insane due to the challenges of heredity, environment, and experiences. But they never become UNSANE. You can't lose your salvation. You can't find your salvation. It finds you.

An unsane person can never be temporarily SANE. The unsane person has no access to saneness because sanity is illustrated as objective morality. Objective morality comes from God. You can't acquire it. It acquires you.

"Objection!" someone says. Christians exclude all other religious definitions of deity. *God defines objective morality, but which God? Who is God? What is God?* Why is Jesus Christ the only way to salvation and the true definition of God?

Because JESUS says so. Don't believe Christians. Believe Jesus. You shouldn't believe anyone else. Why would you? Jesus is a 100 percent bona fide historical person. He was PERFECT. No sin. He claimed to be deity. He let Himself be killed and arose from death three days later. He then appeared to many people and ascended to Heaven.

WHO DO YOU TRUST?

In an overall sense, Connecting The Dots Of Identity 1 and 2 is about subjective morality versus objective morality. Subjective morality is human beings' prerogative to define right and wrong. Not God. Objective morality is God's prerogative to define right and wrong. Not human beings.

What makes God the standard of right and wrong, good and bad? He created human beings! He became a perfect human being! He has ALL the credentials.

If God doesn't exist, as there is no such thing as right and wrong behavior. There is just behavior. That must also apply to evil in the world. Those things that are considered evil, such as war, floods, hurricanes, and fires, are just facts of life. They are not good or bad in themselves. Good-bad and right-wrong are just useful labels of ongoing events in nature.

Similarly, rape, murder, theft, and molestation are not bad. They are just events from forces in nature that stimulate responses in agents. It's all physical. We're meat, from the top down. The body and the brain are composed of material properties. We euphemize cold reality with codes of conduct and in terms of relationships. The universe is an organic machine, and we are particles of the machine. The machine is not intelligent. There is no purpose or teleology. Life is a mysterious accident.

In the Questions and Answers section of this book, one of the questions is *"How can Jesus be the only way to salvation, when CD1/CD2 admits people from every religion and people of no religion will be saved"?*

Until that chapter, when you're wondering why people think and behave the way they do, rather than thinking they're stupid, evil, or out of their minds, think of the chart. They don't know God—yet. What they think they know of Him comes mostly from other people.

General Revelation in nature reveals Him. Special Revelation of scripture reveals Him. Those of us who know Him could be better at communicating Him to others. The unsane are spiritually blind. Our prayers should be to the Holy Spirit to assist us in helping the blind to see. Details follow at the end of this chapter.

Part of the challenge in communicating with people who are suicide candidates is gaining their trust. Telling them it's crazy to think such thoughts may show them you are not the kind of person to entrust with deep personal feelings. We all admit suicide is utterly unsettling to contemplate. It gets you closer to insanity the deeper you think about it, because thinking about suicide exposes you to the act, even if on a miniature scale.

How does a suicidal person override the highest prime directive—the will to live? You never want to know that. In fact, we protect our thoughts from simulating such ghastly imagery. And suicide must be in the top five categories of ghastly imagery. So, we leave it to the professionals who are trained in mental health: psychiatrists, psychologists, neuroscientists, and the healthcare system. The rest of us stay away from suicide. But we may inadvertently expose ourselves to the very thing we abhor.

As of this publication, the sale of firearms is at record levels. The 2020 pandemic, political unrest, political policy, and economic uncertainty contribute to new buyers. New firearms sales indicate people who haven't had firearms safety courses are at risk. Also at risk are the children in the homes of new gun owners. We also know that, of all suicide attempts, firearm use has the highest success rate. So now suicides will be expected to continue the deadly increase from years past. Suicide attempts, suicide completion, suicides from carelessness, negligence, with intent, without intent, with willing assistance, and without willing assistance all continue.

Even after a lifetime of exposure to theism, atheism, and agnosticism, of having those principles explained to me over and over, they never really sank in. There was always a missing element that left the imagery incomplete. *Connecting the Dots of Identity* is not complete either, but it fills in some of the missing elements, even suicide.

As devastating and heartbreaking as suicide can be, it doesn't always have to be bad news. We all die. There are reasons to believe the person that takes their life could not have been in their right mind. This is insanity. We may be helpful during their times of sanity, but only God can save their life. Their life is never in our hands. Other than this, we trust they are 100 percent human beings—Pre-Life Elect Roleplayers. From the MARVI-RPIA point of view, even suicide works out Marvelously.

You Are Not Alone: 1-800-273-8255 24/7 (National Suicide Hotline).

BLIND EYES CHART

The Blind Eyes Chart is an informal attempt to highlight nonphysical aspects of identity-array Roleplay blindness using a questionnaire and a brief essay.

Nonphysical Roleplay blindness refers to spiritual blindness, intentional blindness, and unintentional blindness. This follows from an inability or unwillingness to perceive objective morality, thereby deferring to subjective morality. The intent of the chart is to help clarify the disparity in Roleplayers' perceptions of good/bad and right/wrong.

A thirty-point yes/no questionnaire on spiritual blindness follows with a brief essay defining spiritual, intentional, and unintentional blindness.

Will your answers be based on objectivity or subjectivity?

Will your answers be truthful? Are they YOUR answers, or the answers you think are the “right” answers?

Blind Eyes Chart—Part 1. Questionnaire.

1) Do you consider yourself a theist?

2) Do you consider yourself an atheist?

3) Do you consider yourself an agnostic?

4) Have you publicly confessed to being a theist, atheist, or agnostic to your family, friends, and associates?

5) Would you love God (of the Bible) if God wouldn't send anyone to Hell?

6) Would you love God if God already has your residence in Heaven?

7) Have you ever done a deep search on who God is?

8) Are you interested in learning more about God?

9) Do you believe in angels, good and evil spiritual beings?

10) Do you believe in an afterlife of Heaven or Hell, rather than Oblivion?

11) Do you believe you will go to Heaven at death?

12) Do you believe you will go to Hell at death?

13) Do you believe you will cease to exist at death—Oblivion?

14) Does a person have Free Will to believe in Jesus Christ?

15) Have you read the Bible all the way through?

16) Are you interested in new philosophical ideas?

17) Should you be held responsible for your life, considering you had no control over heredity, nationality, chronological age, or intellect?

18) Is objective morality (right/wrong, good/bad, as defined by God) better than subjective morality (right/wrong, good/bad as defined by human beings)?

19) Should the God of the Bible be the standard of objective morality?

20) Does the God of the Bible exemplify the best moral character?

21) Is objective morality important in government?

22) Is objective morality important in business?

23) Is objective morality important in academia?

24) Is your country founded on good/bad, right/wrong principles for all citizens?

25) Should you have freedom of speech to criticize the government, public entities, or nations?

26) Should freedom of speech be controlled by the government?

27) Should possession of firearms by citizens be illegal?

28) Assuming these questions were answered thoughtfully and truthfully, do they help define your worldview?

29) Are you now more assured of your worldview?

30) Are you now less assured of your worldview?

Blind Eyes Chart—Part 2. Essay.

Host person X's internet program consists of guest person A in segment one and guest person B in segment two.

Host person X asserts the nuances of identity-array Roleplay blindness may help explain why people see things so differently. Two guests are present.

Guest person A disclosed she was visited by a messenger of a certain group to consider withdrawing her political protests for a great sum of money. A suitable position for her, in a nonpolitical setting, will presently follow. She refused. The messenger countered: Name your price! Surely there's a number you think worthy of your sacrifice. Again, she refused.

Host person X says, "Think of a second messenger, or the same messenger, saying in his New York gangster accent, *'You know, it would be a shame if something unfortunate were to happen to you, or your spouse, or your family. People drop dead suddenly, people disappear, accidents happen. We can do this the easy way. Or, we can do it the hard way.'*"

Guest person A went on to highlight her political concerns and what strategy to employ to counteract governmental misconduct. She reiterates the obstacles to address are rules, regulations, corrupt lawyers, judges, courts, and even politicians who may belong to the same political party.

Guest person B in segment two said as much in their interview. Bad people are demoralizing good people. There seems little can be done, and it takes forever to accomplish even minimal progress. The corruption is so entrenched and so pervasive that people actually consider forsaking the voting process. This becomes a contingent strategy by the opposition that enhances their effort of electing their own candidates.

But why are people so corrupt? Why are so many people considered bad politicians, lawyers, judges, policemen, teachers, and businesspersons?

How is it that this group of people see things this way, and that group of people see things the opposite way?

1) *Spiritual blindness*—the unsane (Insanity Chart). There is yet to arrive the Holy Spirit to facilitate objective morality; therefore, personal integrity is compromised by subjective morality.

2) *Intentional blindness*—the sane and the unsane (Insanity Chart). People are able to see but blindfold themselves or are blindfolded by others. They may be blackmailed, threatened, extorted, framed, bribed, bullied, or tricked. How do you respond to threats of losing your reputation, your finances, your family, your health, or your life?

3) *Unintentional blindness*—the sane, unsane, and insane. People are unable to see, but it's not because of spiritual blindness or intentional blindness. They're deluded. They maintain a reliance on beliefs that are contrary to reason or rationale. Vision is obscured by suggestion, expectation, prejudice, insecurity, fear, hate, deceit, and immaturity.

When God is not the standard for good, but humans are, what follows? Does the highest good become the ability to control destiny? If so, this requires power. Power arises from political strategy to be the leading persons in the leading nations of the world. In this regard, the quest to acquire power creates tunnel vision—superseding all other goals. Be number one. Win. It doesn't matter how. The world is the prize.

Blind people are extremely destructive and extremely dangerous. They may hate you. Don't hate them. They're blind. Help them see.

FINISH

Your Blind Eyes Chart test results are being prepared . . .

CHAPTER 18

SUICIDE—PART 3

Do you remember when you first heard of suicide? As you think about it, it probably wasn't near the time you first understood what death was. Initially, we find out death is just the absence of life. Sleep. Disappearance from others. Old age. Then we learn about fatal accidents, fatal illnesses, and the make-believe deaths on TV, in movies, and in games.

Then we discover the very bizarre act of someone killing themselves. No one seems to know why they do it. It's some sort of mental illness.

Here's a question for you. What are the most famous suicides you're aware of? Take sixty seconds to think of five. Or take thirty seconds to think of three. Were any of them celebrities? Famous people would mean famous suicides. Right? That's pretty much what you see when searching for famous suicides in history. Celebrities: writers, singers, and movie stars.

I went on a search to compare what is found on the internet with what my personal most-famous suicides are. What I discovered was variations in suicide definitions.

My most-famous historical suicides were:

1) Japanese Kamikaze suicide airplane attacks on Allied naval fleets in World War II (1944)

2) Religious group of 907 people, dying of cyanide-laced Kool-Aid drink in Guyana (Jonestown, November 1978)

3) Islamist hijacked-airline terrorist attacks in New York, Virginia, and Pennsylvania (2001)

4) *Jesus Christ

You may say wait a minute. These aren't strictly suicides. These are social causes the people considered worth dying for. I will agree. If I expanded my list of famous suicides, it would include murder-by-cop and murder-suicide. They aren't strictly suicides, either. Strictly speaking, suicide could refer to a person who contemplates self-destruction after momentary or prolonged instances of insanity. The deciding factor to commit suicide is a favorable opportunity, or a life event, along with momentary or prolonged lapses in sanity.

And Jesus Christ with the asterisk? Yes, Jesus Christ. The asterisk is because we know Jesus had to take His own life. No one is capable of taking it from Him. Free Will agents and circumstances led to the capture, trial, and execution of Jesus. The details are a convoluted arrangement of prophecy from Old Testament law, Jewish law, Roman law, and demands from the crowds.

Also, the Roman official, Pontius Pilate, rendered a not-guilty verdict of treason. The religious leaders didn't stone Jesus for blasphemy. A prisoner named Barabbas was offered as a festival ritual of releasing one prisoner. The whole trial, execution, and death scenario took place in the earliest hours of the day, until about 3 p.m.

Everyone implicated in the death of Jesus could be considered the lowest of the low human beings. But, as MARVI-RPIA illustrates by verbal abstract impression, they are all simply Roleplayers. They are the result of heredity, environment, and experience coming together in the circumstances of the crucifixion event. None of us today are any better or any worse than any of those people of the past.

Taking your own life with the intent to do so, along with an ability to avert death if so desired, qualifies as suicide. Jesus is a one-only case of suicide. Jesus said he would arise from death and live three days later. To further emphasize Jesus's unique suicide are the OTHER six components of his death. Jesus's seven-part mission that includes suicide may look like this:

1) PROPHECY—Many Old Testament prophecies of the crucifixion.

2) SUICIDE—Multi-motive act of intentional death.

3) HEROISM—Savior of mankind sacrificing His flawless life and body.

4) MARTYRDOM—Died for the Elect.

5) ATONEMENT—Reconciled the error of Adam and Eve by dying and coming to life again.

6) RESURRECTION—Overcame the enemy of life, or death.

7) TRANSFIGURATION—Victorious ascension and return to Heaven.

I memorized the list as PUSHMART. Jesus was Prophesied as a Unique Suicide, a true Hero and Martyr who Atoned for mankind and, after Resurrection from death, later Transfigured and returned to God.

Jesus committed suicide so you won't have to. He conquered death, so death is not our final destination. Jesus's death atoned for all levels of sanity, unsanity, and insanity.

> As the Father knoweth me, even so know I the Father: and I lay down my life for the sheep. And other sheep I have, which are not

of this fold: them also I must bring, and they shall hear my voice; and there shall be one fold, and one shepherd. Therefore doth my Father love me, because I lay down my life, that I might take it again? No man taketh it from me, but I lay it down of myself. I have power to lay it down, and I have power to take it again. This commandment have I received of my Father (John 10:15-18).

And after six days Jesus taketh with him Peter, and James, and John, and leadeth them up into a high mountain apart by themselves: and he was transfigured before them. And his raiment became shining, exceeding white as snow; so as no fuller on earth can white them (Mark 9:2-3).

So then after the Lord had spoken unto them, he was received up into heaven, and sat on the right hand of God (Mark 16:19).

From that time forth began Jesus to shew unto his disciples, how that he must go unto Jerusalem, and suffer many things of the elders and chief priests and scribes, and be killed, and be raised again the third day (Matthew 16:21).

Now the next day, that followed the day of the preparation, the chief priests and Pharisees came together unto Pilate. Saying, Sir, we remember that that deceiver said, while he was yet alive, after three days I will rise again. Command therefore that the sepulchre be made sure until the third day, lest his disciples come by night, and steal him away, and say unto the people, He is risen from the dead: so the last error shall be worse than the first (Matthew 27:62-64).

For thou wilt not leave my soul in hell; neither wilt thou suffer thine Holy One to see corruption (Psalm 16:10).

All they that see me laugh me to scorn: they shoot out the lip, they shake the head, saying, He trusted on the Lord that he would deliver him: let him deliver him, seeing he delighted in him . . . For dogs have compassed me: the assembly of the wicked have enclosed me: they pierced my hands and my feet . . . They part my garments among them, and cast lots upon my vesture (Psalm 22: 7-8, 16, 18).

He keepeth all his bones: not one of them is broken (Psalm 34:20).

They gave me also gall for my meat; and in my thirst they gave me vinegar to drink (Psalm 69:21).

I gave my back to the smiters, and my cheeks to them that plucked off the hair: I hid not my face from shame and spitting (Isaiah 50:6).

He was oppressed, and he was afflicted, yet he opened not his mouth: he is brought as a lamb to the slaughter, and as a sheep before her shearers is dumb, so he openeth not his mouth . . . And he made his grave with the wicked, and with the rich in his death; because he had done no violence, neither was any deceit in his mouth . . . He shall see of the travail of his soul, and shall be satisfied: by his knowledge shall my righteous servant justify many; for he shall bear their iniquities (Isaiah 53: 7, 9, 11).

> And it shall come to pass in that day, saith the Lord God, that I will cause the sun to go down at noon, and I will darken the earth in the clear day (Amos 8:9).

> And I will pour upon the house of David, and upon the inhabitants of Jerusalem, the spirit of grace and of supplications: and they shall look upon me whom they have pierced, and they shall mourn for him, as one mourneth for his only son, and shall be in bitterness for him, as one that is in bitterness for his firstborn (Zechariah 12:10).

You Are Not Alone: 1-800-273-8255 24/7 (National Suicide Hotline).

988 is the 3-digit 24/7 National Suicide & Crisis Lifeline.

CHAPTER 19

SUICIDE—PART 4

As you follow Connecting The Dots Of Identity, a question may arise. If my identity is SAFE IN PARADISE, why not COMMIT SUICIDE? I'm absolutely miserable. Maybe not suicidal, but very down and depressed.

That's a fair question. That may be part of the number one question facing humanity: Should I commit suicide? As French-Algerian intellectual Albert Camus put it, "There is but one truly serious philosophical problem, and that is suicide" (*The Myth of Sisyphus,* 1943).

Why is this? Because life is almost impossible to figure out. Some say this, some say that. Who am I really? Is there an afterlife? What is the meaning of life? Since there is no clear 100 percent correct answer, everyone has to figure life out for themselves. Some people begin dead in the water—literally. Others are aborted, stillborn, and miscarried. Some are born with horrific disabilities. Some are born simple-minded, defective-minded, born in the wrong country, to the wrong family, at the wrong time in history.

You look around in despair at the plight of half the people in the world. Millions of people are starving, at war, in poverty, under government oppression, suffering from the weather, religious persecution, and overall distress.

As for you, today, why should Connecting The Dots Of Identity discourage you from suicide? Some of the same reasons others don't attempt or commit suicide:

Embarrassment – People would label you insane, and this also reflects on your family.

Sorrow for others – The people left behind will suffer from your abrupt death.

Denial – Life isn't at the insanity point of suicide.

Sin – Suicide may be self-murder, a sin in God's eyes.

Fear – There may be an afterlife with a dreadful destination.

If there is an afterlife, is it to provide justice for the unfairness in life? Philosopher Immanuel Kant spoke about this. His thoughts come later.

If there is no afterlife, crime pays. People get away with evil. And for those who die young, well, too bad, tough luck. Those who are good people will have no reward for being good. But, if there is an afterlife, will it be Heaven to gain or Hell to pay? Heaven, no worry. Hell, total worry.

Suicide is a mental illness and plausibly a sin. You have an unreasonable aversion to living because you can't manage life. That's probably a sign of mental illness. Frequent thoughts of suicide are a clear signal to seek help—immediately. Murder is a sin, and suicide is usually self-murder. There's no going back to square one. It's over.

Suicide is always an option. Thinking of it as a last resort is understandable. Before the last resort arrives, consider how your dots of identity have become connected. What has happened in life is not all your fault. *You've been set up—framed. You don't have to accept it.* This is why MARVI-RPIA is being offered.

MARVI-RPIA is not theology. It's an art project. Art is meant for beauty, inspiration, insight, escapism, imagination, fun, interest, emotion, stimulation, and intrigue. Beauty is in the eye of the beholder, as the saying goes, but MARVI-RPIA seeks to be more than beautiful.

Seeing in the Bible that Jesus Christ proclaimed Himself to be 100 percent true, holy, and absolutely reliable, we can cite many of the 100 scriptures regarding the Elect (CD1, Chapter 6)—those persons saved before the world was created. You may rest in the knowledge that your life here on earth is simply a temporary role forced upon you by circumstances beyond your control.

Make the best of what you have, one day at a time. *Don't fret, don't worry, and don't freak out.* Life is not easy, but once you have MARVI-RPIA's rose-colored glasses, one day at a time is still troublesome but not insurmountable.

You're a Free Will Roleplayer. You're participating in a Demonstration of Free Will initiated by Adam and Eve. The Demonstration proves that disobeying God's won't enhance your life. In fact, it may well destroy it.

Your true identity is safe in Paradise. Meanwhile, your identity in time and space consists of a simplistic identity array: spiritual (4), physical (1), mental (1), child (1), and dream (1). Who you are fits into these categories. *Who you are does not have to be a complicated affair that includes your occupation, family role, hobby, appearance, financial status, ethnicity, religion, education, or any such attribute.*

Everything comes packaged in the eight-Identity Array model. The model is derived from the culmination of events leading to you being born. You arrive (or don't arrive if aborted, miscarried, or stillborn) as the person developed by heredity, the environment, and experiences. Welcome. Free Will Roleplaying now continues for at least one more life.

TIMELESS AND ANCIENT SUICIDE

Let's go a little further. A case could be made that suicide is addressed in the very first book of the Bible. Even further back in time, when there was no time, what were the angels thinking?

"Suicide" may have been on Lucifer's mind. If Lucifer's Postulate (Glossary of Colors) has any credibility, it underlies an immortal creature's predicament. If a flawless creature's ultimate desire is complete freedom to behave, and God denies that freedom, is protest futile?

Is there a line between disagreement with God and rebellion against God? If a disagreement reaches a state of insubordination to the point of rebellion, what repercussion follows? Flawless spirit beings, angels, are immortal. They can't die. Hell is created for the Devil and his angels.

But Hell may not exist until Judgment Day, the afterlife of human beings. What happens to insubordinate angels in the interim? Is there limited access to limited areas in Heaven?

Beyond verbal protesting, what if disgruntled angels could simulate nonexistence? Perhaps angels would agree to not congregate, not worship, nor show any sign of life. Would God allow their immobility indefinitely? How long could a living creature simulate nonlife?

A flawless spiritual creature never loses consciousness, voluntarily or involuntarily. So, it's not likely they could refuse to maintain consciousness. *Therefore, suicide for an immortal being seems out of the question.*

What's left? Accept God's Determined Will, or act upon your own Free Will. It may have been at this point God offered His Demonstration.

Lucifer was probably the best person ever created to dispute God's Determined Will versus a flawless creature's Free Will. There was an ideal number of angels, representing a large sample size. *Presented with a Demonstration of Free Will involving flawlessly created HUMAN beings, angels may realize the jeopardy in exercising Free Will.*

God's Determined Will is a secured future. Free Will to oppose God creates an unsecured future. An unsecured future incurs risk. Potentially, life becomes uncertain, imprecise, and apprehensive. *Immortality in such a state could be disconcerting, problematic, and utterly regretful.*

The other suicidal question might have been expressed in the Garden of Eden. Adam and Eve were uncertain if life was worth living without knowledge of good and evil. Does good and evil include knowledge of oneself, of others, of the world, or of God?

If disobeying God means death, what happens after death? Nothing in their experience compares to death. As flawless creatures, they never lose consciousness, voluntarily or involuntarily. They possessed boundless energy, night vision, and no need for sleep. They simply rested from time to time. The few times they ate was from the Tree of Life, and that was more for pleasure than of necessity.

They would never cease to exist spiritually. The spirit of humans and angels don't die. When death occurs, where would their spiritual identity reside? With the Lord? Adam was put to sleep to create Eve. Would death mean sleep? Would they remain asleep? If they physically died, would God resurrect them to physical life again, or spiritual life like the angels? Would they have a similar identity to their former identity when recreated?

Loss of life to Eve and Adam may not have been the deterrent we might assume.

JUDAS AND PETER

From *Connecting the Dots of Identity's* point of view, suicide doesn't accomplish the final escape it portrays. There may be a different escape route worth pursuing—Modern Abstract Religious Verbal Impressionism-Roleplay Identity Array.

If you are able to set aside suicidal thoughts for a while, think about Jesus Christ committing suicide so that you won't. People may remember Judas Iscariot. He was a disciple of Jesus but committed suicide after betraying Jesus. Was Judas 100 percent human? Was Judas simply living out the constraints imposed by heredity, environment, and experiences?

It would be reasonable to read the Apostle Peter also committed suicide. He denied Jesus three times. Assuming Peter believed with his whole heart that Jesus was indeed the Christ, how did he manage to continue living after such a betrayal? Judas couldn't. Why not Peter? Only because Peter was 100 percent human? Only to show the contrast between Jesus praying for Peter and not praying for Judas? Not that Judas doesn't have an SSID counterpart in Paradise. He may have one. *It apparently shows that no one chooses Jesus, even though Jesus is well-known to them. He has to choose you, or you will die without ever choosing Him.*

> And the Lord said, Simon, Simon, behold, Satan hath desired to have you, that he may sift you as wheat: But I have prayed for thee, that thy faith fail not: and when thou art converted, strengthen thy brethren (Luke 22:31-32).

People who are 100 percent human, theists, and atheists have committed suicide. Some for altruistic reasons. Others for less than favorable reasons like poor health, immaturity, stupidity, or negligence. Perhaps most suicides are the result of depression, despair, and hopelessness.

We know suicidal people are not just a danger to themselves. *They are dangerous to non-suicidal people.* Any tactic that may be effective in preventing suicide should be considered. CD1/CD2 is a contender, even if it's unreal, unproven, and unfounded. Effectiveness is what matters.

CD1/CD2 could be a beautiful door opposite the suicide door. Please, please, please consider it.

You Are Not Alone: 1-800-273-8255 24/7 (National Suicide Hotline).

988 is the 3-digit 24/7 National Suicide & Crisis Lifeline.

QUESTIONNAIRE — SUICIDE

Connecting the Dots of Identity isn't about the existence of God.

Connecting the Dots of Identity is about the existence of you.

Who you are is an essential question about everything else.

Do any of these statements apply to you?

____ I HAVE THOUGHTS OF SUICIDE.

____ I'M PRESENTLY LIVING A SLOW SUICIDE.

____ I'M PLANNING OR HAVE PLANNED SUICIDE.

____ I'VE ATTEMPTED SUICIDE BEFORE.

____ I MAY COMMIT SUICIDE IN THE NEXT TWELVE MONTHS.

____ I'M NO LONGER SUICIDAL (MARVI-RPIA HELPED).

____ I WILL PROMISE TO HELP PREVENT SUICIDE AND PROMOTE MARVI-RPIA.

To communicate, check all that apply.

Reproduce previous page. Share it:

JLT

PO BOX 15730

Rio Rancho, NM 87174

johndeuce442@gmail.com

CHAPTER 20

ABORTION

There should NOT be an abortion chapter in Connecting The Dots Of Identity.

I agree. It doesn't belong here.

This is the last chapter of three no-so-pleasant topics: sex, suicide, and abortion. I had absolutely no idea abortion would be included. It seems a rather political hot button. To start, with respect to identity, abortion has a peculiar standing because of its incidence in the history of the United States.

The United States has a unique identity. A famous politician made use of the slogan "Make America Great Again." For many people, America has NEVER been great. Ask Black Americans. Ask Native Americans. Ask Alaska Natives. Ask American women and children of the distant past how great America was for them.

It wasn't that America has ALWAYS been great. It is that America was founded on glorified principles and opportunities that made it the premier country for freedom and opportunity. If any country has the potential to be truly great, it's America.

Every nation of the world receives blessings and calamity. The USA cannot overcome calamity with blessings while abortion continues to be sanctioned by the populace. It's fair to say that is a statement from the religious community. What is also fair to say is that if we're to minimize abortion, our females must have comprehensive SEX EDUCATION, comprehensive LEGAL SUPPORT, and comprehensive LIVING SUPPORT. It may be that the religious community has been negligent in this regard. *We don't support our women and girls nearly enough.*

Over the last twenty years or so, America has been in imminent danger of losing its status as the number one country in the world: the country millions of people would choose to live in. Why? Why is America losing its appeal, losing its image, losing its identity as the leader of the free world?

The identity of its citizens is not grounded in a reliable, sustainable, objective moral framework. Certainly not every citizen is expected to possess good character and love for his fellow man, but as of late, moral character continues to decline. Is morality important? Is lying, okay? Is stealing, okay? Is cheating, okay? Alcohol, drugs, sex, exploitation, coercion, and almost any immoral activity seems worth the risk so long as you don't get caught. It's not immoral if people don't object. It's not wrong if you don't get caught.

Abortion: You got caught. No, not the man. No, not the woman. The BABY got caught.

The REMEDY: Murder the baby. The SENTENCE: Not Guilty.

The man: It was the best choice. The woman: It was the best choice. The baby: —

They say that this is a case of female misfortune. It's WRONG if she has to bear the child. Wrong, she loses her career. Wrong, she loses her lover's favor. Wrong, she can't afford the child. Wrong, the contraception failed.

Wrong, she had poor or no sex-ed exposure. Wrong, that family planning was no plan at all. Wrong, that she was underage. Wrong, that she was raped. Wrong, that she was a victim of incest, exploitation, or coercion.

Admittedly, the rapist, molester, or abuser who impregnates a girl is a despicable criminal. But the girl who aborts the child is a despicable criminal also. Yes, she's distraught, stressed-out, angry, humiliated, embarrassed, and victimized. But kill the baby? *It's almost murder-suicide.* She kills the child, which is 50 percent of her own identity.

The guy, as bad as he is, doesn't kill the baby. She does. Premeditated murder. Oh, it's not murder because science says pre-birth human tissue is not exactly a person. But explanations of science change from generation to generation. However, the discernable detection of human conception should CONFIRM its status as human life, preventing all equivocating.

Trusting in science means no one knows when life begins. *Who's no one?* Scientists? Politicians? Atheists? I'm someone. I know when life begins because the Bible knows when life begins. I'm also speaking for most Christians. They know when life begins. Jesus confirmed the Bible is reliable. Jesus Christ is 100 percent God and 100 percent human. Jesus Christ is a historically reliable figure. He knows when life begins.

There are millions of Christians. There comes a time when Christians must unite to help solve the problem of unwanted pregnancy. There are millions of non-Christians. *They've solved the problem of unwanted pregnancy. It's abortion.*

Abortion is such a big decision. The woman frequently has to make the decision alone. The woman is frequently not mentally prepared to make the "right" decision because she doesn't know who she really is, as defined by Connecting the Dots of Identity. She also must factor in the person who impregnated her, and the person who may be aborted. Whoever else she confides in about her decision may not have sufficient interest or wisdom to be of value.

Fortunately, there are agencies and unsanctioned resources in place that accept newborn babies. The babies are then matched with persons who desire the unwanted child. We understand this is in no way the solution to the nine-month ordeal of childbirth. *This is nine months the mother can never get back. And a baby who is aborted before it can develop never gets its life back.* Adoption is a path to reclaim a large part of life a pregnant woman will lose. Even so, adoption has its own issues. There are rules and regulations. There are preferences for the kind of baby the adoptive parents' desire. There's racial bias, age bias, and appearance bias. Fetal identity drama begins early. Who will want the baby? Why? What kind of parents adopt? How well do adopted children adjust to life?

As you know, this chapter is written by a man counseling a woman on what to do about her body. However, I am speaking in love to daughters, girlfriends, and wives. I'm speaking in love for the unborn defenseless unique identity totally at the mercy of its mother.

Connecting the Dots of Identity speaks to females in three stages of abortion.

Stage 1—Pre-abortion. Not yet pregnant.

Stage 2—Pregnant and contemplating abortion.

Stage 3—Post-abortion.

Stage 1—*Pre-Abortion.* Please read Connecting the Dots of Identity 1 and 2. Your identity is more than you've been taught. Sexual activity is a fact of life, but life is far more than self-gratification and self-fulfillment in the mental/physical realm. You are a spiritual creature.

Stage 2—*Pregnant and contemplating abortion.* Please read Connecting The Dots Of Identity 1 and 2. There are now two role-play identities: your ID and the baby's ID. Are you 100 percent human? Think and behave as if you are. You are not alone and without hope. Be positive. You and the baby have an SSID counterpart in Paradise.

Stage 3—*Post-abortion.* Please read Connecting The Dots Of Identity 1 and 2. The past is irretrievable; don't worry about it. That identity was not you; it's inauthentic. The baby's identity is also inauthentic. What matters now is you should not feel trapped in an identity forced upon you. Life is more than heredity, environment, and past experiences. Go forward as a person understanding that each day is another opportunity to become the Free Will Roleplayer God wants to have.

If you've had an abortion, it's understandable to be very defensive. It wasn't wrong. I'm not a murderer. I'm not a despicable criminal. There is no deceased person. It was simply tissue. Desperate times called for desperate measures. Only a woman can know the specifics of this difficulty.

But as a 100 percent human Roleplayer, you can admit murder because such an act is the type of activity typical of Roleplaying. Every single person comes into the world subject to heredity, the environment, and experiences. Unless the Holy Spirit causes rebirth in that person, they remain subject to natural factors. These factors include insensitivity toward other living beings. The insensitivity covers abuse, rape, incest, and molestation, all the way up to murder.

Pro-choice advocates relegate murder to the legal profession. In that case, abortion is not murder. Abortion is political. It's legislation that provides a legal path for women's rights. But it also has the power to circumvent the conscience that has been compromised. A compromised conscience is difficult to reach. The hope is that sharing an artistic impression of reality may help.

As the science of the abortion debate evolves, the message changes to reflect the latest medical procedures and public policy. Religion involved in the abortion debate has been fairly consistent, all the way back to the Old Testament. But neither the state nor the church wants the other side to dictate the terms.

Meanwhile, legislation is being carefully constructed that includes a provision for AFTER-BIRTH ABORTION. *It's highly unlikely such a crude term would be found in the draft. An abortion after the baby is delivered, or termination of life after birth, would be INFANTICIDE.* Currently, abortion laws in place around the world vary on jurisdiction and application. As it stands, *the incessant inclination to terminate life at ANY stage of development represents a principal goal of the unsane person.*

The unsane are spiritually blind. God hasn't opened their eyes. There is no objective morality. Therefore, subjective morality impedes and lowers the standard of ethics, truth, honesty, and love. What matters more is control, power, and influence.

The chess match between pro-choice and pro-life continues. Pro-choice unsane have no way of opening their own spiritual eyes. That's the province of the Holy Spirit and the sane pro-life defenders. Please do MORE to help our beautiful females out of the abortion quandary.

Is there ever a case for abortion? Of course, but it's a door to a chamber of horrors.

CHAPTER 21

ABORTION POSTSCRIPT

In the Old Testament, God appointed several so-called cities of refuge for the people of Israel (Numbers, Deuteronomy, Joshua). They were intended as a safe haven for the person who committed manslaughter—the unintentional death of an innocent person without malice. The relative of the person who was killed could not take vengeance on the killer if the killer arrived in a city of refuge.

As Israel experienced children born with birth defects, they realized this was probably the result of the Nephilim influence and/or mixed marriages with Gentiles. Gentile nations did not know of or practice laws of cleanliness, sexuality, or godliness. Their lifestyle obstructed the quality of childbirth. Birth defects followed from heredity, the environment, and experiences.

Following Christian Reformed Impressionism as a worldview, ministers of art might advocate abortion cities of refuge. Parents who recognize their child will be born with malignant defects may consider an intermediary that puts the baby to death. The parent(s) are witnesses to the death and reside in the city for several days to honor and mourn the loss of life. The woman may have a second pregnancy or more, but only one additional abortion as detailed in Abortion Cities of Refuge guidelines.

While reading CD1/CD2, reflect on being conceived by different parents in a different country. In the case of rape or incest—do not abort. In the case of pre-birth defects—abort.

An egregious pre-birth condition may make abortion preferable. How many of us would decline to Roleplay such an identity? Elect Roleplayers may act on behalf of their unborn child and resort to such a city. There is anguish, remorse, and sorrow. However, this is the choice they would make for themselves. The question becomes how do you decide? Down syndrome? Defective body parts or bodily functions? On suspicion of abnormalities?

Such a scenario by people who hold an objective moral position cautions us to be mindful of abortion's chamber of horrors.

Furthermore, abortion could be the same as a worldwide life-and-death crisis. The lives of mothers and the lives of unborn children have a high priority. Life is as high a priority as any program being funded, privately or publicly. God will surely curtail our blessings as this tragedy prevails. This should not be a subjective matter. I like what philosopher Gregory Koukl says: "Abortion is taking the life of a defenseless human without proper justification." Unfortunately, taking the life of a person remains a right of females, fought for in pro-abortion legislation.

We must change the present conditions to protect, honor, and cherish unborn children and our female population. Pregnant females are vulnerable, emotional, and trusting. Abortion is an option only the inauthentic identity perceives as viable. It's understandable but unreasonable. The person who doesn't feel trapped in their identity will consider other options.

Meanwhile, we abhor the blight on society that is child pornography. We would never advocate pro-choice child pornography. It's abhorrent. It's illegal. Abortion is also abhorrent. But it's legal, for now. Not many scenarios are worse than sexual activity as a very young child. But one is: the death of a child before it even has a chance to be born. Death by its own mother. And it's legal. This is pro-choice.

Virtually every pro-choice argument is less than a life-and-death decision for the mother. All except one, the possibility of the mother dying in the process of childbirth. The other reasons for abortion regard quality of life. This is where MARVI-RPIA has an opportunity to support women in their struggle to understand their role in the extremely difficult situation of an unwanted pregnancy. Additionally, MARVI-RPIA offers the same support to women in post-abortion life, and a voice of assistance in times of deficient sex education.

Of course, child pornography is an after-the-fact tragedy. The direct tragedy is the adult thinking and behavior that eliminates the rights of children through pornography. Similarly, abortion is an after-the-fact tragedy. The direct tragedy is the thinking and behavior that eliminates the rights of the unborn child through death.

The expectation is there will be strong objection to the MARVI-RPIA point of view on grounds of separation of church and state. The default social standard is a secular point of view. This view rejects any religious reasons for women's rights or the rights of a fetus. A woman's identity should not be based on religious ideology. The identity of a fetus should not be based on religious ideology. What does that leave? Not the facts of science; a human embryo is a human being. That leaves secular ideology, or human tissue, as a legal term. It's an issue for the courthouse. Abortion programs appear protected and semi-funded by organizations and the government. *We ALL participate financially, whether religious or secular.*

The alternative? Make abortion illegal? The argument is that if abortions are illegal, unsafe abortions skyrocket. But abortions cost millions of lives either way, legal or illegal. However, legal abortions could cost many more millions of lives—one million deaths versus fifty million deaths (Abortion Facts and Figures 2021). We should ask ourselves how to address the *option* of abortion, even as females know intuitively, they are only addressing a *result* of an error, but not the error itself.

Archeological evidence suggests many ancient cultures engaged in a superstitious ritual of child sacrifice. Though that evidence may be circumstantial, judging by modern-day behavior, similar behavior prevails. *We would argue only uncivilized, barbaric, heathen cultures would practice human sacrifice to nonexistent gods.*

Yet today women abort, or sacrifice, their children to a god of fate. Fate has shown disfavor to them via pregnancy. They have the option to undo this disfavor through abortion. Restore one's life with the great personal sacrifice of the unborn child. Fate will reward the act. Witch doctors perform the ritual in the safety of clinics throughout the world. Other witch doctors invent drugs that terminate a pregnancy. This is similar to modern paganism.

My body. My choice. *Connecting the Dots of Identity* suggests otherwise. You are not your body. You didn't choose to be your physical identity. The fetus didn't choose its identity. It lives in a life-or-death position inside the mother. There are two bodies. No choices. Just life.

So even though scripture indicates that abortion constitutes the death of an unborn person, and the killer is subject to execution (Exodus 21:22-23), the argument holds the Bible isn't reliable.

Whether Jesus Christ was a real person or not can't be known, and even if He is a historical figure, He has no bearing on present-day affairs. Look around you. Reality says there is no God, no Jesus Christ, and no religion that's helping the world. We are on our own. If God and Jesus do exist, we don't like them, because it's obvious they don't like us.

> If men strive, and hurt a woman with child, so that her fruit depart from her, and yet no mischief follow: he shall be surely punished,

> according as the woman's husband will lay upon him; and he shall pay as the judges determine. And if any mischief follow, then thou shalt give life for life (Exodus 21:22-23).

Sorry, I'm not interested in making Connecting The Dots Of Identity political imagery. But we should acknowledge that the dynamics of identity relate to abortion as well as the sex-ed and suicide chapters addressed earlier. *You should be able to see the dots are certainly connected.*

Poor sex-ed or no sex-ed may lead to an unplanned pregnancy. Unplanned pregnancy may lead to anxiety, stress, and depression. Thoughts of suicide may surface. Where no abortion clinics are available or no abortion medication is available, the girl may risk her life to end the pregnancy by whatever means found. Or, in a successful abortion, 50 percent of herself is the person being aborted. The other 50 percent of herself is subject to suicidal influence.

Certainly, this is a grim scenario. But there are great numbers of women who have no reservations about making abortion readily available worldwide. The position is that women have an absolute right to the availability of safe pregnancy termination.

But hold on a minute. What does this matter if everyone goes to Heaven? Isn't this what *Connecting the Dots of Identity* maintains? *The aborted baby, the mother, the father, the "witch doctors"—everybody is already safe in Paradise.* Right? Yes! But MARVI-RPIA is not theology. It's art. I'm an artist, not a theologian or philosopher. I'm offering an impression that describes identity so that you have confidence in an assessment of who you are, why you're here, and what you should be doing. Impressionism. An art project.

So, yes, in a sense, suicide doesn't matter, and abortion doesn't matter if we all go to Heaven. But for now, today, we don't know. We can't know. We have faith. We trust. We hope. Are there really any better worldviews than Connecting The Dots Of Identity? Have you taken the time to evaluate them? What do you believe? Why do you believe it? Can you know absolutely without question the true nature of reality? Do you know why you're here? Is life an accident? What is knowable?

What can be bleaker than atheism? Life has no meaning. It could end abruptly any second. Agnosticism holds that no one can know what is being, knowledge, or purpose, so they live as atheists. Theism is accused of being no better than those two worldviews because of Hell. At least Connecting The Dots Of Identity is 100 percent optimism. Everyone goes to Heaven because they're already there. No one goes to Hell who is 100 percent human.

Lastly, MARVI-RPIA has a special image to add to abortion. This image includes offers of love for women who have already had an abortion.

There are women who continue to feel bad after an abortion. There are women who are indifferent and women who feel great after the abortion. These feelings may change over time from one aspect to the other. If the abortion experience is perceived as negative and is unresolved, it causes problems in other areas of life.

For the Christian woman, her past indiscretions are set apart from her new identity in Jesus Christ. That old identity does not represent her reborn identity. For the most part, the non-Christian woman still accepts and affirms her past indiscretions as who she is today.

Consider ABORTION GRACE, the next chapter. This entry is very personal and meant to be private support for women who have had an abortion or are thinking of one.

Visit OPTION LINE or call (800) 712-HELP. Twenty-four hours a day, seven days a week.

Or send a text to 313131 to chat with someone right now who can help.

PREGNANCY DECISION LINE. Call (866) 993-0794 for immediate help.

CHAPTER 22

ABORTION GRACE

Recognition:

Today is a formal acknowledgment of an aborted baby.

I honor the person I didn't honor before.

Details:

Given Name of Baby (optional)

Day/Month/Year of Event (optional)

Reason for Event (optional)

Pardon:

The past is not me.

The present is not me.

The future is me.

The past is not the baby.

The future is not the baby.

The future is an individual.

Eulogy:

This is a prayer of forgiveness.

This is a prayer of resolution.

This is a tribute to the baby.

The Demonstration of Free Will is the baby, me, the father, the clinic, and the doctor.

We will be rejoined with our Pre-Life Elect identity in Paradise.

Your Name (optional)

Date (optional)

Since this is a private memento, you may want to search and find an image to associate the memento with. For example, find an image of a nature scene, a work of art, or maybe a doll. Perhaps use an image you already have.

Celebrate a day YOU were not aborted (birthday). Celebrate a day for the aborted BABY (assigned birthday).

If you decide to share your Abortion Grace details, don't be held back by shame, embarrassment, intimidation, or slander. Making mistakes is human. You are not the same person today you were then. This may help empower other women to declare freedom from oppressive expectations. Women aren't solely responsible for control over human reproduction. A man is also responsible. Society is responsible.

Visit OPTION LINE or call (800) 712-HELP for someone to speak with twenty-four hours a day, seven days a week. Or send a text to 313131 to chat with someone who can help.

Call (866) 993-0794 for immediate help with your pregnancy decision. M-F 10-5 EST.

Safe Haven Baby Box 1-866-99BABY1.

Crisis Pregnancy Center for locations and info: cpcmap@uga.edu.

All crisis pregnancy centers (CPCs) offer pregnancy tests and information. Some offer limited medical services, such as ultrasounds.

CPCs also serve Canada, Latin America, Africa, and Europe.

Or you may share with me:

JLT

PO BOX 15730

RIO RANCHO, NM 87174

CHAPTER 23

ABORTION—POST POSTSCRIPT

She is not just carrying the rapist's baby. She is the storehouse for a new identity that is the product of HER family tree and HIS family tree. Those tree branches date back thousands of years. This branch may include Nephilim roots (evil angels), but it surely also includes the root of Adam and Eve. We all trace our roots back to Adam and Eve. This is our heritage. This is the aborted baby's heritage.

On one of the social media sites, someone posted an image of a severely beaten twelve-year-old girl. The girl had been raped and impregnated. It was a horrible image. The writer was outraged that people OPPOSE abortion in cases such as these. *Her childhood. Her innocence. Her future is now RUINED!* (Quora. Shawn Mootoo. Accessed July 20, 2022.)

Being FORCED to become a mother is unfair.

Yes, it is. It's unfair to the mother. It's unfair to the baby.

Being FORCED to be conceived in a young girl's womb is unfair.

Yes, it is. It's unfair to the mother. It's unfair to the baby.

And the mother is only ten, eleven, or twelve years old.

And the baby is only one, two, or three months into conception.

And the mother is only a child; motherhood is too much for her to handle at that age.

And the baby is more of a child, and death is too much for it to handle at its age.

The mother's life will surely be ruined.

The aborted baby's life will surely be ruined.

The fetus is not her child. It's the rapists' child by force.

The fetus is 50 percent HER child PLUS an additional 50 percent her child if the father is absent. That's 100 percent.

The baby becomes a constant daily reminder of an evil event.

All Free Will Roleplayers are daily reminders of evil events in the world.

The father. The mother. The baby. The aborted birth assistants. Everyone.

When a female suffers an unwanted pregnancy, it may be a terrible tragedy. The pregnancy may have been unavoidable, or it may have been avoidable. In the interest of not making matters worse by aborting the baby, understanding WHY such an ordeal takes place helps heal the distress. As bad as things appear to be, it's only because Free Will

Roleplay is in operation. Everyone is simply acting out forces based on heredity, environment, and experiences. This includes you.

Connecting the Dots of Identity paints the picture of an afterlife. This afterlife means the present life is not all there is.

Even though you accept the default worldview until God opens your spiritual eyes, exposure to the MARVI-RPIA concept may appeal to you. Its possible God does have your true identity safe in Paradise. In that case, life in the present loses its finality. It's not your only life. You're a Roleplayer. It's not who you really are. This makes it much easier to accept forgiveness for what's happening to you. *It's not really you. It happens to a character in the demonstration of Free Will.*

Jesus taught to forgive, forgiveness in the manner of seventy times seven. In the case of abortion, that means to forgive the father, the abortion assistants, the baby, and to forgive yourself.

> Then came Peter to him, and said, Lord, how oft shall my brother sin against me, and I forgive him? Till seven times? Jesus saith unto him, I say not unto thee, until seven times: but, until seventy times seven (Matthew 18:21-22).

In the case of life, you should forgive your gender, ethnicity, height, weight, appearance, and IQ. These attributes are not you. They are who you were told you were, and who you thought you were. You don't have to believe that.

Connecting the Dots of Identity is the impression of a renewed childhood, renewed innocence, and renewed future no matter what happens in life. People are in wheelchairs, in prison, and in mental wards. People are in war zones, in hospitals, and slowly dying in horrible living conditions across the world. This is life, but it doesn't mean it's who you are. You're a Roleplayer. Your authentic identity is in Paradise, awaiting the end of the Demonstration of Free Will.

The science of embryology shows the identity of the embryo in its mother's womb is a complete human identity. But science doesn't matter. The Bible shows abortion is a sin. The penalty is capital punishment (Exodus 22). But God doesn't matter.

> If men strive, and hurt a woman with child, so that her fruit depart from her, and yet no mischief follow: he shall be surely punished, according as the woman's husband will lay upon him; and he shall pay as the judges determine. And if any mischief follow, then thou shalt give life for life, Eye for eye, tooth for tooth, hand for hand, foot for foot, Burning for burning, wound for wound, stripe for stripe (Exodus 21:22-25).

Some of you may say Exodus 22 only refers to life lost as the life of the mother, not the unborn child. However, the unborn Jesus, and the unborn John the Baptist in their mother's womb, were considered complete human identities.

> And Mary arose in those days, and went into the hill country with haste, into a city of Juda; and entered into the house of Zacharias, and saluted Elisabeth. And it came to pass, that, when Elisabeth heard the salutation of Mary, the babe leaped in her womb; and Elisabeth was filled with the Holy Ghost (Luke 1:39-41).

What matters to abortion proponents is the legal right of the mother to terminate a pregnancy at any point after conception. The morality of it is purely subjective. There is no objective morality defined as God. Everyone defines it for themselves.

If your spiritual eyes are closed, you think and behave like an animal you believe is your ancestor. Killing someone is a survival mechanism. Additionally, if your spiritual eyes are closed, it may be due to your evil spirit ancestors—the Nephilim. Jesus said to a group of people: Ye are of your father the devil.

> Jesus said unto them, If God were your Father, ye would love me: for I proceeded forth and came from God; neither came I of myself. But he sent me. Why do ye not understand my speech? Even because ye cannot hear my word. Ye are of your father the devil, and the lusts of your father ye will do. He was a murderer from the beginning, and abode not in the truth, because there is no truth in him. When he speaketh a lie, he speaketh of his own: for he is a liar, and the father of it (John 8:42-44).

We don't want God in our politics. We must separate the church and the state. However, this has come to mean people don't want God in public policies. So, humans or the Devil take over. The devil in the sense of no reliance on moral objectivity. People want subjectivity—the ability to define morality as conditions arise.

Instead of compromises or neutral positions regarding church and state, governments have increasingly become anti-church and pro-state.

In one obvious case, this has brought about an extremely grotesque practice. This practice is a mother taking her newborn baby by the ankles and swinging it against a rock to bash its brains out. Okay. Not really. The mother pays someone to do it for her while she goes out of town. Okay.

Not really. She goes in for a procedure at a medical clinic that destroys the baby's past, present, and future. *This is the civilized way of bashing a child's head against a rock. You hire a hit man.*

In a sense, we can't blame the mother, the clinic, or the hit man (or hit woman). When your spiritual eyes are closed, all you can do is depend on others for truth. You hold hands with others who are blind hoping to find the right way. Your eyesight is dependent on the eyesight of your group.

With trust in the most perfect Person who ever lived, died, and arose, Jesus Christ, we can know when our eyes are open. When we have spiritual eyes, we see with X-ray vision. We see right through bull-error. We have microscopic vision, telescopic vision, and wide-angle vision. We have night vision that gives us guidance when darkness is all around.

The momentary topic is abortion, but the bigger issue is your spiritual eyesight. Only God can open our eyes. What should we be doing in the meantime?

ABORTION — POST-POST POSTSCRIPT

One of the gut-wrenching thoughts that came up relative to child pregnancy was the age of the youngest birth mothers. *Internet searches reveal the age as FIVE years old!* Your heart drops into your stomach. It just makes you sick. Five-year-old, six-year-old, and seven-year-old pregnant children, all impregnated by relatives, friends, and strangers. Some fathers are never to be found.

Then, you think of all the children who were raped but did not become pregnant. What kind of degenerate human being would assault, molest, or rape a five-year-old child? Of course, we know people sink even lower and do the same to infants much less than five years old.

Now, the emphasis shifts from abortion to unsane and insane males. *These guys have no objective morality.* They have no respect for their life or the life of others. Why would they? If their worldview features life as an accident, has no purpose, is unfair, cruel, and crazy, what really matters to them?

People who imply only a degenerate would rape a child also imply a degenerate is a totally uncivilized person. Mentally ill. Yet we live in what is arguably the most civilized society in world history. A society that not only rapes babies and children but KILLS them while they're still developing in the womb.

This is not saying the mother is as uncivilized as the degenerate who rapes children. The mother doesn't act alone. She is influenced by the father of the baby, family, friends, doctors, nurses, pharmaceutical companies, her culture, and society. She's also influenced by how the "Good News" of Jesus Christ people treat her.

This is not an attack on those who support abortion. If we don't have safeguards in place that inform, protect, and support our young girls and women, desperate situations provoke desperate measures. Desperate measures often overrule even Christian moral objectivity.

This is not an attack on those who have an atheistic worldview. From the outside, the Christian lifestyle restricts behavior, impedes science, and suppresses nonconformity.

The attack, or challenge, is on those who assume the responsibility to illustrate the Good News of Jesus Christ. The Good News seems to be losing ground to non-theism, agnosticism, and non-Christian ideology.

If you still don't know the Great News about the Good News of Jesus Christ after *Connecting the Dots of Identity*, this confirms the Demonstration of Free Will. God hasn't opened your eyes—yet. Be patient. He knows you.

CHAPTER 24

POLITICS—PART 1

Politics? Church and state—again. Abortion, and now politics.

Yes. Please, be patient.

The church represents God. The state represents human beings. A separation is necessary to preserve freedom from religious oppression on the one hand and secular government oppression on the other. The corporate church has a long history of oppressing the population. Belief in God of various religions was often not only expected, but it was also compulsory. The general public was not literate to any great degree until the recent past. In the distant past, people had to rely on religious leaders to read scripture to them. They had to rely on what was being read until the next reading session. They didn't have many options. We have literacy. We have TV, radio, newspapers, magazines, the internet, and etcetera. They had low literacy and small group meetings.

By the time of the so-called Age of Enlightenment in the 1700s, science and reason challenged the role of the church in government. Science became the new god. Human beings now had a newfound belief in themselves that had been obscured and repressed by the church. Evidence of reality provided by science was more reliable than faith in reality provided by the church. Skepticism of theology as a worldview gradually gave way to disbelief in theology as a worldview. God did not create human beings. Human beings created God. Humans evolved and adapted from forces in nature. God was just a name pointing to the misunderstanding of those forces.

Following from this, your identity is tied to your race. Your race is tied to your ancestor's country of origin. Their country of origin highlights the influences the environment has on the development of physical and other characteristics. *This is typically an overall range of attributes that became known as Caucasoid, Negroid, and Mongoloid. We know them today as White, Black, Hispanic, Asian, and natives of America (American Indian/Native American and Alaska Natives).*

By connecting the dots of identity derived from the ancestors of your country of origin, people strongly identify with racial differentiation. This is reinforced by the people in your immediate family, extended family, and culture.

By extension, the community, city, state, and country you reside in becomes part of your family. Every family bears dysfunction to some degree. As more individuals are added to the family, dysfunction is added. Generally speaking, populations in most communities are increasing. More families lead to larger communities, which increases growth for that location. Public policy is put into place and updated to maintain a standard of living for the people. Who are the people responsible for the standards in a given community? The people who live in the community. The community of individuals is a microcosm of public policy—or politics.

Life in countries around the world lives through the political system. The system is orchestrated by people who are put in power to make decisions for them. The groups of COMMUNITIES comprising cities and towns make up a macrocosm of a political system. Another part of the macrocosm is CORPORATIONS. Corporations are business entities that, by size, wealth, and influence, coordinate with individuals, organizations, and governments to shape politics.

As an individual, you may see yourself as a political avatar. You represent a citizen of a country. Given the nature of your legal status, you may have an official or unofficial voice in government. By way of social media, news reports, and global communication techniques, you can make yourself heard. But what is it that you would want to say? Do you support the status quo? Do you oppose the status quo?

In free market systems, everyone who is qualified to vote should be encouraged to vote. If your point of view is not represented, you should initiate proposals that encourage support for your view. Be a champion of representative government. Be responsible, or support someone who is.

Of course, this perspective has two sides. Representation for good people and representation for bad people. Good people and bad people? Is there such a thing as a good person and a bad person? Science tells us no, there is no such thing. Bad and good is only a euphemism for nonconformity. The scientific explanation for human behavior is simply behavior. Behavior is subjective in the sense that there is no objective standard for everyone across a broad range of human behavior. Therefore, behavior is defined by individuals.

How good and bad are defined is the arrangement of a social contract initiated by individuals for the advancement of society. Laws, rules, and regulations are put in place and enforced to ensure humanity doesn't devolve into anarchy and chaos. This is necessary so that complex, dissimilar behavior is controlled and channeled for the benefit of that society.

In a system of this sort, an absence of the objective standard of good and bad is perilous. Why?

You know why. What can you expect when human beings define good/bad and right/wrong? The most powerful people soon rise to the top. They dictate the definition. The least powerful people have no standing. They simply contribute to keeping the powerful in power.

Theology states that God is the transcendent standard of good and bad. In the Holy Scriptures, God defines good and bad, right and wrong, righteousness and evil. Thou shalt not steal, kill, or bear false witness. Theology declares kidnapping, rape, and treason as evil. It's evil by its nature of being. It is not evil for you, but not evil for me. It's evil for every person. It's not relative to any individual's perspective.

How does this relate to a present-day political identity? It is a facade. *Your political identity is a distraction. It is not you.* Your country, nationality, and race are a hereditary and environmental construct on top of the construct of your life experiences. It is all inauthentic, following in the *Connecting the Dots of Identity* presentation. You are forced into a character by many obtuse influences. The reason for bringing in the political nature of identity is to highlight social psychology. Connecting the dots of individual thinking and behaving (psychology) may help understand group behavior (sociology).

If we isolate groups of behavior strictly by country, we could make a case for political lifestyles. In Country A, we might see significantly fewer restrictions on individuals, businesses, and organizations than in Country B. Country B residents may have no less love for their country than Country 'A' residents. Dissatisfaction with Country B's identity can be similar to dissatisfaction with individual identity. We are taught to love, honor, and reinforce individual identity. Therefore, uneasiness results when feelings of disapproval are voiced about our identity regarding our country because it's essentially our own collective identity.

This is a critical point in national leadership. The ability to communicate the direction of a small group for the good of a larger group further defines the identity of a nation. As the leaders go, or people in power, so go the people of that nation.

MARVIA-RPIA political imagery paints more dots to connect at this point.

If the people of a nation are led to believe their identity is NOT defined by their geographic location, race, or ethnicity, which is an inauthentic imposed identity, *but rather by their authentic identity before they were born, what might we envision?*

Perhaps people who refuse to go to war. Perhaps people who refuse to follow irresponsible government mandates. Perhaps people who refuse religious or secular policy but advocate reasonable neutral policies. If this is not possible, would they seek to change the government strictly by peaceful means? If not, what other un-peaceful means would qualify as legitimate? Is the last resort to leave the nation they've come to love, the only country they've ever known?

Most people cannot. Most people will not. Their country is their identity. They will die for their country. Good country, bad country, rich, poor, large, or small country. It's just not likely they could leave. They would rather stay and suffer what comes.

Connecting the Dots of Identity hopes to change your views. *You are not Russian. You are not Iranian. You are not African.* You are born a citizen of a nation. You had no control over that. Why are you proud? You're

White? You're Black? You're tall? You're cute? You're young? So what? You don't have a reason to be proud. You didn't create yourself. But when we're taught this present life is the only life that has meaning, what more can we expect? Who we are is where we are. Who we are is what we see in the mirror.

Not anymore, not necessarily. *Who we are is NOT what we see in the mirror. Who we are is spiritual. The identity we see is a temporary imposed identity based on heredity, the environment, and circumstances.* It's an assignment. We did not have any notice, give any permission, or contribute to any aspect of being brought to life. We have to make the most of it, and there is no consensus on what is best. Even as we hear what may be best, and even pursue what may be best, there is no equal opportunity for each one to get there.

THE CHRISTIAN LEADER

Who are we assigned to be?

Science tells us there can be no such thing as a morally responsible religious political leader. Forget about it. It will never happen. Deep down, a human being will basically do what is in their own best interest. That is innate human nature. When a person advances moral responsibility, the expectation is to restrict the individual freedom of its citizens to conform to some sort of religious standard. Worst-case examples are the standard of living in certain Middle Eastern, African, and Asian nations. Science asks us: Is that what we want?

A similar case could be made regarding nonreligious nations in the West. *Where subjective moral standards prevail, the toll on the populace is reflected in corruption, crime, and vice statistics.* The freedom to pursue subjective morality leads to instability in personal relationships, social activities, and occupation choices. Define your own morals rather than let religion tell you what is right and wrong. The price of freedom isn't always pleasant, but it's freedom. Meanwhile, the un-pleasantries of freedom escalate annually and have a negative impact on the generation that follows.

The solution? Science—again. Subjective moral standards are led by the belief in science. The education system of global nations favors the scientific explanation of reality: evolution rather than creation. Broadly speaking, evolution is the scientific explanation of how life began. The so-called Big Bang started a process of space, time, and matter. There is no reliable reason to believe in a religious explanation of how life began. Religion is sufficient for some people. It's a simplistic explanation for an understanding of the world. But scientific evidence is a much more verifiable explanation for a worldview.

From the scientific premise of reality, no intelligent factor was involved in creating life. The beginning was an apparent accident, with no purpose, unguided, and as yet a mystery to be solved. How life began is an event scientists continue to explore. They won't accept the beginning was initiated by an intelligent being. *As we are guided by reason and our five senses, no empirical evidence suggests an invisible transcendent entity defines objective morality.* Human beings define it.

Since there is no standard outside human judgment, then each human has their own judgment that defines what is bad, wrong, or evil. If enough people in any community agree that rape, theft, or murder is wrong, then the standard for that community becomes the moral standard. It's a social contract.

Is there anything wrong with these assumptions? Isn't it obvious?

Community standards fluctuate as people rise and fall in the community and redefine morality. The social policy then has no application of long-range moral standards. Moral inequities in the government lead to inequities in the system. The system becomes corrupt.

As non-theist policies advance, the evolution of mankind may not be so evolutionary. It may be *devolutionary.* An argument can be made that as humans evolve and adapt to advance with the next generation, humans devolve to an even greater degree. *The final stage of devolution? Self-annihilation.* Doesn't matter if it occurs by accident, negligence, or intent.

Artificial intelligence eliminates us. We blow ourselves up in war. An experimental laboratory project goes awry, and we're all dead nine months later.

You say no? Humans are not devolving? The classic position of mainstream human evolution is that humans become better with each stage in the evolutionary process. Humans adapt to challenges in life and produce the necessary changes that promote survival for the next generation.

And further, the scientific community disbelieving in the God of the Bible often says this: *Humans are basically GOOD!* We don't need to believe in God to be moral, define our identity, and solve our problems. We will eventually cure diseases, medical conditions, and starvation. We will have a world government, equity, and peace. Finally, we will achieve long life and possibly overcome death from old age.

Oh, really? That sounds more like philosophy, hope, and faith—not science. When you look back in time, it may seem that there was much less crime, much less hate, and much less inhumanity to mankind. But no. Sorry. We all know bad things were happening. In the past, people didn't have the news media to record details of current events. They didn't have the benefit of modern law and law enforcement techniques. People in power, and people out of power, were judge, jury, and executioner.

Bad things continue to happen. Often, they are worse than before and are now readily accessible on the internet. They are not so much a function of a larger population creating more examples. Things are worse as more people accept the premise that individual rights matter more than all the other rights. Each individual defines rights—not family, not culture, not society. This becomes moral subjectivity, where everyone sets their own standard of good and bad. There is no such thing as objectivity regarding individuals. There is only subjectivity. *No one, and certainly no made-up God, dictates what's best for every person.*

A common belief is that society doesn't suffer from anarchy because the goodness of humanity puts social agreements in place. This is enough to define right and wrong. People do what it takes to maintain order and prevent chaos. If society devolves into chaos, nobody wins.

Meanwhile, we continue to see random evil, highly intelligent evil, and idiot evil. We see gruesome evil, political evil, and evil like we've never seen before. If people were basically good people, we should see a DECLINE in law enforcement, a decline in civil and criminal litigation, and a decline in incarceration. We should see declines in rape, robbery, molestation, abuse, abortions, suicides, homicides, and wrongful deaths. Do we see a decline?

Imagine a simple test. *Abolish law enforcement for thirty days in every nation's largest city. Surely, there are many more good people than bad people. Display progress every five days.*

Start the clock ... Good city … Bad city … No city?

While believing in the goodness of mankind, the world is under continual stress. Stress of cyber warfare, chemical warfare, and bio-warfare. There's the stress of financial warfare, food and water warfare, and civil warfare. *We can't tell the difference between natural causes and effects or behind-the-scenes maneuvers of manipulation.*

Every day there's gun violence, terrorism, and assault. Generation by generation, the sanctity of life is losing ground. Why wouldn't it? Life is unfair. Life is a fluke. Life is meaningless. There is no devil, no angels, and no God. Or maybe the God they think they know isn't who He is. Who is He?

God, show yourself!

From a view of theism, it's reasonable to think a political leader should have integrity, be of good moral character, be motivated to serve, and possess skills of sound decision-making. Citizens want the very best for their nation. Their nation is their extended family. A religious person in government isn't necessarily a bad thing. Of course, everyone claiming to be religious isn't religious. On top of this, defining which religion is being followed is a very important factor.

Imagine a person who follows Christian Reformed Impressionism as outlined by Modern Abstract Religious Verbal Impressionism. Such a person would not seek to convert every person to Christianity. They know

God is the One who provides salvation, and that was accomplished before the world was created. This politician promotes a neutral public policy in the interest of the religious and nonreligious rights of the citizenry. No religious agenda is advanced. Would that be feasible? Maybe. Maybe not. It would certainly take a very unique individual and a team of like-minded politicians to make it work.

Is that proposition worth pursuing?

MONEY IS POWER

If that proposition is WORTH pursuing, what VALUE is given to it?

Yes. This means MONEY! It takes a great message, but it takes tons of money, because tons of money will be raised AGAINST any religious or semireligious platform.

You should be able to understand by now that life in most nation-states has become divisive. People are aligning on the side of "us" and "them." As these two sides reach clearer lines of definition, the records of who financially supports each side are of great importance. Financial support is extremely important as it is crucial in the area of communication. Without adequate financing, lines of communication are disrupted, opposed, and compromised.

The enemies of Christians are smart, resourceful, and numerous. They have tremendous wealth, power, and diversity. No feelings of guilt plague them. They will lie, cheat, steal, break the law, and commit acts of heinous proportions. We are in a war. *This war is for the highest stakes imaginable. The world!* If you're able to acquire the power to control the number one nation, such as the United States, you control the world. Therefore, *do whatever it takes to win.*

At this point, all the forces of note are against Christians. There's big business, big technology, individual billionaires, the media, academia, government, and international groups. Only in recent years has the opposition to Godliness become so apparent. How do we fight this?

Consider a group of us becoming the RICHEST Christian organizations in the world. We could be a league dedicated to amassing enough wealth to match the trillions at large against us. *It's only by the power of money that we can fight fire with fire.* We should never suffer because of a lack of finances. Money also provides the incentive for people to get involved in the fight. They deserve compensation for the great risks they take.

Yes, there will be risks. Loss of reputation, loss of freedom due to incarceration, loss of wealth, and possibly loss of life. The fight is for life—the quality and integrity of life. We will need the most trusted of strategists. We would need the equivalent of an Integrity Team, an Oversight Team, and a Reporting Team. Perhaps start with six teams comprised of groups of four:

1. Finance professionals (4)
2. Politicians (4)
3. Attorneys (4)
4. Spiritual Experts (4)
5. Business Professionals (4)
6. Philosophers (4)

This is just a rough draft. YOU tell us how we should proceed.

This is urgent. Christians are being outspent by a wide margin. We do not have the resources or leverage that anti-Christians have. We are getting better at building our own resources, but it takes time. We are running out of time because we don't have our financial resources organized. Let's do something about it. This is urgent.

Contact me:

JLT

PO Box 15730

Rio Rancho, NM 87174

johndeuce442@gmail.com

OR

Don't contact me. Contact each other.

POLITICS 1 — POSTSCRIPT

Man-Woman Man-Machine

As you read this, politics is an even greater issue than you might imagine. The definition of what it means to be human is being systematically compromised. The god of science pushes forward on two main fronts: *the merger of man and woman and the merger of man and machine. How far it goes is all political.*

The merger of males and females has taken a long time to develop. We might call it gender depletion. Gender identity, gender manipulation, and gender redefinition imply a mission to expedite the fall of individualism. You won't define yourself; science will define you. The government will define you. Grammar school won't feature *Fun with Dick and Jane*. It will feature *Fun with X1 and X2*. The new gender will be "it"—neither male nor female.

The merger of man and machine, an assumption of trans-humanism, comes closer each day. Machines, or smart devices, are increasing in every home across the world. How much longer will it be before the device is not IN your hand but IS your hand? Going further, devices will not be in your heart or in your brain, they will BE your heart and BE your brain.

The deceptive messaging will point away from artificial humanity and point to medical altruism. Impairment and diseases will be diminished and finally eliminated. But this is only a ploy for the ambition to recreate humanity. In doing so, at the risk of the demise of human beings, they are compelled to plow full speed ahead into oblivion. *They know more than God because they ARE God.*

Such a scenario is reminiscent of pre-Flood earth. Angels manage to merge with human females. God intervenes. Will God intervene again as humans begin to merge with machines? How much violence and violation of God's natural laws will He tolerate?

It's not that far removed from Lucifer's quest for omnipotence or Adam and Eve's quest for omniscience. Human beings' quest for advancement in knowledge and power WITHOUT the objective morality of God's standard inevitably causes mayhem.

The insidious nature of politics is that all too often, laws are decided behind closed doors, in obtuse language, without full disclosure, and without public awareness. Then, as deals are made and agendas progress, the public may seem informed but, in reality, are completely bamboozled. *Some people don't even care. Just do it. Just win. We trust you.*

This is politics. We feel powerless to change it. *If we don't properly evaluate people in politics, we deserve every horror that comes to us. Of course, we must know on what basis to evaluate our politicians. This comes back to objective morality.* This comes back to trusting God as the standard of morality. And this comes back to the inability of anyone to open their own spiritual eyes. God has to act first. This seems counterproductive to a godly nation and a godly world. Why wouldn't God act first, ALL THE TIME, FOR EVERYONE?

The Demonstration of Free Will has to play out!

Meanwhile, those who have their spiritual eyes open should be doing all they can to beautify the environment by introducing God to others. God works through us to open the spiritual eyes of the unsane and His Elect. It's an uphill battle. The Good News of Jesus Christ doesn't seem to be so great. God doesn't seem to be so good. If there is a God, why does the Devil seem to be winning? Why is there a Hell? Why don't prayers work?

This is the challenge *Connecting the Dots of Identity* accepts. Will you accept the challenge also?

CHAPTER 25

POLITICS—PART 2

But what if the people are so cynical, so distrustful, so set in their ways that they refuse to support a religious politician? They just don't believe religious principles will ever be acceptable across a broad range of people. What platform could a potential religious candidate run on—and win?

Let's start by imagining a MARVI-RPIA Minister of Art who begins a political career at the local level, then the state level, and then at the national top level. The platform is something like *"Make God Great Again."* They say God has already saved us before we were born. Our authentic identity awaits us after we complete the Demonstration of Free Will. God is love. God is fair. God has saved us all. He is back on the throne where He belongs. And, just as good or better, no one goes to Hell since Hell is prepared for the Devil and his angels. But none of us accepts this premise until God opens our spiritual eyes. In the interim, those of us who do see this understand those who don't see this. We still treat them with love, patience, and honor, even though they don't reciprocate. Your support of this platform will help present our country as the number one country in the world.

A vote for a Minister of Art, in the MARVI-RPIA tradition, means the legislative, judicial, and executive policies will reflect a neutral bipartisan religious-secular position. This will be done with the highest regard for every citizen. Nonreligious freedom will be honored. Orthodox religious freedom will be honored. Unorthodox religious freedom will be honored.

The question now becomes: HOW does the Minister of Art politician articulate Christian Reformed Impressionism? After all, the premise is an impression, not a religious doctrine. The author of the project himself does not believe in it. It's art. It is not a belief system. How would such a politician be taken seriously? *His platform is people who behave badly are insane, unsane, or probably less than 100 percent human beings. Angels and human females created giants that may be the ancestors of subhuman people who live among us.*

As if that isn't enough to flummox people, it's possible that we all have dual identities. Identity one is on earth in the present. Identity two is in Heaven. Identity two began before we were born and isn't realized until after we die. Identity one, here on Earth, isn't real.

The atheists will ridicule this platform. The agnostics will agree with atheists. They may not comment at all or comment only in generalities. Unorthodox religions might support Connecting The Dots Of Identity, but orthodox religions simply can't afford to do so. Orthodox organizations must protect the integrity of theology based on evidence compiled over thousands of years.

And then you consider Christian Reformed Impressionism, as illustrated in Connecting The Dots Of Identity, came up overnight, from nothing. How can anyone accept words as art? Is it fiction? Is it nonfiction? Is it literature? Is it not literature? What is it?

They probably won't accept it. Such a political person would have to build their image from examples of transparency, trust, and accomplishments. Otherwise, *Connecting the Dots of Identity* won't be meaningful to most citizens. They have to get to know you. They have to get to know God. That is, they have to get to know the God of *Connecting the Dots of Identity.* It will take time to build the kind of exposure needed to make people aware of this God they've never heard of before. Everyone goes to

Heaven, and no one goes to Hell—unless they are less than 100 percent human. Getting that message out will be difficult and time-consuming.

How much time will it take for CD1/CD2 to realize any significant exposure to the general public? It may take as little as two years. It may take five to ten years. It may require twenty years or more.

On the other hand, it might never see the light of day. Why? It's poorly written. The few people who read it don't get it. It's too esoteric, too convoluted. There are too many pieces in the puzzle. They're hard to put together.

Another possibility is that other people could take components of CD1/CD2 and improve them. They may be able to create the enhancements needed for political applications.

However, to have a significant political influence on society, it may NOT be necessary to be in politics. With insight, good fortune, and a strong enough voice, a person can be a "kingmaker" (or *king breaker*) in other ways. By supporting candidates favorable to a MARVI-RPIA worldview, any Minister of Art may help put people in place who articulate and coordinate public policy.

KINGMAKER

Search, discover, influence, and then support the most likely person to represent sane people of the community. But the opposition will fight with cunning, treachery, and immense resources. There is an underworld group of antagonists. These people absolutely do NOT want a moral leader. Example:

Group A. The people who are immature Christians. They say they're Christians, they go to church, and they try not to do the wrong things, but they are lacking in spiritual maturity. They may not recognize an upstanding moral leader right there in front of them.

Group B. The people who are mistrustful of any Christian political leaders. They are nonreligious, anti-religious, and non-Christian people who refuse to support a Minister of Art proponent. It doesn't matter how popular such a person comes to be. This group has no spiritual eyesight. They see what they want to see or what others tell them they see.

Group C. The persons who may have a mission to influence the world that human beings are a failed experiment. This is Satan's accusation. Humans are NOT better than angels. Humans are going to exterminate themselves. Angels don't murder, steal, or commit suicide. These persons were all good angels until they applauded Adam and Eve's disobedience to God. Adam and Eve pursued the knowledge of good and evil. God condemned Adam and Eve but promised them a future life through procreation. Angels only want equal favor. An attempt was made to secure their own redeemer through procreation with human females. It failed. Though their attempt failed, their disobedience was still less heinous than Adam and Eve's.

Groups A, B, and C follow the Demonstration of Free Will model. They all conform to the forces of heredity, the environment, and experiences. If God does not intercede to change their life, they will continue on the path of opposition to Christian worldviews. They will continue the path of downfall. Such paths lead to downfall for everyone. But on those paths, there are lights that guide—guided by the Lord.

POLITICS AND THE LORD

Guided by the Lord? The Lord of the Alaska Native, Native American, or Australian Aborigine? Buddhist, Hindu, or Muslim? Christian in name only? Are they guided by the Lord?

Yes, if their spiritual eyes are opened. Otherwise, Life continues the Demonstration of Free Will.

So, do politics really matter? Yes, politics matter. Politics matter to protect the quality of life and organize the social structure. For example, what is the quality of life for any nation-state in a given belief system? Belief systems such as: Non-theists, non-Christians, and agnostics? Belief systems like Islam, Hinduism, and Buddhism?

As you know, quality of life depends on who you ask. If the quality is satisfactory, no need to seek change. If unsatisfactory, do you have the systems in place to make changes? What if the systems in place prevent access to make changes for the better? What if "better" is only defined by the systems in place? Then what?

1. Leave the system (temporarily or permanently)?
2. Overthrow the system (peacefully or un-peacefully)?

Regarding individual rights and public policy, how well are the people's rights represented in Government?

Recently, what seems to be trending is a separation between liberal and conservative worldviews. The separation of church and state is coming under review as politics increasingly consume the public spotlight. It may be sooner than later that a time comes when the public will be forced to declare allegiance to a specific political identity.

However, before you can know which political identity is the best choice, what is YOUR identity?

This is how Joshua puts it in the Old Testament:

> And if it seem evil unto you to serve the Lord, choose you this day whom ye will serve; whether the gods which your fathers served that were on the other side of the flood, or the gods of the Amorites, in whose land ye dwell: but as for me and my house, we will serve the Lord (Joshua 24:15).

And the Free Will question becomes: How can you choose to serve the Lord if the Lord must first choose you? Yes, right back to God's election plan of salvation. You are already chosen before you were born.

Those of us who agree that we are chosen and therefore have a responsibility to beautify our environment with the words of God now have a call to action. Get involved in politics!

WHAT IS GOODNESS?

As it stands, morale in the USA is extremely low. We don't trust politicians, we don't trust our family, and we don't trust other Americans. We've lost trust in the ministers of God, and we've lost trust in God. We don't know if there will be a tomorrow, a next week, or a next month. Money may fail, food may fail, and the government may fail. I may be killed. Everybody may be killed.

How can we beautify our environment if we don't have beauty in our hearts?

What political action should we take? This political action: open your eyes to the class of people who OPPOSE objective morality. People in positions of authority who pursue a SUBJECTIVE moral standard have severely limited integrity. Without integrity, corruption permeates government, business, and academia. It influences all segments of society.

The evidence of a corrupted political system is difficult to itemize as the very checks and balances are themselves corrupted. They'll tell you there's nothing to see here. The very few leaders that ascertain and expose corruption won't acquire the support needed to make changes. They will be outmanned, outmaneuvered, and outspent.

The right to rule is being lost to the unsane. If rulership is not soon appropriated by sane people, America may not be recoverable. If America goes down to a second-class or third-class nation, no other nation is likely to ever achieve what America stands for: liberty, individualism, and prosperity. The devolution of humanity is already being seen in the areas of education, entertainment, and business. We have high crime, health problems, and financial turmoil. Every day, every week, every month another crisis is on the news.

It's not enough to recognize unsanity in positions of authority. We have to see in ourselves. If we don't trust so-called Christians who attempt to support objective morality, that is not a bad thing. It's not wrong to resist being ruled over by a morality that doesn't represent individual freedom. *Oppressive restrictions of individual rights in the name of religion are no less tolerable than any restriction of individual rights.* Look no further than the restrictive religious practices of large and small countries around the world.

If you consider opposing objective morality and the transcendent standard of God as the judge of right and wrong, you're only other choice is the standard of human beings. Corruption is what happens when right and wrong are relative—relative to the person and to the situation. At that point, right and wrong don't apply to everyone equally. Its okay for some people to cheat, steal, lie, kill, withhold evidence, deceive, manipulate, and instigate violence. The means justify the end. Just win, no matter what it takes. If people are harmed, that's just collateral damage. Sorry about that.

That mentality permeates the people in authority. They won't tolerate threats to their position. They can't afford to, as too many people are involved and too much is at stake. They're intelligent. They're versatile. They have unlimited resources. *And they despise, they loathe, they HATE goodness.* They don't believe in it. They don't understand it. Goodness is against everything they stand for.

Goodness is weakness. Goodness is what Christians call God. *What's so good about God? The planet Earth is not much more than a stinking public toilet! Christians don't deserve to rule over us. God doesn't care about us. How dare they tell us how to live?* How can they not see the same toilet we see? Why blame us? Blame your God!

So, it's up to you, and those who champion goodness, to redefine goodness. *Connecting the Dots of Identity* wants to be a champion of goodness you may recognize. What's goodness? It has to be taught. It has to be meaningful. It has to be compelling.

WHO REPRESENTS SANE PEOPLE?

The Serpent, Eve, and Adam were flawless beings in the flawless environment of the Garden of Eden. One day, they abandoned their prime directive to maintain the beauty of their environment. They did so to pursue their own individual interest rather than the interest of the environment and other flawless creatures.

God was not number one. Their world was not number one. THEY were number one. They lost trust in God. They gained trust in themselves.

The pastors, the ministers of God, have accepted the mission to introduce God to the public. God is worthy of trusting your life to Him. Though God is incomprehensible and indescribable, the Bible has been given to us. HELP THE BIBLE COMMUNICATE BEAUTY, HOPE, AND LOVE!

Politicians should arise from the people who are taught about God, then represent people taught about God. But until then, they trust more in themselves. The people don't see that God has such a great plan. They see evil everywhere, every day, for every person. They see death ahead. They see Hell ahead for people they may love. They see an unpredictable future. And finally, they have a nagging sense of dread that nothing … can be … known.

So along comes MARVI-RPIA. Not science. Not theology. Art is presented as an impression that may give you hope, ideas, and a beauty that religion and atheism haven't offered.

WAKE UP

But we're running out of time. We need a call to action. A call to action to get involved in politics. It should take the form of a National Emergency—by the people, not the government. We can't depend on the government to save America. They're part of the problem. There are too many unsane politicians entrenched in the government. That's partially our fault for being negligent in evaluating personnel and being uninvolved in the election process. We let corruption happen. We've been uninvolved, naive, and docile. We may not be unsane, but we are spiritually immature or not spiritual at all.

Others tune out politics. We tune out the world. We escape the bad news, the unpredictability, and the stress. We carve out our own little world. How so?

Dating, sex, marriage. Children, television, movies. Social media, games, music. Maybe we throw ourselves into our job. Maybe we put all our energy into how to make money and manage money. You may say it's not being irresponsible to avoid politics. It's being responsible to protect mental health, enjoy life, and improve the basic characteristics of our identity.

What if you began to realize that your identity may not be authentic? What if you begin to realize the country you live in is about to lose its number one status? That loss will have a significant impact on all your favorite escapist tactics to tune out politics and tune out the world. *Then would you participate in politics? It may be too little too late.*

If and when enough of us overturn the unsane contingent of Roleplayers, what follows may include disbelief and surprise. How could corruption go so deep? How was it undetected for so long? How could we have been deceived so badly? With that may come outrage, hostility, and a vengeful attitude toward those that caused so much destruction? *There may be hate for the perpetrators and hate for yourself. Hate THEM for their evil, hate YOURSELF for your stupidity.*

But we must be purposeful, not hateful. We will seek justice for the evil that will be uncovered when the sane recover the nation. We will strive to redesign the justice system to reflect a balanced system of policy for all.

WHAT CAN I DO?

Each of us who come to accept the broad MARVI-RPIA definition of sane and unsane have to cooperate somehow. That means forming a group of people who agree on a common goal. The goal is to recover America from the un-American. In this sense, the sane have to cooperate with an unsane segment of society, the immature Christian, and the non Christian. By the way, un-American is just a generic term. *Surely, people of every country resent injustice and oppression. Assume terms like un-Algerian, un-Armenian, or un-Australian for wherever you live.*

Somehow, we must speak as one voice to show un-American we are not fragmented, uninformed, powerless, afraid, and without resources. We will ORGANIZE, ACT, SUPPORT, and FUND movements to confront and oppose threats that jeopardize national standards of freedom.

Though the USA has been severely compromised by corruption in the legislative, judicial, and executive branches, the government must stand down if millions of people organize in peaceful opposition. However, we must be definitive in our voice and speak as one voice. If enough of us agree on well-defined core principles and purpose, it's possible to achieve significant progress.

As a very *rough, not well-thought-out* action plan, perhaps we could start with something like this:

1) World War XX. There are many undeclared world wars. War of finance, food, resources, drugs, cyber, disinformation, etcetera. The War on America by un-American qualifies. Let's MOBILIZE and DEFEND ourselves—peacefully. This is World War XX.

2) "We Say No" or a similar slogan to organize, protest, and oppose un-American activities as they arrive. How dare they proceed as MILLIONS of us EMPHATICALLY say NO in a coordinated act of solidarity?

3) Support the people who represent American freedom and withdraw support from un-Americans.

4) Communicate to inform the populace of WHAT's happening, WHY it's happening, and HOW and WHEN to make our voices heard. Include alternate communication strategies as the opposition cancels our sources.

5) Organize LOCAL WWXX emergency plans. Draft procedures for what to do in a time of uncertainty, fear, power outage, no communication, or lawlessness.

6) Join together MONTHLY on THREE specific days. One day for a display of POWER to show solidarity. One day for a day of APPRECIATION as a day of prayer. One day for a day of CELEBRATION.

Obviously, such a plan is far from adequate, but it's something. There are enough of you who have much better ideas that should take the initiative and proceed. Please do. *It may already be too late to recover the nation. The government is only the most obvious problem to confront. There are forces behind the scenes that even the government may not be able to control.*

Help. Act now.

THE PLAN B

Will enough sane people renounce their inauthentic identity? If so, it would mean a dedication to sacrifice your life to promote the Great News about the Good News. God is actually godly. He has a Plan A that has to be better than the Plan B of *Connecting the Dots of Identity.*

Why does God's plan have to be better than any person's plan?

Because man's plan is only a crude analogy of how beautiful, holy, loving, and righteous God actually is. We are flawed creatures attempting to define a flawless perfect non-creature, who is God, blessed forever, amen. When we ask why there is unfairness, why there is evil, why there is death, all when a really great God could have deleted such flaws in His creation, *we should get an answer that's probably close to Connecting The Dots Of Identity.*

The reason we suffer could be that it's not really us that suffers. It's our inauthentic identity. The present life is a demonstration, symbolism, an analogy. The Bible is filled with analogies, symbols, rituals, examples, figures, types, and characters. This is so ideas and details of reality translate across the great diversity in human experience.

The Demonstration of Free Will could be the contrast of God's Determined Will represented by the Super-Spiritual Identities (SSIDs) and the First-Class Angels who did not rebel. God's Plan A is perfect. The MARVI-

RPIA Plan B is imperfect. *How could an imperfect being have a better plan than God's plan? It won't be. It can't be.*

Plan B is meant to be something that comforts and supports you. Theists, atheists, and agnostics come to you with every worldview imaginable. With CD1/CD2 Plan B you will be able to connect the dots of identity that are just as good as any and better than most—without saying a word. You have an impression that simulates a worldview as an art project. Not theology. Not philosophy. Not science. You don't believe in art. You like it or you don't.

POLITICS 2—POSTSCRIPT

Is God 100 Percent Moral?

For people who spend their time on spiritual matters rather than politics, the political climate has changed all that. The political climate over the past few years has taken center stage, intruding deeply into individual rights, parental rights, business rights, and religious rights. Involvement is now mandatory.

On the one hand, the government has a responsibility to manage the rights of the minority as well as the majority. On the other hand, what seems to have happened is the state has become antagonistic toward the church. You can't really blame them. *The ungodly never want to be guided by the godly.* The ungodly do whatever it takes to acquire power and retain power, so the godly never have the opportunity to presume judgments on them and restrict their freedom.

Of course, this stands to reason. As crazy as an insanity chart is, it does help show why people misrepresent kindness, justice, love, and honor as

Christian nationalism. People have no way of understanding an objective moral standard until God opens their spiritual eyes. Until He does, we should understand their position:

Number 1: *They don't believe in God—the One who sets the moral standard.*

Number 2: *People who do believe in God have doubts that He's 100 percent moral.*

Since God, Himself, does NOT treat all people fairly and allows the world to devolve into chaos, mayhem, and despair, how is He the epitome of morality? The Bible is full of God's absolute unfairness to man, woman, child, animal, and nation. Moral? *God hasn't proven He is any more moral than human beings.*

So, people in positions of power, wealth, and beauty set their own standards of morality. And God allows them to do so. As people see that God seems just as immoral as the best of the best are, what do they say? They say don't trust God. Don't believe in God. God does not love you. Or they just give up.

Over the years, a disbelief in the moral character of God has grown more apparent. Add to this the political view that religion has no place in public policy. Public policy should be neutral. However, we know this is only a way of saying the default position should always be atheistic rather than theistic or agnostic.

There are disagreements over how much involvement the church should have in politics. The notion is if the church concentrates on theology, this will affect the population, and the population will affect the political leaders. There's no need to pursue a career in politics or other political missions. Just concentrate on the Lord.

However, when looking at the most prominent individuals in the Bible, they were all essentially political figures. People like Abraham, Joseph, and Moses were presidents, prime ministers, and kings. Others like the judges, prophets, and disciples counseled heads of state and kings across many countries.

Then came Jesus Christ. The preeminent explosion in time. The arrival of the King of kings. The whole world has been affected by His leadership and authority. And this is where conflict becomes obvious. There is opposition to the kingship of Jesus Christ. This is the Demonstration of Free Will. We all oppose Jesus Christ … until He overrides our Free Will, and the Holy Spirit gives us new birth.

For now, we can't get discouraged by what we see in the world.

The bad people are bad. They don't know they're bad.

Bad people are unsane. They don't know they're unsane.

They think YOU are the one who should think and behave the way THEY do.

Or they say, "If I'm unsane, what can I do about it? You already say God has to open my spiritual eyes through your efforts. What do you have to offer me?"

Or “If I'm NOT the unsane one and YOU are unsane, what should YOU do about it? Maybe you have to let ME open YOUR eyes—trust that I have the truth.”

The sane have the responsibility to articulate the beauty of right and the ugliness of wrong as the standard God commands. The unsane must depend on God to open their spiritual eyes, but it is much easier to see if godly imagery is comprehensive. *Much of the imagery that the sane present to the unsane is not comprehensive; it's shallow, judgmental, and dismissive.*

Communicate the beauty of God's Plan A. If you have to use MARVI-RPIA's Plan B, do so. Or create another Plan X that highlights God’s Plan A. Use theology. Don’t use theology. Use business, use art, use politics. Be involved. Don’t escape. Don’t ignore. Don’t give up.

In the Old Testament Book of Numbers, God brings His people to possess a land occupied by ungodly people—and giants. God's people became fearful of the giants and didn't trust God to give them victory. So, God said no one over twenty years old will live in that land. Therefore, God's people wandered for forty years in the wilderness until the fearful adults died.

There are monsters in the United States and in every country. God's people must reclaim and repossess the land occupied by the monsters, or so-called giants. We must not fear them. God will bring victory or else we deserve every evil that befalls us. The giants appear absolutely invincible. They are not. We can't let those who are fearful of the giants keep the rest of us in the wilderness for forty years. We are here for a reason.

Unity. Strength. Dedication. Resources. Ingenuity. Do Not Fear. Trust God for victory.

And they returned from searching of the land after forty days... And they told him, and said, we came unto the land whither thou sentest us, and surely it floweth with milk and honey; and this is the fruit of it. Nevertheless the people be strong that dwell in the land, and the cities are walled, and very great: and moreover we saw the children of Anak there . . . And Caleb stilled the people before Moses, and said, Let us go up at once, and possess it; for we are well able to overcome it. But the men that went up with him said, we be not able to go up against the people; for they are stronger than we. And they brought up an evil report of the land which they had searched unto the children of Israel, saying, the land, through which we have gone to search it, is a land that eateth up the inhabitants thereof; and all the people that we saw in it are men of a great stature. And there we saw the giants, the sons of Anak, which come of the giants: and we were in our own sight as grasshoppers, and so we were in their sight (Numbers 13:25, 27-28, 30-33).

But your little ones, which ye said should be a prey, them will I bring in, and they shall know the land which ye have despised. But as for you, your carcasses, they shall fall in this wilderness. And your children shall wander in the wilderness forty years, and bear your whoredoms, until your carcasses be wasted in the wilderness. After the number of the days in which ye searched the land, even forty days, each day for a year, shall ye bear your iniquities, even forty years, and ye shall know my breach of promise. I the Lord have said, I will surely do it unto all this evil congregation that are gathered together against me: in this wilderness they shall be consumed, and there they shall die. And the men, which Moses sent to search the land, who returned, and made all the congregation to murmur against him, by bringing up a slander upon the land, Even those men that did bring up the evil report upon the land, died by the plague before the Lord (Numbers 14:31-37).

CHAPTER 26

MOLESTED BY DEATH—PART 1

All my life, I have lived under the threat of death. First as a non-Christian and later as a Christian. This is a nagging sensation below the level of consciousness. It's stress. One of the ways of alleviating stress is to become aware of the direct cause. If you can do that, stress becomes less of a threat.

I grew up in Anchorage, Alaska, the oldest of six children. In the 1950s and 1960s, my father worked for the Alaska Railroad and was also a Protestant minister. My mother worked in the home and later became active in real estate and social organizations.

Like most children, I learned death meant some terminal illness, an accident, or being forced into unconsciousness by some-one or some-thing. A little later in life came the imminent threat of World War III. Knowing what happened to Japan when the hydrogen bomb was dropped in 1945 and the tensions leading up to the Cuban Missile Crisis in 1962, the end of the world never felt closer. Duck-and-cover school drills were a part of the education system.

As I grew older, I was even threatened with death by my own father. Yes, he was a strict disciplinarian, no doubt by Old Testament law and by how he himself was raised.

Finally, I reached sixteen years old. I felt like an adult. But then, out of nowhere, came the biggest earthquake ever recorded in North America. The epicenter was just outside my city of Anchorage. Magnitude 8.4, but since upgraded to 9.2. Our house was damaged but still inhabitable.

In the following days, earthquake aftershocks and minor tremors reminded everyone that, from now on, Alaska was officially earthquake territory. Psychologically, that was a major trauma that followed me for years. I always wondered—when will the next big earthquake hit? Will I survive it?

The threat of death surfaced again when I was drafted into the US Army. Not yet twenty-one years old, military basic training transformed my adolescence into manhood. I was now ready to kill or be killed. Fortunately, I was blessed to be stationed in Germany rather than Vietnam, where most of the soldiers were being sent in those days.

After the army and visits to Alaska, I relocated to Los Angeles, California. Most underlying threats of death came from exposure to crime, drugs, or traffic accidents. California was also long known for earthquakes. Once again, I lived through several strong quakes and even more sudden, unexpected natural traumas over the years.

Gradually, over time, the Lord opened my spiritual eyes, and I identified as a Christian. Not long afterward, two big events occurred. The first event was radio station host Harold Camping's end-of-the-world prediction for 1994. If so, the advent of the arrival of Jesus Christ meant Judgment Day was here. This was the trauma to end all traumas. As we all know, it didn't occur, but it prompted hours of Bible study to refute it.

The next great threat of death came in 2001. The Islamic terrorists declared war on America. In fact, when a terrorist kills someone who disbelieves in Islam, they are doing God's work. The terrorist could be awarded great honor on earth and even greater honor in heaven. An international declaration of war was on me and anyone like me, here or abroad.

While bearing the burden of the international death threat, the ongoing threat of accidents, crime, illness, and world war continued. And then, something came along that no one had any reason to expect. A worldwide pandemic. Everyone living came under the same death threat. Of course, the media dramatized the pandemic for the sake of ratings. We were in constant fear. We were unaware of what could be relied on as fact. The facts were always changing. The event became political. The event became big business. The event became polarizing for friends, family, even nations.

CONSTANT REMINDERS

Now, with this background on my personal journey of trauma, imagine a similar background for many individuals reading this story. They have them too. Even further, imagine the threat of death that children and females face. Not just the threat of death but situations almost as gruesome. Rape, molestation, abuse, bullying, kidnapping, etcetera. We can also imagine the fear we have that a loved partner may soon die, or parents have that their child may soon die. We fear our mother or father may soon die, or our best friend or a pet may soon die. Even when we hear of a well-known public figure who may die or has died, it affects us.

The trauma of death reaches people who are afraid of dying of starvation or a nagging medical condition. We fear death by drugs, alcohol, and even suicide. Death by bad weather, fires, and accidents never go away. Even when we dream, bullying, assault, and threats of death haunt us.

Living under the threat of death is something we can all relate to. The feeling may be similar to general molestation, only in this case, molestation is by subconscious thoughts of death. Molestation can be worse than abuse, worse than being bullied. Molestation has that connotation of innocence lost, innocence stolen by someone older, someone who takes perverse advantage of the innocent. And like molestation, even if we're aware that thoughts of death distress us, we can't talk about it. Death is not a pleasant subject. Death is disturbing, depressing, and turns to dread. Just don't talk.

Still, the molestation by thoughts of death persists. We are constantly reminded we are going to die. It may come today, tomorrow, next week, next month, or next year. It's stalking us, and we will never get away. It has a hundred disguises. A fall, an auto accident, a medical condition, a criminal, a mentally impaired friend, a spouse, or a lover. It may be some demise we don't anticipate occurring but begrudgingly admit it could be occurring right now.

In the days before radio, television, and the internet, people relied on word-of-mouth communication, letter writing, and the mail system. Thoughts of death didn't have the incessant reminders we have today. Today, being well-informed means paying attention to local news, regional news, and international news. News media outlets have strong incentives to attract and hold attention. Bad news is much more attention-getting than good news. You've probably heard the phrase *"If it bleeds, it leads."* Highlights on drama, suspense, and tension help ratings.

You remember the pandemic beginning in 2020. There were daily death counts. You may be next. Tune in tomorrow for urgent information you need to stay alive.

When we turn away for a reprieve from all the bad news, we have programs featuring death-defying acts of ability, sport, and adventure. Death is mocked. Or we turn to programming that *intentionally* scares us to death—or features a lot of mayhem and death—for entertainment. *It's like having the eyes of God.* We can witness death without any direct participation.

Is the constant molestation by thoughts of death causing insensitivity to death? Probably, perhaps on a minor scale. It is more likely hypersensitivity is being repressed. In this case, it causes underlying stress. Underlying stress has a way of manifesting itself in unhealthy ways. So, what can we do to minimize or stop the molestation? How much control do we have?

Good question. Especially when we may be aware of a particularly troubling verse in the New Testament Book of Hebrews:

> Forasmuch then as the children are partakers of flesh and blood, he also himself likewise took part of the same; that through death he might destroy him that had the power of death, that is, the devil; And deliver them who through fear of death were all their lifetime subject to bondage (Hebrews 2:14-15).

The devil has the power of death. That is an underlying feeling prominent in most churches and even outside the church.

The Bible? The church? When speaking of molestation by death, where do you find more death per square inch than anywhere else in the world? THE BIBLE! Now, what?

Yes, the Bible may be further molestation. *On the other hand, the Bible, as a figurative molester, is telling you ahead of molesting you that your repulsive experience prepares you to avoid a far worse experience in the future.* This requires your trust. This requires your cooperation. This requires your understanding that the experience is relative to your inauthentic identity, not your authentic identity. The experience is

Roleplaying. It's a temporary ordeal. It is not an assault on your one and only identity. Your exposure to death is relevant to the big picture. Without a big picture that provides an adequate reason for the molestation by death, the molestation enhances—not softens—death.

HELPLESSNESS OF ONLY ONE LIFE TO LIVE

Worldometers.info and other second-by-second online counters display deaths (and other statistics) from multiple sources. You see how many people are dying this instant from abortions, alcohol, or malnutrition. Other categories allow the ability to compare and contrast reasons for death. In a sense, this is similar to seeing a global presentation of death infinitely broader than the Bible presentation.

The Bible isolates examples of death for our edification. The world counters isolate examples of death for our interest. Knowing the number of suicides, homicides, or abortions should be of interest to assist in addressing responses to the numbers.

Here are three things to consider:

1) Be aware that Satan does not directly hold the power of death over every individual. God has absolute authority over death. Satan and his Second-Class Angels only act as God allows. Death is the result of Adam and Eve's error in the Garden of Eden. We inherit death from them. The Demonstration of Free Will is the causal factor of why we die. *This would still be the case if Satan and his devils did nothing. All of us have set in motion everything needed to continue death. Satan's power is in using our circumstances against us.* This contributes to the stress of death.

2) Jesus Christ conquered death. He became a human being, led a sinless life, let Himself be killed, and was raised from death to guarantee our eternal life.

3) According to the images presented by Connecting The Dots Of Identity, our Super-Spiritual Identities (SSIDs) are in Paradise before the foundation of the world. This is our authentic identity. Presently, we are Roleplayers demonstrating the effects of Free Will initiated by Adam Eve. This Demonstration of Free will leads to death. We are actors forced into a role, but it's only a temporary deadly role.

The helplessness of having only ONE LIFE seems to be the driving force of molestation by death, the stress of death, and the escapism of death.

The medium of art, CD1/CD2, portrays an image that may give us hope for a SECOND LIFE.

This second life considers the present life under the constant threat of death and defines it as inauthentic. Being inauthentic, the stress of death loses impact. The second life, having the new position of authentic identity, is the life that relieves the stress of an inauthentic identity. My unauthentic identity rightly deserves stress. It is a demonstration of the error Adam and Eve made. All of humanity inherited death.

However, this life forced upon us by heredity, environment, and circumstance is simply Roleplaying. Being male or female, black or white, good-looking, or unattractive is a role dumped in our lap. We didn't choose our parents, our race, or our intellect. It's unfair, haphazard, and frustrating. Science says it's the best we can expect from such a phenomenon as life. The good news and the bad news is that everything ends at death. *Religion has a similar explanation but adds there will be pie in the sky for some and the depths of hell for others in an afterlife.*

Apart from those presumptuous scientific and religious points of view comes *Connecting the Dots of Identity*. If, as MARVI-RPIA illustrates, we are all safe in Paradise, then life is infinitely more bearable. God is back on His throne after WE took Him off. We know, absolutely without question, that if God is God, His Life-Plan-A is 100 times better than the MARVI-RPIA Life-Plan-B. Plan B is SUPER, but it does have holes in it. If you and others contribute to this Christian Reformed Impression art project, we can patch the holes and beautify our environment. How to contribute?

Read *Connecting the Dots of Identity* books.

Share *Connecting the Dots of Identity* books.

Create MARVI-RPIA-type impressions of your own.

Establish MARVI-RPIA-type Image Galleries.

POSTSCRIPT

In that last paragraph, the initial words were not “Plan B is SUPER.” The initial words were Plan B is drop-dead gorgeous. Why would that be a bad phrase? The word dead. It's like “heart-stopping” or “killer.” Why use death words for something that's good? Death words have been downplayed, and the offensive connotation somewhat mitigated. But it's still deadweight. No, sorry, but it's still the unsolvable problem lingering in our subconscious.

CHAPTER 27

MOLESTED BY DEATH—PART 2

The data tells us *150,000 people died yesterday, 150,000 people will die today, and 150,000 people will die tomorrow.* They die of stroke, diabetes, and heart conditions. They die from auto accidents, homicide, and suicide. They die in 100 different ways, some labeled unknown. We know this, even though there is no daily death count on the news shows. We really don't want to know. The media knows you don't want to know. But certain deaths are brought to your attention. It's politics. Its ratings. It's controlling public perception.

Underneath the certainty that we will die—maybe tomorrow, maybe next month, or maybe next year—is a nagging sensation. This is all insane. Life is insane. I am insane. *To think about not having control over my own life, that someone can take my life from me any day of the week and I have no say so, makes me furious.* I'm frustrated. I'm fearful. So, I push it out of my mind. However, there are things I can do that minimize the feeling of helplessness. I can live in a safe neighborhood. I can practice safety protocols. I can be alert and project an awareness of my surroundings.

But what about other people? What about those of us who don't or can't improve from the conditions of heredity, environment, and experiences? These people occupy positions on the so-called Insanity Chart mentioned in Chapter 17. Near the bottom of the chart are people who have committed suicide, are planning suicide, or are suffering the consequences of attempted suicide. Those contemplating suicide, we could say, belong in the category of an insane person, even if it's temporary insanity.

Other people on such an insanity chart may include people we hardly ever see. They are not in public very much. They might be said to be those who "self-medicate" or require prescription medication to function adequately on a regular basis. This would include any of the many legal substances or illegal substances available.

Insane people on the chart are seen as dangers to society. Their concern for others may be minimal. We know people who are suicidal are extremely dangerous because they will kill themselves and possibly others without feeling. But people who are insane but don't acknowledge their insanity are not as much a danger to themselves as they are a danger to others.

By the way, the same could be said for those considered "unsane" on the Insanity Chart. They denounce moral objectivity. There is no God. We are God.

A woman who has no qualms about abortion—killing her baby—should be considered insane. A large portion of the world vehemently disagrees. Abortion is not insanity. In abortion there's nothing human, nothing alive, no person is being killed. Abortion is a medical procedure regarding the mother's body. Abortion is simply a personal medical decision between the patient and the medical professional.

In the case of abortion, the definition of insanity does not apply. This is simply a case of individual rights. *God is not first. Family is not first. Other persons are not first. I am first.* Self-interests must always have an essential primary status. This is discretionary and recognized in almost every country in the world.

Anyone who has had an abortion, thinking about abortion, or is pro-abortion isn't insane by common definitions. The Insanity Chart is only a simplistic way to show how closely related suicide, poor judgment, and self-centeredness are. It also defines UN-sanity.

On charts showing the leading causes of death worldwide, *abortion is not listed. When abortion is listed, it is the number one cause of death worldwide.* The number two cause of death worldwide is heart disease. The top ten causes of death are linked to poor medical health conditions. Suicide and homicide come in around numbers fifteen and sixteen, depending on the source. *And suicide is TWICE the number of homicides!* Twice the number!

Apologies to those affected by abortion. Abortion was singled out as an example of how insanity could be applied where we wouldn't normally apply it. Insanity levels on an insanity chart apply to many other people we're all familiar with. Suicide and homicide are rather obvious contenders for insane persons. Add to the list people who:

- continue interpersonal toxic relationships;
- engage in risky, dangerous behaviors;
- advocate and follow certain political ideologies;
- abuse drugs, alcohol, and other products with impunity;
- extreme hoarders;
- child/adult molesters; and
- Many more.

Being insane is not meant to be pejorative. Being insane is simply a state of mental impairment. It may be momentary. It may be temporary. It may be a gradual loss of rational thought processes over time. No one is immune to doing stupid things here and there. We're not always 100 percent correct on everything. The point is to get away from name-calling. *Simply calling someone (or something) insane isn't helpful. They say the same about you.* Instead, let's isolate imagery that highlights momentary, temporary, or prolonged states of mental impairment.

Here is the Insanity Chart again from Chapter 17:

INSANITY CHART

SANE

The status of Pre-Life Elect individuals (Holy Spirit Identity-HSID) who possess a Christian worldview while continuing the Demonstration of Free Will through heredity, environment, and experience. They affirm objective morality as the standard of thinking and behaving based on the transcendent, universal, top-down imperative from God of the Bible. The sane include people who are Holy Spirit immature, spiritually minded people who have yet to receive the Holy Spirit, and people whose mental impairment prevents them from consistent Christian participation.

UNSANE

People who ascribe to atheists, agnostics, and non-Christian worldviews. They are spiritually blind but broadly mentally competent. Their profile is a cynical, derisive, contemptible view of objective morality. They reject the standard of thinking and behaving based on the transcendent, universal, top-down imperative from God of the Bible. They are against godliness unless God overrides their Free Will. They portray the Demonstration of Free Will through heredity, environment, and experience. (See Blind Eyes Chart)

INSANE

Group A: The group of people who are 100 percent human that suffers mental impairment from heredity, environment, and experience. They may be sane, adult Christians, but in general, they are mentally irresponsible. Additionally, the unsane also may suffer insanity from the effects of heredity, environment, and experience.

Group B: The group of people who are less than 100 percent human. Their mental identity also suffers the effects of heredity, environment, and experience. These are most likely ancestors of the Nephilim.

INSANITY LEVELS ON THE SANENESS SCALE:

Level 0: Inconclusive.

Level 1: Those who show poor judgment on many issues though they share agreement with sane persons on particular issues.

Level 2: Delusional. Persons who are conniving, untrustworthy, and immoral. Showing limited empathy for anyone but themselves or their group. Risk of danger.

Level 3: The simpleminded, slow, and easily influenced. They exercise poor judgment. Risk of danger.

Level 4: Unless they are medicated, they don't cope well with reality. Poor social skills. Risk of danger.

Level 5: People who have limited freedom, under guardianship, or care of a responsible person. Danger.

Level 6: Institutionalized. Those with limited self-awareness, who can't discern right from wrong. Danger.

Level 7: Dangerous to their own person and others. Moody. Irrational. Unstable. High risk of danger.

Level 8: Attempted suicide. Suicide prone. On life support/coma. High risk of danger.

Level 9: Committed suicide.

Level 10—Nephilim ancestor. Their thoughts and actions are characteristic of inhuman behavior. Not 100 percent human. High risk of danger.

We all know people are crazy. There is great diversity in how people think and behave. In trying to discover an underlying reason for what makes them this way, nothing seems to quite satisfy. When setting aside the distinct case of mental disability, what might the Insanity Chart offer? If a person is sane, if a person is reasonable, it's because they follow the Christian objective moral standard. This makes sense if God is the standard of morality. They're not necessarily doing what THEY think is right. It's what GOD says is right that matters.

But what if most of the world is NOT Christian? What if atheists, agnostics, nonreligious people, and non-Christians comprise a larger group than Christians? Are Christians authorized to define sanity? Are most people sane and Christians insane? Unsanity loses its significance.

But that doesn't really matter. Unsanity is just a term to show a contrast between objective and subjective morality. What matters is who has the credentials to define what is objective morality—what is right and wrong. That would be Jesus Christ. He has ALL the credentials and the ONLY credentials ever demonstrated. We know this from oral tradition, written tradition, and scientific discovery. Find out for yourself; don't rely on others.

The issue of God failing to be a moral standard goes something like this:

God hates, God punishes, and God kills. God loved Jacob and God hated Esau. Good people suffer evil and bad people are rewarded. God is nowhere around as babies die, fires and hurricanes destroy, and war wipes out thousands of people. This can't be considered good moral character if God is omnipresent, omnipotent, and omniscient.

There's another angle. It's not all insanity. It's not all chaos. It's Free Will. It's inauthentic identity. It's what happens when the Serpent, Adam, and Eve exercise Free Will to disobey God. The animals, the people, and the environment became cursed. The consolation is that God saved everyone BEFORE He created everyone.

This is not conventional theology. That's why it takes artistic expression to paint a picture of a Plan B. The Plan B is a crude image of God's Plan A. But Plan B may help people see that all is not what it appears to be. *Spiritual reality may be the true reality.*

In a certain sense, it's unfair to paint people as insane who simply think and behave as heredity, environment, and experience dictates. We all qualify as insane (or unsane) as we demonstrate our Free Will to live as best we can. This only changes if and when God intercedes to make us a new creature.

You believe in abortion. You are insane. You do not believe in abortion. You are insane also. You molested ten children over the course of eight years. You're insane. You organized five chapters of Big Brothers and Big Sisters in your state. You're insane too. You're a top-level person in a drug cartel. You're insane. You're a top prosecutor who disrupts drug organizations across the world. You're also insane.

You only become sane when coming to the state of being "born-again." The Holy Spirit comes into your life verifying you are a Pre-Life Elect person. *The made-up term "unsane" is to move away from the mental impairment connotation associated with "insanity." Unsane people are mentally competent but spiritually blind.* Like a suicidal person, unsane people are a threat to themselves and to others; they just don't realize it. They are Roleplayers of Free Will who have yet to be born-again by the Holy Spirit.

This is the part of life that molests sane persons. The unsane and the insane bring death all around us. It's the same way of life that we, as sane persons, formerly lived. We would love to rescue the insane and unsane from their plight, but salvation is not in our hands. This has already been accomplished before the world was created. God uses us as a witness for the Good News of Jesus Christ, but until God opens their eyes, they don't see.

Okay. So, it seems that insanity (or unsanity) is a range of people thinking and behaving "normally" before God comes into their life. Secondly, we're subconsciously affected by death.

Yes. Being aware of death statistics assists us in having a better perspective on what death means to us. From this, our worldview directs how we manage life.

In understanding why so many people die from diseases—number one to number ten on most lists—we might say it's because of heredity, environment, and experiences. This is what life has given you. Why fight it? Atheism says it's pointless. Life has no meaning, and it will end abruptly. Theists say there's pie in the sky. God loves you. Just accept Him.

And then . . . *Connecting the Dots of Identity*. If you are less than 100 percent human, no wonder you think and behave the way you do. Your ancestors were Nephilim. It doesn't mean you're doomed to Hell. But it does help explain why some people seem so inhumane.

On the other hand, if you simply Roleplay your heredity, environment, and experiences without God opening your spiritual eyes, it becomes apparent why you think and behave the way you do. Otherwise, your life will change or is changing so that you are a new person—one of the Pre-Life Elect.

As subconscious thoughts of death molest you, whether sane, unsane, or insane, your inauthentic identity must manage the underlying uneasiness. We try to learn from others what they have done that could help us improve. It begins with the worldview we have adopted as our spiritual identity (SID) went from SID-Neutral to SID-Positive or SID-Negative. The process starts in childhood and continues through the adult years of life.

Gradually, the acceptance of theism, atheism, or agnosticism begins to form. The hard push from heredity, environment, and experience accentuates the Demonstration of Free Will.

POSTSCRIPT

In the meantime, the news reports will continue with the latest tragedy of sudden and unexpected death. The pressing question starts with ways in which the tragedy could have been prevented.

Was the tragedy a weather-related accident? Was it negligence of some kind? Was the event a factor of a mechanical flaw, a medical emergency, or the victim of malicious intent?

Malicious intent. Think about that for a few minutes. This relates to molestation by death. Malicious intent such as murder, war, terrorism, and insanity. When you consider how the incidence of sudden and unexpected death might be decreased, one place to start may be insanity.

At certain levels of insanity (or unsanity), no amount of communication is effective. An insane person or group of insane persons will commit acts of mayhem no matter what. This group includes terrorists, religious groups, nonreligious groups, and criminals. Whether they use guns, chemicals, bombs, fire, or other agents, the goal is manipulation or destruction.

Considering the category of sane persons, how do we, as sane persons, prevent the next tragedy from showing up in the news cycle? The usual talking points have been gun control, politics, and mental health.

Gun Control. Guns are not the problem. Guns are related to the problem. There will always be bigger and better guns, more long-range guns, and guns that don't use bullets. As policymakers apply rules and regulations based on national ideology, debates ensue for a strategy that appears meaningful for the nation. In the background, we see other weaponry gaining ground. Cyber weaponry, biological weaponry, water, food, and financial weaponry.

Insane people don't understand the principle of an armed citizenry. Some unsane understand but are spiritually blind, intentionally blind, or unintentionally blind (Blind Eyes Chart). Sane people may also be blind, but in the main, they never want to be in a position where weaponry for personal use is prohibited.

Politics. As political party's direct legislative, judicial, and executive branches oversee the safety of the citizenry, the role of politics is to reflect the will of the people. But the people are weak and uninformed. It takes strong, informed leaders to administer the nation's interests. They must placate special interests, apply hidden agendas, and evade answers to yes or no questions. A nation's political system is as good as the people in charge of staffing it. Unsanity seems to rule. Subjective morality. Relativism. Just win.

Mental Health. When life no longer matters, it suggests that every effort to find meaning has failed. It's possible to restore meaning if the agent is not mentally impaired—insane. If the agent is unsane, this is the province of the Holy Spirit and the sane to help open the unsane's spiritual eyes. In the meantime, the province of mental health has been the healthcare professionals and the pharmaceutical companies. We can "buy time" by treating symptoms rather than the cure. But how much time can we buy? Do we know the cure? In the meantime, being molested by death continues as world affairs offer no promising solutions.

Connecting the Dots of Identity doesn't stop the continuous molestation. CD1/CD2 is meant to console you. Molestation comes with the Demonstration of Free Will. Death is all around, all the time. The Bible is filled with death. Though we are subject to death, death is NOT the end. Death has been conquered by Jesus Christ. Our Roleplay inauthentic identity dies but not our true authentic identity God saved before the world was created. This is part of God's magnificent Plan A. CD1/CD2 is an inferior Plan B. It's just another way of proclaiming the Great News about the Good News.

CHAPTER 28

MOLESTED BY LIFE

In times past, you had to bear the anguish, grief, and despair of being molested. Not just sexually molested but molested by experiences. Experiences that you may not even remember so clearly. Other experiences are as fresh as yesterday. Being molested by life is what happens to you through no real fault of your own. You are just being yourself, and bad things come along and assault you.

For example, a person takes advantage of you. Your family takes advantage of you. Your job, your neighbors, your friends. Your church, your school, your city take advantage of you. You didn't do anything wrong. Someone did wrongly to you. Sometimes it's a matter of miscommunication. Sometimes it's a matter of prejudice. Sometimes it's a matter of hate, negligence, or just plain stupidity.

The reason to add an additional chapter regarding molestation is to address a recurring theme in society. The theme is loss of quality of life due to some past unresolved trauma. The trauma lingers and is always subconsciously affecting other aspects of your life. Only when the particular trauma is directly addressed is there a realization of how deep the trauma actually is.

As *Connecting the Dots of Identity* portrays, your life is more than what has happened to you since you were born. Don't let your inauthentic identity define your present life. What happened in the past is past. It is bad. It is miserable. It does truly hurt. *However, it is not really a part of you. It is part of the Roleplayer you. It's Free Will.* It's Roleplaying your Free Will while the Free Will of others occurs. Once we come to realize we may be an elect person of God, we have a second adventure of life. This present life is not our only life experience.

From this point of view, it doesn't matter as much what has happened to us. It is not an assault on us. It is an assault on a Roleplayer, an inauthentic identity. We move on. We know life is a demonstration of Free Will. Once the demo is over, we will assume our authentic identity in Paradise. The future is separate from the present and secured by the Perfect Roleplayer Jesus Christ.

Jesus's role was to redeem mankind. He was promised by God to correct the error of Adam and Eve through procreation. Jesus Christ arrived on the scene. He lived a perfect life that Adam and Eve did not live. He let Himself be killed so He could conquer death by resurrection. Jesus taught that we are spiritual creatures in a temporary physical form. Jesus taught us to sacrifice our temporary life. Be an example to others. Love your neighbor. Love your enemy. Work with the Holy Spirit to help open the eyes of the spiritually blind.

Jesus confirmed the authenticity of scripture. He was the embodiment of God's holy words. All the words of the Bible are the words God wants us to have. Scripture teaches throughout the Bible the principle of Election and Predestination. *Connecting the Dots of Identity* is not a new age vision, a new message from God, or a new church denomination. It's based on an impression from scripture that we can trust the historicity of Jesus Christ. We can trust we were truly saved before God created the world.

Connecting the Dots of Identity is the Great News about the Good News. Election and Predestination mean God has saved us before we were even born. *Connecting the Dots of Identity* helps illustrate this image that has never been seen. This is the Pre-Life Elect identity God has guaranteed. *Admittedly, this pre-life identity is an impression, but it is an impression that has precedence. A hundred verses from Holy Scripture (Connecting the Dots of Identity-1, Chapter 6) indicate God saved persons before the foundation of the world.* As an artist, it is not forbidden to render this image if the image is not submitted as doctrine. It isn't. It's submitted as art.

GET OVER IT

You've probably heard that you can't drive your car while looking in the rear-view mirror. And you've probably heard of Lot's wife in the Old Testament Book of Genesis. She was told by the angel not to look back after leaving Sodom. She looked back and turned into a pillar of salt. Among other things, salt was a staple in those days as a food preservative. *Don't preserve the Past. Detach yourself.* That was not you.

It's heartbreaking to see how devastated people are by life's circumstances. They feel their lives are ruined beyond repair. They make matters worse by dwelling on revenge. They make matters worse by debilitating self-hatred. They make matters worse by reliving the trauma over and over. *You've got to let it go. You've got to get over it.* It's not helpful to keep it alive. Box it up and discard it as another example of Free Will Roleplay. Do your best. Don't take it so personally.

But you object. You say I was hurt. I will never be the same. I CAN'T get over it.

And you may continue to be "damaged goods." One way to resolve it is to see it as happening to someone who is not you. That was a past you. Not the current you. The present you are aware that the past you were a victim of heredity, environment, and experience. *The present you are able to disassociate the past you from the present you.* Presently, identity is NOT rooted in the recent past or present. It is rooted in the future. This is the authentic identity in Paradise. Today is a temporary demonstration of global Free Will. Everyone is affected by everybody else's Free Will. I don't have to take it so hard. I'm just a character who's been given a role to play. I didn't choose the character. I didn't want the role. But I'm forced to be in the drama of life.

Another objection to letting go and moving on in life is the resentment against the molesters. *How can those who cause harm join with me in the afterlife residing in Paradise?* That doesn't seem right.

It isn't right. The people who are in Paradise have no direct connection to people who Roleplay bad people. In Roleplay, we are all varying degrees of bad. It's a function of Free Will imposed on us all the way back to Adam and Eve. *The SSIDs in Paradise were NEVER Roleplayers.* The worst Roleplayers who transition to Paradise were only playing a role. They were set up. They were set up by heredity, environment, and circumstance. The only reason they continue their evil ways is that the Holy Spirit has not met them. Only then will they be born-again—begin the change to a new creature. The reason the Holy Spirit does NOT meet them is to show no one is able to become a new creature unless God intercedes. Mankind will ALWAYS choose its own will.

So, Hitler, Mao, and Stalin won't hug and kiss you in Paradise. When these evil ones die, if they are 100 percent human, *their Roleplay ends. That identity perishes. It doesn't go anywhere.* If these evil ones are not 100 percent human, they cease to exist. They have no soul, no spirit. They don't transfer to an afterlife. If they were angels who assumed human form, they join Satan and his demons in Hell.

The people who cause us harm may be sane or unsane. It may be the case of temporary insanity, prolonged insanity, or permanent insanity. They don't know what they're doing. Unless God intercedes to cause their rebirth, they continue being the result of heredity, environment, and experience—just like you. Our resentment at being harmed should be tempered by the many examples we have in scripture.

(1) Adam and Eve's son Abel is an Elect person. He's killed by his own brother Cain (Genesis 4:8).

(2) Lot's wife is judged unworthy to live yet both his soon-to-be incestuous daughters are worthy to live (Genesis 19:26, 36).

(3) Naboth is framed and murdered by Queen Jezebel for not surrendering his garden to the wicked King Ahab (1 Kings 21:13).

(4) John the Baptist is beheaded for being a righteous minister to the kingdom he is minister to (Matthew 14:10).

(5) Bathsheba is seduced, raped, and impregnated; and her husband is murdered by the same great man of God—King David (2 Samuel 11).

These are only five of innumerable cases that describe inequities in life. We don't get to judge what is right, what is fair, or what is supposed to happen. Life is unpredictable. It's cause and effect. It's an evolving drama of Free Will characters.

> And Cain talked with Abel his brother: and it came to pass, when they were in the field, that Cain rose up against Abel his brother, and slew him (Genesis 4:8).

> But his wife looked back from behind him, and she became a pillar of salt . . . Thus were both the daughters of Lot with child by their father (Genesis 19:26, 36).

> And there came in two men, children of Belial, and sat before him: and the men of Belial witnessed against him, even against Naboth, in the presence of the people, saying, Naboth did blaspheme God and the king. Then they carried him forth out of the city, and stoned him with stones, that he died (1 Kings 21:13).

> And he sent, and beheaded John in the prison (Matthew 14:10).

> And David sent messengers, and took her; and she came in unto him, and he lay with her; for she was purified from her uncleanness: and she returned unto her house. And the woman conceived, and sent and told David, and said, I am with child... And he wrote in the letter, saying, Set ye Uriah in the forefront of the hottest battle, and retire ye from him, that he may be smitten, and die (2 Samuel 11:4-5, 15).

DOOMED ROLEPLAYERS

Don't take life personally. It's only a role. It's temporary. So what you were molested? So what you were bullied? You were humiliated, embarrassed, and ridiculed. You were beaten, starved, and deprived of your childhood. You didn't matter. You didn't fit in. You were ready to give up. Don't. You're not the only one. Millions of people are in these same groups. This life is not all there is. Your identity is not what it appears to be. The best people in the world have bad things happen to them. The worst people in the world have good things happen to them.

We should mention a few of those who were not good people. They also were Roleplayers, simply living out the dictates of heredity, environment, and experience. We have no apparent indication the Holy Spirit interceded on their behalf. *Their life has damnation written all over it.*

Some of the “bad” Roleplayers in Scripture:

Goliath

> And there went out a champion out of the camp of the Philistines, named Goliath, of Gath, whose height was six cubits and a span (1 Samuel 17:4).

> Therefore David ran, and stood upon the Philistine, and took his sword, and drew it out of the sheath thereof, and slew him, and cut off his head therewith. And when the Philistines saw their champion was dead, they fled (1 Samuel 17:51).

Pharaoh

> And the Lord hardened the heart of Pharaoh King of Egypt, and he pursued after the children of Israel: and the children of Israel went out with a high hand (Exodus 14:8).

> And the waters returned, and covered the chariots, and the horsemen, and all the host of Pharaoh that came into the sea after them; there remained not so much as one of them (Exodus 14:28).

Korah

> And the sons of Eliab; Nemuel, and Dathan, and Abiram. This is that Dathan and Abiram, which were famous in the congregation, who strove against Moses and against Aaron in the company of Korah, when they strove against the Lord: And the earth opened her mouth, and swallowed them up together with Korah, when that company died, what time the fire devoured two hundred and fifty men: and they became a sign (Numbers 26:9-10).

Jezebel

> Wherefore they came again, and told him. And he said, This is the word of the Lord, which he spake by his servant Elijah the Tishbite, saying, In the portion of Jezreel shall dogs eat the flesh of Jezebel: And the carcass of Jezebel shall be as dung upon the face of the field in the portion of Jezreel; so that they shall not say, This is Jezebel (2 Kings 9:36-37).

King Zedekiah

> And the army of the Chaldees pursued after the king, and overtook him in the plains of Jericho: and all his army were scattered from him. So they took the king, and brought him up to the king of Babylon to Riblah; and they gave judgment upon him. And they slew the sons of Zedekiah before his eyes, and put out the eyes of Zedekiah, and bound him with fetters of brass, and carried him to Babylon (2 Kings 25: 5-7).

These Roleplayers might say life was very unfair to them. What chance did they have? Did God elect them before the foundations of the world? Did they know anything about being born-again? Do they have a Pre-Life Elect identity awaiting them in Paradise?

We don't have to worry about that. God took care of everyone before He created everyone. Reformed theology teaches this. But Reformed theology doesn't answer questions any better than other denominations. *To make matters worse, it confounds inquirers with the absence of Free Will but the certainty of Hell.*

Christian Reformed Impressionism comes in with imagery that paints over Reformed theology. Initially, it may not appear much better. Art isn't always a model of clarity and beauty.

TRUE ANCESTRY

Life that lasts for only a day is created for a reason. It matters or it would not be created. Think positive. No matter how bad things are or seem to be, God is omnipresent. He is always near. We must trust He will make things right even when it's surely all wrong.

Some of you may say I will trust God, but I don't know what Roleplay character I am. I don't know my father. I don't know my mother. My ancestral line is undiscovered. I don't know thc history of my ethnicity. I want to know more about my inauthentic identity.

These pressing issues are distractions from your real identity. Your ancestors of record, of importance, of historical value, are a very limited group. They are:

1) Mister and Missus Noah

2) Mister and Missus Ham

3) Mister and Missus Shem

4) Mister and Missus Japheth

And one other group has a bearing on identity.

5) Mister Angel and Missus Human Female (Nephilim)

Everyone born afterward has hereditary relevance to these groups of people. Adam and Eve would be the primary relatives of hereditary distinction, but that was compromised by the angels producing offspring with the daughters of Adam and Eve.

Why would God allow human beings to be corrupted by evil angels? We must get the right answer from God. We could guess and say angels and humans share similar identities.

There are two groups of flawless beings who will never fall:

1) First-Class Angels who did not exercise Free Will to disobey God.

2) Super-Spiritual Identities (SSIDs) who were saved before the world was created. They are the Elect.

The flawed groups include:

- Humans who are alive but are flawed living creatures.
- Humans who have died and await the Last Day.
- Second-Class Angels who live but are doomed to Hell when the Demonstration of Free Will ends.
- Third-Class Angels who are relegated to the Abyss. This group left Heaven to marry human females in the interest of creating an angel redeemer.

The violation of God's natural procreation order led to a corrupted planet of beings. God destroyed all but eight people.

The Demonstration of Free Will is preserved as Noah and his family repopulate the earth. By the nature of procreation, small traces of Nephilim "material" come through the population. Inhuman thinking and inhuman behavior continue to plague humanity. This may be what can be expected when flawless living creatures have Free Will to disobey God. As bad as things come to be, and destroying all but eight people on the planet is about as bad as bad has ever been, we can still be so thankful that life has a *part two*. What we experience in *part one* of life is necessary to prove the error of choosing our own will for life rather than God's will for our life.

We shouldn't focus on woe-is-me in the here and now. We move on. We accept that we're in a demonstration of Free Will. Free Will is essential to life. All of us Free Will agents must demonstrate the error Adam and Eve made. *Adam and Eve AND the Serpent were flawless. FLAWLESS! Therefore, their error to disobey God must be conclusively and exhaustively proven wrong.*

The error of exercising Free Will to disobey God must play out. The essence of perfection in a living creature is to have autonomy. We must be free to think and behave apart from God's intrusion on our ability to be independent of Him. *Give us liberty or give us death.* That may be how Eve and Adam eventually felt. There must be no restriction on our knowledge. Why can't we know good and evil? Every intelligent creature loves to learn, loves to improve themselves through advancement in knowledge.

Once it's sufficiently proven that God knows best for every flawless living creature—whether angel or human—then the Demonstration of Free Will ends. This coincides with the error Second and Third-Class Angels made to exercise Free Will to disobey God. A group of angels observed Adam and Eve challenging God. God allowed Adam and Eve to die but prolonged their lives and also promised an Antidote for their misbehavior.

The angels took a chance God would have the same mercy on them. First-Class Angels did not disobey God. Second-Class Angels, Satan, and group did disobey God but didn't leave Heaven to seek an angel redeemer by procreation with human females. Abaddon (Apollyon) and Third-Class Angels did undertake the “daredevil” mission.

All to suggest that no matter what happens to you, or has happened to you, it’s not really you. You are only a temporary Roleplayer of Free Will. The real you are in Paradise reserved for the End of the Demonstration of Free Will. Your *real* name. Your *real* identity.

For now, be mentally patient. Be mentally strong. Your body is not you. Your experience is not you. You are safe before you were born. A hundred Bible verses say as much (CD1-Chapter 6).

CHAPTER 29

QUESTIONS AND ANSWERS 1-10

Question 1: If Pre-Life Elect individuals exist outside time and space, why are we forced to live the Error of Free Will Roleplayers—life after life, year after year?

Answer: Ask that question to Second-Class Angels (Lucifer and group), Third-Class Angels (Abaddon and group), the Serpent in Eden, and Adam and Eve. They were highly motivated and made a commitment to pursue the interests of a flawless creature rather than the interests of God. This was their Free Will to do. An attribute of a flawless living creature is to be autonomous from God. God denied unlimited Free Will but granted restricted Free Will.

Why they chose to exercise Free Will is something only a flawless creature can answer. We are all flawed creatures. Our answers are notwithstanding. The fact that the Free Will Demonstration continues may indicate the necessity of observable history to a specific degree with innumerable lives. And maybe your life, or my life, will end the Demonstration.

The Free Will Demonstration also included the First-Class Angels–those who refused to exercise Free Will to pursue their own interests above God's interest for their lives. They observed the Serpent, Adam, and Eve fall. They observed Second-Class and Third-Class Angels approve of the choice made in the Garden by the flawless human creatures. Apparently, an angel's initial choice of yay or nay is final. They have no Mediator, Fail-safe, or Redeemer.

In the case of the Pre-Life Elect individuals, they are strictly determined. No Free Will test or observation of Free Will drama exists for them. They will never fall.

So, Roleplay continues as conclusive proof that Free Will leads to death unless the Holy Spirit intercedes. How many lives prove this? How many years? Will human beings devolve to the last seconds of mass self-destruction before God brings Judgment Day? Maybe.

For now, we tend the garden of human beings as Adam and Eve were responsible to do in Eden. We participate in the Demonstration of Free Will, exhibiting the dynamics of heredity, environment, and experiences. From this comes religious views, nonreligious views, and anti-religious views.

Roleplayers function as proof of lives that receive and do not receive the Holy Spirit. No one chooses God no matter what the circumstances, no matter the human population figures, and no matter what period in history. Unless God intercedes before death, at death, or afterward, no one will come to God.

This is the absolute beauty of God saving us before He created the world. Imparting the Holy Spirit to some of us and not all of us shows the stark contrast in identity. The embryo, the newborn, and the toddler who can't choose aren't excluded. God takes all the action. For those who could choose but won't, God overrules their Free Will. For others, He doesn't do so. That doesn't mean they're damned. If they're 100 percent human, they have a corresponding Super-Spiritual Identity in Paradise. If they are not 100 percent human, they cease to exist. Oblivion.

Question 2: Do those in Heaven look down on us, are aware of us, know us, help us?

Answer: It's funny that Christian and non-Christian etiquette often implies people who die are in a better place, looking down from Heaven. However, it's not unreasonable to assume the world is mostly non-Christian. There is no real Heaven, or real Hell, and any god you create is God for you. The Christian position is that no one in Heaven except God has access to us. The heavenly hosts have access, but only by permission or direction from God. No deceased Free Will Roleplayers have access to us. No Pre-Life Elect (SSID) have access to earthly affairs.

If deceased persons have access to earthly affairs, wouldn't that be the height frustration? Not only that, but it would also be impertinent, obscene, and intrusive to observe earthly affairs from Heaven. Nothing constructive could come from such awareness. The Trinity and all the angels are the observers of consequence, not you and me.

The theme of CD1/CD2 is don't look back on who you are. It's inauthentic. Your heredity, environment, and experiences formulate who you come to be. You're here, but it could all end tomorrow. CD1/CD2 imagery is an authentic identity in the future based on Election-Predestination from scripture. Looking back is constructive in the sense it shows the Demonstration of Free Will. Given the images of Determinism as portrayed by SSIDs and First-Class Angels, Free Will is a devastating error. The Serpent, Eve, Adam, Second-Class Angels, and Third-Class Angels prove this.

You probably remember what happened with Lot's wife (Genesis 19). The angels rescued her from the cities of destruction. She was safe in Zoar! And then, she looks back—against the instructions of the angels. Do you connect any dots about why looking down from Heaven isn't good?

> And it came to pass, when they had brought them forth abroad, that he said, Escape for thy life; look not behind thee, neither stay thou in all the plain; escape to the mountain, lest thou be consumed . . . Haste thee, escape thither; for I cannot do anything till thou become thither. Therefore the name of the city was called Zoar ... But his wife looked back from behind him, and she became a pillar of salt (Genesis 19: 17, 22, 26).

Question 3: Do infants go to Heaven?

Answer: No. The reason infants don't go to Heaven is that they are not infants to God. God sees whole persons, a complete identity. This includes a person before conception (Pre-life Elect and Non-Elect Roleplayers), after conception (born, stillborn, miscarried, aborted), and in the afterlife. We can only observe the identity of chronological age.

What about Jesus saying don't despise little ones because their angels behold God?

We might assume ALL angels behold God; perhaps even angels who are in the Abyss chained in darkness. Children are Roleplayers like all of us. They are complete identities, just undeveloped. We should always be mindful of them. We should always respect them as individual people in total. This must include the human identity in the womb.

> Take heed that ye despise not one of these little ones; for I say unto you, That in heaven their angels do always behold the face of my Father which is in heaven (Matthew 18:10).

Then why does Psalm 127 say children are a blessing? Happy is the man who has his quiver full of them.

> Lo, children are a heritage of the Lord: and the fruit of the womb is his reward. As arrows are in the hand of a mighty man; so are children of the youth. Happy is the man that hath his quiver full of them: they shall not be ashamed, but they shall speak with the enemies in the gate.

What if this refers to fertility? Happy is the man whose quiver (maleness) is full of them (virility). Inability or unwillingness to procreate may not be a sin, but even today it's often seen as an indication of spiritual disfavor, except when self-imposed to honor the Lord or as a result of poor health. Unhappy is the man who is infertile or suffers from sexual dysfunction. Unhappy is the man who is physically weak regarding his enemies.

We know, intuitively, that children are only a blessing in the figurative sense. It can't mean the literal sense. If children are literally a blessing, they would all grow up to be blessings. No one can curse whom God blesses. They stay blessed. In the Book of Genesis, God blesses Noah and his three sons Shem, Ham, and Japheth. Later, in the same book, Noah curses Canaan, Ham's son.

In most cases, children grow up to be examples of evil. It's their nature. They are conceived in evil. They are sinners from the womb. If God doesn't intervene, none of us would change our ways. We would continue in evil from childhood.

The blessing of children is the position that children represent in procreation. They provide the means God employs to facilitate 100 percent human Jesus Christ. He is the Blessed Child, the blessing of children.

The method of procreation is the second blessing—procreation from Adam and Eve. By this, we exemplify God's creative process of life. God creates humans. Humans create humans. Human offspring provide the Demonstration of Free Will via billions of lives. But these individual lives are obviously not all individual blessings.

Ninety-nine-point-nine percent of pastors quote Psalm 127 as children are blessings whether they have children of their own or not. On the other hand, they also affirm that most people are bound for Hell. Ministers of God's word readily acknowledge God kills children. They cite the Flood, Sodom, Gomorrah, and cities nearby. They're also forced to acknowledge the many groups of people God wiped out down to the last child and pregnant woman.

Remember when God said He would spare Sodom (and other cities) if fifty righteous were there? Are forty, or thirty, or twenty, down to ten righteous persons found in those cities? How many hundreds of people lived in those cities? How many thousands? How many children were alive in those cities? How many women were pregnant? Not even ten could be found who were considered to be a blessing? Do you say the children were indeed blessings but became martyrs? The righteous become collateral damage when in the company of great evil?

> And Abraham drew near, and said, Wilt thou also destroy the righteous with the wicked? Peradventure there be fifty righteous within the city: wilt thou also destroy and not spare the place for the fifty righteous that are therein? (Genesis 18:23-24)
>
> And he said, Oh let not the LORD be angry, and I will speak yet but this once: Peradventure ten shall be found there. And he said, I will not destroy it for ten's sake (Genesis 18:32).

Are children blessings when they kill their parents? Murder ten people and then commit suicide? Set their parents' house on fire? Are children blessings by being drug addicts, alcoholics, and thieves? Is a child a blessing when it's born with severe birth defects?

What about a curse? Are children ever a curse? Was Cain cursed by God? Canaan was cursed by Noah. Was Judas Iscariot cursed by Jesus? Elisha cursed young children and bears appeared and ravaged them.

> And he went up from thence unto Bethel: and as he was going up by the way, there came forth little children out of the city, and mocked him, and said unto him, Go up, thou bald head; go up, thou bald head. And he turned back, and looked on them, and cursed them in the name of the Lord. And there came forth two she bears out of the wood, and tare forty and two children of them (2 Kings 23-24).

The Bible has many examples of holy men whose children were not holy. Aaron's children Nadab and Abihu. Samuel's children Joel and Abijah. Eli's children Hophni and Phinehas. We read about Goliath (1 Samuel), Sihon, and Og (Deuteronomy). Were they blessings?

Think of King David (Absalom), Adam and Eve (Cain) and God Himself (Adam and Eve). Children misbehave and corrupt the meaning of blessing no matter who the parents are.

The Bible recounts a story in Mark where a child has been demon-possessed for some time.

> And they brought him unto him: and when he saw him, straightway the spirit tare him; and he fell on the ground, and wallowed foaming. And he asked his father, how long is it ago since this came unto him? And he said, of a child. And of times it hath cast him into the fire, and into the waters, to destroy him: but if thou canst do anything, have compassion on us, and help us. Jesus said unto him, if thou canst believe, all things are possible to him that believeth. And straightway the father of the child cried out, and said with tears, Lord, I believe; help thou mine unbelief. When Jesus saw that the people came running together, he rebuked the foul spirit, saying unto him, Thou dumb and deaf spirit, I charge thee, come out of him, and enter no more into him. And the spirit cried, and rent him sore, and came out of him: and he was as one dead; insomuch that many said, He is dead. But Jesus took him by the hand, and lifted him up; and he arose (Mark 9:20-27).

The Fifth Commandment to honor your mother and father regards honoring the position of motherhood and fatherhood. This is not the same as giving honor to a person who is dishonorable. That would simply honor evil. Every parent is not a blessing any more than every child is a blessing. Child blessings can fail? Can any blessing fail?

The focus is not on the person (children or parents) but on the means of procreation that brought about Jesus Christ and the Roleplayers of the Free Will Demonstration.

Traditional Christian teaching holds that, for married persons, the edict is to be fruitful and multiply. That hasn't been abrogated. So, no birth control? Family planning is against scripture? The vision of MARVI-RPIA maintains this is strictly between husband, wife, and the Lord. Considering the salvation plan is set before the world began, your role in procreation is grace, not works. God isn't dependent on you to make babies. He can raise children from stones, atheists, or artificial insemination.

> And God blessed Noah and his sons, and said unto them, be fruitful, and multiply, and replenish the earth (Genesis 9:1).

> And think not to say within yourselves, We have Abraham to our father: for I say unto you, that God is able of these stones to raise up children unto Abraham (Matthew 3:9).

> Honor thy father and thy mother, as the Lord thy God hath commanded thee; that thy days may be prolonged, and that it may go well with thee, in the land which the Lord thy God giveth thee (Deuteronomy 5:16).

> The wicked are estranged from the womb: they go astray as soon as they be born, speaking lies Psalm 58:3).

Question 4: Is there an age of accountability?

Answer: No. Age of accountability implies the age of a person when held accountable for their actions. Below a certain age, perhaps twelve years old, they are not responsible for their behavior due to physical or mental limitations. This concept is incompatible with Christian Reformed doctrine and the biblical principle of grace. There is nothing a person is, does, or thinks that determines salvation. Salvation is 100 percent grace, 0 percent works.

The fetus, the baby, and the toddler aren't considered saved or damned based on chronological age. True, they may not have opportunities to do wrong things, but salvation is not based on behavior. On top of that, everyone is CONCEIVED in sin before they are born (Glossary of Colors – Creationism/Traducianism/Designationism). Sinners all. The grace of God covers the fetus, infants, and toddlers; the mentally and physically challenged; and everyone else. They are all Roleplayers. Whether they are Non-Elect or Pre-Life Elect, we don't know, but age does not matter.

Question 5: Why did perfect creatures such as Lucifer, Serpent, Adam, and Eve sin?

Answer: The general answer is Free Will, but that doesn't constitute the absolute answer. Any answer given comes from imperfect creatures. By the way, Connecting The Dots Of Identity uses the term "flawless" creatures rather than "perfect" creatures. Only the Father, the Son, and the Holy Spirit are perfect. Flawless creatures, such as the First-Class Angels who did not sin, chose not to sin. The other flawless creatures who did sin chose to sin. On what basis did all flawless creatures execute their decisions? It would seem that the process entailed creating simulations, then evaluating simulations based on risk/reward. Or, in the case of First-Class Angels, perhaps they simply refused to speculate on Free Will and trusted God for direction in their life. We can only guess.

Connecting the Dots of Identity-1 paints detailed imagery of Lucifer, the angels, the Serpent, Adam, and Eve's transition from flawless to flaw. The Glossary of Colors also lists details.

Question 6: Did Adam and Eve consummate their marriage Pre-Fall?

Answer: No! But the Bible plainly says in Genesis that God said to be fruitful and multiply BEFORE Adam and Eve committed sin. Also, before the fall, God introduces the words father, mother, wife, and one flesh . . .

> And God blessed them, and God said unto them, be fruitful, and multiply, and replenish the earth, and subdue it: and have dominion over the fish of the sea, and over the fowl of the air, and over every living thing that moveth upon the earth (Genesis 1:28).

> Therefore shall a man leave his father and his mother, and shall cleave unto his wife: and they shall be one flesh. And they were both naked, the man and his wife, and were not ashamed. (Genesis 2:24,25)

The CD1/CD2 imagery of Adam and Eve in Eden is flawless human beings. Before the Fall, there is no need to *procreate.* No need to *replenish* and *subdue* the earth. No need for *father, mother, wife, one flesh.*

The two humans were flawless. The Garden was flawless. The Earth was flawless.

Adam and Eve were in a childlike sexual stage of innocence. They had no idea that they were naked, much less what function genitalia could have. At this point, there was no need for waste elimination. Whenever they chose to consume food, the food of the Garden was so pure it did not produce waste. Moreover, even the thick AROMA of the Garden with the magnificent Tree of Life sustained them. Flawless bodies. Flawless environment. Flawless food.

As for procreation, it was the *Fail-safe System* if human beings committed sin. In such an event, the human race would die but continue to live via procreation from the parents. Procreation would produce the Redeemer who would correct the error of sin.

If you assume consummation did occur pre-Fall, certainly, pregnancy will follow forthwith. This was God's mandate. What follows is the timeline in the Garden of Eden for Adam and Eve now shrinks. *In nine months the first child will be born.*

For Adam and Eve to consummate their marriage on day one and conception begins for Cain on day one or day two, the days of flawless life in the Garden decrease starting from nine months in the future. No children are recorded living in the Garden.

The test of the Demonstration of Free Will, exemplified by the Tree of the Knowledge of Good and Evil, is now accelerated by the arrival of baby Cain in nine months. Apparently, the splendor of the flawless Garden of Eden, flawless Adam, and flawless Eve only lasts less than a year. Sin must have occurred within the nine-month window. Pregnant Eve is deceived. Adam doesn't divorce her. They are expelled from the Garden.

Cain is born nine months and a few days after Adam and Eve were created. If Cain is born within this timeframe, he would be less than one year younger than his parents. It's a bit humorous to think when Adam is a few days old, Eve is a few days old, and nine months later, Cain is a few days old. There will come a brief three-month window when *all three are the same age.* When Cain turns terrible two years old, Adam and Eve are two years nine months old. They're all age two—a trio of terrible twos.

But wait a minute. If Cain was conceived by flawless parents, *he would be flawless*, NOT born in sin. And . . . his Free Will was still unlimited. He could obey God OR disobey God. Even outside the Garden, he could still be flawless. But . . . Cain would then be in a similar position that Adam was when confronted with Eve's transgression. Should he eat of the forbidden tree? No! He can't! The Garden is inaccessible, guarded by Cherubim. There is no return to the tree. *So, Cain can't sin by the same method as his parents.* Now what? Remain flawless? Not at all.

Cain's legacy is well known in scripture. His offering was unacceptable to God. He killed his brother Abel. He was banished from his family.

It seems unnecessarily complicated to assume sex occurred pre-Fall. It could be true. It's a popular orthodox teaching. But I'm not a pastor or a teacher. I'm an artist. I share impressions. What do you see?

> So he drove out the man; and he placed at the east of the garden of Eden Cherubims, and a flaming sword which turned every way, to keep the way of the tree of life (Genesis 3:24).

> And Adam knew Eve his wife; and she conceived, and bare Cain, and said, I have gotten a man from the Lord (Genesis 4:1).

Question 7: Were Adam and Eve Elect Roleplayers? Were they saved?

Answer: Yes! They certainly retained a portion of what they lost in the Garden of Eden, and what they possessed in the Garden was glorious, majestic, and spectacular. Their children are some indication of how well Adam and Eve represented God to them. Abel turned out well. Cain did not. Further down the ancestral line, many turned out great. Adam and Eve were still alive to influence everyone in the families for 900-plus years. This includes the families from Seth and the families from Cain. Good people and bad people were on both sides. Finally, only Noah and his immediate family are chosen to survive the Flood.

However, *Connecting the Dots of Identity* says yes, they are saved. They were Elect Roleplayers. They were certainly 100 percent human. No one became less than 100 percent human until the Nephilim were created.

Question 8: When will The End occur? The Rapture? Judgment Day?

Answer: MARVI-RPIA has no imagery for the End of the World except, perhaps, at the end of the Free Will Demonstration. MARVI-RPIA illustrates a Free Will Demonstration that eventually proves, conclusively, that God understands the thoughts and feelings of a creature, though He Himself is not a creature. Lucifer challenges this as being impossible. Only a created being can know what it's like to be a creature. Lucifer was thankful for being alive, but unless unrestricted behavior exists, the creature will never live his own life. It will be God's life through the creature. A puppet. A robot. An automaton.

God advises Lucifer that omnipotence (unrestricted behavior) without omniscience (unrestricted knowledge) and holiness (I AM), is detrimental to the creature, other creatures, and the environment. Nevertheless, God creates a Demonstration with flawless creatures who have limited Free Will. Adam and Eve chose their own will rather than God's will. They accepted death rather than the knowledge of good and evil withheld from them.

Angels observe the Demonstration. Some angels agree with Adam and Eve. They also reject God's will for their life. The error of doubting God's ability to know what is best for a created being plays out in the lives of human Roleplayers. They all evolve from Adam and Eve, including Virgin Mary. This also includes Jesus, even though He is 100 percent human from Mary and 100 percent God from the Holy Spirit.

Jesus Christ corrected the error of Adam and Eve. The Free Will Demonstration begins the first portion of years, before Jesus was born, under the teaching of the priests, the prophets, and God Himself. The Demonstration under the second portion of years is influenced by Jesus Christ's arrival in time.

The end of the Free Will Demonstration may signify the End of the World, the Rapture, and Judgment Day. Your Roleplay life may help make this happen. Other than that, the teaching of eschatology (theology of the end-of-the-world events) includes what can be known from prophecy. Prophecy means the declaration and fulfillment of God's word.

What Bible prophecies have been fulfilled? How many remain unfulfilled? Research on Bible prophecy suggests there is no clear answer. You may do your own research and discover a reasonable solution.

The New Testament Bible Books of Matthew, Mark, Luke, and John overlap many verses to reiterate the same teaching. This is a snapshot in Matthew of when the End will come—Judgment Day.

> But of that day and hour knoweth no man, no, not the angels of heaven, but my Father only. But as the days of Noah were, so shall also the coming of the Son of man be. For as in the days that were before the flood they were eating and drinking, marrying and giving in marriage, until the day that Noe entered into the ark, And knew not until the flood came, and took them all away; so shall

> also the coming of the Son of man be. Then shall two be in the field; the one shall be taken, and the other left. Two women shall be grinding at the mill; the one shall be taken, and the other left. Watch therefore: for ye know not what hour your Lord doth come. But know this that if the good man of the house had known in what watch the thief would come, he would have watched, and would not have suffered his house to be broken up. Therefore be ye also ready: for in such an hour as ye think not the Son of man cometh (Matthew 24:36-44).

The second aspect of the End, or Judgment Day, regards individuals affecting the timing of the End.

> And this gospel of the kingdom shall be preached in all the world for a witness unto all nations; and then shall the end come (Matthew 24:14).

What gospel? What kingdom? What end comes?

The Good News of the kingdom is that salvation was accomplished before the world was created. Jesus came to preach this. He is the guarantee by living a sinless human life, conquering death, and preparing Heaven for us.

Shall be preached in all the world, and then the end. Conventional thought was every person in every town, village, or community had to receive the message of Jesus Christ. From this, no one could ever claim they never had the opportunity to know about God.

General Revelation means God is revealed in nature and by intuition.

Special Revelation means scripture is expressed as God's holy word.

However, Christian orthodoxy teaches the written word, in some form or format must be seen, heard, or touched to be effective.

You can see we are right back to heredity, environment, and experience dictating the chances of recognizing Jesus Christ as the only way to salvation—and therefore dictating the timing of when the end comes. The End can NEVER come if EVERY person born all over the world must hear about Jesus Christ. By the way, this hearing is almost always a reference to physical hearing, not spiritual hearing. Physical hearing, the ear, perceived sound, is not grace. It's works. Something YOU must do to be saved.

Never mind that children are born into Muslim, Hindu, or Buddhist families and die without ever hearing of Jesus. Never mind that children are born and die too mentally impaired to conceptualize anything. Never mind the fetus dies before birth.

Once again, there is no such thing as an "age of accountability," a free pass to Heaven for all "special cases." God doesn't see age, mental ability, or circumstances. Salvation is accomplished before the world was created.

The Demonstration of Free Will could be the stage setting up The End. Once the demonstration is sufficient to prove the error of mistrust in God by flawlessly created beings (Serpent, Eve, Adam, angels) why continue further?

MARVI-RPIA imagery is similar to the Book of Revelation—a dramatic picture of scripture. On Judgment Day, there are no books, no writings, no billions of people being presented with evidence of why they are Hell-bound. That is hardly a literal event taking place in a spiritual reality outside of time. Or is it? The artistic impression conveyed in *Connecting the Dots of Identity* is there is no "day" of judgment. Judgment has already occurred.

In a split second of the present time, the Demonstration of Free Will ends. Elect Roleplayers transition to Heaven. Non-Elect Roleplayers cease to exist. The Devil and his angels are relegated to Hell.

You could say Judgment Day is every day. It was, it is, and it will be an event that confirms which lives transition to which destination. An assignment event. The analogy of people receiving a conviction, a sentence, and delivery to their destination is a memory aid in story form. Matthew 7:22, where people state their case for entry into Heaven, doesn't seem very likely. Will begging help your case? Will presenting evidence help your case? Please. There is nothing you could possibly say. Your LIFE is your words. Your life WAS your words. If there would be any speech at all, it would be from God.

We know God named everyone before He created the world—angel names and human names. Judgment comes to evil angels and Non-Elect Roleplayers. The Elect are not judged; they're Elect before the foundation of the world.

> Not everyone that saith unto me, Lord, Lord, shall enter into the kingdom of heaven; but he that doeth the will of my Father which is in heaven. Many will say to me in that day, Lord, Lord, have we not prophesied in thy name? And in thy name have cast out devils? And in thy name done many wonderful works? And then will I profess unto them, I never knew you: depart from me, ye that work iniquity (Matthew 7:21-23).

Finally, we read that the End will be like the last days of Noah before the Flood. From the MARVI-RPIA imagery, those last days meant the Nephilim were destroying humanity as humanity went about daily life. Perhaps today, the unsane of the world are destroying humanity as the sane go about daily life. A possible difference is that, as Elect Roleplayers, we know what to expect. We aren't bewildered or surprised. We have purpose, confidence, and the leverage of a simulated worldview that doesn't depend on theism, atheism, or agnosticism.

Jesus Christ may return when things are going well, or He may return when things are going horribly. We're working for His Majesty. We're always ready. We're not blind.

Question 9: Will I be reunited with loved ones in Heaven?

Answer: How many people think they're going to Heaven? How many people think if they do go to Heaven, their loved ones will be there? The whole point of Heaven is being with those you love and those that love you. You will see them. Will they be as you knew them before? How did you know them? By looks and personality? How will that change in Heaven?

You probably know in the back of your mind it doesn't make sense to see loved ones as you knew them on Earth. That actually might be fine for momentary identification purposes, but what if that person were blind, crippled, or deaf? Overweight, underweight, or incapacitated? Unattractive, deformed, or elderly? Wouldn't that be a sorrowful reminder in Heaven? If the loved one's appearance is simply a name tag type simulation, it seems that could be an option, although a crude vision of Heaven.

Let's say your loved one is very obese, very unattractive, and very old. Nothing wrong with those attributes in themselves. That was the person you loved. That's how life turned out for them. But wouldn't you rather see them very healthy, very beautiful, and very young? Of course. You want the very best for them. They want the very best for themselves. This is Heaven!

You may be reunited with loved ones and not know them as you knew them. Think of going to a party where everyone there knows you and loves you and vice versa. There is no need to know everyone by name, by family, by occupation, by ethnicity, by reputation. Those things don't matter anymore. What would you want to talk about? The only things you can think of would be the things you knew: your life on Earth. Are those topics to have in Heaven? Is the past life accessible? The things that matter in Heaven will be loving reunions in a loving environment.

But don't worry. God has all this worked out in a wonderful fashion. Read more in Connecting The Dots Of Identity, Chapters 40 and 41, Heaven 1 and Heaven 2.

Question 10: Does God love me?

Answer: God of the Bible DOES love you—the Pre-Life Elect you. The Elect Roleplayers of the present and future are loved by God (Holy Spirit-HSID). The Non-Elect Roleplayers are also loved by God in the sense they share in the General Revelation of God. General Revelation through the natural order of the world—health, prosperity, family, relationships, occupation, experiences, etcetera.

Showing love may be enforcing harsh penalties on people for the sake of love for the community. Non-Elect people share with the Elect in day-to-day life. Hate means a deviation from the standard of love. If God doesn't love you, it doesn't mean He hates you. He has an intense dislike for what you represent—disobedience to Him.

It means you represent the opposite of what He wanted for Adam and Eve. God hates that, not you. You are simply demonstrating Free Will.

Can't God just overrun that identity? Yes, He could. But that wouldn't allow Free Will. There could be an objection that God created puppets. God created robots, automatons. They would not be free-living creatures. Free Will has to play out with real lives. If it turns out you have an SSID counterpart in Paradise, the Super-Spiritual Identity, at the Last Day you join your true self in Heaven.

If you do not have an SSID counterpart, that may indicate you are not 100 percent human. In this case, when you die, your Roleplay inauthentic identity ends. You cease to exist. There is no afterlife. No Heaven. No Hell.

In a way, that is love. No one has control over being born less than 100 percent human. Will God send someone to Hell if they have no choice in being born to godless parents, in a godless culture, without sufficient resources to know Him?

"God loves you" continues to be a popular phrase. Such phrases will always continue. Are they helpful? Maybe. The issue would seemingly be more meaningful if God is defined in such a phrase, and you are defined in such a phrase.

> I pray for them: I pray not for the world, but for them which thou hast given me; for they are thine . . . I have given them thy word;

and the world hath hated them; because they are not of the world, even as I am not of the world (John 17: 9,14).

CHAPTER 30

QUESTIONS AND ANSWERS 11-20

Question 11: Why didn't God start over when Adam and Eve sinned? Or when the good angel Lucifer sinned?

Answer: How do you know God didn't start over? Maybe God ran 100 simulations of Adam and Eve, 100 sins of the Serpent, and 100 sins of Lucifer in Heaven contemplating rebellion. Maybe God ran 1000 sins, 100,000 sins, or even a trillion simulations.

Of course, God doesn't have to do that. He's omniscient. He oversees the best scenario for an outcome to occur. All is as it should be as flawless creatures have the opportunity to exercise Free Will. This includes the First-Class Angels who did not sin. And don't forget, God has in reserve the Pre-Life Elect before he created the world.

We, the Free Will Roleplayers, are the participants in a Demonstration of freedom for flawless living creatures. Perhaps it started with Lucifer's Postulate (Glossary of Colors), though Lucifer's identity was not inauthentic Roleplay. His identity is authentic. Lucifer humbly inquired about the freedom to behave as desired. God instructed that it would not be good without omniscience. God is now proving that point with us, the flawed creatures in physical space and time. The Serpent, Adam, and Eve demonstrate the error of pursuing freedom without omniscience as they sought omniscience through knowledge of good and evil, which God forbade.

God WILL start all over. It's called the afterlife.

Question 12: Where does evil come from? Why does it exist? What is it?

Answer: The impression *Connecting the Dots of Identity* has is that evil began in the Garden of Eden. Evil had its origin in the form of Free Will decisions by three flawless living creatures. The Free Will decision was a pursuit of self-interest rather than God's interest for their life. The Serpent chose self-interest, Eve chose self-interest, and Adam chose self-interest. Why was that evil? *Those choices of self-interest led to the death* of the three flawless creatures, the offspring of the now-flawed creatures, and the curse of the environment—the world.

The same Free Will option existed in Heaven before the world was created. The angels inquired about unlimited behavior. God counseled them that such a pursuit was detrimental to other creatures and the environment. They desired God to rectify any transgressions on the fly, as in an autocorrect feature. God rebuked them. He is God. He is not a 24/7 on-call repairman. He loves them. He knows what's best for them. *It wasn't evil to inquire, and it wasn't evil to desire.*

God offers a Demonstration. Flawless living creatures will be given their own world, Free Will to think and behave, and close companionship with Him. Will they trust His will for them, the same goodwill He provides the angels, or will they choose their own will?

The Demonstration of Free Will in the Garden of Eden featured an attraction. The attraction facilitated self-interest. This was the Tree of the Knowledge of Good and Evil. Such knowledge could be said to approach a form of omniscience, knowing everything that is good and everything that is not good.

However, such knowledge has a high price. It will cost the creatures their lives. Eve and Adam did choose death rather than have their freedom of knowledge restricted.

The Demonstration of Free Will project God produced included a "prearrangement," of male and female gender. Should the flawless living creatures' decline God's will and bring about death, God promises an Antidote through procreation. Procreation continues the Demonstration of Free Will. The offspring of Adam and Eve are a product of heredity, environment, and experiences.

Being in observation of God's Demonstration, a specific group of angels also risked death by exercising Free Will to pursue their own interests for their lives rather than God's will for their life. This group left Heaven to "marry" human females. A second group did not leave Heaven but remained to accuse God. Their accusations:

- God's design of flawless humans and angels is a flawed design. Otherwise, they would be content.

- God favors humans more than angels. Humans are in God's image; angels are not. God promised humans a Redeemer should they disobey, but not angels. This is discriminatory and shows prejudice.

Evil now comes in the form of *human rebellion and angel rebellion.* The human rebellion caused the world environment to be cursed, as well as mankind. Angel rebellion also caused humans to have a second curse. This came in the form of hybrid angel-human offspring—the Nephilim. The world becomes so corrupt and filled with violence (violations of God's natural order) that God destroys everyone except eight people in the Flood.

Evil in the spiritual world is evil spirits opposing God's plan for human beings.

Evil in the spiritual world is an accusatory posture toward God and His creation.

Evil in the physical world is human-to-human opposition. It is inherently a lack of care for the environment of other humans. It also suffers the worldwide effects of evil spirit wickedness.

The everyday kind of evil we presently experience are acts to abuse, despise, defame, slander, humiliate, bully, restrict, silence, incarcerate, and eventually exterminate those who engage in criticism, insubordination, or opposition to authority. Furthermore, evil is the expression of unsanity (Insanity Chart).

Evil is an ideology of rejecting objective morality. God is not credible as the overall standard of right and wrong. Scripture documents God's immoral acts of unfairness, cruelty, and abuse of power. Until the Holy Spirit opens our spiritual eyes, we doubt God's moral character.

Evil has potential where Free Will is present. Free Will is necessary for the life of a flawless living creature. Thank God His salvation plan saved us before He created the world. *Evil is rampant, but it's a part of the Demonstration of Free Will.* Once the Demonstration ends, we will be with Him in Paradise.

Question 13: What about Mormons, Catholics, Jehovah's Witnesses, Muslims, and those of the Jewish faith? Are they saved?

Answer: Religious affiliation is irrelevant to the person possessing salvation. The Bible teaches salvation is not sought for, not earned, and not acquired by acts of the individual. Salvation comes by the will of God. Grace, not works. At some point, depending on the spiritual maturity of a person, they typically remain in any church if what is being presented is not in opposition to who they perceive God to be. In other words, they seek resources that contribute to their spiritual maturity, wherever they may be.

There is never a danger of losing salvation by being in the wrong church, the wrong religion, or the wrong country. We are not saved by what we know or what we do. Error in the understanding of religion is universal. Error in the understanding of reality is universal. As Free Will Roleplayers, our responsibility is always to do the best we can with what we have. That may be a little, or that may be a lot. The objective is the Demonstration of Free Will.

And, as the Bible indicates, salvation was accomplished before the foundation of the world. Religion, or the absence of religion, has no bearing on 100 percent human beings—the ones Jesus Christ redeemed.

Question 14: Who were the sons of God in the Bible, especially in the Book of Genesis?

Answer: MARVI-RPIA takes the position that the sons of God were angels. That differs from the conventional, conservative view that the sons of God were the descendants of Seth, Adam and Eve's next child following the death of Abel and the exile of Cain. The other lesser accepted opinions are sons of God are men of great fame or the person who follows God's ways.

> And it came to pass, when men began to multiply on the face of the earth, and daughters were born unto them, That the sons of God saw the daughters of men that they were fair; and they took them wives of all which they chose (Genesis 6:1-2).

Contention comes from the story in Genesis, where the sons of God chose the daughters of men to marry. The result was the so-called Nephilim—children from the "marriage." A scientific explanation would be angels and humans are not able to procreate. They are not the same species of living beings. Therefore, humanly speaking, it is not possible for them to produce offspring. Of course, science doesn't recognize the existence of angels. And then, Jesus states angels do not marry and are not given in marriage (Matthew 22:30).

Connecting the Dots of Identity-1 goes into great detail regarding the Nephilim. Also, see the Glossary of Colors regarding Nephilim.

> Jesus answered and said unto them, Ye do err, not knowing the scriptures, nor the power of God. For in the resurrection they neither marry, nor are given in marriage, but are as the angels of God in heaven (Matthew 22:29-30).

How do angels procreate with human females?

By simulating human behavior, possessing humans, sorcery, and ingenuity. The violation of God's natural laws was accomplished by recklessness, impudence, and experimentation.

Question 15: Why are there so many religions?

Answer: There are at least two explanations. One refers to people pursuing what they think religion should be based on the religion they have been taught or were exposed to. The other is how historical religious documents, oral traditions, or spiritual insights are interpreted and advanced, thereby becoming acceptable as doctrine.

The first example is essentially what works out to be simply human diversity. When God mandated humans proliferate and cover the earth, it was for good reason—the Demonstration of Free Will. How someone interprets what is supernatural, transcendental, mysterious, or something greater than human potentiality is subjective . . . personal.

It's important that people pursue individual interests as a factor of their heredity, environment, and experiences. This is how differentiation arises in occupations, hobbies, the arts, education, and religion. People reflect their interests based on their identity—their Free Will Roleplay identity. Of course, that spills over into how they perceive the world: their worldview. That includes religion as well as an absence of religion (atheism or agnosticism).

The second example, the interpretation of historical religious beliefs, is, generally, a function of disagreements on issues that remain within the core beliefs of religion. Core beliefs such as one God, Jesus Christ, prayer, good behavior, a day of worship, church attendance and support, the sacraments of baptism and communion, Bible study, life after death, Heaven, and Hell. The more beliefs that are added or subtracted illustrate why religions diverge or converge around a particular belief about the supernatural.

Question 16: What good is prayer? Can we change God's mind?

Answer: We can NOT change God's mind! That is a very GOOD thing. Would you really want billions of people changing God's mind throughout the day and night? NO! Are you wise enough to give God suggestions for what is best for you or others when God already has His plan in place? No.

But the Bible itself says prayer changes things. Yes, and the things that are perceived as change are actually God's sovereign will. Also, WE are changed through prayer. This change is our ongoing Christian maturity as we learn to communicate to God with our heart, mind, and the assistance of the Holy Spirit.

God tells us to pray, expects us to pray, teaches us to pray, and desires us to pray. Prayer is the expression and confirmation of our relationship with God. Prayer is much more than words. Verbal expression assists in organizing our thoughts, our interest, and our intention. When we seek to communicate with God, our thoughts guide our words. We know good communication requires a reasonable level of skill on the part of the parties. Poor communication can be acceptable if one of the parties understands the limitations of the other party.

You can communicate effectively with your young child or even a pet animal, but the level of communication is limited. Yes, you may be like a pet, compared to God, when it comes to communicating. Your communication suffers due to a lack of familiarity with God and with scripture. The better you know a person, the easier it becomes to communicate.

You also know that communication isn't all verbal. Body language is important. Your attitude is important. Prior behavior is important. Consider the sacrifices you've made to spend time with other people, the "gifts" you've brought, the care you show, and the effort you put forth. All this expresses the value of the relationship.

So, it's not just what you say in prayer, it's also behavior—what you do. Not only that, it's what's in your heart. Do you know God? Do you love God? Do you even like God?

It's been pointed out that most people in the world know more about their favorite sports team, favorite celebrity, favorite hobby, favorite music, or favorite TV show than they do about Jesus Christ, *the number one Person of all persons.* Everyone should know the smallest details about Jesus Christ, forward and backward, even if they aren't Christian. Jesus Christ was/is utterly amazing! He is/was perfect!

Do you stay in touch with God? Are you always asking for something and seldom giving? When you give a gift to God, do you give your best? I'm speaking now of your gift of singing, cooking, public speaking, finances, hospitality, or any particular expertise you may have. Do you only give a minimum, the leftovers, or the weak, lame, and speckled from the flock? Is this offering acceptable to God? Is this how you give to people you love? What if you offer from the best things you have? A real sacrifice to you. Wouldn't God especially honor that?

Pray with your heart. Don't worry about the words. You don't have to close your eyes, get on your knees, fold your hands, remove your hat, bow your head, or stop what you're doing.

Jesus gave the Lord's Prayer as a guide (Matthew 6:9-13). It's only a guide. Whatever words you use, the Holy Spirit shares them. They—God the Father, God the Son, God the Holy Spirit—assist you in communicating. Don't be afraid to communicate anything to them. Anything! Don't fret if you don't receive what you expect as a reply. Always keep communicating, no matter what.

The Lord's Prayer, then the Lord's Prayer as an impression:

The Lord's Prayer:

> After this manner therefore pray ye: Our Father which art in heaven, Hallowed be thy name. Thy kingdom come, Thy will be done in earth, as it is in heaven. Give us this day our daily bread. And forgive us our debts, as we forgive our debtors. And lead us not into temptation, but deliver us from evil: For thine is the kingdom, and the power, and the glory, forever. Amen (Matthew 6:9-13).

The Lord's Prayer as an Impression:

The Ultimate One is the Father who identified us before He created the world.

His name should be hallowed by all, even as we don't perceive His name.

We are already in the kingdom, but His will to be done on earth is the Demonstration of Free Will.

As it is in Heaven could refer to the Super-Spiritual Identities (SSIDs) and the First-Class Angels who did not rebel against God.

As Free Will Roleplayers, we pray to be responsible caretakers of the Garden of Earth, which is compromised by sane, unsane, and insane other persons.

We are dependent on the earth and our fellow man to have sustenance.

This life indicates an inauthentic identity that resolves to our authentic identity with God forever.

Amen.

The Lord's Prayer, even more simply, might be: God, we honor you and We thank You. Knowing that we were saved before we were born gives us the patience, strength, and confidence to live and die for you. Amen.

As mentioned earlier, your prayers are already answered. You're in Paradise as a Pre-Life Elect person! For now, we are Roleplayers demonstrating Free Will. Say hi to God. He loves it when you take even a few seconds to acknowledge Him.

> Likewise the Spirit also helpeth our infirmities: for we know not what we should pray for as we ought: but the Spirit itself maketh intercession for us with groaning which cannot be uttered. And he that searcheth the hearts knoweth what is the mind of the Spirit because he maketh intercession for the saints according to the will of God (Romans 8:26-27).

> Ask, and it shall be given you; seek, and ye shall find; knock, and it shall be opened unto you: For every one that asketh receiveth; and he that seeketh findeth; and to him that knocketh it shall be opened (Matthew 7:7-8).

> Be careful for nothing; but in everything by prayer and supplication with thanksgiving let your requests be made known unto God (Philippians 4:6).

Question 17: What is the greatest challenge facing Christianity?

Answer: The greatest challenge may be hard to isolate. Christianity is one of five major worldviews. There's Islam, Christianity, Hinduism, Buddhism, and non-theism (no religion). All worldviews present religious challenges. Additionally, not everyone who purports to be a Christian is a Christian. Secondly, the broad realm of Christianity itself may be a significant impediment to its growth and vitality. We all see many flavors of Christian churches and Christian organizations. Christianity may be a label that lacks specificity.

As an example, *Connecting the Dots of Identity* epitomizes a concept found throughout scripture—the Elect. The Elect are the ones predestined to salvation before the foundation of the world. No orthodox religious source exists that gives credence to an ONTOLOGICAL status of the Elect. The Pre-life Elect has no obvious designation of being other than AFTER the world is created. Once created, you are then the embodiment of someone who was destined to be saved. Any identity acknowledged BEFORE birth is inexplicable. Therefore, the Elect is an implied, immaterial, indistinct IMPOSSIBLE identity until conception occurs in the first stage of life.

MARVI-RPIA illustrates that if the Pre-life Elect does exist—outside time and space—Christian orthodoxy still stands. The Elect as Roleplayers doesn't threaten mainstream Christianity. The challenge for MARVI-RPIA is to constantly reiterate this is an artistic impression—meant to BEAUTIFY Christianity, not redefine it.

MARVI-RPIA looks at two separate identities, one pre-Christian (before you're born-again) and one post-Christian (after you're born-again). Also, dual identities exist when comparing the identity in dreams to the identity in the awakened state. Same person, two identities.

This view, along with other views following the MARVI-RPIA imagery, opens up aspects of God's salvation plan, the origin of sin, Free Will, Heaven, and Hell. Meanwhile, Islam, Hinduism, atheism, agnosticism, and religious and nonreligious worldviews will continue to criticize and vilify Christianity. That is understandable. That testifies to the Error of Free Will from Adam and Eve. People make decisions based on ideas of who they think they are. Who they think they are is the identity from heredity, the environment, and experiences.

All Christians have an obligation to make the world a better place by promoting Christianity. Making the world a better place should not be subjective. Making it better should include objective standards that appeal to every individual, thereby making it better for the neighborhood, city, state, and country. However, making the world a better place is not in everyone's best interest. Their own best interest, not the interests of others, comes first. This is the subjectivity of standards, what is best is relative to the individual.

What is best is not a standard based on a transcendent entity beyond the individual. There is no intelligent entity beyond the individual. That may be the great Christian challenge: *how to communicate God to people, a transcendent entity representing moral objectivity.* How to communicate "goodness" for the sake of the environment. The environment is our family, friends, associates, neighborhood, city, state, nation, and world.

Question 18: Are atheists reasonable to accuse God of unfairness if He sends people to Hell because they are born in circumstances beyond their control?

Answer: The atheists would be reasonable, and their accusation would be correct if God does that. God does NOT do that. Salvation does not depend on what you know or what you do. Salvation is by grace to those whom God has elected before they were born. What we observe is the person who is a product of their heredity, environment, and experiences. This traces back through every ancestor, culminating with Adam and Eve.

Adam and Eve exercised their Free Will to disobey God's will for their lives. The result was death, a slow death, which they passed to their progeny. Every person thereafter demonstrates individual Free Will and death. Adam and Eve were flawless creatures. They had Free Will, an essential attribute of a flawless living creature.

An atheist, a nonbeliever, *might blame Adam and Eve for being unfair.* They're the ones who caused the blueprint of a flawless human being to be corrupted. But don't blame God.

Consider that the corrupted blueprint was carefully monitored and guided so it produced the Virgin Mary for the Holy Spirit to father Jesus Christ. God is unfair? God is more than fair. He is more than fair by telling us in scripture that He saved us before He created the world. Yes, you. Yes, me. This physical world is a drama of Free Will. It's inauthentic. Our authentic identity awaits in Paradise for the End of the Demonstration of Free Will.

Question 19: But what about Goliath, Jezebel, Judas Iscariot, and Pontius Pilate? What about whole groups of people exterminated in the Flood, Sodom, Gomorrah, and ethnic groups annihilated by the people of God, the Israelites? Are any of them the Elect ones? Are they all simply Free Will Roleplayers as designated by the error of Adam and Eve, all now headed for Hell?

Answer: The teaching of Christian Reformed theology, which is the teaching of orthodox biblical principles, does not tell us on what basis the Holy Spirit intercedes in a person's life. We also do not have 100 percent accuracy of who is an Elect person or when a person becomes Elect. Two extremes of an Elect person are John the Baptist in his mother Elizabeth's womb and the thief on the cross with Jesus in the last seconds of life.

Connecting the Dots of Identity offers an impression of the persons mentioned in the question that is posed here. The impression is they are all elect!

They all go to Heaven because they are ALREADY in Heaven. The persons we're familiar with, the Free Will Roleplayers living after the world is created, are all the Demonstration of Free Will. This began with the Serpent, Adam, and Eve. The Pre-Life Elect has no awareness of the Free Will Roleplayers. The Free Will Roleplayers have no awareness of the Pre-Life Elect.

Hell was created for the Devil and his angels. No 100 percent human being goes to Hell. Anyone less than 100 percent human—anyone with "dominant-phantom-Nephilim-genetic immaterial"—will cease to exist at death. They have no soul, no spirit. No afterlife will apply to them.

Question 20: Where do we go when we die?

Answer: Christian teaching follows two paths. One path is for "good" people and the other path is for "bad" people. Good people go to Heaven, right away. Bad people go into "soul sleep" until Judgment Day, or they regain consciousness in Hell. Other worldviews have an assortment of explanations including nothing happening when you die. It's the end. Oblivion.

Another view is that everyone goes into a state of tranquility outside time and space. Reincarnation is another popular theory.

The MARVI-RPIA mural projects imagery for the so-called good people, bad people, and other people.

Good people are 100 percent human beings. They are the Elect. God granted salvation to them before the foundation of the world. They are "sane" Roleplayers. Their Roleplay identity demonstrates the effects of heredity, environment, and experience.

Bad people are also 100 percent human beings. They're "unsane" Roleplayers, those who reject objective morality. Their Roleplay identity demonstrates the effects of heredity, environment, and experience. In the afterlife, they will be joined with their authentic identity in Paradise.

The other people are less than less-than-100 percent human beings. They may be evil spirits impersonating humans or born compromised by Nephilim ancestors.

The Bible says Hell is created for the Devil and his angels. So, 100 percent human beings don't go there.

A person born less than human can't be at fault for being born. A person less than 100 percent human would not have a soul or a spirit. *Jesus became human to redeem humans, not angels, angel-human hybrids, aliens, or animals.* At death, these persons would simply cease to exist. There is no afterlife.

Scripture implies to be absent from the body is to be present with the Lord (2 Corinthians 5:8). However, the Lord is omnipresent. We are all present with the Lord right now. Given that persons of God may be in Paradise, such as Enoch, the thief on the cross, and Virgin Mary, all Elect Roleplayers may transition there. The Bible also says that when we die, the spirit goes back to God (Ecclesiastes 12:7).

When you search the Bible for people who died and were brought back to life, were they with the Lord in that afterlife? Lazarus, Dorcas, Eutychus, the other six. What would they be able to say about the afterlife? Are they again with the Lord when brought back to life? Yes. Is the Lord with all of us now? Yes, He is omnipresent.

Where do we go when we die? No explicit location? Is this a definition of Heaven, where the Lord dwells? Maybe. Where does the Lord dwell? Does He dwell? Having a spiritual identity in a spiritual world may mean that location is irrelevant.

Are we active or inactive in the afterlife? When you are resting, meditating, or sleeping, you are NOT typically described as active. This may describe an aspect of the afterlife.

If we are active, the activity outside time and space, in the spiritual world, may not be expedient to describe. If it were expedient, wouldn't we know more? Some people think they do know more. Okay.

> Therefore we are always confident, knowing that, whilst we are at home in the body, we are absent from the Lord: (For we walk by faith, not by sight) We are confident, I say, and willing rather to be absent from the body, and to be present with the Lord. Wherefore we labour, that, whether present or absent, we may be accepted of him (2 Corinthians 5:6-9).

> Then shall the dust return to the earth as it was: and the spirit shall return unto God who gave it (Ecclesiastes 12:7).

CHAPTER 31

QUESTIONS AND ANSWERS 21-30

Question 21: Why does God say he loved Jacob and hated Esau? Doesn't the Bible state that God is no respecter of persons?

Answer: This question addresses part of the reason to publish Connecting The Dots Of Identity. The Roleplay of human beings is to demonstrate the Error of Free Will. Adam and Eve began the evolution of human beings with a corrupted version of the unimpaired Free Will they possessed before partaking of the Tree of the Knowledge of Good and Evil.

Every person evolving from Adam and Eve represents a collection of unique attributes caused by heredity, environment, and experiences. The amount of control a person has over their identity is limited, fragmented, and spread over time.

In this regard, God could say He loves what has contributed to making Jacob who he is and hates what has contributed to making Esau who he is. It's not the individuals; it's the factors involved that influence identity. The most influential factor is sin. The Free Will Demonstration of declining God's will must play out. When God does intervene in the Demonstration to involve specific Roleplayers, this is not favoritism. It may seem so, but the characters are in place by procreation from Adam and Eve. God intervenes to show the contrast between not intervening and intervening.

But if God doesn't hate the individual, Esau for example, but hates what makes Esau the person he is, why does Esau go to Hell?

Esau doesn't go to Hell, assuming Esau is 100 percent human. The real Esau, Pre-Life Elect Esau, is already safe in Paradise. Esau and Jacob were twins; they had the same parents.

Only a less-than-100 percent human Roleplay Esau would be in jeopardy of Hell. Being less than 100 percent human may indicate being demon compromised. In the worst-case scenario, that would mean joining the Devil and his angels in Hell.

The purpose of a Roleplayer is to demonstrate Free Will based on heredity, environment, and experience. All are hateful unless they are Elect—saved before they were born. Non-Elect persons have no control over being brought to life. They have no control over choosing God to save them. They may even hate the thought of God in their life.

If people could choose God as their Savior, why wouldn't they? No fear of Hell. Heaven is guaranteed. God loves them. Easy choice.

But anyone who CAN choose God proves they have the ability to do so. That leaves out the people who DON'T have the ability: embryos, infants, toddlers, the mentally impaired, and the simple-minded. It leaves out people in remote villages who never hear of Jesus Christ. It leaves out people subjected to nonreligious views and counter-religious views. It leaves out all but the most intelligent and capable individuals.

Don't worry about whom God hates. It's only a figure of speech. Hell is created for the Devil and his angels. Hundred-percent human beings are saved before they were born. Less than 100 percent humans cease to exist at death per MARVI-RPIA imagery.

> I have loved you, saith the Lord. Yet ye say, Wherein hast thou loved us? Was not Esau Jacob's brother? saith the Lord: yet I loved Jacob, And I hated Esau, and laid his mountains and his heritage waste for the dragons of the wilderness (Malachi 1:2-3).

> As it is written, Jacob have I loved, but Esau have I hated (Romans 9:13).

Question 22: But doesn't the Bible also say that God is the one who creates us in the womb, causes conception or inhibits it, and knows us before we are born?

Answer: Yes, the Bible indicates God is the One who controls Pre-Life, Life, and the Afterlife. God allows conception or inhibits conception and may intercede in His plan for individual Roleplayers.

God creating us in the womb could refer to the spiritual identity (SID), not physical identity (PID). The terms Traducianism, Creationism, and Designationism refer to WHEN a soul is created—before, at, or after conception—and HOW it's created—by God or by the parents. See Glossary of Colors for further explanation.

We know we are all born in sin. This is from our parents, and that goes all the way back to Adam and Eve. If God creates us in the womb physically, *that would mean God creates us as sinners.* God is not the creator of sin. Adam and Eve are. So, God apparently determines spiritual identity (SID) before or after physical identity (PID).

Secondly, the imagery presented by MARVI-RPIA is God is the One who has designed and created the flawless human blueprint. Once the product was in place, human beings reproduced the product as procreation. Human beings make changes to the blueprint by alterations, adjustments, and rearrangements, thereby corrupting, distorting, and misrepresenting the original flawless human blueprint.

So, when people say they are the way they are because God made them that way—no. Adam and Eve made you that way. Sin made you that way. Your ancestors, the environment, and your experiences made you that way.

Christians say the same thing. *God made you the way you are so that you may glorify Him.* Then you look at people in your neighborhood, your city, and around the world. How do they look? They have all manner of deformities, injuries, and misfortune. This is so God will be glorified? No. God may work THROUGH any situation to show His glory, but that's not WHY the person is in dire straits. The inauthentic identity—blindness, lameness, deafness, etcetera—is a factor of Adam and Eve. This is a factor of sin. God is glorified by working over, under, around, and through sin. God is glorified by forgiving sin, which is salvation.

> And as Jesus passed by, he saw a man which was blind from his birth. And his disciples asked him, saying, Master, who did sin, this man, or his parents, that he was born blind? Jesus answered, neither hath this man sinned, nor his parents: but that the works of God should be made manifest in him (John 9:1-3).

> Then the word of the Lord came unto me, saying, before I formed thee in the belly I knew thee; and before thou camest forth out of the womb I sanctified thee, and I ordained thee a prophet unto the nations (Jeremiah 1:4-5).

> Know ye that the Lord he is God: it is he that hath made us, and not we ourselves; we are his people, and the sheep of his pasture (Psalm100:3).

> For thou hast possessed my reins: thou hast covered me in my mother's womb. I will praise thee; for I am fearfully and wonderfully made: marvelous are thy works; and that my soul knoweth right well. My substance was not hid from thee, when I was made in secret, and curiously wrought in the lowest parts of the earth. Thine eyes did see my substance, yet being imperfect; and in thy book all my members were written, which in continuance were fashioned, when as yet there was none of them (Psalm 139:13-16).

> And now, saith the Lord that formed me from the womb to be his servant, to bring Jacob again to him, Though Israel be not gathered, yet shall I be glorious in the eyes of the Lord, and my God shall be my strength (Isaiah 49:5).

> Did not he that made me in the womb make him? And did not one fashion us in the womb? (Job 31:5)

> For he shall be great in the sight of the Lord, and shall drink neither wine nor strong drink; and he shall be filled with the Holy Ghost, even from his mother's womb (Luke 1:15).

The follow-up question will eventually refer to Exodus 4:11. God has chosen Moses to lead Israel out of Egypt. Moses admits he is unfit as a public speaker. God says that is no excuse. Who, but God, has made man's mouth? Who has made the blind, lame, and deaf but Jehovah God? So here in the book of Exodus, it seems that God creates in the womb those persons who are born blind, lame, deaf, and with other physical/mental disabilities.

Even without *Connecting the Dots of Identity*, we know this isn't literal. *God created man's mouth in the sense He created human mouths. God created flawless human beings—Adam and Eve.* God created every human attribute with no imperfections. Eyes, nose, mouth, ears, fingers, legs, etcetera. When Adam and Eve sinned, not only were they impaired, but their offspring also became impaired. The effect of this worsened as impaired offspring begat impaired offspring. As if this wasn't bad enough, the entire environment was also cursed. This means air, water, land, animals, food, and drink were compromised. Impairment is a feature of living.

God allows, not causes, defects to occur before birth, at birth, and after birth. God then makes over man's mouth, eyes, ears, legs, etcetera, in ways He sees fit to fulfill His will. God asks Moses, am I not the Lord? If He is the Lord, He is certainly beyond adequate for any endeavor. We know *God made the Serpent's mouth (Genesis 3:1) and He made the mouth of Balaam's donkey (Numbers 22: 28, 30). Even where there are no material mouths made, immaterial mouths of angels are also made by God.* We know God's designs are flawless. The consequences of Free Will and how God intervenes is another story.

> And Moses said unto the Lord, O my Lord, I am not eloquent, neither heretofore, nor since thou hast spoken unto thy servant: but I am slow of speech, and of a slow tongue. And the Lord said unto him, who hath made man's mouth? Or who maketh the dumb, or deaf, or the seeing, or the blind? Have not I the Lord? Now therefore go, and I will be with thy mouth, and teach thee what thou shalt say (Exodus 4:10-12).

> Now the serpent was more subtil than any beast of the field which the Lord God had made. And he said unto the woman, Yea, hath God said, you shall not eat of every tree of the garden? And the woman said unto the serpent, we may eat of the fruit of the trees of the garden: But of the fruit of the tree which is in the midst of the garden, God hath said, you shall not eat of it, neither shall ye touch it, lest ye die. And the serpent said unto the woman, you shall not surely die: For God doth know that in the day ye eat thereof, then your eyes shall be opened, and ye shall be as gods, knowing good and evil (Genesis 3:1-5).

> And when the ass saw the angel of the Lord, she fell down under Balaam: and Balaam's anger was kindled, and he smote the ass with a staff. And the Lord opened the mouth of the ass, and she said unto Balaam, What have I done unto thee, that thou hast smitten me these three times? And Balaam said unto the ass, because thou hast mocked me: I would there were a sword in mine hand, for now would I kill thee. And the ass said unto Balaam, Am not I thine ass, upon which thou hast ridden ever since I was thine unto this day? Was I ever wont to do so unto thee? And he said, Nay (Numbers 22:27-30).

Question 23: Why did God kill so many people at once—the Flood, Sodom Gomorrah, and enforce genocide on so many nations like the Midianites in the Book of Numbers? A lot of innocent people died. God seems amoral.

Answer: The reason for killing so many at once isn't obvious except in the matter of the Flood. In that case, the human blueprint became compromised for the second time. Initially, it was compromised by Adam and Eve in the Garden and secondarily by sons of God with human females. Only eight persons were selected to repopulate the earth. Even then, one or more of the eight may have been responsible for carrying forward any negative "Nephilim substance."

As the situation became dire for a 100 percent human being to arrive in the future to be the mother of the Redeemer, the Virgin Mary, emergency surgery on the population was carried out.

As for the other examples of widespread human eradication, MARVI-RPIA paints two pictures.

One, to separate the chosen people of God from other people. *A specific line of individuals is necessary to arrive at the Virgin Mary.* A specific chosen people meant these people had to adhere to strict guidelines for posterity. The salvation of the human race was dependent on the Messiah arriving on the scene at a specific time in the future. Groups of people living outside the chosen group of Israel were living by their own standards and not God's standards. As the Bible states, before there were rulers and kings in those days, people did what was best in their own eyes (Old Testament Book of Judges).

Imagine living in a land where there is no police, ambulance, hospital, court, jail, judge, or king. No laws except the survival of the strong. Add to this the effect of people seeking every opportunity to become a god themselves. The most intelligent people used guile. The most beautiful used sex. The most diligent used ingenuity. The most devious practiced crime. And the evilest used sorcery, magic, voodoo, mysticism, the occult, divination, and such. From this last group, you may suppose human beings fell prey to evil spirits—angels. These are the Second-Class Angels that did not join the Third-Class Angels associated with the Flood, now imprisoned in chains of darkness.

As various groups of people in the land were affected by evil, anarchy, and lack of organized medicine, they suffered from diseases. Not only did the people suffer, but so did the animals, food, and water. Sick people meant more disease. Plagues, viruses, germs, bacteria, uncleanliness, mental illness, and disabilities must have been common. Proper care of deceased persons may not have been followed, possibly by superstition or by reasons of sorcery.

Sexual disease without medicine or protocols to follow could decimate a community practically overnight. This could include diseases from group sex, pedophilia, coprophilia, necrophilia, and bestiality for example. Cannibalism and human sacrifice were also a scourge. When pets and livestock become infected, what do you do? Kill all of them or take a chance? Soon there are plagues, famine, and desperate people in deep trouble with no reliable resources to count on.

Remember, there were no widely held medical practices in those times.

Thousands of years passed before anyone knew of the germ theory of disease. No one knew about sterilization. No one even knew about hand washing. There was no running water! There were no standard medications. No antibiotics, anesthesia, antiseptics, disinfectants, or vaccines. There were no standardized medical instruments, equipment, or facilities.

The history of medicine teaches us the plight civilized and uncivilized people faced from ancient times until the relatively recent past. Even if ancient researchers suspected organic causes for disease, they had no reliable methods of proof and certainly no organized communication for collaboration. It wasn't until people like Francesco Redi (1626), Agostino Bassi (1773), and Louis Pasteur (1882) came onto the scene that medicine began to overrule ritualism, tradition, and dangerous practices.

Two, the other picture MARVI-RPIA paints for widespread death at God's hands regards the devolution of humanity by wickedness. While God is building a hedge of protection around His chosen people by commands and rituals, the rest of humanity is in the process of creating their own community standards. Free Will Roleplayers simply act out their identity based on heredity, the environment, and experiences. Wickedness becomes the rule rather than the exception in the land. *Wickedness must not overrun God's chosen people or their location.* But why make an example by the death of this group over another group?

When you consider how many different groups of people there are around the world—at every time in history—it's not unusual to single out one or ten or one hundred groups. The fact that God names this group and that group does not for one moment mean all the other groups across the world are innocent. We're only seeing samples of the whole. The man who picked up a few sticks on the sabbath, Nadab and Abihu, Jezebel, Athalia, and Nabal. God could have chosen from many others. These are examples for our edification. We should know there were many more individuals and groups the Bible does not name. As the book of Acts hints, God is extremely patient, merciful, and kind.

CD1/CD2 paints the picture of all those who perished directly by God, through the chosen people of God, or the wicked slaying the innocent, are all Roleplayers. Hundred-percent humans are already saved before they were born. We are in a Demonstration of Free Will. It has to play out.

> And the times of this ignorance God winked at; but now commandeth all men everywhere to repent (Acts 17:30).

> In those days there was no king in Israel, but every man did that which was right in his own eyes (Judges 17:6).

In those days there was no king in Israel: every man did that which was right in his own eyes (Judges 21:25).

When thou art come into the land which the Lord thy God giveth thee, thou shalt not learn to do after the abominations of those nations. There shall not be found among you any one that maketh his son or his daughter to pass through the fire, or that useth divination, or an observer of times, or an enchanter, or a witch. Or a charmer, or a consulter with familiar spirits, or a wizard, or a necromancer. For all that do these things are an abomination unto the Lord: and because of these abominations the Lord thy God doth drive them out from before thee. Thou shalt be perfect with the Lord thy God. For these nations, which thou shalt possess, hearkened unto observers of times, and unto diviners: but as for thee, the Lord thy God hath not suffered thee so to do (Deuteronomy 18:9-14).

Thou shalt not suffer a witch to live (Exodus 22:18).

Manasseh was twelve years old when he began to reign, and he reigned fifty and five years in Jerusalem: But did that which was evil in the sight of the Lord, like unto the abominations of the heathen, whom the Lord had cast out before the children of Israel. For he built again the high places which Hezekiah his father had broken down, and he reared up altars for Baalim, and made groves, and worshipped all the host of heaven, and served them. Also he built altars in the house of the Lord, whereof the Lord had said, In Jerusalem shall my name be forever. And he built altars for all the host of heaven in the two courts of the house of the Lord. And he caused his children to pass through the fire in the valley of the son of Hinnom: also he observed times, and used enchantments, and used witchcraft, and dealt with a familiar spirit, and with wizards: he wrought much evil in the sight of the Lord, to provoke him to anger (2 Chronicles 33:1-6).

Regard not them that have familiar spirits, neither seek after wizards, to be defiled by them: I am the Lord your God (Leviticus 19:31).

And the LORD spake unto Moses, saying, Vex the Midianites, and smite them: For they vex you with their wiles, wherewith they have beguiled you in the matter of Peor, and in the matter of Cozbi, the daughter of a prince of Midian, their sister, which was slain in the day of the plague for Peor's sake (Numbers 25:16-18).

And when they shall say unto you, Seek unto them that have familiar spirits, and unto wizards that peep, and that mutter: should not a people seek unto their God? for the living to the dead? (Isaiah 8:19)

And while the children of Israel were in the wilderness, they found a man that gathered sticks upon the sabbath day (Numbers 15:32).

And all the congregation brought him without the camp, and stoned him with stones, and he died; as the Lord commanded Moses (Numbers 15:36).

And Nadab and Abihu, the sons of Aaron, took either of them his censer, and put fire therein, and put incense thereon, and offered strange fire before the Lord, which he commanded them not. And there went out fire from the Lord, and devoured them, and they died before the Lord (Leviticus 10:1-2).

> And when she looked, behold, the king stood by a pillar, as the manner was, and the princes and the trumpeters by the king, and all the people of the land rejoiced, and blew with trumpets: and Athaliah rent her clothes, and cried, Treason, Treason. But Jehoiada the priest commanded the captains of the hundreds, the officers of the host, and said unto them, have her forth without the ranges: and him that followeth her kill with the sword. For the priest had said, let her not be slain in the house of the Lord. And they laid hands on her; and she went by the way by which the horses came into the king's house: and there was she slain (2 Kings 11:14-16).

> And it came to pass about ten days after, that the Lord smote Nabal that he died (1 Samuel 25:38).

> And it came to pass that night, that the angel of the Lord went out, and smote in the camp of the Assyrians an hundred fourscore and five thousand: and when they arose early in the morning, behold, they were all dead corpses (2 Kings 19:35).

Question 24: What if I am not an Elect person?

Answer: You don't know if you are not an Elect person. You don't know who Elect person is. Election is all of God's knowing and doing. We know Election comes at different points in a person's life. *The range given in scripture is the earliest point with John the Baptist and the latest point with the thief on the cross with Jesus.* We don't know precisely when it comes because when it is evident to us, that is just confirmation that salvation was with us all along. We didn't have convincing evidence before or were too spiritually immature to recognize it.

You may not at all be interested in religion or the Christian worldview. It's foolishness to you. Christianity is unscientific, myth, superstition, fiction, coercion, and delusion. The reason you feel the way you feel is the effect of being a Free Will Roleplayer. Your identity was forced upon you by circumstances. Under certain circumstances, you could be living as a Muslim, Hindu, or Buddhist. You could be in some remote village, a third-world slum, or down on skid row. Some of you may be wealthy, famous, or in high-level government. You were given a spiritual identity, a set of parents, a body, and a mind. Your mission: to exercise Free Will.

Connecting the Dots of Identity has it that if you are not an Elect person, you may not be 100 percent human. The One-Drop Nephilim-Blood Rule applies (Glossary of Colors). You have been compromised by the spirit of evil—the Evil Spirit Identity (ESID). Initially, Hell was created for evil spirits. It is doubtful any 100 percent human being will go to Hell because a 100 percent human being's identity is already in Heaven. Everyone conceived/born is a Roleplayer. They came to life without their knowledge or permission. They were assigned a role dictated by the people who lived before them all the way back to Adam and Eve. MARVI-RPIA paints a glitch in the ancestral line with the Nephilim. Heredity may include compromised human tissue with evil spirit phantom-genetic immaterial.

In a way, it doesn't matter about your ancestral line. Even if it did, the other factors of environment and experience also have a significant influence on identity. Finally, scripture says you don't have the power to get yourself saved; you don't have the power to get yourself lost. You provide the Demonstration of Free Will with your life—one day old (or less) or one hundred years old (or more). You are not puppets. You are not robots. You're a living creature proving the error of a flawless creature's Free Will to disobey God.

All 100 percent humans should have a corresponding Pre-Life Elect identity in Paradise. Every 100 percent human being who ever lived will go to Heaven, because they are already there! No 100 percent human being goes to Hell. It's prepared for the Devil and evil spirits.

> Then shall he say also unto them on the left hand, Depart from me, ye cursed, into everlasting fire, prepared for the devil and his angels (Matthew 25:41)

> For if God spared not the angels that sinned, but cast them down to hell, and delivered them into chains of darkness, to be reserved unto judgment (2 Peter 2:4).

Question 25: If I'm a Non-Elect Roleplayer, a person who is not 100 percent human, would I know it?

Answer: Probably not. When thinking back through life, no memory is likely to stand out as particularly inhuman. Even people who absolutely loathe some act they committed in the past have no reason to fear a demonic influence. Sin is sin. We all sin. Some sins are significantly worse than others. Some sins seem harmless but have long-range effects. The worst characters in the Bible are not that far removed from people we know. It's best to focus on the positive. Life is just a temporary role. I'm human.

But how do you defend against Satan, aka the Great Deceiver? *When you are deceived by the master of deception, you have absolutely NO idea you're deceived.* And we KNOW hypnosis works. It acts on individuals below the threshold of consciousness. Another problem is the use of language. It's an effective tool for politicians, network news, and social media to influence thoughts and behavior.

So, I'm an easy target? No, not really. As a Non-Elect Roleplayer, none of those things matter. God intervenes, or He doesn't. If He doesn't, you simply won't know. At death, you will have reached the final stage of your role. Your identity ends. No authentic identity awaits you.

However, there may be every indication that you are not Elect, but you actually are Elect.

An example is the Apostle Paul before he was converted. As the person called Saul, he was on his way to persecute Christians when He met Jesus Christ. As Saul, he had no idea he was an Elect Roleplayer. He was acting out his identity. He had no interest in being anything like the people he was persecuting. God entered his life, and he was a changed person—180 degrees.

Again, your role is not you. If you are at all concerned about being a Non-Elect Roleplayer, less than 100 percent human, or heading for Hell, that is a good sign you are Elect. If you aren't concerned, don't care, or don't believe in an afterlife, that's just a part of your role. Is Paradise in your future? Most likely, but only God knows. The impression painted by MARVI-RPIA is that even the worst of us are only playing a role imposed on us. It is an inauthentic identity. Our authentic identity is in Paradise, awaiting the end of the Demonstration of Free Will.

> And as he journeyed, he came near Damascus: and suddenly there shined round about him a light from heaven: And he fell to the earth, and heard a voice saying unto him, Saul, Saul, why persecutes thou me? And he said, who art thou, Lord? And the Lord said, I am Jesus whom thou persecutes: it is hard for thee to kick against the pricks. And he trembling and astonished said, Lord, what wilt thou have me to do? And the Lord said unto him,

> Arise, and go into the city, and it shall be told thee what thou must do (Acts 9:3-6).

Question 26: If all go to Heaven and none go to Hell, who are vessels fitted for destruction in Romans 9?

Answer: Vessels fitted for destruction imply human beings. Free Will Roleplayers are conceived, born, live their lives, and are destroyed by death. Some Roleplayers are not born—the aborted ones, the stillborn ones, the miscarried ones. They are all physically destroyed. Did God make them that way? No. God made flawless human beings. The human beings themselves corrupted the flawless human being blueprint. When the blueprint is corrupted, you then have "vessels fitted for destruction." They all die temporarily. Then, an afterlife.

God allows corrupted offspring in order to provide the Redeemer who is the Remedy for the destruction of the vessels. God intercedes in the lives of vessels fitted for destruction as they participate in the Free Will Demonstration, proving the error of disobeying God with multiple lives in multiple situations.

> What if God, willing to show his wrath, and to make his power known, endured with much longsuffering the vessels of wrath fitted to destruction: And that he might make known the riches of his glory on the vessels of mercy, which he had afore prepared unto glory (Romans 9:22-23).

Question 27: Is the afterlife the way to achieve justice for all the unfairness life presents?

Answer: In watching the YouTube video of R.C. Sproul, I learned how Immanuel Kant perceived the afterlife.

Kant: Humans must have an objective behavioral standard.

Dostoevsky: If no standard, all you have is just preferences.

Kant: If any ethic is present, you must have JUSTICE. If no justice, then "crime pays." Right behavior is rewarded, bad behavior punished. To get ultimate rewards for good or bad behavior (fairness for individual identity), there would have to be:

1) AFTERLIFE. Otherwise, life makes no sense. Good people die young, bad people live a great life for years.

2) One who is RIGHTEOUS (assures perfect justice).

3) One who is OMNISCIENT (unlimited knowledge/wisdom of all facts).

4) One who is OMNIPOTENT (power to carry out enforcement of justice).

(RC Sproul /YouTube/*Defending Your Faith Part 23*/Kant's Moral Argument.)

From this, philosophy presents a way of understanding what the afterlife provides. Alongside philosophy, major religions offer rewards and punishments in the afterlife. A variety of religions don't follow major belief systems, and, of course, atheists and agnostics have their perspectives.

MARVI-RPIA supports the contention held by the number one Person who ever lived (lives): Jesus Christ. Jesus taught the afterlife was, is, and will be.

Question 28: How has Connecting The Dots Of Identity concept of an ontological Pre-Life Elect individual been overlooked these two thousand years since Jesus taught the imperative of spiritual identity?

Answer: The most obvious answer is that there can be no such entity as a pre-life being. Pre-life must mean before life—there is yet to be life. Life is existence. There can be no substantive quality of existence if there is no definition of personhood. The Trinity are Persons. The heavenly hosts, angels, are persons. Human beings are persons. If there are two identities, one inside time and one outside time, this would mean two persons instead of a single person.

Single personhood is the basis for almost every concept of individual existence. Dual identity must account for a living person and also a nonliving person who possesses some sort of status. This doesn't support a rational definition of being. To be is to be alive. One life. To not be is to be nonexistent, or dead. You are either alive or not alive. If not alive, there is no existence. You can't be and not be at the same time and confidently assert a rational relationship.

The Bible plainly teaches that before the world was created, God mandated specific individuals were guaranteed salvation. God had knowledge of PERSONS He chose. The Bible does not disclose on what basis God chose certain ones. The Bible does NOT say God knew in advance who would become salvation worthy and chose individuals based on omniscience. No. That would mean God looked and saw that some people were better than other others. They were either born better or somehow made themselves better than all the rest. The Bible says NONE will EVER choose God, not one. God must select them.

By recognizing personhood before the world is created, the first problem is dual personhood. Person one can't be alive before the world is created and allow Person Two to exist at the same time. If Person One was never alive/never died, how can they have existence? God's knowledge of them, being undefined, remains undefined by Bible scholars. Offerings of a definition invite speculation and unorthodox conjecture. This undermines the integrity of scripture.

Connecting the Dots of Identity is outside and apart from orthodoxy. MARV-RPIA is an art project, not theology. MARVI-RPIA is the result of the last two thousand years culminating in an impression of Christian Reformed theology. The mural MARVI-RPIA paints onto the architecture of the Bible dares to imply ontological status to the Pre-Life Elect. Why NOT do this? MARVI-RPIA developed the framework to present the Elect in a context that does not violate the principles of Jesus Christ's teaching.

Jesus taught you are not your body. Spiritual life is reality. Physical life is a shadow of reality and temporary. Spiritual life is eternal. Nothing you think or do can save you. Adam and Eve doomed you to death, and to Hell, if that were possible. It isn't for the Elect. The Son of God was sent to undo Adam's effect on humanity. The Son did so.

Life continues as a Demonstration of the Error of Free Will. After enough lives prove this, the End will come. Maybe.

In defense of the many excellent bible scholars who advocate the Christian Reformed view of predestination, they have never constructed a foundation that addresses issues Connecting The Dots Of Identity (ostensibly) resolves. However, they aren't obligated to resolve them. Orthodoxy simply tries to articulate what the scripture articulates. No more, no less.

Connecting the Dots of Identity is under no such obligation. Art is the freedom to beautify, stimulate, and inspire. Verbal word pictures mean artistic license to illuminate language in the pursuit of enlightenment, splendor, and hope.

By the way, the foregoing underscores the grand debate on the Order of God's Decrees. The terms used are Infralapsarian and Supralapsarian (Glossary of Colors). Christian theology asks the question: How can God elect someone before the world is created? Before they are born? The Elect person has no existence before birth.

Connecting the Dots of Identity doesn't know how. MARVI-RPIA creates an image of how it could be. That is, the SPIRIT of God's Plan A rather the God's LITERAL Plan A.

God acknowledges SPECIFIC individuals who were, are, and will be saved BEFORE He created the world or any person. They are the Elect PERSONS, not a collective group of people.

Persons conceived AFTER the creation of the world are Roleplayers. Some die in the womb, die soon after birth, or bear the burden of birth defects. Others are born beautiful, intelligent, and rich. As Roleplayers, they all have the same awesome mission: demonstrate Free Will. Prove the Error of *flawless* human beings disobeying God.

Whenever someone comes along saying they found something the church has missed for 2,000 years, you know they are not trustworthy.

But the church hasn't had a way of describing ontological status without being heretical. MARVI-RPIA does have a way. It's an art project. It's an impression. It's not heretical, because it's not asserting to represent biblical doctrine. It's NOT trustworthy. Don't believe it. I, the author, don't believe it. However, it may be undeclared leverage against the assertions of atheists, theists, and agnostics.

Art appreciation. You like it or you don't.

> As it is written, there is none righteous, no, not one: There is none that understandeth, there is none that seeketh after God. They are all gone out of the way, they are together become unprofitable; there is none that doeth good, no, not one. Their throat is an open sepulchre; with their tongues they have used deceit; the poison of asps is under their lips (Romans 3:10-13).

> While we look not at the things which are seen, but at the things which are not seen: for the things which are seen are temporal; but the things which are not seen are eternal (2 Corinthians 4:18).

> For there shall arise false Christs, and false prophets, and shall shew great signs and wonders; insomuch that, if it were possible, they shall deceive the very elect (Matthew 24:24).

In Chapter 6 of *Connecting the Dots of Identity-1*, 100 Bible verses are given to show how prevalent Election/Predestination is. An internet search will readily prove Election/Predestination is widely featured throughout scripture. The problem has been accepting this principle. It's utterly unacceptable to 95 percent of the world. Who would accept that God only elects some to Heaven and everyone else goes to Hell? Mankind has no

Free Will; everything is predestined. This means God is not fair, not moral, not love.

Connecting the Dots of Identity aspires to change this unacceptable view via Modern Abstract Religious Verbal Impressionism-Roleplay Identity Array. God IS wonderful. He IS beautiful.

Question 29: Scripture teaches your body is the temple of the Holy Spirit. *Connecting the Dots of Identity* declares Jesus's number one message is you are NOT your body. How is this resolved?

> What? Know ye not that your body is the temple of the Holy Ghost which is in you, which ye have of God, and ye are not your own? (1 Corinthians 6:19)

Answer: One, the Holy Spirit (HSID) does have a specific time to arrive and abide with the Elect person. It's a reference point—a symbol of identity but not authentic identity.

Two, the Holy Spirit is omnipresent as He makes Himself a part of the congregation in their places of worship. It's a way of saying the Holy Spirit is participating with people. It is not so much a physical process as it is a spiritual relationship. Your body is a temporary physical location. God and the Holy Spirit are omnipresent. They are inside and outside your physical, mental, and spiritual location. This includes the time you have yet to meet the Holy Spirit. It doesn't mean He is not present with you. There's just no specific relationship.

The Holy Spirit could be likened to a bridge going from inauthentic identity to authentic identity or from a house (old identity) to a temple (new identity). In life, we have a residence, a house, but we are not the actual house we live in. When we are born-again, our body is like a new spiritual environment. Our house is a spiritual environment. Our car is a spiritual environment.

There should be an awareness of the Holy Spirit wherever we go, wherever we are. The whole point of spiritual awareness is to REMOVE the focus from the inauthentic PHYSICAL Roleplay identity. We live WITH it; we don't live IN it. It's not us. We are actually a SPIRITUAL identity.

The physical aspect of sin involving the body plays back into role-play identity. The admonition is to abstain from thinking and behaving by compulsion. Don't succumb. Your body wants comfort, pleasure, entertainment, and leisure. This is not the function of a temple. Respect it. Honor it. But you have a role to play. The role is only partially physical. The role is mental and spiritual.

Spiritually, your physical body can't defend you in spiritual attacks, spiritual wrestling matches, or spiritual beatdowns. You are in a constant spiritual fight. You need the Holy Spirit to win. Until the Holy Spirit arrives, you lose every fight, even while seeming to win. Don't be deceived.

> My flesh and my heart faileth: but God is the strength of my heart, and my portion forever (Psalm 73:26).

> Thus saith the Lord; cursed be the man that trusteth in man, and maketh flesh his arm, and whose heart departeth from the Lord (Jeremiah 17:5).

The light of the body is the eye: if therefore thine eye be single, thy whole body shall be full of light. But if thine eye be evil, thy whole body shall be full of darkness. If therefore the light that is in thee be darkness, how great is that darkness! (Matthew 6:22-23)

Therefore I say unto you, Take no thought for your life, what ye shall eat, or what ye shall drink; nor yet for your body, what you shall put on. Is not the life more than meat, and the body than raiment? (Matthew 6:25)

Watch and pray, that ye enter not into temptation: the spirit indeed is willing, but the flesh is weak (Matthew 26:41).

And he said unto his disciples, Therefore I say unto you, Take no thought for your life, what ye shall eat; neither for the body, what ye shall put on (Luke 12:22).

For as we have many members in one body, and all members have not the same office: So we, being many, are one body in Christ, and every one members one of another (Romans 12:4-5).

Know you not that you are the temple of God, and that the Spirit of God dwelleth in you? If any man defile the temple of God, him shall God destroy; for the temple of God is holy, which temple ye are (1 Corinthians 3:16-17).

What? Know ye not that your body is the temple of the Holy Ghost which is in you, which ye have of God, and ye are not your own?

For ye are bought with a price: therefore glorify God in your body, and in your spirit, which are God's (1 Corinthians 6:19-20).

For we know that if our earthly house of this tabernacle were dissolved, we have a building of God, a house not made with hands, eternal in the heavens. For in this we groan, earnestly desiring to be clothed upon with our house which is from heaven: If so be that being clothed we shall not be found naked. For we that are in this tabernacle do groan, being burdened: not for that we would be unclothed, but clothed upon, that mortality might be swallowed up of life. Now he that hath wrought us for the selfsame thing is God, who also hath given unto us the earnest of the Spirit. Therefore we are always confident, knowing that, whilst we are at home in the body, we are absent from the Lord: (For we walk by faith, not by sight): We are confident, I say, and willing rather to be absent from the body, and to be present with the Lord (2 Corinthians 5:1-8).

Put on the whole armor of God that ye may be able to stand against the wiles of the devil. For we wrestle not against flesh and blood, but against principalities, against powers, against the rulers of the darkness of this world, against spiritual wickedness in high places (Ephesians 6:11-12).

Question 30: Why does Christian Reformed theology promote changing your life when your life is already determined? If it's predestined, you really can't change.

Answer: Yes, and the accompanying questions about why preach the gospel, why promote Christianity, or why not do whatever you feel like doing if all is determined in the afterlife?

Organized non-Reformed religion teaches you can make the change from bad to good. Repent of your sins. Choose God. You control your salvation. There is no determinism.

Reformed theology teaches Election/Predestination. We are saved before the foundation of the world. But they are inconsistently adding that you MUST do this, do that, or do the other to be saved. And—you must STOP doing this, that, or the other to be saved.

In the defense of Reformed theology, behavior matters in the sense that what you do reflects your born-again status. If your behavior is incompatible with scriptural principles, it indicates your born-again status may not be valid.

Secondly, the Holy Spirit utilizes theists to influence atheists and agnostics. For God to directly intrude into physical reality would eliminate Free Will to deny, refute, or disbelieve Him. There would be no further need to continue the Demonstration of Free Will. Realization of God would be obvious. So, He makes use of us, the sane ones, to help open the eyes of the unsane.

Nonreligion implies you can make the change from bad to good or good to bad. It then inconsistently adds that, based on materialism/physicalism, life began from nothing, is unguided and purposeless, and goes back to nothing. But if that is so, everyday life suggests undefined forces are acting on living agents who are under an illusion of Free Will. Apparently, the illusion protects sanity. Thoughts of no legitimate choices, no unique identity, and no purpose induce despair, depression, frustration, resentment, rage, recklessness, murder, and suicide.

A positive view of determinism, the absence of Free Will, is the theme of CD1/CD2. *Connecting the Dots of Identity* portrays the limited Free Will of the inauthentic identity. This means choices in life are only freely made under the influence of heredity, environment, and experience. Materialism/physicalism stops at this point. Limited Free Will continues, as the ability to choose godliness has been removed by the sin of Adam and Eve. The authentic identity in Paradise that CD1/CD2 illustrates as Super-Spiritual Identities, SSIDs, is determined; no Free Will to disobey God exists. Similarly, First-Class Angels exercise Free Will by forever accepting God's determined will for their lives.

So, the Free Will life of Elect Roleplayers, those God guaranteed salvation before the foundation of the world, is demonstrated by those who have Holy Spirit Identity (HSID) status—the born-again Christians. This includes those yet to meet the Holy Spirit. How these people live is a function of their worldview status, either objective morality or subjective morality. The crude Insanity Chart of CD1/CD2 presents this status as sane, unsane, or insane individuals.

So, yes, Christian Reformed theology teaches the ability to change life ONLY in the ways it is free to change. Those ways are LIMITED. PURE Free Will formerly possessed by the Serpent, Adam, and Eve became corrupted by sin. Sin NEVER goes away. It's always present.

God makes a specific intervention in the life of the Roleplayer. You don't change, God changes you. You don't want to change. God changes you. You don't expect such a thing as being "born-again." You're born-again.

As far as behaving in any manner you so desire, once you realize your born-again status, careless behavior is inconsistent with being born-again. To be born-again, receiving the Holy Spirit Identity, is the definition of being a new creature. You have no interest in your spiritually blind, selfish, former identity. *The Trinity—Father, Son, and Holy Spirit—assist you in moving from spiritual identity-negative (SID-NEG) to spiritual identity-positive (SID-POS).* This should show progress from spiritual immaturity toward spiritual maturity. No human being is sinless, but now sin is abhorrent. Gradually, spiritual maturity confirms the change from old ways to new ways.

For other Elect Roleplayers, life goes on as usual. God does not make His presence known. The contrast is to show no one will choose God of their own will.

Meanwhile, CD1/CD2 is trying very, very, very hard to make a significant contribution to life. This is why I'm in the world. This is why you're in the world also. We are the result of a flawless creature's deathly decision and God's grace and mercy to rescind it.

> Let not sin therefore reign in your mortal body, that ye should obey it in the lusts thereof. Neither yield ye your members as instruments of unrighteousness unto sin: but yield yourselves unto God, as those that are alive from the dead, and your members as instruments of righteousness unto God. For sin shall not have dominion over you: for ye are not under the law, but under grace. What then? Shall we sin, because we are not under the law, but under grace? God forbid. Know ye not, that to whom ye yield yourselves servants to obey, his servants ye are to whom ye obey; whether of sin unto death, or of obedience unto righteousness? But God be thanked, that ye were the servants of sin, but ye have obeyed from the heart that form of doctrine which was delivered you. Being then made free from sin, ye became the servants of righteousness (Romans 6:12-18).

Fatalism

Though the word "fatalism" is commonly used to refer to an attitude of resignation in the face of some future event or events which are thought to be inevitable, philosophers usually use the word to refer to the view that we are powerless to do anything other than what we actually do.

("Fatalism," *Stanford Encyclopedia of Philosophy*, plato.stanford.edu/entries/fatalism/, December 18, 2002. Accessed April 2021).

Determinism

The doctrine is that all events, including human action, are ultimately determined by causes external to the will. Some philosophers have taken determinism to imply that individual human beings have no Free Will and cannot be held morally responsible for their actions.

("Determinism," Definitions from Oxford Languages, lexico.com/en/definition/determinism, April 2021.)

Defeatism

The attitude, policy, or conduct of a person who admits, expects, or no longer resists defeat, because of a conviction that further struggle or effort is futile. Pessimistic resignation.

("Defeatism," Dictionary.com, dictionary.com/browse/defeatism, April 2021.)

CHAPTER 32

QUESTIONS AND ANSWERS 31-40

Question 31: Is blasphemy against the Holy Spirit the unforgivable sin because it's committed by a person who isn't 100 percent human?

Answer: According to the image MARVI-RPIA paints, only a person who is not 100 percent human could commit such a sin. A 100 percent human might say the same words but without any conviction. They lack an understanding of the terms involved in the charge. Being human means every Roleplayer has a corresponding SSID in Paradise. They are not in jeopardy of being unforgiven for any sin. The anti-Christian Saul, who was transformed into the Apostle Paul, admitted he was a blasphemer (1 Timothy).

Jesus was accused by the religious authorities, the Pharisees, of acting on behalf of the Great Deceiver. The Pharisees themselves were deceived by the Great Deceiver, or perhaps his accomplices. A 100 percent human being may be deceived and an accomplice of Satan, but only temporarily, and only by permission from the Lord.

When thinking of any number of heinous, gut-wrenching, unthinkable acts that man could commit or has committed, why is blasphemy of the Holy Spirit the one unforgivable sin? These are only words, not acts. "Sticks and stones may break my bones, but words will never hurt me."

Blasphemy is unforgivable, considering we know words have power. Jesus is called the Word. Words brought the world into being. We do not have the power of words that we could have. That is a good thing. People distort speech. People distort print. As the New Testament Book of James points out, who can tame the tongue?

Jesus, 100 percent man, acted by the power from above—by God. To simply SAY His power was from Satan was not the same as UNDERSTANDING what that meant. Do not take His name in vain. Be mindful of your words. Revere Him. Never curse Him. The Trinity is holy, holy, holy! Blasphemy is a warning.

The demons know that Jesus is not Satan. However, demons know they are already unforgiven. Blasphemy doesn't harm them any further. Demons act to accuse and oppress humans to prove humans are not worthy of God's favor. They assert that humans are just as bad as or worse than angels. That accusation would have to apply to Jesus, who is also a human being.

Jesus as 100 percent human was the Redeemer that Third-Class Angels sought to emulate by marrying human females. Apparently, they couldn't comprehend that Jesus would be 100 percent deity also. An affront to Jesus is also an affront to the Holy Spirit. The Holy Spirit acted as the Father of Jesus's human identity.

> And I thank Christ Jesus our Lord, who hath enabled me, for that he counted me faithful, putting me into the ministry; who was before a blasphemer, and a persecutor, and injurious: but I obtained mercy, because I did it ignorantly in unbelief (1 Timothy 1:12-13).

> In the beginning was the Word, and the Word was with God, and the Word was God (John 1:1).

Jesus answered and said unto them, Verily I say unto you, If ye have faith, and doubt not, ye shall not only do this which is done to the fig tree, but also if ye shall say unto this mountain, Be thou removed, and be thou cast into the sea; it shall be done (Matthew 21:21).

Wherefore I say unto you, all manner of sin and blasphemy shall be forgiven unto men: but the blasphemy against the Holy Ghost shall not be forgiven unto men. And whosoever speaketh a word against the Son of man, it shall be forgiven him: but whosoever speaketh against the Holy Ghost, it shall not be forgiven him, neither in this world, neither in the world to come (Matthew 12:31-32).

But when the Pharisees heard it, they said, this fellow doth not cast out devils, but by Beelzebub the prince of the devils. And Jesus knew their thoughts, and said unto them, Every kingdom divided against itself is brought to desolation; and every city or house divided against itself shall not stand: And if Satan cast out Satan, he is divided against himself; how shall then his kingdom stand? (Matthew 12:24-26)

But the tongue can no man tame; it is an unruly evil, full of deadly poison (James 3:8).

But Jesus held his peace, And the high priest answered and said unto him, I adjure thee by the living God, that thou tell us whether thou be the Christ, the Son of God. Jesus saith unto him, Thou hast said: nevertheless I say unto you, hereafter shall ye see the Son of man sitting on the right hand of power, and coming in the clouds

> of heaven. Then the high priest rent his clothes, saying, He hath spoken blasphemy; what further need have we of witnesses? Behold, now ye have heard his blasphemy (Matthew 26:63-65).

Question 32: *Connecting the Dots of Identity* seems to conflict with the scriptures that teach only a few will be saved and many lost. How is this answered?

Answer: The teaching a few will be saved:

> And I heard the number of them which were sealed: and there were sealed an hundred and forty and four thousands of all the tribes of the children of Israel (Revelation 7:4).

It is fair to say the 144,000 is a symbol of a number saved, and that the tribes represent a group of people saved. The terms "few" and "many" apply depending on the context.

> Then said one unto him, Lord, are there few that be saved? And he said unto them, Strive to enter in at the strait gate: for many, I say unto you, will seek to enter in, and shall not be able (Luke 13:23-24).

You notice that Jesus didn't answer yes or no. He didn't say many will be saved. He didn't say few will be saved. He spoke of INDIVIDUAL salvation, not GROUP salvation.

The Minister of Art might say, "What kind of question is that? The question should be, am I saved?" You're the only person that matters when it comes to salvation. If you are saved, then you can help others to salvation.

Scripture uses the words "few" and "many" to describe similar scenarios. For example, FEW saved relative to a general number, and MANY saved relative to a specific number. It doesn't make scripture contradictory. The way to read scripture is from the view of the whole Bible. Jesus says to strive to go the difficult path away from destruction. This sounds like a "works doctrine" of a man getting himself saved. That can't be the correct message. Rather, it would seem to imply a focus on yourself.

The Bible indicates the world is not interested in the things of God. People who profess to follow the Lord Jesus Christ make up a small portion of the world. The people who ARE Christians versus those who SAY they're Christians make up an even smaller portion. MARVI-RPIA agrees with this. Secondly, MARVI-RPIA imagery is that EVERYBODY who goes to Heaven is still a remnant of the EVERYBODY who goes to Hell. Hell was created for the Devil and his angels. Angels represent an innumerable number.

The premise is there are many more angels in existence than humans. Humans exist in segments of time, while angels are in existence all at once. Have you ever heard the question "How many angels can dance on the head of a pin"? Do you remember the scripture of an angel answering Jesus that his name was Legion: "For we are many"? Additionally, the heavenly hosts have been unnamed and relegated to "angels" to represent ALL spirit beings.

How many lives, Super-Spiritual Identities (SSIDs) and angelic identities, were identified before God created the world? Elect Roleplayers would represent every person created from Adam in the Garden of Eden to the last person created to end the Demonstration of Free Will. Think of First-

Class Angels, Second-Class Angels, and Third-Class Angels. Think of all the heavenly hosts God created who are not necessarily named in scripture.

What role did the Nephilim play in corrupting human offspring? How many humans are 100 percent human? How many Non-Elect Roleplayers are living at any given time, compared to the Elect Roleplayers? Seemingly, HSID persons are always in the minority. Evil is everywhere; virtue only here and there. Additionally, the Roleplay identity we have and see in others is imprecise. We aren't able to tell who is human and who is not. We may not even know that about ourselves.

The general feeling for mature Christians is that there aren't many people in the world who understand what Christianity means. Christians struggle with other Christians. Many Christians behave like non-Christians.

We do know God saved us before He created the world. That is our consolation. Who we are now is a character by force of heredity, environment, and experiences. Our tendency is to follow the broad path of destruction. We only follow the narrow path to life by the Holy Spirit leading us. In this regard, we don't devise our own path and follow through with the directions we've plotted. We rely on spiritual guidance.

Another altogether different view is this: Suppose a 10 trillion population level at the time of the Flood in Noah's day (*Connecting the Dots of Identity-1*. Flood 1, 2, 3). Ten percent is 1 trillion. Five percent is 500 billion. *One percent is 100 billion. A few saved could be 10 percent, 5 percent, or even 1 percent.* Think of the total number of people who have lived since Adam and Eve. Are a few saved? Are many saved?

> But when he saw Jesus afar off, he ran and worshipped him, And cried with a loud voice, and said, what have I to do with thee,

Jesus, thou Son of the highest God? I adjure thee by God, that thou torment me not. For he said unto him, Come out of the man, thou unclean spirit. And he asked him, what is thy name? And he answered, saying, my name is Legion: for we are many (Mark 5:6-9).

Then shall he say also unto them on the left hand, Depart from me, ye cursed, into everlasting fire, prepared for the devil and his angels (Matthew 25:41).

After this I beheld, and, lo, a great multitude, which no man could number, of all nations, and kinds, and people, and tongues, stood before the throne, and before the Lamb, clothed with white robes, and palms in their hands (Revelation 7:9).

Question 33: The theology of Universalism is bad enough (Glossary of Colors). It says everyone goes to Heaven and no one goes to Hell. But Universalism contradicts two biblical principles. Everyone does NOT go to Heaven. People WILL end up in Hell. *Connecting the Dots of Identity* denies Universalism. *Connecting the Dots of Identity* is Christian Impressionism, not theology. It's an art project. But the pressing question is how can such an art project be so irresponsible? It "shows" people they are going to Heaven because their authentic identity is already there. Isn't that the height of danger? The height of irresponsibility? There's no need to be born-again. There's no need to be concerned about sin. There's no need to worry about Hell.

Answer: *Connecting The Dots of Identity* as an art project is intended to offer imagery that enhances life. The function of art is not to impose definition but to expose definition by progressive expression. *Unfortunately, people are already influenced by what they feel and what they hope. They choose what Bible scriptures they like and dismiss scriptures they don't like.* God would never send a baby to Hell. God would never deny Heaven to someone who truly wants it. I'm not a bad person. My parents mean well, my children mean well, my friends mean well. Only people who don't believe in God are denied Heaven and sent to Hell. This is how many people feel.

People don't read their Bible. People don't understand religion. *They make up their own religion.*

The imagery of MARVI-RPIA is meant to share an impression of what God's Salvation Plan might appear to be. It is an unorthodox rendition of the Bible, and no doubt an absolutely crude example of what God's actual Salvation Plan is. Anyone who believes *Connecting the Dots of Identity* is theology is missing the point. It is not theology. It is an art project. The biblical doctrine of Election and Predestination is beyond what most people grasp. Churches teaching this from scripture leave most people cold.

They have no Free Will? If they have no Free Will and God already chose some and rejected others, what's the point in having the church? Why did Jesus arrive? There are many questions and no answers that satisfy. None of it really makes sense.

So, it may be irresponsible to present imagery of scripture that helps explain Election and Predestination. *But it seems more irresponsible to do nothing and to continue seeing people lose hope, lose faith, and lose confidence in the God of the Bible.*

Modern Abstract Religious Verbal Impressionism paints a picture of Connecting the Dots of Identity. Your identity is important to God. The world is important to God. Life is not out of control. Everything is as it should be. It should be great to have another model that helps us understand what is happening and why. We have a lot of models, some individual models, and some worldwide models. Perhaps *Connecting the Dots of Identity* will motivate people to read the Bible. Is Christian Reformed Impressionism a reasonable impression of the Bible (Glossary of Colors)? If it is, there is a reason for great joy in the concept of Election and Predestination. It can work. God is more beautiful than we ever imagined.

If Connecting The Dots Of Identity becomes influential enough that people depend on it for their salvation, it won't matter. Their salvation is already secure and has been since before they were born. If people think and behave badly because they now think they're guaranteed Heaven, it doesn't matter. Salvation was a foregone conclusion before the world was created.

If there is concern about bad people never becoming good people, don't worry. Bad people are either Elect Roleplayers—having a corresponding Pre-Life Elect identity in Paradise—or bad people who are less than 100 percent human or of Nephilim ancestry. Ancestors of Nephilim may join Satan and his demons in the afterlife. If Hell is created for the Devil and his angels (Matthew 25:41), the implication from *Connecting the Dots of Identity* is no 100 percent human goes there. The persons who are cast into Hell are all one "family" of evil spirits.

A *figurative* image of Hell, as only for the Devil and his angels, is presented at the time of the Flood. Who's in Hell—the Abyss? Only *Abaddon and Third-Class angels!* Not the Nephilim. They died. Oblivion. Not human 100 percent beings. They died. No Abyss. No Oblivion. *Why didn't God relegate EVERYONE to chains of darkness? The Abyss. Hell. It's the end of the world.*

> For if God spared not the angels that sinned, but cast them down to hell, and delivered them into chains of darkness, to be reserved unto judgment (2 Peter 2:4).

> And the angels which kept not their first estate, but left their own habitation, he hath reserved in everlasting chains under darkness unto the judgment of the great day (Jude 1:6).

> And they had a king over them, which is the angel of the bottomless pit, whose name in the Hebrew tongue is Abaddon, but in the Greek tongue hath his name Apollyon (Revelation 9:11).

The concern around "favoritism" echoes the reason people reject predestination. If you are predestined for Heaven, you are forever in God's favor. Why not sin to your heart's content? Nothing will change your heavenly destination. They just don't understand the depth of predestination. They don't understand being born-again.

If you are a born-again Christian, why do you still commit sins? They don't understand spiritual warfare, the progression from spiritual immaturity to maturity, and those who are Christians in name only.

Yes, there is favoritism. But to understand favoritism, as grace from God, is to understand God's salvation plan. That is not easy to understand. This is the reason Modern Abstract Religious Verbal Impressionism-Roleplay Identity Array is featured in Connecting The Dots Of Identity.

> Then shall he say also unto them on the left hand, Depart from me, ye cursed, into everlasting fire, prepared for the devil and his angels (Matthew 25:41).

Question 34: Will there be sexual activity in Heaven that includes same-sex activity?

Answer: Can there be same-sex activity when there is no gender differentiation? There is likely to be dynamic sensual activity, but not necessarily between two persons. The activity may be the opportunity to simulate sexual activity by assuming a "body" and exploring a "menu" of scenarios. You design a scenario, or scenarios are designed based on an assumed identity, a so-called inauthentic "virtual" identity.

Sex in Heaven may resemble the New Jerusalem—a tangible experience. No permanent gender identities there. Points of contact may "model" physical experiences but be nonphysical, or "virtual." *In this sense, activity may be non-personal.* It's pristine, it's refined, and it's intuitive. It's a transformed sensual act that does not resemble the rudimentary one-on-one or group activity of earthly life. This new activity is more of a constant head-over-heels, love-at-first-sight experience that continually evolves. It doesn't build up and taper off. It will be "new." It will be "mysterious." It will be "exciting." The relationships will be mutual, never one-sided, unless you want that built into your scenario. Don't worry: Heaven will be queer enough for anyone and straight enough for anyone. It will certainly be atypical, unnatural, and extraordinary.

> And I saw a new heaven and a new earth: for the first heaven and the first earth were passed away; and there was no more sea. And I John saw the holy city, new Jerusalem, coming down from God out of heaven, prepared as a bride adorned for her husband (Revelation 21:1-2).

Question 35: Will bestiality, pedophilia, rape, and snuff also be on the sexual activity menu?

Answer: Can there be fornication where there is no deceit, no lust, no coercion, no jealousy, no hate, and no exploited partner? Can there be adultery when there is no marriage? Can there be pedophilia when there are no children? Can there be bestiality when there are no beasts? Can there be rape when there are no victims? Can there be snuff when there is no murder?

In Heaven, there are no malicious thoughts, intentions, or acts. In the pursuit of fun, entertainment, recreation, pleasure, and adventure, *God provides unimagined and unlimited attention to details that engage the intellect in expression.*

But how could a heavenly menu include homosexuality, bestiality, pedophilia, rape, and murder?

It doesn't! Those are malicious terms for despicable acts on earth. In Heaven, those terms translate to other products, simulated productions, and non-real other events. As a child, we should not be exposed to sexual intercourse, autopsies, severe birth defects, human and animal torture, medical surgeries, or explicit horror films. A child's mind is not suited to comprehend such discoveries. Similarly, we can't comprehend limited options forbidden on Earth and unlimited options not forbidden in Heaven. *At this time, it's "too adult" for our childlike world to grasp.* We are not prepared for it.

Here on Earth, computer graphics simulate all manner of imagined scenarios. We have superheroes, monsters, aliens, time travel, life on other planets, pornography, world wars, murder, theft, assault, and deceased persons brought to life. These are not intended to be real. We do not expect actual events. *We expect the simulated event to be realistic.*

And the final consolation to our apprehension is that we won't remember any negative aspects of former things, sexual or otherwise. They will be like a bad dream, fading away from memory. We will have brand-new sensual interests.

Give God credit. He will have thought of everything. The Heaven we usually hear of, unfortunately, is like many church services—bor-ring.

Question 36 A: If a pastor, minister, or preacher is so devoted to being a servant of God, why is it that 90 percent of them are married, giving half or more of their focus to their wife and children rather than the Lord? God is not that attractive? Sex and children are more important than God?

Answer: First, let's look at three scripture references.

> One: I say therefore to the unmarried and widows, it is good for them if they abide even as I. But if they cannot contain, let them marry: for it is better to marry than to burn (1 Corinthians 7:8-9).
>
> Two: A bishop then must be blameless, the husband of one wife, vigilant, sober, of good behaviour, given to hospitality, apt to teach . . . One that ruleth well his own house, having his children in subjection with all gravity; For if a man know not how to rule his own house, how shall he take care of the church of God? (1 Timothy 3:2, 4-5).

> Three: But I would have you without carefulness. He that is unmarried careth for the things that belong to the Lord, how he may please the Lord: But he that is married careth for the things that are of the world, how he may please his wife. (1 Corinthians 7:32)

First, from what the scriptures teach, we know sexual activity is forbidden outside marriage. If you are interested in a sexual relationship and/or have an interest in children, you must marry.

Secondly, if you are called to be a leader in the church, especially to pastor a church, you must be a husband of one wife (1 Corinthians 7:32-33).

So, the initial question could be is the compulsion for sex and/or children so strong that it takes precedence over things of the Lord?

The answer has to be yes: the sexual impulse is so strong that it's easier to marry than fight temptation or fall into sexual sin. Your body will then belong to your spouse, and vice versa. You must also accept the possibility of children.

That is all certainly understandable until you think about the number of pastors who are married. You might guess that if someone was called to serve the Lord BEFORE they become married, the number of men who chose to remain unmarried might be half—50 percent. As the men mature and continue in life, perhaps the compulsion to marry increases to 75 percent of pastors being married. Now only 25 out of 100 pastors are dependent on God to fulfill their lives. But 25 of 100 is not likely the highest number. Only 10 of 100 is more likely. *So, 90 of 100 are not able to remain single.*

How many pastors can you name who are single? Does it seem 90 percent are married? Is 90 percent a reasonable number? Is it more like 99 percent? *Are the remaining 1 percent on dating sites?*

There's absolutely nothing wrong with 100 percent of pastors being married. Nothing wrong with 10 percent being married. It's easy to get married. It's NOT easy to be single. This is explored in previous chapters.

Question 36 B: Are married pastors sexually weak because they marry to defend against temptation, making them also spiritually weak?

Answer: Probably. But we all respond to influences of heredity, environment, and experiences. Until the Holy Spirit intercedes, we demonstrate the effects of Free Will. Even after HSID, as a new creature, the other aspects of our identity are still a factor. Being weak spiritually or sensually has still produced many great men of God. They have managed to make significant contributions to society despite being compromised by marriage and children. *They will be quick to point out that they would be distracted from their pastoral role if they were not married.* They would not be able to focus on their mission. We have to take their word for it.

Question 37: If the Dream Identity (DID) is part of the inauthentic identity, who I am in dreams is not really me. Does the Minister of Art imply I should disown, renounce, and disassociate my awake identity from who I am in my dreams?

Answer: Yes. Dreams are weird, interesting, frightening, mysterious, exhausting, elusive, frustrating, maddening, and much more. A lifetime of analysis and centuries of studies haven't made us any more convinced that reliable dream interpretation exists. Perhaps the best clue is from scripture. *Only God can accurately interpret dreams.*

This Minister of Art has kept a dream journal for many years. Only the most vivid and meaningful dreams go into the journal. There may be weeks or even months between entries. Finally, in recent years, the realization came that the dream identity is NOT me. That realization helped illustrate one-eighth of the Roleplay Identity Array impression—the Dream Identity (DID).

Of all the identities in the eight-part array—SSID, HSID, SID, MID, PID, CID, DID, and ESID—the Dream ID is particularly inauthentic. It is NOT me in the dreams no matter how real, how comprehensive, or how detailed my character is. Yes, there in dreams is my mother, my father, my siblings, my friends, my house, my car, etcetera. *But they are not real, and neither am I.*

How do I know it's NOT me? *I don't have Free Will!* There is no agency, an ability to initiate change or direct an outcome. I'm not active—physically or mentally. *I'm a passenger, a sightseer.* Even spiritually, I'm not active. Only God acts. We are uninterested and spiritually blind until He acts. This is confirmed as dreams shift back and forth through time. Time BEFORE I met the Holy Spirit, time of spiritual immaturity, and up through the present and beyond. Even back to my childhood identity (CID), I may dream.

So, perhaps a dream represents your subconscious mind projecting the inauthenticity of your imposed identity—your identity from heredity, environment, and experience. *You dream an inauthentic identity that's built upon an inauthentic identity.* An identity that continues heredity, environment, and experience, then extends the identity with fabrication, supposition, and impossibility.

As in real life, things seem to make sense, but they don't. You seem to be real in your dreams until you wake up. Rather than trying to figure out the dream, it may be better to laugh it off, even the nightmares. Laugh and say, *So what*? That dream person is never me. It's always a subconscious construct. And further, dreams are a reminder that I don't have full access to any inauthentic identity. Therefore, I'll focus on the identity I'm known by—the person God identified as saved before I was born.

My dream is not me. My past is not me. The present is not me. I'm a Super-Spiritual Identity in the future, guaranteed by the Greatest Person Who Ever Lived and Lives.

Meanwhile, just improvise. Be the best Roleplayer possible.

Question 38: Can a person receive the Holy Spirit (HSID) after they die?

> For then must he often have suffered since the foundation of the world: but now once in the end of the world hath he appeared to put away sin by the sacrifice of himself? And as it is appointed unto men once to die, but after this the judgment: So Christ was once offered to bear the sins of many; and unto them that look for him shall he appear the second time without sin unto salvation (Hebrews 9:26-28).

Answer: Though there are exceptions to the rule, the rule is once you're dead, your afterlife fate is sealed. You are destined for Heaven or for Hell.

However, in orthodox Bibles, there are ten examples of people who arose from the dead. We also have numerous examples in the medical records of deceased persons who recovered.

Do these exceptions modify the rule? No? Maybe?

In laying out the imagery of Connecting The Dots Of Identity via MARVI-RPIA, attention is given to people who do NOT receive the Holy Spirit before they die, seconds before death, or at death. Their Roleplay identity has ended. If they are 100 percent human, their SSID counterpart awaits in Paradise. If they are not 100 percent human, they cease to exist. No afterlife.

Christian orthodox teaching is salvation is no longer possible after death. That teaching may be true, but it may not matter.

If salvation has been accomplished BEFORE the world was created, and that includes every 100 percent human being, it follows that God is the loving God we know Him to be. No one goes to Hell because they are already guaranteed Heaven. Hell is created for the Devil and his angels. Our present life is a demonstration of Free Will initiated by Adam and Eve. We simply Roleplay our identity based on heredity, environment, and experiences. Our Roleplay identity ends, and we die.

The intercession by the Holy Spirit (HSID) BEFORE death simply shows the contrast between those who reject God and those who accept God despite former rejection. Grace versus works.

> (1) “And the Lord heard the voice of Elijah; and the soul of the child came into him again, and he revived” (1 Kings 17:22).

> (2) “And he went up, and lay upon the child, and put his mouth upon his mouth, and his eyes upon his eyes, and his hands upon

his hands: and stretched himself upon the child; and the flesh of the child waxed warm. Then he returned, and walked in the house to and fro; and went up, and stretched himself upon him: and the child sneezed seven times, and the child opened his eyes" (2 Kings 4:34-35).

(3) "And it came to pass, as they were burying a man, that, behold, they spied a band of men; and they cast the man into the sepulchre of Elisha: and when the man was let down, and touched the bones of Elisha, he revived, and stood up on his feet" (2 Kings 13:21).

(4) "And he came and touched the bier: and they that bare him stood still. And he said, Young man, I say unto thee, Arise. And he that was dead sat up, and began to speak. And he delivered him to his mother" (Luke 7:14-15).

(5) "And he put them all out, and took her by the hand, and called, saying, Maid, arise. And her spirit came again, and she arose straightway: and he commanded to give her meat" (Luke 8:54-55).

(6) "And when he thus had spoken, he cried with a loud voice, Lazarus, come forth. And he that was dead came forth, bound hand and foot with grave clothes: and his face was bound about with a napkin. Jesus saith unto them, Loose him, and let him go" (John 11:43-44).

(7) "And he saith unto them, be not affrighted: Ye seek Jesus of Nazareth, which was crucified: he is risen; he is not here: behold the place where they laid him" (Mark 16:6).

(8) "And the graves were opened; and many bodies of the saints which slept arose, And came out of the graves after his resurrection, and went into the holy city, and appeared unto many" (Matthew 27:52-53).

(9) "But Peter put them all forth, and kneeled down, and prayed; and turning him to the body said, Tabitha, arise. And she opened her eyes: and when she saw Peter, she sat up. And he gave her his hand, and lifted her up, and when he had called the saints and widows, presented her alive" (Acts 9:40-41).

(10) "And there sat in a window a certain young man named Eutychus, being fallen into a deep sleep: and as Paul was long preaching, he sunk down with sleep, and fell down from the third loft, and was taken up dead. And Paul went down, and fell on him, and embracing him said, Trouble not yourselves; for his life is in him. When he therefore was come up again, and had broken bread, and eaten, and talked a long while, even till break of day, so he departed. And they brought the young man alive, and were not a little comforted" (Acts 20:9-12).

Question 39: Does *Connecting the Dots of Identity* imply people who claim to be agnostic regarding knowledge of God are actually atheists?

Answer: Yes. Life is a demonstration of Free Will. Free Will lost its objectivity when Adam and Eve chose their own will instead of God's will for their life. Subjective Free Will by theists, atheists, and agnostics mean they all think and behave based on heredity, environment, and experiences. Moving from SID-Neutral to SID-Negative or SID-Neutral to SID-

Positive has no bearing on whether the Holy Spirit will confer HSID status. Salvation has already been granted before the world was created.

Atheists deny the God of the Bible exists. Agnostics deny God defined by the Bible can be known. Agnostics affirm God is incomprehensible. No one has the capability to know such a being—if He exists.

But agnostics are not neutral. They don't live as Christians part of the time and as atheist part of the time. They live as atheists. *They don't have the option to open their own spiritual eyes and live as a Christian.* Even LIVING as a Christian is not the same as BEING a Christian. A non-Christian may think and behave in a superior fashion to an immature Christian, but the immature Christian has the Holy Spirit. The non-Christian does not—yet.

This is further proof that salvation is not chosen. No one is able to choose it. It chooses you.

Atheists BELIEVE there is no God. If there was, it would be impossible to NOT know Him.

Agnostics BELIEVE God isn't knowable. TRUE … until God opens their spiritual eyes.

Theists BELIEVE there is a God. They only KNOW God when He opens their spiritual eyes.

Modern Abstract Religious Verbal Impressionism-Roleplay Identity Array offers a temporary structure in the deconstruction/deconversion process of theism, non-theism, or agnosticism.

Deconstruct—to doubt, disbelieve, and discard a worldview. A neutral position is attempted while evaluating a worldview to pursue.

Deconvert—Abandon specific principles of a belief system and adopt a neutral or favorable belief system in the interim.

You often hear deconstructionists and those who speak of de-conversion profess they were true followers of Christianity, 100 percent, with all their heart, for many years. They paused their commitment to Christianity in order to reevaluate why they still believe it. This evaluation could strengthen their commitment or be the first steps to be uncommitted. The reasons for the reevaluation vary from person to person.

However, these people fall into the same group as atheists and agnostics. How so? They are not in control. The Holy Spirit is in control. As CD1/CD2 illustrate, *no true follower of Christianity can deconstruct or deconvert. It is not in our power to choose to be a Christian or choose not to be a Christian.* This is GOOD! If it were a matter of choice, we would NOT choose Christianity. This is why God overrules Free Will or allows it.

And those who don't choose God are not damned. They just prove that, unless God intercedes, they pursue their inauthentic identity as dictated by heredity, environment, and experience. When their life ends, assuming they are 100 percent human, they transition to an authentic identity in Paradise. Their Roleplay identity served its purpose.

> Wherefore I give you to understand, that no man speaking by the Spirit of God calleth Jesus accursed: and that no man can say that Jesus is the Lord, but by the Holy Ghost (1 Corinthians 12:3).

Question 40: How can Jesus be the only way when Connecting The Dots Of Identity admits people from every religion and people of no religion will all be saved?

Answer: When Christians declare Jesus is the only way to salvation, they are reiterating Jesus's words. “Jesus saith unto him, I am the way, the truth, and the life: no man cometh unto the Father, but by me” (John 14:6).

Some people think Jesus was saying *His way* meant the way Jesus lived His life. His life was devoted to God as a sacrifice to bring peace, love, hope, faith, and healing to the world. That’s the way to live. Some people think Jesus was misquoted. The Bible isn’t inerrant. Some people think Jesus was great, but He wasn’t a deity.

Most people don't believe the only way to be saved is to believe in Jesus Christ. That’s obvious.

Connecting the Dots of Identity portrays Jesus as the Promise from God in the Garden of Eden. God promised a Redeemer of fallen Adam and Eve by childbirth in the future. This is how salvation will be guaranteed to those identified before the world was created.

Jesus was before the world was created. We were before the world was created. The angels were before the world was created.

Jesus is *absolutely* the only way to salvation. People are guaranteed salvation because God saved them before He created the world. People from every religion and people who hate religion were saved by Jesus because He is the Promised Redeemer to save mankind—100 percent human beings.

Jesus is the ONLY one who is capable of being the Redeemer. His identity confirms it. He lived a sinless life. He performed miracles, taught scripture, and lived scripture. He was publicly killed and publicly affirmed to live again. It doesn’t matter what other religions or atheism proclaim about other ways to salvation or the absence of salvation. They only prove the Error of Free Will imposed by heredity, environment, and experience. Their worldview continues unless and until the Holy Spirit intervenes to change their identity.

We just read in John 14:6 that Jesus said I AM the truth. What is truth? It's not just the kind of certainty we have from two plus two equals four. That is truth, but it's not intelligence. Without a comprehensive application of intelligence, we get misunderstandings. We all have a misunderstood concept of Jesus until the Holy Spirit opens our spiritual eyes. Jesus, as a Person of the Trinity, was omniscient. That meant He knew the truth about reality. None of us know reality. What we know is how well we represent what is real to us. This is how we get our laws, principles, and models of the physical, metaphysical, and abstract world. We can never achieve omniscience. Our intelligence is not fixed. Intelligence is on a sliding scale as we learn, unlearn, and forget.

Basing our intelligence on the truth of Jesus Christ is close enough to omniscience. By doing so, we will enhance the quality of life, thereby enhancing the length of life. The magnificent illustration of this is Jesus raising people from death. Jesus is the only way to *recover* life. Jesus is the only way to *eternal* life. *Jesus is the only way!* Do we trust Jesus? We do if He takes the initiative. He has—before the world was.

CHAPTER 33

QUESTIONS AND ANSWERS 41-50

Question 41: What does it mean when we are told the Bible, and the Bible ALONE, is the word of God?

Answer: The word of God is the "best" translation from the "original documents" by the "original authors." The author is God, using biblical characters to produce what He wanted mankind to know. Jesus Christ quotes it.

After the Bible was "completed" in the Book of Revelation, the last verses in Revelation caution not to add or take away from "this book." In context, this book meant the whole Bible, not just the Book of Revelation. If you add or take away anything from Revelation, you've added or taken away from the Bible. All the books relate to each other. It's a complete historical narrative.

> For I testify unto every man that heareth the words of the prophecy of this book, If any man shall add unto these things, God shall add unto him the plagues that are written in this book: And if any man shall take away from the words of the book of this prophecy, God shall take away his part out of the book of life, and out of the holy city, and from the things which are written in this book (Revelation 22:18-19).

The beauty of accepting this premise is that no matter what other spiritual edification arises over the years since the Book of Revelation was completed, we can ignore it. Trust the Bible—ONLY the Bible.

There will ALWAYS be visions, miracles, anointed ministers, prophets, tongues, and angel visitations. There will always be religious wonders. However, as long as we trust in the Bible and the Bible alone, we can be assured of what is reliable.

If religious experiences are 100 percent truly from God as they are stated, then these godly revelations should be added to the scriptures. The book of Joe Blow, the book of Anonymous, the book of Susie Q, and so on. Absolutely. Why not? *We all want to know what more God has to say and what more He has to reveal.* And throughout history, controversy has swirled over which documents qualified as sacred religious documents and which religious artifacts and relics were authorized as legitimate.

Imagine how large the Bible could become if God didn't protect it: 990 books of the Bible, or 2.5 million books of the Bible. The New International Consolidation of Bible Books. The Old Testament, New Testament, and the Up-To-Date Testament. There would be no standard Bible. The Bible could NEVER be reliable because it changes every year, every month, every week, every DAY! Everyone would have their own translation.

Additionally, and even more detrimental to the holiness of scripture, *is evil spirit infiltration*. The Devil is known as the Great Deceiver. He's known to employ ministers of light. Being ageless, cunning, and having nothing to lose, they undermine human life. They've probably memorized the whole Bible and other religious documents. They depend on people not knowing the word of God. If you ONLY read and rely on the Bible, *your chances of deception plummet.*

> And the great dragon was cast out, that old serpent, called the Devil, and Satan, which deceiveth the whole world: he was cast out into the earth, and his angels were cast out with him (Revelation 12:9).

> And no marvel; for Satan himself is transformed into an angel of light. Therefore it is no great thing if his ministers also be transformed as the ministers of righteousness; whose end shall be according to their works (2 Corinthians 11:14-15).

Trust in the Bible is problematic because few people read the Bible. Few people know the Bible. Few people believe the Bible is the word of God. The Bible is not easy to read. It's difficult. It didn't have to be. God could have made the Bible like a first-grade storybook. Why didn't He? Free Will. *If salvation was made obvious, and God wanted every person saved by the time they were ten years old, it would be easy for Him to do.* But He wants Free Will to play out. He doesn't appear on TV, on the internet, or radio. He doesn't appear in the sky or visit you in your dreams. Angels don't go door to door bringing the Good News to each residence.

If God really doesn't want any to perish, NONE would perish. Atheists bring this up all the time. *God isn't the God Christians say He is.* If He is, why is there such calamity in everyday life? Why is there random death? Why Hell? Why am I here? Why all the mystery?

As the Bible plainly says in many different scriptures, no one understands the Bible until God opens their spiritual eyes. God chooses those He saves. Those not chosen prove that their own Free Will is more important than God's will for their life. They don't know God and have no interest in knowing Him.

The Bible, and the Bible alone, tells this story. You cannot get this from General Revelation, God revealed in nature. You cannot get this from God revealed in other people, other religious documents, or God revealed by angels. *This message of Election/Predestination is only revealed in scripture.* He saved us before we were born. The reason not to open ALL spiritual eyes is so Free Will runs its course.

Question 42: Is it helpful to ask people to recite the sinner's prayer or say it ourselves to publicly affirm Jesus Christ?

Answer: "And it shall come to pass, that whosoever shall call on the name of the Lord shall be saved" (Acts 2:21).

There is apparently no specific scripture or sequence of words that define a sinner's prayer for salvation. The term "sinner's prayer" is meant to convey a person's admission that they are a sinner, they want forgiveness for their sins, and publicly affirm a desire for Jesus to come into their life as Savior.

Such a prayer, whether public or private, helps acknowledge a point of decision. At this point, the uncertainty, embarrassment, or shame of Jesus Christ is overcome. But not necessarily. Sometimes coercion or intimidation is a part of the motivation to act on a sinner's prayer.

The principle of Election/Predestination underscores nothing that is thought, said, or done contributes to salvation. God does all the work by grace. We do not contribute to salvation. We only receive it. The reason the sinner's prayer is so popular is that understanding Election/Predestination is very difficult. Affirming such a prayer comes from a belief in being destined toward salvation. You're now safe.

The sinner's prayer is a tool that represents Free Will to choose God or not choose God. *This puts salvation back in the hands of the person.* The belief in Election/Predestination is obfuscated. Belief isn't necessary if the sinner's prayer is about choice.

Question 43: Are people who claim to be astrologers, mediums, fortune tellers, etcetera less than 100 percent human? Could they be relatives of the Nephilim?

Answer: We know the Bible condemns activity or association with such practices that are associated with evil spirits. Whether or not such persons are less than 100 percent human—ancestors of the Nephilim—we can't say. If evil angels produced offspring with human females by whatever means devised, some of the offspring did survive the Flood. The scriptures disclose this plainly (Genesis 6). The "One-Drop Rule" could apply through ancestral lines until today.

(Glossary of Colors – Nephilim, One-Drop Rule)

You may ask: Why would a person pursue an occupation or hobby featuring spirits, the dead, wizards, witches, magic, and ancient knowledge of the underworld? *Certainly, no GOOD spirits would be involved with humans in this regard. That would leave only evil spirits.* Are good people, 100 percent humans, involved in practices of evil?

Yes, absolutely. Free Will includes an interest in the spiritual world. If the Holy Spirit does not meet you, you may be deceived into the underworld. Even after meeting the Holy Spirit, a person's spiritual immaturity may not discern the risk to themselves or others. However, the Elect cannot be deceived and fall, although they may certainly be oppressed. Even a demon-possessed person can be restored to God. But why take chances?

There were giants in the earth in those days; and also after that, when the sons of God came in unto the daughters of men, and they bear children to them, the same became mighty men which were of old, men of renown (Genesis 6:4).

The Emims dwelt therein in times past, a people great, and many, and tall, as the Anakims; which also were accounted giants, as the Anakims; but the Moabites called them Emims… (That also was accounted a land of giants: giants dwelt therein in old time; and the Ammonites call them Zamzummims; A people great, and many, and tall, as the Anakims; but the Lord destroyed them before them; and they succeeded them, and dwelt in their stead (Deuteronomy 2:10-11; 20-21).

Thou shalt not suffer a witch to live (Exodus 22:18).

A man also or woman that hath a familiar spirit, or that is a wizard, shall surely be put to death: they shall stone them with stones: their blood shall be upon them (Leviticus 20:27).

If there arise among you a prophet, or a dreamer of dreams, and giveth thee a sign or a wonder, And the sign or the wonder come to pass, whereof he spoke unto thee, saying, Let us go after other gods, which thou hast not known, and let us serve them; Thou shalt not hearken unto the words of that prophet, or that dreamer of dreams: for the Lord your God proveth you, to know whether ye love the Lord your God with all your heart and with all your soul. Ye shall walk after the Lord your God, and fear him, and keep his commandments, and obey his voice, and ye shall serve him, and cleave unto him. And that prophet, or that dreamer of

> dreams, shall be put to death; because he hath spoken to turn you away from the Lord your God, which brought you out of the land of Egypt, and redeemed you out of the house of bondage, to thrust thee out of the way which the Lord thy God commanded thee to walk in. So shalt thou put the evil away from the midst of thee (Deuteronomy 13:15).

> There shall not be found among you any one that maketh his son or his daughter to pass through the fire, or that useth divination, or an observer of times, or an enchanter, or a witch. Or a charmer, or a consulter with familiar spirits, or a wizard, or a necromancer. For all that do these things are an abomination unto the Lord: and because of these abominations the Lord thy God doth drive them out from before thee (Deuteronomy 18:10-12).

We know everyone who engages in such things as astrology, enchantment, or magic is not inherently evil. We enjoy mystery, deceit, and trickery as entertainment. It's fun. It displays skill. The issue is how deeply involved are people seeking knowledge and discernment from good spiritual sources versus evil spiritual sources. How do you know the difference? You don't know the difference until God opens your spiritual eyes. Even the Elect could be deceived if that were possible. It isn't.

> For there shall arise false Christs, and false prophets, and shall shew great signs and wonders; insomuch that, if it were possible, they shall deceive the very elect (Matthew 24:24).

Question 44: Is church attendance mandatory for Christians?

Answer: Church attendance is NOT mandatory. However, the church will be quick to point out:

> "And let us consider one another to provoke unto love and to good works: Not forsaking the assembling of ourselves together, as the manner of some is; but exhorting one another: and so much the more, as ye see the day approaching" Hebrews 10:24-25).

The general assembly of God's chosen people was an important part of communal life in the Old Testament. To be separated from the family of God meant being at the mercy of pagan communities. Within the religious communal lifestyle was the worship service. This became a separate assembly devoted to specific aspects of religious meaning. God was directly involved in making those services known to His people.

As rituals, traditions, and expectations passed into the New Testament, the role of organized religion became more personal than communal. A personal responsibility now applied to the observation of a day to honor the Lord. How do you honor the Lord?

You honor the Lord by associating with other like-minded Christians. This is association by physical means, virtual means, or spiritual means. You honor the Lord by associating with others to assist in ministering to those in need.

It may not be so pleasant as you learn to coordinate with people. You may not like a particular group, or they may not like you. The church is made up of those who may not have great social skills. There are people in churches who are prejudiced. There are people in churches who are selfish, condescending, and aloof. People are shy, mentally challenged, or even a nuisance. People come into the church from all backgrounds. Thankfully, most of them learn to get along better as they socialize and spiritually mature.

You can accomplish great things on your own, and many people do so. But when mobilized with others of like mind, even greater things can be accomplished. As a group, you might visit prisons, provide service to convalescent homes, or attend civic events. You could minister at homeless camps, be a comfort at hospitals, or make a difference to select charities. It can be intimidating to go alone on some of these missions. As a group, the focus is not as much on the individual. Additionally, group access many facilities is easier to acquire than inquiring alone.

Another benefit of church attendance is family-centered activities. The capability to network with other families is especially beneficial. You'll have exposure to job opportunities, housing opportunities, financial planning, and life counseling. On top of that, your children will have access to other Christian children. You'll also have a broader prospect of education for your children as you consider homeschooling, public, and private schools.

The act of neglecting to assemble implies a disassociation with other Christians and a disinterest in supporting those who do assemble. The implication is an act to *renounce* or *cease* attendance. Using scripture to threaten those who have IRREGULAR church attendance is not responsible behavior. Don't be intimidated. *Besides, church attendance isn't tied to salvation. No behavior is.* Church attendance is simply a way of participating in worship services and partaking of the privileges offered by the church.

> Not forsaking the assembling of ourselves together, as the manner of some is; but exhorting one another: and so much the more, as ye see the day approaching (Hebrews 10:25).

There are specific opportunities only available in local churches, and for that reason attendance is necessary. This is where church membership applies. Membership lays out what is expected if one is to be a participant in that local body. Having the opportunity to be baptized and join in communion of the Lord's Supper (Eucharist) remain two of the most important reasons for membership. Prayer, singing, and scriptural edification don't require church attendance, but it's certainly enhanced by being present.

A Christian should always have a desire and responsibility to support the church. A physical presence may be strongly encouraged every single week. If the church takes that position, accept it, respectfully challenge it, or else decline membership. Assume the status of a visitor.

Money underwrites the foundation and growth of the church. As we commit to giving financial support on a regular basis, this is essential to Christian teamwork. The church makes use of our giving in many ways we can't. *This is our obligation to show love and an opportunity for the church to show love.*

What's often overlooked in a church profile is discipline. The role of discipline is to hold accountable those persons who have become members of the church. They profess to be Christian, yet come into questionable circumstances. By establishing a schedule of disciplines, the church protects its integrity and the integrity of Christian principles. No one likes to be disciplined, but levels of discipline are very helpful as a teaching opportunity to the congregation.

Okay. So, you're going to join a church. Which church? How do you find a good church? You probably know the answer already. It's the same way you find anything good. Do you want a good spouse, a good car, or a good house? Do you want a good job, a good phone, or a good computer? You do the research. For the church, you outline essential features a church should provide. You find a reasonable place to invest your time and resources as you continue your spiritual education. *And if you don't find a good church, just find a church. You aren't obligated to stay there. Stay long enough for an assessment and relocate only if a better church qualifies.*

Don't put the church on a pedestal. The people there are like most other people. They may not make you feel welcome. It may feel awkward every time you attend. But you go to make the church a better place for you, your family, and the community. You're a teamplayer. You're not on staff, you're not the coach, and you're not the team owner. Just do your best.

Now, finally, what should you wear to church? Dress up, dress down, does it matter? Here are five things to consider:

1) A church is a HOUSE OF GOD. It's an honor, a privilege, and an exceptional opportunity to join others in personal acknowledgment of His Majesty. Appropriate attire befitting the worship service should include respect for the venue.

2) Making an attractive visual presentation to the community and especially the church BEAUTIFIES the attendance experience. God loves beauty. We love beauty.

3) When attending events that feature ROYALTY, the attendees dress in a manner befitting the occasion and the nobility. Who is more royal or noble than God?

4) To DRESS UP for church service demonstrates your probable destination to others as you leave home on a weekend. You're probably not going to work, especially if your family is with you. *You become a witness to others* that you're sacrificing part of your day for church. Otherwise, you appear as 95 percent of people leaving home on Saturday

or Sunday. As people tend to dress down more than dress up these days, nice clothing makes a good impression.

5) Children of the King should present themselves as KINGLY CHILDREN. Look no further than children of royalty in the natural realm. They represent the crown. Children of royalty in the spiritual realm also represent the crown. Look ordinary, or look exceptional?

No money? No nice clothes? Don't worry. People at church shouldn't judge you. They may even help you buy clothing or buy clothing for you. Speak to the elders of the church.

Do you live in a country where clothing is not a luxury? Do you live in a country where Christianity is oppressed or dangerous? This reminder applies to people who have become lax in their attitude toward the worship service. There are other ways to express appreciation and beauty where options are limited.

> Then said he unto Zebah and Zalmunna, What manner of men were they whom ye slew at Tabor? And they answered, as thou art, so were they; each one resembled the children of a king. And he said, they were my brethren, even the sons of my mother: as the LORD liveth, if ye had saved them alive, I would not slay you (Judges 8:18-19).

> Remember the sabbath day, to keep it holy. Six days shalt thou labour, and do all thy work: But the seventh day is the sabbath of the Lord thy God: in it thou shalt not do any work, thou, nor thy son, nor thy daughter, thy manservant, nor thy maidservant, nor thy cattle, nor thy stranger that is within thy gates: For in six days the Lord made heaven and earth, the sea, and all that in them is,

and rested the seventh day: wherefore the Lord blessed the sabbath day, and hallowed it (Exodus 10:8-11).

And he said unto them, the sabbath was made for man, and not man for the sabbath (Mark 2:27).

Let no man therefore judge you in meat, or in drink, or in respect of holyday, or of the new moon, or of the sabbath days (Colossians 2:16).

If thou turn away thy foot from the sabbath, from doing thy pleasure on my holy day; and call the sabbath a delight, the holy of the Lord, honourable; and shalt honour him, not doing thine own ways, nor finding thine own pleasure, nor speaking thine own words: Then shalt thou delight thyself in the Lord; and I will cause thee to ride upon the high places of the earth, and feed thee with the heritage of Jacob thy father: for the mouth of the Lord hath spoken it (Isaiah 58:13-14).

Question 45: What is the CD1/CD2 position on aliens, UFOs, and angels?

Answer: Angels are spirit beings with the ability to intrude into time and space. This ability is only limited by God's permissive will. Considering some angels oppress, possess, and influence human beings, it isn't unreasonable to assume they could be a source of unexplained phenomena.

Secondly, it's highly unlikely God created any other life forms apart from the Genesis account in scripture. *The pinnacle of life revolves around three specific beings: the Trinity, angelic spirit beings, and human beings.* Only to a lesser extent do plants, animals, and other living creations matter.

The Trinity created life to share a part of Their Essence. It was imperative that the life created was flawless, autonomous, and possessed Free Will. Autonomy and Free Will involve the risk that flawless creatures would oppose God's authority, and, thereby, become flawed creatures. The solution was Determinism, which overrules Free Will. Determinism imagery is the Pre-Life Elect individuals recognized "before the foundations of the world." This imagery is rendered as Modern Abstract Religious Verbal Impressionism. It includes the so-called First-Class Angels who did not disobey God.

As non-determined flawless creatures, Adam and Eve were prepared in time and space as a Demonstration of Free Will. In the Garden of Eden, the forbidden Tree called the Knowledge of Good and Evil accelerated the Demonstration. Eventually, Adam and Eve exercised Free Will to disobey God.

The observation of the Demonstration also affected the lives of flawless spirit beings outside time and space. The spirit beings who applauded the disobedience to God were divided into two groups. One group (Third-Class Angels) left Heaven. One group (Second-Class Angels) did not. Third-class Angels that left Heaven to live on Earth were imprisoned for violation of God's procreation laws. They are not suspects of aliens, UFOs, or unexplained phenomena. Second-Class Angels that did not leave Heaven could be labeled Suspect Number 1.

Suspect one is Satan and his fallen angels.

They could be responsible agents regarding aliens, UFOs, and unexplained phenomena. This category is made up of fallen angels or ancestors of angel-human hybrids—the Nephilim.

Suspect Two is 100 percent human beings who are unsane.

The insidious nature of Suspect Two persons is unsanity. By definition, they lack access to moral objectivity. They take advantage of unsuspecting and easily deceived people. *The unsane distract their acts of unsanity by attributing them to aliens, UFOs, and unexplained phenomena.* Why not? There's no evidence disproving alien existence. Going further, they enforce secrecy regulations that prevent oversight and inhibit transparency. Ascertaining the truth about anything of consequence is misleading and confusing. The progression to national emergency powers by corrupt authorities is an ever-present danger to a "free" society. Do as you're told. We have the data. Trust us.

As the unsane develop in ungodliness, science, and trans-humanism, what is known of their prowess is never fully disclosed. *Progress may be so far advanced that it appears as otherworldly or nonhuman.* Add to this the less than 100 percent human beings that augment the Underworld of things (UoT) and we have no idea of what is what.

The fact that God's main focus is on human beings is paramount in scripture. *If there are a trillion life forms on a trillion different planets, so what?* It doesn't matter to us on Earth. The Bible story is about us. Even the spirit beings, angels, are not as important as human beings. Jesus Christ became 100 percent human for the sake of humans, not angels, angel-human hybrids, aliens from space, or animals. The Bible has us on record as the center of attention throughout any universe.

So, when we are told aliens from other planets, solar systems, or the universe are always potential threats, *don't accept it.* The threat is certainly from evil spirits, less than 100 percent humans, or 100 percent human beings. This is another reason why relying on scripture gives us optimism, encouragement, and confidence. We're not weak. We're not gullible. We're not fearful.

Question 46: How can the Minister of Art publicly recommend lying about being a Christian when threatened with death? Lying is bad enough to keep you out of Heaven, but will you deny your Lord and Savior Jesus Christ? Would you disrespect the historic Heroes of Faith and risk condemnation of your own soul?

> And what more can I say? Time is too short for me to tell about Gideon, Barak, Samson, Jephthah, David, Samuel, and the prophets, 3 who by faith conquered kingdoms, administered justice, obtained promises, shut the mouths of lions, quenched the raging of fire, escaped the edge of the sword, gained strength after being weak, became mighty in battle, and put foreign armies to flight. Women received their dead—they were raised to life again. Some men were tortured, not accepting release, so that they might gain a better resurrection, and others experienced mocking and scourging, as well as bonds and imprisonment. They were stoned, they were sawed in two, they died by the sword, they wandered about in sheepskins, in goatskins, destitute, afflicted, and mistreated. The world was not worthy of them. They wandered in deserts and on mountains, hiding in caves and holes in the ground. All these were approved through their faith, but they did not receive what was promised, since God had provided something better for us, so that they would not be made perfect without us (Hebrews 11:32-40.

Answer: Every Christian is familiar with Bible verses that recount examples of people who were murdered simply for being people of God. In the distant past, we've heard of Christians publicly murdered unless they deny biblical doctrine and accept the reigning de facto doctrine. In the recent past, Christians have been beheaded, hanged, and assassinated only for being Christians or refusing to denounce Christianity.

Why would it matter what I say if threatened with death? What if I recant, deny, disavow, equivocate, or LIE about being a Christian? So what?

I can't lose my salvation! I can't gain my salvation. It's not up to me. It's up to God!

I could swear on a stack of Bibles.

I could blaspheme the name of God.

I could curse God and die.

God knows my heart. God knows me.

So, I lie about it. I don't get killed. I live another day to rededicate myself to the Lord, spread His Good News, and seek His forgiveness for all my sins.

What of the other captured Christians in my group who castigate me for my despicable behavior? I don't blame them. I honor them. We just disagree on what salvation means. Salvation has not been well understood for hundreds of years. It's an ongoing process.

But what about the dire warning from Jesus that if you deny Him, He will deny you?

> Also I say unto you, whosoever shall confess me before men, him shall the Son of man also confess before the angels of God: But

> he that denieth me before men shall be denied before the angels of God. And whosoever shall speak a word against the Son of man, it shall be forgiven him: but unto him that blasphemeth against the Holy Ghost it shall not be forgiven. And when they bring you unto the synagogues, and unto magistrates, and powers, take ye no thought how or what thing ye shall answer, or what ye shall say (Luke 12:8-11).

This probably refers to those who have yet to be saved. It's a notice of caution. Or it admonishes those who will not be saved—Non-Elect Roleplayers. *Jesus won't deny those who are Elect, no matter what they say or do.* Those who truly INTEND to deny Jesus, and it's their WILL to deny Jesus, have no idea who Jesus is. Their knowledge is all hearsay. They've never met Jesus Christ.

In the book of Isaiah, King Hezekiah reminds us only those who are alive exemplify the good news. Only those living praise God (Isaiah 38).

> Behold, for peace I had great bitterness: but thou hast in love to my soul delivered it from the pit of corruption: for thou hast cast all my sins behind thy back. For the grave cannot praise thee, death cannot celebrate thee: they that go down into the pit cannot hope for thy truth. The living, the living, he shall praise thee, as I do this day: the father to the children shall make known thy truth (Isaiah 8:17-19).

Speaking as the Minister of Art, not as a theologian, denial of Jesus Christ is not a guarantee of damnation.

The Apostle Peter denied Christ three times. It did not affect his salvation.

The Syrian military general Naaman, cured of leprosy by Elijah, *was pardoned in the past and also pardoned in the future for allegiance to his king during worship service to a false god.*

> And when they had kindled a fire in the middle of the courtyard and sat down together, Peter sat down among them. Then a servant girl, seeing him as he sat in the light and looking closely at him, said, "This man also was with him." But he denied it, saying, "Woman, I do not know him." And a little later someone else saw him and said, "You also are one of them." But Peter said, "Man, I am not." And after an interval of about an hour still another insisted, saying, "Certainly this man also was with him, for he too is a Galilean." But Peter said, "Man, I do not know what you are talking about." And immediately, while he was still speaking, the rooster crowed. And the Lord turned and looked at Peter. And Peter remembered the saying of the Lord, how he had said to him, "Before the rooster crows today, you will deny me three times." And he went out and wept bitterly (Luke 22:55-62).

> And Naaman said, Shall there not then, I pray thee, be given to thy servant two mules' burden of earth? For thy servant will henceforth offer neither burnt offering nor sacrifice unto other gods, but unto the Lord. In this thing the Lord pardon thy servant, that when my master goeth into the house of Rimmon to worship there, and he leaneth on my hand, and I bow myself in the house of Rimmon: when I bow down myself in the house of Rimmon, the Lord pardon thy servant in this thing. And he said unto him, Go in peace. So he departed from him a little way (2 Kings 5:17-19).

In speaking of deceit or not bearing a true witness, Rahab, the harlot, hid the godly spies from the ungodly people of the city and directed the ungodly group away from God's group.

> And the king of Jericho sent unto Rahab, saying, Bring forth the men that are come to thee, which are entered into thine house: for they be come to search out all the country. And the woman took the two men, and hid them, and said thus, There came men unto me, but I wist not whence they were: And it came to pass about the time of shutting of the gate, when it was dark, that the men went out: whither the men went I wot not: pursue after them quickly; for ye shall overtake them. But she had brought them up to the roof of the house, and hid them with the stalks of flax, which she had laid in order upon the roof (Joshua 2:3-6).

We know kings and military generals like Joshua, leader of the Israelites, utilized many deceitful military tactics to defeat their enemies. On the other hand, we also know God's commandment number nine is not to bear false witness against our neighbor (anyone).

> Thou shalt not bear false witness against thy neighbour (Exodus 20:16).

Plus, we know the devil is the father of lies.

> Ye are of your father the devil, and the lusts of your father ye will do. He was a murderer from the beginning, and abode not in the truth, because there is no truth in him. When he speaketh a lie, he speaketh of his own: for he is a liar, and the father of it (John 8:44).

And we know what happened to Ananias and Sapphira.

> But Peter said, Ananias, why hath Satan filled thine heart to lie to the Holy Ghost, and to keep back part of the price of the land? Whiles it remained, was it not thine own? And after it was sold, was it not in thine own power? Why hast thou conceived this thing in thine heart? Thou hast not lied unto men, but unto God. And

> Ananias hearing these words fell down, and gave up the ghost: and great fear came on all them that heard these things . . . And it was about the space of three hours after, when his wife, not knowing what was done, came in. And Peter answered unto her, tell me whether ye sold the land for so much? And she said, ye, for so much. Then Peter said unto her, how is it that ye have agreed together to tempt the Spirit of the Lord? Behold, the feet of them which have buried thy husband are at the door, and shall carry thee out. Then fell she down straightway at his feet, and yielded up the ghost: and the young men came in, and found her dead, and, carrying her forth, buried her by her husband (Acts 5:3-5, 7-10).

There are many biblical examples of people who misrepresented the truth, withheld the truth, or were unaware of the truth. What seems to matter is Roleplay identity. Are we sane, unsane, or insane (Insanity Chart Chapters 17 and 27)? Do we glorify God or ourselves? If we are sane, that is, a Christian, we do not risk losing salvation.

This is because salvation is not based on thinking and behaving. Salvation is not a result of what you think or do. Salvation was accomplished before you were born.

We all do the best we can based on heredity, environment, and experience. Our limitations are a factor of our resources—mental and physical. The goal for success in life may be measured by the quality of life. Quality of life may be measured by victory over enemies and alliance with friends and lovers. Victory over enemies means winning the war. Christians are at war every day.

Examples in scripture of wartime military strategy feature the use of deceit. Deceit is vital in assuring victory. Not only is deceit useful, but we're also obligated to use such tactics. Christians are ALWAYS at war with the enemies of God. We must win, and we will win.

An objection to the denial argument might point back to those who are remembered and honored for their heroism. They did NOT deny the Lord. Their lives testify to the value of standing for Christ in the face of death.

In either case, don't be concerned about losing your salvation by saying the wrong things. You can't get yourself saved and you can't get yourself lost. God is omnipresent. He is always with you. Do not fear.

Question 47: Is it permissible to use Connecting the Dots Of Identity as a substitute for teaching salvation if church attendance is not feasible?

Answer: No. MARVI-RPIA should not be used in place of a church, a pastor, or reading the Bible. Go to church, support church leadership, and read your bible. (*See the disclaimer on the copyright page at the beginning of this book.*)

Attending a church is extremely important to every Christian. The function of a church is to be a resource for the community of Christians. This community is made up of an organization that provides the essentials and nonessentials to ensure people participate in spiritual reality. This includes the establishment, support, and importance of the function of the church. We must all have tangible accountability to a church body of some sort. This is vital to individual responsibility and providing an example to others who may be religious or nonreligious.

MARVI-RPIA is “background” support for spiritual thought. It is not a house of God.

It is not an organization intended to represent a standard for worship. Meeting together physically or by other means to share a common initiative is encouraged. Discouragement comes in when there are efforts to replicate the worship services of a church. Modern Abstract Religious

Verbal Impressionism is meant to be informal spiritual services. *Informal, not formal.*

By the way, you may use the MARVI-RPIA name when you gather, but don't gather as a church, tabernacle, temple, chapel, or house of worship. Terms like museum, gallery, or mission may be more appropriate.

> For where two or three are gathered together in my name, there am I in the midst of them (Matthew 18:20).

Remember, MARVI-RPIA is NOT as good as or better than God's plan for humanity. MARVI-RPIA is its own "plan." The MARVI-RPIA portrait paints an image that portrays everyone going to Heaven, and no one who is 100 percent human going to Hell. The Demonstration of Free Will Roleplay shows why life is so unfair and how that is resolved by placing the blame on Adam and Eve, where it belongs, and exonerating God. God intercedes on behalf of some lives, not all, showing that no one can or will choose God. God has to choose them, or they are never born-again.

We know that whatever God's plan ends up being, it is the right plan, the best plan, the plan that we all should want considering who God is. From this, no plan we could devise will be better than God's plan. So, however magnificent the MARVI-RPIA plan is, and it is magnificent, GOD'S PLAN WILL BE SO MUCH BETTER! That is worth whatever we go through here.

The author of Connecting the Dots Of Identity, John Louis Thomas, is on record as saying even he doesn't believe in MARVI-RPIA. It's an impression. It's an art project. It draws on the Bible for verbal expression, but the Bible is inspired by God. MARVI-RPIA is not inspired by God. It's impressionism, a perception of reality by the author.

Question 48 A: Would the Minister of Art attend a same-sex wedding?

Answer: Is this question because I said I could marry a transgender person? Okay. Fair question. I'll answer it.

No, if my absence is acceptable as non-support of the lifestyle rather than non-support of the person. No, if there isn't a close relationship with either partner.

Yes, if my absence will be misconstrued as hate for the person. It may take more time to demonstrate that I don't hate them, and I don't hate same-sex marriage.

A Christian is obligated to exemplify biblical standards. The Bible forbids Christians to marry non-Christians—don't be unequally yoked (2 Corinthians). Orthodox ministers usually refrain from presiding over such marriages. A similar principle applies to same-sex couples in that they don't exemplify the moral standard of holy matrimony. Traditional orthodox marriages were between couples who were committed to religious ideals, so the integrity of the family unit remained intact.

Couples that married outside the church did not hold to religious family values, preferring to define their own values.

Though committed to religious ideals, married couples have no religious assurance from sin, divorce, or dysfunctional family life. Same-sex couples have even less assurance. The responsibility of a Minister of Art is to contrast the ASSENT and CELEBRATION of same-sex marriage from the WILLINGNESS to be physically present at the wedding. As a Minister of Art, I may be present.

Being present in a person's life is being present to not only DECLARE disapproval of the gay lifestyle but REVEAL disapproval in a comprehensive, meaningful way.

To not attend same-sex weddings in protest of the couple's sinful behavior suggests not going to ANY weddings due to the couple's sinful behavior. *All weddings consist of sinful couples.* We all sin. Why single out LGBTQ? Selective discrimination based on the most obvious transgressions while ignoring other transgressions exposes bias and inconsistency.

The religious official who won't marry same-sex couples or couples of different worldviews is protecting their religious principles. They also want to protect the community. A so-called "mixed" marriage has a connotation of incongruity or disparate parts. Such relationships don't last.

We know mixed marriages may also include low to high-risk relationships OTHER than religion. Think of race, ethnicity, wealth, looks, fame, age, or intellect. An official who presides over the marriage ceremony may or may not discriminate on whom to marry. When religion is EXCLUDED from the marriage ceremony, arrangements to marry run the gamut from an elopement to a mass wedding event. There are plenty of options.

The matter of protecting religious rights is important. A minister should not be legally compelled to officiate a same-sex wedding any more than a baker or photographer be compelled to provide same-sex wedding services. There is no intent to discriminate against homosexual PERSONS. The intent is to avoid PARTICIPATION in an event that is objectionable to a religious person. People detest the homosexual lifestyle FORCED upon them. People also detest the RELIGIOUS lifestyle forced upon them. An optimum solution would be some form of neutrality. As a Minister of Art, I prefer to not attend ANY weddings, but that's another subject.

> Be ye not unequally yoked together with unbelievers: for what fellowship hath righteousness with unrighteousness? And what communion hath light with darkness? (2 Corinthians 6:14)

Question 48 B: Would the Minister of Art officiate a same-sex wedding?

Wow! I wasn't expecting that. Let me think for a second...

Yes, I would, assuming:

1) I obtained a license to officiate.

2) I acquired a suitable venue, a MARVI-RPIA Art Gallery for example.

3) The same-sex couple

a) Spiritually transitions from same-sex to an opposite-sex relationship;

b) Physically identify as an opposite-sex couple;

c) Good Bible students

d) Read Connecting The Dots Of Identity 1 and 2 well enough to articulate its impression; and

e) Performed well on the Insanity and Blind Eyes charts.

I'm not qualifying my answer because I have high moral character. I don't. Rather, I'm representing a moral agent. The answer personifies a spiritual assessment. It doesn't reflect my personal opinion about the LGBTQ community. I love the LGBTQ community—at least those who want the best for me the same way I want the best for them. We all want freedom from oppression. We want to live our lives as we see fit.

Scripture declares how God wants people to live. Most people are NOT going to do as scripture says. They don't see why they should, and won't see why they should, until the Holy Spirit meets them. In the meantime, I'm not trying to beat you up with scripture. I'm sharing an impression of scripture. The impression is life isn't necessarily as bad as it seems. It could actually be beautiful, regardless of what theists, atheists, and agnostics proclaim.

By the way, this Minister of Art is already on record saying he could marry a transgender person, not necessarily *would* marry. Can't speak for other Ministers of Art.

Question 49: The Minister of Art does not attend funerals. Why not?

Answer: Yes, I do think funerals are helpful to people. They come face-to-face with the event they dread the most—death. But we don't face it alone. Others are present. The unofficial affirmation of a funeral is that no one lives forever. Secondly, it reminds you that you could be next, so make the most of your life.

As a Minister of Art, I have instructed for myself:

- *No funeral service.*
- *No organ donation.*
- *No church service.*
- *No cremation but burial in a military cemetery.*
- *No public display of my dead body.*

Have you arranged your final goodbye?

Currently, the main reason to attend a funeral is to show respect to the deceased and accompany the survivors. That may or may not be true.

The greater well-known tradition probably began with people who knew the deceased best would arrive to confirm the identity of the departed. In order for the assets and liabilities to transfer, the community needed to ensure the deceased was, in fact, dead and certify their identity. So a funeral was the way of resolving any conflict on who died, when they died, and verifying witnesses who were present.

Another matter was: if people knew this person was gravely ill, family and friends would certainly come to visit. If this person soon died, people who knew them were already present for a social gathering. For those deceased who are well-known, a ceremony presents a positive departure that helps offset the loss of that person in the family and the community.

As a Minister of Art, you may imagine how discouraging it would be to attend a funeral and the subject of Heaven and Hell given the usual treatment—slight and none!

This is understandable for those who don't believe in an afterlife. There is no Heaven. There is no Hell. But it seems funerals, for the most part, strongly suggest a positive transition from life to death. The suggestion is always a "better place," Heaven or Oblivion. Never Hell. Considering a funeral is not a religious worship service and the attendees are not especially religious, this protocol is excusable.

However, *Connecting the Dots of Identity* includes the impression of funerals. This impression portrays the funeral service as perfunctory on one hand and obscure on the other. There's a tradition we must follow, then comes the awkwardness about the inevitability of death.

Except in an unusual circumstance, my attention will nonetheless be elsewhere.

The funeral may be an opportunity to present the Great News about the Good News as a Minister of Art would like to do, but perhaps not. It depends. Meanwhile, this is the time for assisting with the needs of those still living.

As you know, it's not unusual for loved ones to pass away, leaving others to grieve, and then the double-whammy of underwriting their financial affairs rolls in. Considering death often comes at unexpected times, unexpected expenses can mount up fast. It's not just funeral expenses; it could be the loss of income that death takes from the survivors. Our responsibility is to be sensitive to the situation, be willing and able to offer financial aid, and be loving in our relationships BEFORE death intrudes.

So, no, I will not be at your funeral. As you read above, no one will be at my funeral. If some of you are put off by that, not agreeing with my feelings, not understanding my position, I'm sorry. My intent is to be respectful and comfort you, now, while you're still alive. I hope that will come across to you over time.

Don't worry. Should your demise occur, you can rest assured many of your family, friends, and associates will be at your final service. My absence shouldn't matter very much. If it does, please feel free to contact me. I'm open-minded.

Question 50: What is a MARVI-RPIA Art Gallery like?

Answer: MARVI-RPIA art galleries are anything and any place people desire. It may be a building, a home, or a designated open area. They are wherever people gather at specific times to appreciate spiritual impressionism. It's a time for Art Appreciation classes. Tentatively, last Friday and Saturday of the month, from 7 p.m. to 8:30 p.m. are suggestions.

People decide their own format. It may include:

- Seating, Meditation, Reading
- Art (modern/abstract/religious)
- Music (instrumental only – classical, jazz, ethnic, world, religious)
- Selected reading from the Bible without comment (no preaching)
- Selected reading from *Connecting The Dots Of Identity* 1 and 2 without comment (no preaching)
- *Connecting The Dots Of Identity* books (donation or free)
- Food, clothing, and children's items donation box
- Financial donation box
- Refreshments (snacks, bread, crackers, oil, water, juice, coffee, tea, soda, wine)

Currently, there is no MARVI-RPIA Art Gallery. If donations are made, they are applied to the promotion of Christian Reformed Impressionism, public policy, and world missionary support.

To assist:

MARVI-RPIA

PO BOX 15730

RIO RANCHO, NM 87174

JLT Author Profile (an extension of Q/A)

1. Marital status: Single-Never Married

2. Children: 0

3. Age: 11-28-47

4. Health: Excellent

5. Apple or Android: Android

6. Mac or PC: PC

7. Console, PC, Handheld, Online, or Mobile (Game): PC

8. Racing, Roleplay, Action, or Puzzle (Game): Racing

9. Football, Baseball, or Basketball (Sports): Auto Racing

10. Psalms, Hymns, or Contemporary (My playlist): No

11. Classical, Instrumental, or Jazz (My playlist): Yes

12. Muslim, Atheist, or Hindu (Girl Date 1): Yes

13. Conservative, Liberal, or Independent (Girl Date 2): Yes

14. Asian, Caucasian, Hispanic, Native, or Negro (Girl Date 3): Yes

15. Netherlands, Armenia, or Dominican Republic (Girl Date 4): Yes

16. Museum, Movie, or Picnic (First Date): Museum

17. Breakfast, Lunch, or Dinner (Second Date): Breakfast

18. Chocolate, Vanilla, or Strawberry (Ice Cream): Yes

19. Crunchy or Creamy (Peanut Butter): Crunchy

20. Mountains, Beach, or Top-Floor Penthouse (Residence): Mountains

21. Surrealism, Cubism, or Impressionism (Art): Yes

22. Dogs or Cats: Yes

23. Wine, Beer, or Spirits: Wine

24. Cake, Pie, or Donuts: Cake

25. Pancakes, Waffles, or French toast (Breakfast): Waffles

26. Pizza, Hamburger, or Burrito (Lunch): Hamburger

27. Chinese, Mexican, or Italian (Dinner): Home-cooked

28. Chinese, Mexican, or Italian (Dinner Out): Mexican

29. Coffee, Tea, or Juice (Mornings): Cold Water

30. Pepsi, Coke, or 7UP: Water (natural sparkling)

31. Japan, Nigeria, or Saudi Arabia (30-Day Visit): Nigeria

32. China, Africa, or India (Christian Mission): China

33. Ford Mustang, Chevrolet Camaro, or Dodge Challenger: Challenger – Ghoul

34. Gas, Electric, or Hybrid (Automobile): Gas (love electric – hate losing privacy/freedom)

35. Batman, Superman, or Flash (Comic Hero): Flash

36. Audemars Piguet, Rolex, or Omega (Wristwatch): Rolex (Daytona)

37. *Existenz*, *Atomic Blonde*, or *Zathura* (Movie): Zathura

38. *Matrix*, *Star Wars*, or *2001*: *A Space Odyssey* (movie): *2001: A Space Odyssey*

39. Piano, Guitar, Bass, or Drums (Musical Instrument): Upright Bass

40. R.C. Sproul, Gregory Koukl, or Harold Camping (Apologist): Harold Camping

41. Christopher Hitchens, Richard Dawkins, or Daniel Dennett (Atheist): Pinecreek Doug

42. Tablet, Laptop, or Smartphone (Gift): Laptop

43. Eve, Mrs. Noah, or Virgin Mary (Interview): Mrs. Noah (Eve and Virgin Mary are too elite)

44. Noah, King David, or John the Baptist (Interview): Noah

Many more questions and answers could be included. Rather than me adding more, it's probably better to see what you, the readers, post. Your postings on social media of your own *Connecting the Dots of Identity* Q/A should be interesting. Now that you know the imagery of Christian Reformed Impressionism, we're all anxious to see how the imagery develops.

EPILOGUE

Your intuition tells you that God is love, God is righteous, and God is doing everything He should be doing. But you have doubts because everything in the world seems to be uncontrolled, disorganized, and perplexing. The church says this is because God is INCOMPREHENSIBLE. They say, "Don't worry. God has a marvelous plan for you."

And even though Jesus was here teaching about God with 100 percent accuracy, the Person who is the most intelligent 100 percent human being is also 100 percent deity. Jesus is also INCOMPREHENSIBLE!

The takeaway is that Jesus is incomprehensible, but we are given what is needed to fulfill God's plan. This includes the document we have conveying God's words to us: the Holy Bible.

So now what? Do you say the Bible doesn't seem like such a great cause for celebration? You would have a good point. Genesis, the first book of the Bible, introduces us to the catastrophe of all catastrophes. Adam and Eve fall and take all of us with them. Then, in that same book, God kills everyone in the Flood except eight people. Following this, God confuses the universal language and scatters the population. As if this wasn't enough to end any celebration of the Good News of the Bible, racial differentiation was added to the human being project. All this without further complicating the story with the infiltration of evil angelic beings—the Nephilim.

So goes some of the headlines of the "Good News." Why aren't people turning cartwheels in merriment every Sabbath Day? The whole point of procreation was to produce the Redeemer: Jesus Christ. He arrived. We are redeemed. Hooray! Now turn cartwheels? Not yet.

Jesus was executed by people He was born to redeem. How ironic. And we can't forget about Hell. Adam and Eve brought death to humanity. That wasn't bad enough. No. Hell is the final penalty for sin. Now can you cheer about the Good News of Jesus Christ? Not yet.

How good is the Good News? How high can Christians jump for joy?

Is this challenge the fault of the religious leaders who proclaim the Good News? Is this God's fault for not opening our spiritual eyes? Or is this our fault somehow, even though what we know, or what we do, doesn't contribute to our salvation?

Connecting the Dots of Identity is meant to give trust to your intuition about who God SHOULD be. What you've heard about God from theists, atheists, and agnostics may be misleading. MARVI-RPIA paints God as an IMPRESSION of spirituality. This doesn't mean the impression is better than your religious worldview, your atheist worldview, or any other worldview. It's an artistic impression.

Is your intuition positive? Is your intuition negative? Is your intuition neutral?

Modern Abstract Religious Verbal Impressionism-Roleplay Identity Array.

Great News about the Good News. Is it great? It doesn't matter. Intuition matters.

You don't have to put 100 percent trust in your intuition. You don't have to trust the author of this book. Your 100 percent trust should be in Jesus Christ. Do you know who He is? If you do, your trust is where it should be.

If you don’t know who Jesus Christ is. Be patient. *He knows you.*

DOOMILOGUE

Connecting the Dots of Identity-1. Connecting the Dots of Identity-2.

Danger! There may be DOOM on the horizon.

Initially, CD1/CD2 seems innocuous. It seems actually pretty great. Everyone goes to Heaven, and no one goes to Hell, except the Devil and his angels. What's not to love about that? But after two years, five years, ten years, what may develop is a cult-like following that blossoms into a full-fledged religion. *A religion of doom!*

Oh, yes, the author says he doesn't believe it; it's only an artistic impression. You don't believe in art. You should believe in theology. Believe your Bible. He says he's only SHARING his views about Christian Reformed religion, not TEACHING. However, we only have to look at world history to see the result of objectionable religious ideals. Well-meaning people, hopeful people, and gullible people will follow all manner of myths, beliefs, and teachings. They bet their lives on yet another questionable belief system that may be worse than any of the others.

The argument can be made that the religion of Universalism also teaches that everyone goes to Heaven, and no one goes to Hell. Loosely held beliefs similar to Universalism must have existed for hundreds of years. Their underlying belief is that God loves everyone, and no one will be tormented in Hell forever.

Atheism professes a related view in that God doesn't send people to Hell forever. God doesn't send anyone anywhere. There is no God. And for every Christian person, there are probably just as many non-Christian persons. They conclude it's not reasonable to assume life is based on stories from the Christian Bible. This is why atheism is popular, along with billions of people in non-Christian religions.

So how much devastation has Universalism and non-theism caused? How much harm have the ten to twenty major world religions caused? How much harm will CD1 and CD2 cause? *The worst harm has to be HELL!* Advocating there is NO possibility of Hell when there IS a possibility of Hell is the ultimate irresponsible proposition. Think about it. The WORST harm!

And then, if authentic identity is in Paradise and inauthentic identity is in the present, why continue life? What's the point? To prove Free Will is an error? Adam and Eve proved it. They lived 900-plus years. Two weeks outside the Garden of Eden would have them saying a thousand times, "We are so sorry! We were wrong! We admit God's Determined Will for our life is better than our choice for Free Will. We are dying. The earth is dying." And dying each day continues.

So many millennia after creation, and 2,000 years after Jesus Christ, humanity should know by now to accept God's Determined Will. But our Free Will is a corrupted Free Will, inherited from Adam and Eve. We must be born-again by the Holy Spirit. Otherwise, there is no interest in God's Determined Will. We can't speak for the angels. They don't have a Redeemer. Their identity is authentic. Their Free Will is final for all eternity.

Meanwhile, a human ontological identity as defined by CD1/CD2 is the identity referred to as existing before the foundation of the world. This conclusion is altogether without precedent. Such an assumption is considered heresy—a direct opposition to orthodoxy. The author makes frequent disclaimers that CD1/CD2 isn't theology. It's art.

This “art” hopes to reduce suicide, reduce abortion, hopelessness, depression and reduce despair. *What if it does the opposite?* What if the thought of assurance in Paradise produces a “disconnect” with present life? The present life has no eternal consequence.

Don't steal, rape, rob, or murder. That's bad. If you get caught, you must pay the earthly penalty. If you don't get caught, you're a bad person to do bad things, but you will be forgiven. It was done in ignorance. You will be forgiven in the afterlife.

And it's possible the people that do continue to go to church could become disillusioned with orthodoxy after CD1/CD2 influences. People walk out in the middle of the sermon. People don’t attend other church services. Doubt about orthodoxy begins its progressive advance.

The orthodox erosion begins with large-scale churches. Then the medium- to smaller-scale churches fall off in membership. *Finally, erosion begins in the Christian Reformed Church itself, the very church that professes Election and Predestination.*

The Orthodox Church expects everyone to follow tradition. You must do this, you must do that, and you must do the other things to please God. The whole system is based on performance. You hear of CD1 and CD2. God has already saved you. The identity you embody in the present is only to demonstrate the Error of Free Will. There's NOTHING you can do in the present that contributes to your salvation. That was done in the past before the foundation of the world.

So, why go to church?

Why participate in the sacraments of baptism and communion?

Why join the choir, go to Bible study, or become an elder or deacon?

Why encourage a pastor whose teachings are less convincing than CD1/CD2?

Why encourage a pastor whose teachings are against CD1/CD2?

Doom! People stop going to church, stop reading their Bible, and stop supporting religious organizations. They may stop working, stop having families, stop being good. Eat, drink, and be merry. Pie awaits in the sky. I'm not me; I'm a construct of heredity, environment, and experience. So what if World War III starts next week?

If I am one of the so-called SANE, I'm not able to open the spiritual eyes of the UNSANE. Only God can. In the interim, the unsane are taking over the world. The polls always show there is a large segment of the world population that affirms a Christian identity. However, when taking a deep dive into the particulars of what Christianity is, a great number don't understand Christianity. Why?

A multitude of factors, perhaps led by Christian immaturity. The church itself carries a large portion of the blame for that. With the lack of leadership in Christian education and in converting the unsane, what else should we expect? God uses Christians to assist in the unsane becoming sane. If CD1 and CD2 come to prominence, will that be beneficial or detrimental to the world? Beneficial if the concept is godly, detrimental if it is not.

Will the Orthodox Church be undermined by yet another "improvement" on the word of God? Will other churches suffer also? Time will tell.

Connecting the Dots of Identity. Bloom, doom, or never blossom?

Doom!

CLOSING PRAYER

Prayer changes things. In the scriptures, there are some twenty verses encouraging prayer. For what should we pray?

It's not unreasonable to see that the unsane people in the world are gaining the advantage in key areas of influence—finance, politics, business, academia, media, entertainment, etcetera. What are sane people to do?

One, commandeer those segments of society for THEISM, or at least for NEUTRALITY.

Two, pray for God's intercession into the hearts of the unsane.

Commandeering those segments of society will take time. How much time do we have?

And for what SPECIFICALLY should we pray?

How do we prepare for the possibility of Hell or Heaven in the afterlife? How do we prepare for World War III, a fatal global pandemic, or an overthrow of humanity by artificial intelligence?

The general public would probably be the last to know of an impending global catastrophe. In the background, people who have no moral objectivity, the unsane, forge ahead without regard for ethical consequences.

There may be automated vehicles on the highway with human-appearing drivers. Human and nonhuman persons may have already replaced their well-known counterparts. The smart device we own may be hypnotizing us through gradations of euthanasia.

This doesn't necessarily mean the end has begun, *but the end has begun.* Previous CD1/CD2 chapters illustrate a breach in God's natural order of procreation that caused the Flood—the first end-of-the-world scenario. Do we have 120 years before the second end-of-the-world scenario? Do we have 120 months? 120 weeks? 120 hours?

> And the Lord said, my spirit shall not always strive with man, for that he also is flesh: yet his days shall be an hundred and twenty years (Genesis 6:3).

> But as the days of Noah were, so shall also the coming of the Son of man be. For as in the days that were before the flood they were eating and drinking, marrying and giving in marriage, until the day that Noe entered into the ark, And knew not until the flood came, and took them all away; so shall also the coming of the Son of man be (Matthew 24:37-39).

We know conclusively that people who were DIRECTLY related to Adam, Eve, Seth, Jared, Enoch, and Methuselah were alive at the time of the Flood. How much closer to godliness could anyone be? Yet, all these people drowned in the Flood. They were executed. *Apparently, godly human males and females didn't recognize the seriousness of the breach in the natural order of procreation that was occurring.* They didn't question, investigate, interrupt, or stop the Nephilim operation … until it was too late.

Are we in a similar situation?

Is pregnancy and delivery by human males any more preposterous than angels and humans creating offspring?

Is procreation by angels and human females, the Nephilim, any more unbelievable than human and artificial intelligence producing less than 100 percent human offspring?

By the way, many people are so desperate to become pregnant they may not care if the child is slightly less than 100 percent human. Worse than this, they may not be informed that the child will be less than 100 percent human. Meanwhile, scientific references to reproductive technology, which include issues of impotence, infertility, human cloning, and advancements in trans-humanism, read like science fiction. In the years 1970 to 2000, reproductive science outgrew science fiction to become science nonfiction. From the year 2000 to the present day, science nonfiction is now science EXTREME reality.

Most of us have heard about the most famous End of the World scenario, the return of Jesus Christ. It is both beautiful and dreadful in its essence. Believers in Christ transition to Heaven and nonbelievers will transition to Hell. Believers have been known to pray earnestly for this Last Day. They finally have their reward for trusting in His name. It's regretful that many of their family, friends, and associates didn't believe. The whole nonbelieving world will now suffer forever in a fiery lake of torment. They were warned.

Part of the impression MARVI-RPIA paints is that:

1) The End may be brought about by humanity itself, as in the Flood.

2) The End could be when Jesus Christ has reached the perfect number of Roleplayers. The Error of Free Will needs no further proof.

In the sense that prayer changes things, CD1/CD2 could propose influencing The End by diminishing further Roleplay participation. We finally agree that God's will is best, not our own will. *We surrender the directive to continue creating more Roleplayers via procreation.* No further proof of the Error Adam and Eve committed is necessary. Of course, if it's NOT about proving the Error of Free Will, and it's NOT God's will to decrease procreation, it certainly won't happen, whether we surrender our right to procreate or not.

Then again, people who love CD1/CD2 might advise a reluctance to discontinue procreation. It may not be the prudent direction to pursue. Significant decreases in the population of any first-rate country come with consequences. This means discussion among those in first-rate countries to articulate details of the consequences. Oh, and there's the point of an extremely powerful human impulse for love, family, and … sex.

However, if enough of us come to accept some version of what is illustrated by CD1/CD2, we could possibly influence God to bring The End BEFORE we cause our own gruesome downfall. *We can now pray for The End with a clearer conscience than before.* We don't have to worry about human beings going to Hell forever. Hell is only for Satan and his devils.

Keep in mind Connecting The Dots Of Identity is just an impression. It is not theology. *However, if prayer changes things as scripture indicates, and if we don't feel comfortable praying for The End, shouldn't we at least pray that God's Plan A will be as good or better than CD1/ CD2 Plan B?* God's Plan A as taught by orthodox theology for 2,000 years may be appropriate, but is it comprehensive? Think of Salvation, Election-Predestination, and Hell.

Final words of a rather long closing prayer: God's Plan A will be as good as or better than CD1/CD2 Plan B.

Isn't that a worthwhile prayer? Let's pray together...

AFTERWORD

War is raging in the world. War is ALWAYS raging in the world. It may not affect us today, or it may cause our death tomorrow. It's such a tragic situation. People don't seem to be willing to take the legitimate steps to de-escalate the tension between warring factions. If there is a willingness to negotiate a resolution, the "war machine" intervenes. Money and power are major influences in continuing the hostilities. Another major factor is the cultural identity of the groups in conflict.

Cultural identity meaning the interests of the *people-in-general* or the interests of the *people-in-power.* The people in general have personal interests represented as a cultural history. Their ethnicity, family traditions, family legacy, and local property, make up present-day life. They feel obligated to preserve this.

The people-in-power are represented by special interest groups who pursue an agenda that seeks to maintain power and wealth. They have no true allegiance to their constituents. It's all rhetorical posturing. Their integrity was compromised long ago.

Wars continue as long as the people-in-general tolerate the people-in-power. By the time objection to the powerful reaches a point of conflict, it is usually too late to save the situation by removing them. When leadership is replaced, the new leadership may not be much of an improvement. The people-in-general must have the integrity to evaluate integrity in leadership. After that, there have to be enough people with integrity to develop a platform of integrity.

A method to minimize conflict between warring factions or nations could be characterized by a political figure who employs the imagery of

MARVI-RPIA. Historically, such an idea could be summarized by the concept of the *Philosopher King.* This is attributed to ancient Greek philosopher Plato three hundred years before Jesus Christ.

The impetus to pursue the concept of a philosopher king is to support a person who embodies the principles of pursuing truth, knowledge, and logic while utilizing political strategy to achieve progress and well-being for the populace. There are two major obstacles to such a political structure:

1) The initial establishment of this person in power.

2) Groups that attack the establishment of this person.

Hope for national integrity must begin with you and me. The quest for a unifying factor that promotes integrity might begin with a version of a philosopher king, such as an Artist King. *A Minister of Art. No, not me. You!* Yes, you. You don't have to do all the work. We will assist you. We will support you.

But when people-in-general look in the mirror, what do they see? They see their family, their race, their ethnicity, gender, culture, height, weight, and age. Underneath, or on top of this, they see their religious identity, their national identity, and their occupation. These things and many other things are reflected as they look at who they think they are… who they're told they are.

CD1/CD2 paints a picture from scripture that means all these images are NOT you. They all DIE. *They die because they are not REAL.* The real you were identified before the world was created. You are safe in Paradise. *The real you NEVER dies because the real you are SPIRITUAL!*

The people who say they KNOW what reality is do not all agree. There are many worldviews. There are theists, nontheists, and agnostics. None of their worldviews are invulnerable. They all have significant misgivings. Of course! They're not omniscient. They're guessing. Jesus, as a Person of the Trinity, wasn't guessing. He was omniscient. He arrived in time and space to teach us that we are spiritual beings, and that Heaven is at hand.

CD1/CD2 also has significant misgivings. However, if more of us contribute to promoting and improving the image, perhaps we can improve the integrity of people. A believable image of God as the epitome of moral objectivity helps refute human beings in that role. A believable image of Christian Reformed Impressionism, based on 100 Bible verses, helps put God back on the throne. Everyone 100 percent human is already in Heaven. Only the Devil and his angels go to Hell. Less than 100 percent humans cease to exist.

In the meantime, life goes on. Then, one day, out of nowhere, while out shopping in various cities across the nation, groups of terrorists roll into selected shopping centers. Guns drawn and firing, they murder people and capture hostages. Retreating to designated locations, they make their demands known. War has come to each of those cities—and the nation.

What am I supposed to do? Fight back? Yes, some would. Some would be killed. Some hostages would be killed. This could happen this year, next year, or in two to three years.

However, by challenging the insistence of an inauthentic identity based on life as authentic, it may be possible to redirect our focus on forgiving the past and upgrading the future. It will be imperative to purge corrupt people and organizations currently in power. As we become more adept at being responsible for our own identity, it will be easier to evaluate, defund, and prosecute corrupt persons. By our irresponsibility, we put them in power. Now we must remove them.

But who's willing to give up their ideology? Their religion? Their worldview? Very few. To a great degree, the family you are born into defines your worldview. The country where you grew up defines your worldview. The formal and informal education you receive defines your worldview. CD1/CD2 paints a worldview that disassembles the imposed inauthentic identity. In its place in an identity that absolves the past. That person was not you. That person was a compilation of heredity, environment, and experience. With a renewed outlook that identity is based in the future, the present is rediscovered.

You're not locked in to continue on a course based on the past. You can make a clean break and start anew. Forgive the past. Build a present and future based on moral objectivity—integrity. It may be possible if enough people accept the Great News about the Good News.

Just imagine if the youth of certain countries began to disassociate themselves from the religious identity that heredity, environment, and experience have imposed on them. They agree to open up their religious location, culture, and relics to the world. Religious descriptions of God should NOT be based on heredity, environment, and experience. God doesn't require strict adherence to customs, rituals, or appearance. There is no need to ostracize, shame, condemn, berate, or kill in the name of religion. We presume God does not require us to behave as though we are special and everyone else is not.

But hostility will continue because it's the ideology of past generations and the present generation. Our physical land on the world map is our physical and metaphysical identity. Who we are is where we are. *Only the next generation of people can break the cycle of an imposed identity based on custom, ritual, and genealogy.* You would have to say: I am me, an individual. I am not all of you. I am not my ethnic progression of ancestors.

A Muslim cannot convert a Jew, Christian, Hindu, Buddhist, or atheist to Islam. And they cannot convert a Muslim to their religion. There are exceptions, but this is the natural order. This is what God achieves with a Demonstration of Free Will.

If God of the Bible created humans flawlessly but they became flawed, isn't it possible for God to have a plan for flawed humans? Wouldn't such a plan be similar to CD1/CD2? It's okay if there are many religions. It's okay if there are atheists and agnostics. *We're all demonstrating Free Will. We CAN'T all have the same worldview.* It's not possible in a world of billions of people—people identified by heredity, environment, and experience.

But fighting to death over property and doctrines is the situation in Israel, Palestine, Armenia, Azerbaijan, Yemen, and other nations and countries. The world sees that this behavior reflects religious diversity, religious disagreement, and religious acts of violence. It's a long history. People have deep-rooted memories.

They did this and that to us. We were innocent. The law says we have a right to exact vengeance. If we forgive or do nothing, they will assume that as weakness. They will exploit us. The law requires penalties for wrongdoing. Jesus taught compromise and forgiveness but accountability in matters of justice. We demand justice after years of restraint and patience. *If justice is delayed, inadequate, or unfair, then matters will be settled outside the law. But matters are never settled.* So, hostility never ends. Never say never?

Well, if a significant number of people are ALLOWED to open their spiritual eyes, here is what they could perceive:

If God is a God of love, honor, fairness, control, and forgiveness, He would NOT make distinctions in religion. The Muslim, Hindu, Buddhist, Jewish, Christian, and Atheist would ALL go to Heaven; none to Hell. How so? God knows they are all demonstrating the effects of heredity, environment, and experience. A person's religion, or absence of religion, is all a factor of when they're born, where they're born, and to whom they're born. *There is no religion better than another. Yes, there's only ONE way to salvation, Jesus Christ, but He accomplished salvation before the world was created.* There were no religions then. Everyone is already saved.

Life has to be something similar to this to make sense. CD1/CD2 is a Plan B impression of God's Plan A. If there is a true God, He would make it obvious which religion was His choice for humanity. There wouldn't be ten major and fifty minor religions. We would ALL know which one God wanted us to follow. *But He doesn't make it obvious.* Why? *Possibly so that flawed human beings demonstrate the result of flawless human beings exercising Free Will to disobey God. There must be proof that God's Determined Will (see Glossary) is superior to a flawless human beings' Free Will.*

It's 100 percent natural for people to base their worldview on heredity, environment, and experience. This is the expectation. Otherwise, why wouldn't God make Himself sufficiently known to everyone so none would be mistaken? Do you think He wants people to be mistaken? Well, He does allow it:

1) Certain people are spiritually immature.

2) Certain people are not 100 percent human.

3) Certain people are Roleplayers who have yet to meet the Holy Spirit.

Today, we simply glorify Him as having made provision for our salvation before the foundation of the world. Today, we simply make the best of what we know to improve the environment of people. Adam and Eve were given the task to maintain, be fruitful, and multiply the Garden of Eden. The Tree of the Knowledge of Good and Evil was there as a test of Free Will. While going about their tasks, Ego-Skepticism set in. Who am I? Why am I here? What is reality? They had doubts. They began to trust themselves rather than God. This is what we may do when we don't trust Jesus Christ, sent by God, to confirm we are spiritual beings, temporarily in physical time and space.

The Promise to Adam and Eve after the fall has been fulfilled. Jesus arrived. Love God. Love your neighbor. Love your enemy. Love yourself. If we don't change our perspective on how we understand God, religion may be the cause of the ultimate act—the end of the human race.

Please don't allow heredity, environment, and experience to continue dictating your religious worldview. That is your inauthentic identity. Your authentic identity is known by God before He created the world. The present is only a Demonstration of the Error of Free Will versus God's Determined Will.

Religion isn't about war. Religion isn't about God loving us and wanting what we want. Religion isn't about us being the best people. Religion is love. Compromise. Cultivating the Garden of People. When the response is to Old Testament examples of God commanding wars, strict rules of behavior, and one chosen people, it was to direct a path leading to specific individuals.

The dots must connect from Adam to Noah to Abraham to Judah to King David to the Virgin Mary to Jesus Christ.

In the Old Testament Book of Deuteronomy, the other nations had developed associations with evil spirits. How did they get involved with spirits? No, not Third-Class Angels. They're in chains of darkness—the Abyss. Second-Class Angels are suspects. Also, the ancestors of the Giants, the Nephilim, are suspects. They're not 100 percent human. So both would be candidates to influence 100 percent humans to practice the occult.

God forbade Israel from doing so. Nothing must interfere with the path to Jesus Christ. Angels collaborated with human beings in the days of Noah. The Nephilim was the result of angel and human female offspring. This defined the violation of God's procreation law. Such violence could be the reason God brought the End of the World—the Flood. This kind of violence must not end the world before the promised Messiah is born.

> There shall not be found among you any one that maketh his son or his daughter to pass through the fire, or that useth divination, or an observer of times, or an enchanter, or a witch. Or a charmer, or a consulter with familiar spirits, or a wizard, or a necromancer. For all that do these things are an abomination unto the Lord: and because of these abominations the Lord thy God doth drive them out from before thee . . . For these nations, which thou shalt possess, hearkened unto observers of times, and unto diviners: but as for thee, the Lord thy God hath not suffered thee so to do. The Lord thy God will raise up unto thee a Prophet from the midst of thee, of thy brethren, like unto me; unto him ye shall hearken (Deuteronomy 18:10-12, 14-15).

The nations who were harmed by God to prevent them from interference were simply demonstrating Free Will. God was working through that to accomplish His Promise. *No one who was 100 percent human was damned to Hell. They were just Roleplayers.* They will transition to Paradise. The damnation was a result of Free Will, and the damnation was death.

Once Jesus is on the scene, He says "I am the Promise. I'm God. I'm human. I'm Roleplaying. You're Roleplaying. This is all a Demonstration of Free Will from Adam and Eve. I am the new Adam. You're a result of heredity, environment, and experience. This creates an inauthentic identity. You're a spiritual being in physical time and space. Your authentic identity is spiritual. *I arrived to fulfill God's promise of a Redeemer to Adam and Eve. I arrived to affirm salvation was accomplished before the foundation of the world."*

Jew and Gentile don't matter. Male and female don't matter. This generation or that generation does not matter. Love God. Love your neighbor. Love your enemy. Love yourself. *That's your religion!*

Man-made? The Bible doesn't say this. Jesus doesn't say this. Bible scholars don't say this.

CD1/CD2 says this. God structured religion to guarantee the appointment of Jesus Christ. Then Jesus spoke in parables. PARABLES! And religion was re-created. CD1/CD2 is a parable.

> All these things spake Jesus unto the multitude in parables; and without a parable spake he not unto them: (Matthew 13:34)

We don't expect a one-world religion. We don't expect people to understand all religions, or no religions are the same. The differences are the Demonstration of Free Will based on heredity, environment, and experience. Religion gives us guidelines, structure, and history. *But religion is not our identity, and it doesn't save us. It's man-made.*

> There is neither Jew nor Greek, there is neither bond nor free, there is neither male nor female: for ye are all one in Christ Jesus (Galatians 3:28).

We have a hard time trusting God. The idea that He saved us before the foundation of the world only comes if He opens our spiritual eyes. One hundred Bible verses from *Connecting the Dots of Identity-1*, Chapter 6, are not persuasive. Those who do see cannot open the eyes of others. We need the Holy Spirit to initiate the process. CD1/CD2 is trying to open your spiritual eyes. *What do you see?*

Please help make this worthy of consideration for young children, teens, and young adults. They don't have all the investment in ideology that adults are protecting. We have a chance of averting the ongoing steps to WWIII. *WWIII is going to happen!* It's just a matter of when. On purpose. By accident. By a thousand cuts...

BOOK REVIEW

A popular A.M. radio station in the USA has a morning show hosted by a fascinating fellow along with his producer. Here is an impression of him giving Connecting The Dots Of Identity a book review. It might come across in one of his morning segments as follows:

Okay, coming up in the nine o'clock hour, we're going to spend some time talking about a book that recently came out with an odd twist on a religious theme. The title is Connecting The Dots Of Identity. The working name is MARVI-RPIA, which is the subtitle. This acronym stands for Modern Abstract Religious Verbal Impressionism-Roleplay Identity Array. What's it about? Well, it's supposed to be a way of making written religious material represent imagery of the Bible—like a mural on a building. MARVI-RPIA is the paint, the Bible is the building. But MARVI-RPIA is not claiming to teach the Bible. It's just an impression of the Bible.

We'll take a quick break and be right back with the story. This is the *Famous Fascinating Fellow Show*.

(Commercial)

We're back, and the first thing I'll say about *Connecting The Dots Of Identity*, the book under review right now, is that I don't know if it really works or not.

Producer: Did you actually read the book?

Host: No, it's really not my cup of tea, you know, religious books. So, I dug around on the internet. As everybody knows, we do infotainment here, and a religious book would be bor-ring to our listeners. Two of the sources I used were the reviews on N5Sense Books and on 10 AM Books.

Producer: Yeah, I don't know, the whole idea seems hard to get your head around. I did buy the book but haven't yet read it. I'm intrigued by how I have those eight Roleplay identities and won't get that one-way ticket to the hot place forever. Host: Yeah, and no Hell might be the reason people would read this. Well, that and also everybody goes to Heaven. Wow! What a concept. Everybody goes to Heaven. Nobody goes to Hell.

Let's start with this. The author, John Louis Thomas, has developed religious imagery he calls art. He bills himself as the Minister of Art. It all begins with a rather obscure religious doctrine called Christian Reformed Theology. Thomas takes artistic liberty to offer a modern abstract impression of the doctrine. Reformed theology isn't a new spiritual concept. It goes all the way back at least to Saint Augustine (400 AD), up through Saint Thomas Aquinas (1200 AD), and then sees a great re-emphasis by Martin Luther (1500 AD). The re-emphasis brought about the Protestant Reformation. This marked the opposition to the Catholic Church, which held great power from the Middle Ages.

Following Martin Luther's belief system in re-establishing the definition of salvation and the means of salvation, John Calvin (1500 AD) expanded and further defined the tenets of "grace" rather than "works" for salvation. Grace means God's gift of salvation and works means you acquire salvation on your own. You may have heard of Calvinism. It has an infamous reputation in religious circles owing to its hardline regarding so-called predestined persons. Predestination is a term for God selecting certain people for salvation before He created the world. These people are guaranteed to go to Heaven. The corollary is that those not chosen cannot go to Heaven. That only leaves Hell.

Seems unfair. Right? Right! And this is one of the many reasons why people don't become religious; they become agnostics or atheists. God is not fair. Life is not fair.

Now, back to MARVI-RPIA. Thomas says yes, God does say quite plainly in scripture that He has predestined certain individuals to salvation before they were born. Thomas calls them Super-Spiritual Identities—SSIDs. But the Bible does NOT say God predestined others to Hell. But by not choosing others, what happens to them? The answer? Thomas says they may not be 100 percent human! I'll explain that when we come back from this short break. This is the *Famous Fascinating Fellow Show*.

(Commercial)

Host: Okay. We're back. I can't believe I'm talking about a religious book on the air. Well, I guess it's supposed to be an art book, but whatever.

Producer: Yeah, and the author says he doesn't believe it himself, even though he wrote it.

Host: Right. He doesn't believe it, the readers don't believe it, I don't believe it, but okay, let's continue.

Now, how is it that people may not be 100 percent human? Here's how that goes. Before the world was created, God created angels. Lucifer, before he is Satan, humbly asks God if created beings are truly free if restricted in behavior? Lucifer advances the notion that God could allow unrestricted behavior and simply correct errors on the fly as beings are behaving. God reminds Lucifer that He is God and not a 24/7 repairman, but He will provide a Demonstration of Free Will using flawless living creatures—human beings.

God creates the world, our planet, the Serpent, Adam, and Eve. Flawless creatures reject God's will for their lives, choosing freedom or death. They die, but in God's mercy, it is a slow death. The greater mercy is a promise to provide an Antidote for their error through procreation. That would be Jesus Christ. The angels observe, and a group of them leave Heaven to seek a similar solution for angels should they ever disobey God. In the Book of Genesis, angels and human females procreate, creating children called Nephilim. The plan fails. The earth becomes corrupted. God drowns everyone in the Flood except Noah and his family. There are now three classes of angels.

First-Class Angels remain loyal to God's will for their lives. Second-Class Angels, led by Satan, do not abandon Heaven to mate with human females. They remain to accuse God of angel and human design flaws and favoritism toward humans above angels. Third-Class Angels, led by Abaddon, are the ones who leave Heaven in the interest of providing a fail-safe for angels like the humans are promised and "marry" human females.

Quite the drama, isn't it? Okay, let's keep going. It's pretty wild so far.

Producer: I'm a little confused but not bored.

Host: Adam and Eve's offspring become Free Will Roleplayers. They inherit a flawed physical and mental identity in a flawed physical environment of air, water, land, plants, animals, weather, and etcetera.

Their consolation is one day a Savior will redeem humanity, and all will be flawless again. In the interim, the proof of the Error of Free Will is depicted with real lives in an innumerable manner of combinations and permutations. Unless God intervenes to change any person's life, all lives continue in sin and damnation.

Because God has chosen people before He created the world, the Pre-Life Elect, they are safe in Heaven. The Free Will Roleplayers that are born-again join with a corresponding pre-life identity at Judgment Day. Those who are not born-again may also join their pre-life identity. They simply provided the contrast to show no one comes to God of their own will. Their Roleplay ends. If a person has no corresponding pre-life identity to join, the implication is this person is not 100 percent human. This person is subject to the One-Drop Nephilim Blood Rule. This is a euphemism for a human with evil spirit ancestry. At death, they simply cease to exist. No soul. No spirit. No afterlife.

Producer: I think I know some of those people.

Host: Yeah, me too. Okay. You might be asking why Jesus Christ arrives if salvation is already guaranteed to individuals. Well, because Jesus Himself is a Roleplayer. Jesus as 100 percent human arrives to save 100 percent humans—not angels, not angel-human hybrids, not aliens, not animals. He redeems Roleplayers as part of the Free Will Demonstration which occurs inside time and space. The Pre-Life Elect individuals exist as a separate reality outside time and space. The focus is on the Error of Free Will (from Adam and Eve that Jesus corrects) versus Determinism (God's Elect persons outside time).

So, what do you think? Any chance? In Thomas's defense, he doesn't claim to be a theologian, philosopher, teacher, pastor, or even a writer. He is an artist, a minister of art. MARVI-RPIA does seem to have a Dan Brown

Davinci Code religious fiction about it. It is quite a stretch. But if it's just art, a mural on a building, you don't have to like it. In fact, Thomas is on record saying he himself doesn't believe in MARVI-RPIA. It's not a belief system. It's art. It's an impression. Speaking as a Catholic person, and my producer is a Jewish person, we don't see it.

When I was on the internet, one of the well-known church leaders made kind of an interesting observation. He said the Demonstration of Free Will is the whole reason for living. The ability to disobey God is proof of a creature's autonomy and reason to continue life. If you ever suspect you are an automaton or a puppet of God, you will lose the will to live. This goes for angels, humans, and even animals, as proven by the Serpent in Eden. Proof of Free Will must be demonstrated with multiple life forms in multiple scenarios in multiple permutations. And then, to show contrast, God intercedes in select people's lives, showing that unless God changes that person, interrupting their Free Will, that person will always choose their own will rather than God's will for their life.

Of course, Connecting The Dots Of Identity says as much by implying the First-Class Angels and the Super-Spiritual Identities, the SSIDs, must also have God's determination for them or they too wouldn't be safe. The SSIDs are the name for identities God saved before He created the world. They correspond to every 100 percent human conceived on earth. JLT's impression doesn't give them life; it gives them ontological status. Orthodox religion teaches the ones saved before the world was created are humans who are conceived here in the present. They're NOT humans who were never conceived, either in the past or in the future.

Okay, we're late for the break, and I think we're just about out of time anyway.

Producer: Okay, then I'll say this real fast. As far-fetched as MARVI-RPIA seems, the actual Bible stories are even further out there. This version seems more likable than what I hear from the churches.

Host: Well, it's not going too bad! N5Sense Books has it at number nine in sales and 10 AM Books has it at number twelve. *Connecting the Dots of Identity-2* just came out, and it follows up on *Connecting the Dots-1* with commentary on sex-ed, abortion, and politics. I think a lot of readers may be put off by any religious slant on those topics, including me. Well, there you go. We're way late for the break. This is the *Famous Fascinating Fellow Show*. Be right back.

QUOTES OFF THE RECORD

(1) "Hate to say this, but Sunday sermons will never sound the same."

Youth Group Leader

(2) "A stupid book. Don't waste your time. Much ado about nothing. Tempest in a teapot. Neither fish nor fowl. Couldn't make heads or tails of it."

ScowlerSpammer12

(3) "Undeclared leverage for the atheist, agnostic, and theist assertions."

@such&such&such

(4) "The Insanity Chart and the Blind Eyes Chart tell me all I need to know to graduate."

Student@life.school

(5) "The Glossary of Colors is a portrait in itself."

Artist

(6) "Extremely dangerous! Everyone goes to Heaven and no one goes to Hell is NOT what the Bible says. Don't bet your soul against what the church has taught for 2,000 years!"

Bishop Metro Media

(7) "I'm turning over in my grave."

Saint Augustine

(8) "Me too."

Martin Luther

(9) "Me too."

John Calvin

(10) "Me too."

Michelangelo

(11) "*CD1/CD2* is the highest quality religious art you can buy."

Art 4 - The Upper Class

(12) "*CD1/CD2* is like *The Da Vinci Code*, *The Matrix*, and *The Greatest Story Ever Told*, with a dash of *Twilight Zone*."

Unorthodox Temple TV

(13) "Do you have ANY IDEA what NOT going to Hell means to millions of people? No, not denial of Hell. Not refuting Hell. Not ignoring Hell. A reasonable explanation of WHY Hell would exist. It's not for US. We're just Roleplayers. It's for the Devil and his angels. We couldn't think that much about Heaven, the virgin birth, the resurrection, or the afterlife, probably because of a RESENTMENT of Hell. It is always Hell constantly molesting us below the level of consciousness.

"The first End of the World, the Flood, who went to Hell (the Abyss)? Not the Nephilim. They drowned, then oblivion. They're not 100 percent human. And not 100 percent human beings. Some of them were saved (eight people). All the others' Roleplay assignment ends. They transition to SSIDs. *Only the evil angels went to Hell!* Why not everyone?

Thank you. Thank you. Thank you. At least we now have hope, even if it's not orthodox."

zero@zero.zero.

OVERVIEW

Thirteen Points of History

1) Life—angels and humans

2) Fall—angels and humans

3) The promise of redemption—humans

4) Nephilim—human and angel offspring

5) Flood—violation of God's procreation plan

6) Babel—language and communities created

7) Days of Peleg—earth divided, countries, and races begin

8) Creation of God's chosen people Israel

9) Prophecy of Messiah

10) Jesus Christ Arrives

11) Ongoing Demonstration of Free Will since the beginning of life

12) Judgment Day—End of Demonstration of Free Will versus God's Determined Will

13) Afterlife in Heaven, Hell, or Oblivion

Twelve Points of Christian Reformed Impressionism

1) Spiritual life is created as the heavenly hosts (angels).

2) Lucifer's Postulate—life may not be worth living while God restricts freedom.

3) God proposes a Demonstration of Free Will—Elect are recognized (SSID). First-Class Angels trust God's will.

4) The Serpent, Adam, and Eve initiate the Free Will Demonstration, exercising the choice to disobey God.

5) The Fall of Adam and Eve brings about Roleplay/identity array from heredity, environment, and experience.

6) Third-Class Angels seek an angel redeemer via offspring with human females causing the Flood.

7) Proof of the Error of Free Will and inability to choose God is shown by the Holy Spirit's arrival or not.

8) Proof of the Error of Free Will is illustrated by the contrast of objective morality to subjective morality.

9) Afterlife refers to 100 percent humans, less than 100 percent humans from Nephilim, and Satan with his angels.

10) Heaven, Hell, or Oblivion as destinations in the afterlife.

11) *Connecting the Dots of Identity* is an impression of God's relationship with angels and humans.

12) Modern Abstract Religious Verbal Impressionism is the art of Christian Reformed theology.

Seven Shortcuts of Christian Reformed Impressionism

1) Life Created
2) Lucifer's Postulate of Freedom
3) Demo of Free Will excluding SSIDs and First-Class Angels
4) Roleplay ID Array based on heredity, environment, and experience
5) Less than 100 percent human beings derived from Nephilim
6) Objective versus Subjective morality as Sane versus Unsane worldviews
7) Afterlife as Heaven, Hell, or Oblivion

Seven Shorter Shortcuts of Christian Reformed Impressionism

1) Life

2) Lucifer

3) Demo

4) Roleplay

5) Nephilim

6) Unsanity

7) Afterlife

IMAGE GALLERY PORTRAITS

|*Minister of Art*|

|*Sane – Insane – Unsane*|

|* Insanity Chart*|

|*Blind Eyes Chart*|

|*Supralapsarian – Sublapsarianism*|

|*Christian Reformed Impressionism*|

|*MARVI-RPIA*|

|*GOD'S DETERMINED WILL*|

|*FREE WILL DEMONSTRATION*|

|*Roleplayer – Team Player*|

|*Single-Persons Champion – Godly Marriage Material*|

NOTES

Chapter 1—Improbable Image

Two identities never connected/never seen: Pre-Life Elect & Less-than-100 percent human

Nephilim-Shmephilim.

Chapter 2—Too Good To Be True

Pre-Life. Life. After-Life. Science is de facto religion.

Chapter 3—Position of Patience.

Personal influencers on thinking (Hitchens, Hume, Koukl, Pinecreek Doug).

Leverage.

Walk Out On Sermon.

Chapter 4—Position Of Patience - Postscript

Robert A Cook. Walk *With The King*. Radio Broadcaster. King's College. NY.

Position of Patience – Post Postscript

Rich Young Ruler Sermon.

Chapter 5—Artistic Ministry.

Woman caught in adultery sermon.

Minister of Art.

Suicide and an ethnic youth.

Free Will Flawless Creatures.

Chapter 6—Opportunity.

Strategic demolition of your inauthentic identity.

A new life by accepting your authentic identity in Paradise. All prayers already answered.

Two engagement rings. Review of Great News about Good News.

Chapter 7—Sex Education 1

Planned Parenthood and Center for Disease Control for comparison. Planned Parenthood (USA/Global) – "Leading expert for more than 100 years." Center For Disease Control – The Centers for Disease Control and Prevention's Division of Adolescent and School Health (DASH) has established evidence-based approach schools can implement to help prevent HIV, STDs, and unintended pregnancy among adolescents.]

MARVI-RPIA Sex-ed Classes.

Male Roleplay. Female Roleplay. Parent Roleplay.

LGBTQ rights.

Chapter 8—Sex-Ed 2

Roleplayer vs Team Player.

Singleness as a gift?

Adam was NOT lonely before Eve.

Boo-hoo, nobody loves me.

Chapter 9—Sex-Ed 3

Homosexuality normal?

Minister of Art marries a transgender?

Thinking about sex is adultery?

Gender identity

Chapter 10—Sex-Ed 4

Did God make me gay?

4 of 5 senses in darkened room.

Homosexuality against nature – providing prophecy, the Redeemer, and Roleplayers.

Ultimate Team Player

Chapter 11—Sex Ed 4 – Postscript

Jack's older brother Karla is transgender.

If gender identity markers removed.

Gender identity, gender expression, Roleplay identity.

Chapter 12—Sex Ed 4 – Post Postscript

Same-sex marriage exaggeration.

Godly Marriage Material. Single-Persons Champion.

Team Player. Team Companions.

Chapter 13—Sex-Ed 5

Is homosexuality a capital offense for Sodom and Gibeah?

Homosexuality vs Inhospitality.

What sins are worse than homosexuality?

Chapter 14—Sex-Ed 6

Transgender child.

Er, Onan, Tamar, and Judah.

Born effeminate a sin?

No female pastors. Alistair Begg. Truth for Life. 2023.

Woman in man's body (and vice versa). God doesn't care about inauthentic identity – but OK to investigate it. Gender assignment, identity, and expression. Bi-sexuality in the population. Men become pregnant as the second violation of God's natural order (The Flood).

Chapter 15—Sex-Ed 7

Advocating marriage and children.

Free Will implies evil.

Apostle Paul's wife. Alistair Begg. Truth for Life. 2023.

Single-Persons Champion.

Minister of Art & Transgender Relationship.

Sex Monster. Human Torch of sensual burning. Sex Monster Weapons.

Warning! A Sex Talk! Explicit content!

Chapter 16—Suicide 1

Native American

Overview of suicide rates, news stories, and public perception.

A desperate escape from inauthentic identity.

Chapter 17—Suicide 2

MARVI-RPIA as a suicide program that has to work.

Insanity Chart.

Blind Eyes Chart

Chapter 18—Suicide 3

Famous suicides.

Jesus commits suicide.

Chapter 19—Suicide 4

Albert Camus. *The Myth of Sisyphus*, 1943.

Main reasons people don't commit suicide.

Ancient Suicide – Lucifer, Adam & Eve, Serpent

Judas Iscariot and Apostle Peter

Chapter 20—Abortion

Planned Parenthood (USA/Global) - "Leading expert for more than 100 years". https://www.plannedparenthood.org/about-us/facts-figures.

Centers for Disease Control.https://www.cdc.gov/healthyyouth/whatworks/what-works-sexual-health-education.htm.

Three stages of abortion status.

Specter of infanticide.

Chapter 21—Abortion Postscript

Abortion Facts and Figures 2021.https://www.prb.org/wp-content/uploads/2021/03/2021-safe-engage-abortion-facts-and-figures-media-guide.pdf.

Support for women before pregnancy, at pregnancy, and seeking an abortion.

"Abortion is taking the life of a defenseless human without proper justification". Gregory Koukl. Stand to Reason (str.org). 2019.

Child sacrifice custom.

Chapter 22—Abortion Grace

Support for women who've had an abortion.

Chapter 23—Abortion Post Postscript

Quora. Shawn Mootoo. Accessed July 20, 2022.

Abortion and the Ancient Practice of Child Sacrifice. Andrew White. Journal of Biblical Ethics in Medicine Vol.1 No.2. Pg.27-42. Accessed 2021.

Identity as a pregnant female and identity as an embryo.

12-year-old rape victim. Youngest birth mother (5 years old).

Chapter 24—Politics Part 1

Church vs State vs Science.

Identity of National Policy.

National allegiance of inauthentic identity.

Human devolution? Humans are good?

Individual values of national leaders.

A MARVI Christian Leader

Money is power.

Trans-humanism – The End again.

Chapter 25—Politics Part 2

Ministers of Art as national leaders. Less-than-100 percent-human political opposition

Government identity? Kingmaker-king breaker.

Don't understand goodness. Avoid politics.

Un-Americans. World War XX.

Is God 100 percent Moral? Giants in the land.

Chapter 26—Molested By Death Part 1

John Louis Thomas bio.

Many faces of death.

Power of death – Satan, God, or humans?

Responses to death.

Only one life?

Help patch MARVI-RPIA holes.

Chapter 27—Molested By Death Part 2

Insanity Chart (also Chapter 17)

Who is insane? Gun control, politics, mental health.

Chapter 28—Molested By Life

Get over It (your experience).

Essential Dynamic Ancestors (Adam/Eve, Nephilim, Noah, et al)

Molested examples (Abel, Lot's wife/daughters, Naboth, Bathsheba, John the Baptist)

Life examples (Goliath, Pharaoh, Korah, Jezebel, King Zedekiah)

Chapter 29—Questions and Answers 1-10

Q/A 1

Why continue the Demonstration of Free Will?

Q/A 2

Deceased persons have no access to earthly affairs.

Q/A 3

No infants in Heaven. Children are NOT blessings of the Lord.

Q/A 4

There is no "age of accountability" for children guaranteed salvation.

Q/A 5

Lucifer, angels, the Serpent, Adam, and Eve were not perfect creatures before falling into sin.

Q/A 6

Did Adam and Eve consummate their marriage Pre-Fall?

Q/A 7

Do Adam and Eve receive salvation? Probably.

Q/A 8

When is Judgment Day (eschatology)? The number of Last Free Will Roleplayer matches the number of Pre-Life Elect in Paradise?

Q/A 9

Meet loved ones in Heaven? May not be what you expect.

Q/A 10

Does God love everyone? Maybe. Maybe not.

Chapter 30—Questions and Answers 11-20

Q/A 11

God started over after Lucifer, Serpent, Adam and Eve sinned.

Q/A 12

Evil came from simulation.

Q/A 13

People from every religion are elect – probably.

Q/A 14

Sons of God (especially regarding the book of Genesis) are considered angels.

Q/A 15

Many religions are a good thing.

Q/A 16

Prayer has a purpose.

Q/A 17

Challenge facing Christianity.

Q/A 18

God is more than fair.

Q/A 19

Goliath, Judas Iscariot, and Pontius Pilate Roleplay.

Q/A 20

Our place when we die.

Chapter 31—Questions and Answers 21-30

Q/A 21

Jacob loved – Esau hated by God.

Q/A 22

God creating each of us in the womb isn't right.

Q/A 23

Was God being fair when He committed genocide on many nations? Did He?

Q/A 24

So what if I'm not elected to salvation?

Q/A 25

Vessels fitted for destruction.

Q/A 26

Would I know if I'm not saved?

Q/A 27

Justice in the afterlife?

Q/A 28

Connecting the Dots of Identity overlooked by the church for 2000 years?

Q/A 29

The body is the temple of the Holy Spirit or not?

Q/A 30

Determinism compromised?

How to change life if life is predetermined?

Chapter 32—Questions and Answers 31-40

Q/A 31

Is blasphemy a human issue?

Q/A 32

Are few saved?

Q/A 33

Irresponsible to teach all in Heaven none in Hell?

Q/A 34

Same-Sex in Heaven?

Q/A 35

Aberrant sex in Heaven?

Q/A 36A

Why are 99percent of Pastors Married?

Q/A 36B

Are pastors spiritually weak?

Alister Begg. Cleveland Parkside Church. *"Truth for Life"* media program. Cleveland, Ohio

Q/A 37

Refuse Dream Identity

Q/A 38

Holy Spirit after death?

Q/A 39

Agnostics are atheists?

Q/A 40

Jesus the only way?

Chapter 33—Questions and Answers 41-50

Q/A 41

ABOUT THE AUTHOR

Born in Los Angeles, California (1947), John Louis Thomas grew up in Anchorage, Alaska. He returned to Los Angeles before retiring in 2009, then relocated to New Mexico in 2017. For twenty-five years, he's been a member in good standing of Christian Reformed churches. During the pandemic of 2020, church attendance was suspended and hasn't yet resumed. Single. No children. Ketogenic diet since 2012.

He is an advocate of the "Rewrite the Bible by Hand" project, having completed all twenty-seven books of the New Testament in 2020. Incomplete writings from Genesis to 2 Samuel exist. He has completed writings from Genesis to Deuteronomy and 1 Kings to Malachi. Currently, he is rewriting the Book of Joshua (2024).

Back of the book cover photo: 2023.

Contact:

John Louis Thomas

900 Pinetree Rd SE #15730

Rio Rancho, New Mexico 87124-9998

johndeuce442@gmail.com

Team Player to JLT? Team Companion to JLT?

Do we match? See age, chastity, ethnicity, location.

Inquiries – please submit on 3x5 index card or postcard.

Business inquiries:

Chad Mulligan

rednlove2@gmail.com

Other books by John Louis Thomas:

Connecting The Dots Of Identity-1. 2024.

Websites:

unorthodoxtemple.com

rednlove.com

johnlouisthomas.com

www.ingramcontent.com/pod-product-compliance
Lightning Source LLC
LaVergne TN
LVHW020646110826
845149LV00012B/1932

* 9 7 9 8 9 9 0 7 4 8 7 1 2 *